INTERNATIONAL RELATIONS THEORY

THIRD EDITION

Sara Miller McCune founded SAGE Publishing in 1965 to support the dissemination of usable knowledge and educate a global community. SAGE publishes more than 1000 journals and over 800 new books each year, spanning a wide range of subject areas. Our growing selection of library products includes archives, data, case studies and video. SAGE remains majority owned by our founder and after her lifetime will become owned by a charitable trust that secures the company's continued independence.

Los Angeles | London | New Delhi | Singapore | Washington DC | Melbourne

INTERNATIONAL RELATIONS THEORY

THIRD EDITION

Oliver Daddow

Los Angeles | London | New Delhi
Singapore | Washington DC | Melbourne

Los Angeles | London | New Delhi
Singapore | Washington DC | Melbourne

SAGE Publications Ltd
1 Oliver's Yard
55 City Road
London EC1Y 1SP

SAGE Publications Inc.
2455 Teller Road
Thousand Oaks, California 91320

SAGE Publications India Pvt Ltd
B 1/I 1 Mohan Cooperative Industrial Area
Mathura Road
New Delhi 110 044

SAGE Publications Asia-Pacific Pte Ltd
3 Church Street
#10-04 Samsung Hub
Singapore 049483

Editor: Natalie Aguilera
Editorial assistant: Delayna Spencer
Production editor: Katie Forsythe
Copyeditor: David Hemsley
Indexer: David Rudeforth
Marketing manager: Sally Ransom
Cover design: Stephanie Guyaz
Typeset by: C&M Digitals (P) Ltd, Chennai, India
Printed by CPI Group (UK) Ltd, Croydon, CR0 4YY

© Oliver Daddow 2017

First edition published 2009. Reprinted in 2010 (twice)
and 2011
Second edition published 2013
This third edition first published 2017

Library of Congress Control Number: 2016955368

British Library Cataloguing in Publication data

A catalogue record for this book is available from
the British Library

ISBN 978-1-4739-6657-4
ISBN 978-1-4739-6658-1 (pbk)

At SAGE we take sustainability seriously. Most of our products are printed in the UK using FSC papers and boards.
When we print overseas we ensure sustainable papers are used as measured by the PREPS grading system.
We undertake an annual audit to monitor our sustainability.

CONTENTS

ABOUT THE AUTHOR

Oliver Daddow is Assistant Professor in British Politics and Security at the University of Nottingham. His research interests are in interpretivist international relations, British foreign policy – especially Brexit and the Europe question – and discourse analysis. He is the author of *Britain and Europe Since 1945: Historiographical Perspectives on Integration* (Manchester University Press, 2004) and *New Labour and the European Union: Blair and Brown's Logic of History* (Manchester University Press, 2011). He edited *Harold Wilson and European Integration: Britain's Second Application to Join the EEC* (Frank Cass, 2003). With Jamie Gaskarth he edited *British Foreign Policy: The New Labour Years* (Palgrave Macmillan, 2011), and with Mark Bevir and Ian Hall he edited *Interpreting Global Security* (Routledge, 2014). He has written book chapters and peer-reviewed journal articles across his research interests, including in *Government and Opposition*, *International Affairs*, *International Relations*, *Journal of Common Market Studies*, *Journal of European Public Policy*, *Political Quarterly*, *British Journal of Politics and International Relations*, *Cambridge Review of International Affairs* and *Review of International Studies*.

ACKNOWLEDGEMENTS

This book began life at the British International Studies Association Conference at St Andrews in December 2005. It was during a chat with David Mainwaring in the publisher's exhibition that we spotted a potential gap in the market for a pedagogically inclined book aimed at students new not just to the study of IR in general but to the increasingly diverse field of IR theory in particular. I can safely say that had that conversation not taken place this book would certainly not have been written – such are the fortuitous vagaries of academic life. This latest edition has been produced following further discussions with my editors at Sage, Amy Jarrold and Natalie Aguilera. Natalie was an equally inspirational editor on the second and this edition. My thanks to everyone at Sage who, as usual, worked on the manuscript on my behalf, especially Katie Forsythe, my diligent Senior Production Editor and David Rudeforth, my indexer for the book. A host of anonymous reviewers gave some excellent feedback on the second edition. They suggested refinements in the way I covered the existing material and proffered some novel ideas on new material that would aid student learning about each theory. I hope they will feel I have done their suggestions justice.

Adrian Gallagher read through some of my first stabs at trying to summarize these theories in a couple of thousand words and his astute comments were most helpful, particularly on the detail of English School theorizing. Thanks, finally, to all my various cohorts of students who have, over the years and probably to varying degrees, both enjoyed and suffered my sometimes clunky attempts to distil the complexity of this subject matter into manageable sized chunks for academic consumption. The lecture and seminar room is where one finds out what works to clarify things, and crucially what does not work, and this book is the product of that constructive and enjoyable process of teaching and learning. Many elements of both formal and informal feedback on my teaching have helped me refine this text enormously. Magnus Evjebraten, Matthew Breeds and Chris Hills were particularly helpful in the early stages.

INTRODUCTION: WHY YOU SHOULD BUY THIS BOOK

I have written this book with one very clear mission in mind: to help students new to the study of International Relations Theory (IRT) find their way in to what can be a fascinating subject of study at university level – but one that requires a good deal of thought and engagement with lots of complex material. Everyone has a view on the major issues in international relations today, whether it be the war in Iraq, the Russian invasion of Ukraine, Brexit, the election of Donald Trump, or the Middle East Peace process. Theorists in International Relations try to make sense of these developments by collecting evidence from past and present, spotting patterns and connections, developing models, and creating generalizations about how **states** act to secure their interests in an increasingly globalized world. Understanding how and why theorists do this is the principle task for any student of International Relations, and this book will help you do just that.

IRT can be a beguiling field of study for two reasons. First, because of the sheer number of theories on offer, all claiming to tell the 'truth' about international events, about what makes the world of international affairs 'tick'. How do we know which **theory** is 'best'? Second, there is no getting away from the fact that IRT can and often is difficult for new students because, although many of you will come to it from a Politics or History background, and will have a handle on some or all of the issues being studied, few of you reading this book will have dealt with the issues from a theoretical vantage point before, especially if you are studying at undergraduate level. It is important to remember, therefore, that you are not alone if you find yourself struggling with theory. No one gets it overnight. Success in academia comes in increments and is sometimes a slow process; you may encounter setbacks and difficult periods. An element of bloody-mindedness is certainly required! But if you stick with your studies in IRT you will reap the rewards. Many school- and college-level courses deal with issues in international relations such as **globalization**, war and peace. What sets apart university-level courses is the 'theory' element. If you can get to grips with theory early on at university you should go very far.

A note on terminology: 'International Relations', written with capitalized 'IR', denotes the formal study of international relations. In other words, There is a discipline of International Relations which studies international relations going on 'out there' in the world. In different universities, courses in IR go by the names 'international politics', 'global politics' or 'world politics', each containing varying amounts of theory. This book abbreviates International Relations Theory to IRT.

And this is why IRT is such a fascinating and rewarding field of study. We might not realize it when we watch news reports about international terrorism, American–China relations, the crisis in Syria, or the death of Fidel Castro in Cuba, but a form of theory underpins all political and media coverage of global politics. Politicians, the commentariat and news media tell us which **actors** are important, frame how they are interacting on the global stage, speculate on their motivations for doing so, and debate the impact of decisions made and treaties signed for the future shape of world politics. Sometimes the discussion centres on routine, day-to-day decisions, at other times policy-makers are responding hastily to a crisis. The point is that in selecting to present the views of a few actors, in a certain way, and with an editorial slant that can cue you, the consumer of news, to view some actors or causes more sympathetically than others, theoretical choices have been made. After reading this book you will, I hope, be in a better position to 'see through' some of the dominant ways in which the world is simplified for understanding through these significant but often hidden theoretical choices. As a result, the book should help you discover how and where you can acquire the skills of critical engagement with the world around you on your course in IRT. And let's face it, if students of politics and international affairs cannot take a critically informed perspective on those who govern us around the world, who can?

The book has therefore been written for the newcomer to IRT. It helps you manage your learning and is structured in such a way to make it easy to dip in and out of. It can be a scary prospect beginning the study of new subjects. There are long reading lists to plough through, unfamiliar concepts and technical language to learn, difficult ideas to digest, and many new ways of thinking to master – all in a relatively short space of time. The volume of reading and depth of information required to succeed can be overwhelming for any student. This book should help you manoeuvre your way through the intricacies of IRT in three ways. First, it summarizes the main components of the theories you are likely to encounter on your course. Second, it shows how all these theories interrelate and influence each other in an emerging dialogue over time. Third, it introduces the background to each theory and gives you a clear sense of how this apparent jumble of ideas and approaches all 'fit' together in the discipline, as it has developed over the years. The book provides you with a clear overview of your IRT course that will allow you to fill in the detail as and when required. Furthermore, it offers practical advice and guidance on dealing with assessed essays and exams, including tips on avoiding plagiarism.

HOW TO USE THE BOOK: TAKING OWNERSHIP OF YOUR LEARNING ABOUT IRT

This book is designed to help you succeed in your undergraduate or postgraduate level course in IRT. Theories of IR will crop up in many and sometimes unexpected places during your degree programme; they are not only studied on courses specifically called 'International Relations Theory'. Theoretical perspectives will likely feature in courses variously titled International Politics, International Relations since 1945, World Politics since 1945, the Contemporary World Arena, Globalization, Foreign Policy Analysis and Methods in International Relations. Any module on International Security or Security Studies is also likely to have a strong theoretical component based around debates between Realists and 'the rest', on, for example, the utility of nuclear weapons as security guarantors in the modern world. Theoretical issues underpin the material on all these courses, and this book should therefore be useful whether your course is specifically on IRT or whether you need it as a handy introduction to the theories that crop up on cognate Politics and IR degree-level modules.

The principal aim of the book is to help you appreciate how to learn effectively about IRT, and in so doing it should help you succeed at coursework assignments, pass your exams, and overall to get the best out of your course in IRT. It has been designed and written to provide you with an accessible guide to the topics, themes and issues you will encounter on a typical IRT course. It discusses the ways of thinking, writing and presenting evidence your tutors will be looking to see when they assess your written work and/or oral presentations (depending on the mode of assessment for the module you are on). I have not written the book to be another textbook on IRT – there are plenty of very good ones on the market already. Nor is this book meant to be read instead of textbooks, academic journal articles, books and other readings for your course. Given the succinct nature of my coverage of the theories, this book should be read as a basic introduction *before*, and, if necessary, *alongside* the more advanced and in-depth scholarship which you will undoubtedly need to engage with to impress your tutors. They will be encouraging you to go beyond textbook treatments of all the subjects you encounter at university level. The introductory nature of my coverage, together with the skills element of the book, means that you should also find it useful to return to this book as you near the end of modules dealing with IRT, as you begin preparing for essays, exams and other assessed work. In sum, I hope this book is both primer and refresher, and that it is easy to navigate in and out of when you need to support your learning about IRT.

Students of IR and IRT are well served by a host of textbooks coming at the subject from a range of perspectives. These textbooks, in turn, synthesize many long and often complex writings from academic research monographs and articles published in scholarly journals, where you will find the latest cutting-edge research on the subject. This book is intended to support the information and learning skills you develop by reading the main course texts and that 'original' theoretical and empirical work on IRT. It will familiarize you with the basics of the discipline and give you an 'insider' (tutor) perspective on how to prepare and deliver effective essays and exam answers. In terms of the key skills tested in such assessments, the book helps you organize your thoughts, critically analyse evidence from a variety of sources, plan persuasive and logical arguments, and express those arguments clearly in speech and writing.

The aims of this book are:

- To introduce you to the subject matter of International Relations.
- To survey the key theories of International Relations.
- To provide help in developing the essential skills needed to meet the learning outcomes on courses in International Relations that have a theory component.
- To act as a study aid alongside the textbook and more advanced reading you should be doing on your course.

There are many different theories of IR and it is rare to find a course that covers all of them. The time allowed at universities to deliver individual modules is very tight indeed and your tutor will have to make choices about which theories to teach you and which to leave out or cover only briefly. Tutors will not be expecting you to know everything about every theory, but they will be looking for a serious engagement with the theories they do cover with you. I would strongly advise you to consult the information about your particular course in IRT as soon as it is available, and to compare what you will cover on your course with the contents of this book. You will then only need to concern yourself with the chapters of the book that are directly relevant to your studies. Concentrate your efforts mainly on the theories that are relevant to the course you are studying but feel free to branch out where you feel you wish to go: wider reading is a very under-rated concept in the modern university and students who go that extra mile always stand out from the crowd!

> There are many more theories in the study of International Relations than there are weeks in the average semester to study them all. Make sure that you know from the beginning of your course which theories you need to know in detail, and which are either not covered or less important to the overall make-up of your studies. Knowledge of other theories is useful but not a prerequisite for success, so plan your time and channel your energy and reading time wisely.

NAVIGATING YOUR WAY AROUND THE BOOK

This book is divided into three parts. Part I gives you an orientation to the field of IR and IRT across three chapters. Chapter 1 introduces the contested subject matter of IR, including some history on the development of the discipline. It argues that if you grasp the reasons for scholarly disputes over the object of study and how to study it, you will quickly understand why so many theories about IR have flourished over the years. Chapter 2 begins by introducing why academics use theory. It moves on to debate why it is important to study IR theoretically and how we evaluate all of the theories on offer. Chapter 3 introduces the fundamental concept of **anarchy** in IR, looks at how theorists have tried to break down the subject matter of IR, and shows you how to think like an IR theorist by considering what it is that IR theorists do. By the end of Part I you should be comfortable with what to expect of a whole or part course in IRT, and to have begun thinking about the big questions that animate scholars working in this fascinatingly diverse discipline.

Part II is the real nitty-gritty of the book, in which I present an overview of the main theories you will encounter when you study IRT. You may cover some, you may cover them all, so feel free to pick and choose the relevant chapters as you see fit. Chapter 4 explores Liberalism, Chapter 5 considers Realism, while Chapter 6 introduces the updated variants of each of them, Neoliberalism and Neorealism. Chapter 7 delves into English School theory and Chapter 8 summarizes Social Constructivism. After that we move to theories that deal with issues in IR overlooked or ignored by these earlier 'mainstream' theories. Chapter 9 is on Marxism, Chapter 10 covers Critical Theory, Chapter 11 examines Feminism, Chapter 12 introduces Poststructuralism, Chapter 13 examines Postcolonialism and, finally, Chapter 14 considers Green International Theory. By the end of Part II you should have a solid foundation of knowledge about each theory of IR and know where to look to find more detail about them.

Each chapter in Part II contains the following features:

- In order to highlight key points in each chapter I have inserted a series of 'Tips boxes' (example below) which will <u>help you remember</u> the most important issues raised in each chapter.

> Remember, this book should not be seen as a substitute for the coverage of the theories you will get from lectures, seminars and course readings but as an accompaniment to them.

- I have also included hints in the form of 'Common pitfall' boxes. These come from my experiences of teaching IRT and watching how students learn about it (or not, as the case may be!). Avoiding these pitfalls will help you enormously.
- Scattered throughout the book are 'Taking it further' boxes (see p. 7), where issues of particular significance within the discipline are developed in a little more detail than in the body text. I hope these will be useful in stimulating you to read more widely around the issues they raise.
- For each of the chapters on the substance of IR theories I have provided a list of key terms associated with those theories. You might wish to keep a list of these terms in a high profile place in your course notes, adding to them weekly. A constantly growing inventory of all the different definitions and interpretations placed upon key terms by IR academics will help you in two ways. First, it will help you understand the 'language' scholars use to debate issues in IR and IRT. Second, you will generate a stock of informed, original and critical reference material for use in your coursework and exam essays. Learning pithy definitions of key terms from established scholars goes a long way.
- I have provided a series of 'Questions to ponder' at the end of each of the chapters, together with a brief overview of how you might wish to set about tackling each one. Thinking about how you carve up essay and exam questions is a real skill to develop at university. My summary of what tutors look for should help you appreciate where you need to be in your written work in terms of evidence, argument, structure and communication.
- At the end of each chapter there are 'References to more information'. These are lists of sources you could read to deepen your understanding of the issues raised in the chapter. Your tutor will doubtless provide you with an extensive reading list for each theory so the two together should give you plenty to go on. I have tried to include less well-known sources along with the canonical texts. It is usually obvious from the title what the book or article is about, but for some entries I have included a few pointers by way of explanation.

Part III is all about study skills. It offers advice and practical guidance in study, writing and revision skills so that you can present your knowledge in the most effective possible way in university level essays, exams and other coursework assignments, such as individual or group presentations. Chapter 15 helps you get the best out of theory in lectures and tutorials. Chapter 16 discusses the difficult process of planning and writing academic essays. It encourages you to appreciate the importance of essay structure and modes of argumentation, and gives you practical steps to help deliver well-balanced, well-argued and clearly structured answers. Chapter 17 illustrates the main points from the previous chapter by giving examples of best practice from real IRT essays I have marked in the past (and, yes, the students are still living to tell the tale). It ends with tips on avoiding the serious academic offence of plagiarism.

> Developing good essay technique is vital for succeeding at courses in IRT. The ingredients of a good coursework essay are the same that go into cooking up a good exam answer.

Chapter 18 covers the two things you need to do to succeed at exams: revise effectively and clearly communicate your thoughts in writing under severe time pressure. By the end of Part III you should be in a position to prepare robustly argued, finely balanced, critically informed and academically sound coursework submissions. You should also be in a position to reflect on how to make the most of your revision time and how to do the very best you can in an exam on IRT. At the end of the book, you will find the Glossary, References and Index. New terms appear in bold throughout the book and their meaning is clearly explained in the Glossary.

RUNNING THEMES

There is a wide assortment of IR theories, all of which claim to make sense of the subject or at least some significant aspect of it. Throughout your course you will be exposed to, and expected to engage with, aspects of all these debates about the functions and value of theorizing international relations. Here are five of the most common dimensions of the debate about theory you will probably encounter:

1. **The nature of theory** – while there are many elements of overlap, there is no single view common to all scholars of IR on what theory *is*. The word 'theory' is often used interchangeably with terms like 'approaches', 'perspectives', 'traditions', or even 'images'. The absence of a commonly agreed vocabulary indicates the depth of the real and ongoing disputes over what 'makes' a theory and when a particular body of writing is sufficiently well developed to constitute a distinct theory of IR.
2. **Ontology** – What is 'out there' to be studied, or the object of study. The problem, issue or set of events different theorists are trying to explain will necessarily affect both what bits of IR they study and the nature of the evidence they bring to bear to develop, test and refine their theory. The question of **ontology** is therefore vital: do you think different theorists are viewing the same world (do they share an ontology of IR), or are they 'seeing' different worlds (are their ontologies of IR at odds with each other)?
3. **Epistemology** – or the theory of knowledge. The stuff of international relations is not as tangible and easy to put under a microscope as, for example, atoms are for physicists, molecules are for chemists, or fingerprints and bodily fluids are for Crime Scene Investigators. IR theorists often involve themselves in quite heated disputes

about **epistemology**: what counts as reliable evidence about a particular problem area. Theoretical debates in IR often revolve around a critique by writers in different theoretical traditions of the evidence used by writers in competing traditions. Putting these writers into dialogue in your essays and exam answers is *the* best way of accumulating marks for being 'critical'.

4. **Logic and argument** – IR theorists use narrative arguments to try and persuade readers of the strength of their case. This process usually has two dimensions to it. First, the theorist has to construct a theory that flows logically from the ontological assumptions s/he has made about what was being studied and the evidence gathered: the theory must have *internal* logic. Second, the theorist will often also question the ontology, epistemology, simplifying assumptions, interpretations and evidential base of other theorists: this is the *external* dimension where rival theories look outward to try to shore up their claims to analytical accuracy by knocking down rival theories.

5. **Positivist/normative divide** – returns us to disputes about the nature of theory. For **positivists,** the study of the social sciences can proceed using the same methods as in the natural sciences to produce generalizations, predictions and laws about IR. **Normative** theorists question the applicability of methods drawn from the natural sciences and tend to be more open about the agendas to which they write and the uses to which their theories might be put in the 'real world' of politics and public policy.

'Theory' is a disputed term. Think about how each writer you study either defines the word in their work or what they would implicitly understand 'theory' to mean. You should soon see how they might position themselves in unfolding disciplinary discussions about the uses, nature and foundations of theory. Keeping different definitions of 'theory' will be top priority if you choose to build an inventory of key terms in IRT and their definitions.

TAKING IT FURTHER

IR is a huge field of study globally. Naturally a course on IRT will reflect the intrinsic diversity of the field. It is testament to the scale of the task at hand (theorizing the world, to put it simply!) that we have so many theories asserting that they afford an objective, 'scientific' account of the broad sweep of international relations. Investigating the subject at university level will provide you with a flavour of the main debates that have shaped the field as well as the latest cutting-edge research. The onus is on you to do as much wider reading as you see fit to expand your knowledge base and follow up on the aspects of IR and IRT that interest you the most. To this end I have interspersed the book with 'Taking it further' sections covering material that may well lie outside the scope of your course, but which add depth or a new dimension to the themes we cover in the main text. Taking things further in this way is useful in three ways. First of all, following up wider debates and points of interest will help you understand more about how the individual theories you examine on your course fit together to make the discipline of IR.

> ## COMMON PITFALL
>
> Many students tend to 'play it safe' and concentrate only on the essential textbook reading for their course. It is advisable to go that extra mile and seek out the original academic readings that get quickly summarized in the textbooks as a way of helping you develop your critical capabilities and familiarity with the original IRT texts.

Second, you will learn more effectively about this subject – any subject for that matter – if you spend time thinking seriously about the underlying disputes about how to study a subject, what 'counts' as evidence, and how to present your findings appropriately in an academic context. Reflecting on what you have learnt and reading around a topic will help you better understand the material you cover on your IRT course, as well as helping you think through the big philosophical and theoretical issues associated with research and debates in politics and the social sciences more generally. Reading what scholars have had to say about how to study IRT will help you come to a position within these debates and help you articulate and justify your opinion in essays and exams.

The third reason is perhaps the most important to you at this stage of your studies: showing your module tutor that you have *actively engaged with IRT.* An active and informed dialogue with yourself and your peers about the nature, value and role of IRT will come across clearly to your tutor when they mark your work. The average student might know what some of the theories say about IR, whereas the better student will be able to dissect the assumptions of each theory and be able to critique the theories using information they have taken from wide reading around the subject. Even better students will know the gist of what key writers say, and be able to put writers from different theoretical traditions into conversation with each other. In exams you will not necessarily be expected to show the same level of depth and critical capability, but you will need to take a stance on a given issue or theory and justify your interpretation with logic and evidence from key writings. Trying to gain an overall impression of the recurring debates that animate the discipline will help develop your intellectual abilities no end.

> It is important not to forget that the theorists whose work you study have been influenced by events in the world at their respective times of writing. Try to identify the influence of practice on theory when you read academic books and articles. We will unpack some of this context specific material in the chapters on each theory, as well as in the history of the discipline section in Chapter 1.

QUESTIONS TO PONDER

As you plough through the lecture and seminar readings for your course in IRT it is advantageous to consider the kinds of IRT-related questions you might have to answer in exams or essays during and/or at the end of the module. Essay questions with deadlines will usually be available at the beginning of your module, but if they are not included in your course resources from the outset, your course tutor may be willing to let you have copies of past essay titles to ponder, before the fresh ones are published. For exams the obvious resource is past exam papers, so check your course materials early on in your studies and scrutinize them carefully. These will show you the kinds of themes, issues, concepts and ideas that your tutor will push through the lectures, and invite you to reflect upon in assessed work.

The nub of the matter is to take an *active* approach to your learning about IRT. Learning from books and articles is not just about concentrating on the fabric of the particular theory you are covering that week, although that is obviously the most significant reason for reading and attending lectures and seminars. Active learning means reflecting on a host of related issues. For example, think about the questions that spurred the authors you read to put pen to paper – why did they decide to write their pieces and what do *you* think about their response? Is their interpretation valid, fair, based on sound evidence and argued effectively? How would *you* prepare an answer to the question they set themselves and where would *you* look for evidence? Breaking down the various sections of their books and articles to help you understand how they did came to write them can inform your view on the appropriateness of their position. What issues would *you* have thrown into the mix to perhaps help that author make his/her argument more effectively? Are there any case studies from the contemporary world of politics and international affairs that shed light on the theoretical problems being explored from a more historical vantage point? Consciously applying theory to present problems is a valuable skill to develop.

At the end of each chapter I suggest a few questions that arise from the material covered; these are the kinds of level of question that will come up in essays and exams. I suggest some ways in which you might approach answering them but it is up to you to flesh out my suggestions with further detail. These questions are designed to encourage you to engage with the issues discussed and to help you see how important it is to be an active consumer of academic literature rather than a passive receiver. Learning to take an active approach to reading and digesting this material will help you, not just on your course in IRT, but on all your studies at university.

REFERENCES TO MORE INFORMATION

Your course tutor will recommend a series of textbooks, journal articles and other resources to help you learn about theories of IR. Different tutors organize course material differently. On the one hand, you might have a reading list that is divided up theory by theory, lecture by lecture, or seminar by seminar, making it easy for you to locate the relevant reading for each week. On the other hand, some tutors prefer to give you a long list of readings and let you choose from them which sources you want to read in preparation for each of the lectures and seminars. On top of your general lecture reading, some tutors might invite you to dissect one or two specific readings in advance of seminars, as a basis for discussion within the group on the day. All approaches to course design and delivery have their strengths and weaknesses. The first approach puts the readings on a plate, so to speak, speeding up your search for the appropriate texts by saving you having to root around in the library and online to find the relevant material from an aggregate course list. The second approach puts more onus on you to find the relevant sources for each week, so while it takes more time, it enhances your information retrieval and wider research skills. Directed seminar reading is good for promoting in-group discussion but can, it is said, limit the opportunities for better students to explore from the list the readings that interest them the most.

However your course reading lists are designed there are certain core textbooks that are absolutely invaluable aids to the study of IRT and several are referred to below in this book. The following three textbooks come with online resource centres and are aimed directly at undergraduate students:

Baylis, J., Smith, S. and Owens, P. (eds) (several editions, 6th edn 2014) *The Globalization of World Politics: An Introduction to International Relations*. Oxford: Oxford University Press.

Dunne, T., Kurki, M. and Smith, S. (eds) (several editions, 4th edn 2016) *International Relations Theory: Discipline and Diversity*. Oxford: Oxford University Press.

Jackson, R. and Sørenson, G. (several editions, 6th edn 2015) *Introduction to International Relations: Theories and Approaches*. Oxford: Oxford University Press.

Undergraduate and postgraduate students can all get something out of the following:

Brown, C. and Ainley, K. (several editions, 4th edn 2009) *Understanding International Relations*. Basingstoke: Palgrave.

Brown, C., Nardin, T. and Rengger, N. (eds) (2002) *International Relations in Political Thought: Texts from the Ancient Greeks to the First World War*. Cambridge: Cambridge University Press.

Burchill, S. et al. (several editions, 5th edn 2013) *Theories of International Relations*. Basingstoke: Palgrave.

Carlsnaes, W., Risse, T. and Simmons, B.A. (eds) (2012) *Handbook of International Relations*. 2nd edn London: Sage.

Der Derian, J. (ed.) (1995) *International Theory: Critical Investigations*. London: Macmillan.

Griffiths, M. (ed.) (2007) *International Relations Theory for the Twenty-First Century*. London: Routledge.

Griffiths, M. (ed.) (2011) *Rethinking International Relations Theory*. Basingstoke: Palgrave Macmillan.

Groom, A.J.R. and Light, M. (eds) (1994) *Contemporary International Relations: A Guide to Theory*. London: Pinter.

Holsti, K.J. (1995) *International Politics: A Framework for Analysis*, 7th edn. Englewood Cliffs, NJ: Prentice Hall.

Jørgensen, K.E. (2010) *International Relations Theory: A New Introduction*. Basingstoke: Palgrave Macmillan.

Linklater, A. (ed.) (2000) *International Relations: Criticall Concepts in Political Science*. London: Routledge.

Little, R. and Smith, M. (eds) (2006) *Perspectives on World Politics*. Abingdon: Routledge.

Nardin, T. and Mapel, D.R. (eds) (2008) *Traditions of International Ethics*. Cambridge: Cambridge University Press.

Nicholson, M. (2002) *International Relations: A Concise Introduction*, 2nd edn. Basingstoke: Palgrave Macmillan.

Nye, J.S. and Welch, D.A. (several editions, 10th edn 2016) *Understanding Global Conflict and Cooperation: An Introduction to Theory and History*. London: Pearson.

Reus-Smit, C. and Snidal, D. (2010) *The Oxford Handbook of International Relations*. Oxford: Oxford University Press.

Smith, S., Booth, K. and Zalewski, M. (eds) (1996) *International Theory: Positivism and Beyond*. Cambridge: Cambridge University Press.

Steans, J. et al. (several editions, 4th edn 2010) *An Introduction to International Relations Theory: Perspectives and Themes*. London: Longman.

Sterling-Folker, J. (ed.) (2013) *Making Sense of International Relations Theory*, 2nd edn. Boulder, CO: Lynne Rienner.

Vasquez, J.A. (eds) (several editions, 3rd edn 1996) *Classics of International Relations*. Upper Saddle River, NJ: Prentice Hall.

Viotti, P.R. and Kauppi, M.V. (eds) (several editions, 5th edn 2013) *International Relations Theory*. Harlow: Pearson.

Weber, C. (several editions, 4th edn 2013) *International Relations Theory: A Critical Introduction*. London: Routledge.

When studying IR it is useful to have a working knowledge of international history, at least since 1945 and preferably back to 1900. The following books will give you the gist of the story:

Best, A., Hanhimaki, J.M., Maiolo, J.A. and Schulze, K.E. (several editions, 3rd edn 2014) *International History of the Twentieth Century*. London: Routledge.

Calvocoressi, P. (several editions, 9th edn 2008) *World Politics Since 1945*. London: Longman.

Keylor, W.R. (several editions, 6th edn 2012) *The Twentieth Century World: An International History*. Oxford: Oxford University Press.

Martel, G. (ed.) (2010) *A Companion to International History 1900–2001*. Oxford: Blackwell.

Reynolds, D. (2000) *One World Divisible: A Global History Since 1945*. New York: W.W. Norton.

Williams, W.C. and Piotrowski, H. (several editions, 8th edn 2014) *The World Since 1945: A History of International Relations*. Boulder, CO: Lynne Reinner.

Young, J.W. and Kent, J. (2004) *International Relations Since 1945: A Global History*. Oxford: Oxford University Press.

Textbooks naturally concentrate on some theories at the expense of others and treat the theories they do cover slightly differently. That said, they all survey core sets of issues associated with the nature of theory, the strength of theoretical claims to knowledge about IR, and their overall contribution to the development of the discipline. They tend to use examples from the 'real world' of politics and international affairs to bring the theories to life. This book is a companion to your textbooks rather than a replacement for them, so make sure that you use your textbooks to put the flesh on the bones of what I say here.

There are lots of journals devoted to the study of IR and IRT. Academic journal articles contain the latest cutting edge research in the field, which later gets distilled and simplified in textbook treatments. Here are some of the most popular journals in IR. You should be able to access electronic versions of these journals through your university library: *Alternatives, American Political Science Review, British Journal of Politics and International Relations, Cambridge Review of International Affairs, Ethics and International Affairs, European Foreign Affairs Review, European Journal of International Relations, International Affairs, International Feminist Journal of Politics, International Organization, International Relations, International Security, International Studies Perspectives, International Studies Review, International Studies Quarterly, Journal of International Affairs, Millennium: Journal of International Studies, Political Studies, Review of International Studies* and *World Politics.*

SUMMARY

There is a lot of reading out there about IRT: do not let this make you apprehensive. One of the most frequent reasons for students not engaging with IRT is the fear that because they cannot know everything about a theory they are wary of taking those first vital steps to understanding it. A way around this pitfall is to read widely from day one of your course; it then becomes routine, part of your day-to-day academic lifestyle (we will return to this in the skills section of the book). Target your reading by parcelling up what you need to do into manageable chunks. Every student reads at different paces, works differently and thinks differently. There are no hard and fast rules on how much preparation is enough for each of the seminars and coursework assignments on your course, but it should be pretty obvious when you are putting in the effort and when you are not.

When you are comfortable and up to speed with the basics of IRT, a complementary skill you need to develop is that of knowing when you have done enough to understand the basics of each theory and how you might critique that theory. Make sure you have a thorough knowledge of your module guide and attend all the course lectures and seminars because they will give you a good insight into what your tutor expects from you on that front. It is important that you work out for yourself as soon as you can in your university studies how *you* work best and how you best prepare for handing in assignments and revising for exams. This book will help you develop these **transferable skills (generic skills),** as well as helping you come to terms with the diverse, sometimes infuriating, and always enjoyable world of IRT.

PART I

INTRODUCTION TO YOUR COURSE IN IR THEORY

It is sheer craziness to dare to understand world affairs. (Rosenau and Durfee 1995: 1)

This book guides you through the general field of IRT in whatever form you encounter it at university. It aims to explain the big questions that have animated so many writers over the years to try to make sense of the 'craziness' of international relations. It is useful to try and think about the key points of dispute and debate between scholars working in the same discipline, and that is in effect what I am trying to do in this book. First, because it helps you appreciate the debates that have driven forward the discipline over the years. Second, it equips you with the weaponry to critique scholarly ideas and opinions on their own terms rather than with the benefit of hindsight. Reading this book will encourage you to develop both these skills: understanding academic theories and critiquing them.

This part of the book is organized around underlying disciplinary debates about IRT. In Chapter 1 we survey the field of IR as an academic pursuit: what is that we are studying when we say we are studying IR? In Chapter 2 we add in the contested issue of theory: what is a theoretical approach to IR and why is it beneficial? Chapter 3 prioritises theoretical debates in IR, in particular those stemming from the foundational problem of 'anarchy' in the **international system**. We then cover the 'story' of the discipline and especially how we map theories, how we evaluate theories and the possibility of building an IR 'super theory'. The chapter draws to a close with a few tips on how to think like an IR theorist. By the end of the chapter we have raised a whole host of uncertainties and questions about IRT. This is a field of study in which no one can really agree either on the appropriate subject matter, or on how best to study it. If you can grasp the reasons for these disputes and offer up convincing evidence that you have taken a position on them, you are likely to succeed at your course because you will have been engaging actively with each theory at quite a sophisticated level. As Chapter 3 suggests, learning to think like an IR theorist is the surest route to success.

CORE AREAS

1

WHAT IS INTERNATIONAL RELATIONS?

> Even by those who have authored them, the emergence of theories cannot be described in other than uncertain and impressionistic ways. Elements of theories can, however, be identified. (Waltz 2010: 10)

It is demanding to build a theory in any field of academic endeavour. Whether it be a social science like IR or a natural science like physics, biology or chemistry, theories by their nature are simplified versions of a deeply complex reality. As Kenneth Waltz goes on to argue in the passage quoted above from his path-breaking *Theory of International Politics* (originally published in 1979), it is a giant leap to go from causal speculation based on empirical testing to the construction of theoretical formulations that enable one to arrange newly observed facts through a theoretical lens. 'To cope with the difficulty, simplification is required' (Waltz 2010: 10).

In the process of theory development, we are trying to comprehend the complexity of relations between, say, State X and State Y by breaking down into manageable chunks the elements of their interrelationships that most intrigue us. Necessarily, theories fall prey to criticisms about their coverage, their depth and their relevance to the 'real world' they are trying to explain. It is worth remembering, therefore, that all theories come with a health warning: no theory can explain everything about the world and nor should we expect it to. Even the most ardent supporter of theory has to admit the limitations of theory: 'in order to have a theory, you'll have to have a subject matter, because you can't have a theory about everything. There's no such thing as a theory about everything' (Waltz, quoted in Kreisler 2003). In other words, a theory about everything is a theory about nothing – a futile exercise from which nothing useful can be gleaned.

Theoretical disputes are common even in disciplines where scholars are trying to theorize the same event or set of events which they agree are happening, or have happened, in the 'real world'. What, then, if scholars disagree on the essence of the 'reality' they are trying to explain? What if they can't come to a basic consensus on what makes the world go around, or why humans behave the way they do, or why states might choose war over peace? What then for supposedly comprehensive theories that enable us to make predictions about what might happen in the future on the basis of our existing theoretical knowledge about the world?

> Engaging with underlying concerns about the construction, function and value of theory will help you appreciate the nature of the scholarly enterprise in IRT because:
>
> ● It helps you see the problem through the eyes of the authors you study.
> ● It enhances your ability to critique each theory.
> ● It helps you 'think' like an IR theorist.

On your IRT course you may well have the chance to study these kinds of **metatheoretical** issues in some detail. I hear you ask, What is metatheory? 'Metatheories take other theories as their subject' (Reus-Smit 2012: 530). Metatheory is theory about theory. IR metatheory, therefore, is theory about IRT. For example, you may have lectures and seminars on the constituent elements of theoretical work at the start and end of your course. To back that up, seminars will doubtless incorporate discussion not only about the substance of each theory that has been developed about IR, but also the assumptions theorists make about how the world works. You might also delve into why theorists in one tradition end up disagreeing with other groups of theorists from other traditions, especially if they put forward competing visions of what it is important to explain in international affairs.

Certainly many of the textbooks you read will, usually in the introductory and concluding chapters, engage with metatheoretical issues in some detail (for instance, Dunne et al. 2016; Jackson and Sørensen 2015). Hence, being aware of **metatheory** – what it is and how it helps you understand IRT – will help you begin to think like an IR theorist.

> Metatheory 'quite simply means theoretical reflections *on* theory' (Jørgensen 2010: 15, original emphasis). Metatheory considers the nature, role and practice of theorizing. Metatheorists look upon all the competing theories about a certain topic and try to understand how all the theorists they study are making sense of their subject. This then helps them come to a considered assessment on the nature and significance of theoretical contributions in a given field. Benno Teschke explains it perfectly – metatheory is a reflexive enterprise, 'not simply thinking with a theory, but rather thinking about the nature of theory' (Teschke and Cemgil 2014: 606).

In this chapter I try and answer three big questions that have motivated scholars to theorize IR over the years. First, what is 'the world' of international relations that we are studying? Second, what is International Relations as a structured discipline of academic study? Third, who or what are the major actors we need to study in IR? Answering these questions helps us understand more about the role of theory in studying a subject like IR, and we cover that in the next chapter after this disciplinary scene setter.

WHAT IS THE WORLD OF INTERNATIONAL RELATIONS?

> Accurate and reliable measurements are of little value unless they measure the proper variables; and, unfortunately, our speculations about changing global structures involve variables that are not readily observed. (Rosenau 1976: 8)

Every academic discipline requires a subject that practitioners agree will be the focus for study: no subject matter means no discipline. This statement might seem obvious or trite. Yet it has many intriguing ramifications for social or 'soft' science subjects, such as Politics, International Relations, History, Media and Communications and Sociology, because looking across these endeavours we do not find much agreement on what the 'core' of each discipline is, or should be. So when I ask 'what is the world of international relations?', I am trying to alert you to what I call the problem of the subject matter of IR: what are we actually looking at and attempting to theorize in this discipline? As A.K. Ramakrishnan rightly points out, 'Generating knowledge requires the knower to identify and speak about an object' (1999: 132). In IR this proves contentious because, as R.B.J. Walker (1995: 314) has astutely observed, most of the debates we engage in 'arise far more from disagreements about what it is that scholars think they are studying than from disagreements about how to study it'.

To explore this further, we can take a cue from literature on the philosophy of social science by comparing the study of the social (or behavioural) sciences on the one hand with the study of the natural (or physical) sciences on the other (see Scriven 1994). This will enable us, first, to draw some preliminary conclusions about the problematic nature of the subject matter of IR and, second, to gain insights into the reasons why theoretical disputes recur in the discipline, helping to drive forward the search for knowledge about contemporary global politics.

> If you have friends at university studying in different departments (social or natural sciences) try asking them about their respective disciplines: what do they study and how? Is the subject matter of their discipline and how to study it generally well recognized, or is it contested? Who decides these things? Compare their experiences to your experience of studying International Relations.

Let us start with simple, dictionary-style definitions of the principal natural sciences:

- Biology – the study of living organisms.
- Chemistry – the study of the composition, properties and reactions of substances.
- Physics – the study of the properties of matter and energy.

These disciplines are clearly not monolithic. That is to say, they are divided into communities of scholars working in component sub-disciplines, each with their own scope for inquiry. For instance, physics breaks down into astrophysics, nuclear physics, quantum physics and others. Chemistry is divided between organic and inorganic, physical, analytical and biochemistry; biologists can do genetics, anatomy, physiology, biotechnology and others. Nor are the natural sciences immune from some pretty fevered debates about disciplinary development and cohesion. These are especially marked around novel findings or approaches that challenge existing **paradigms** and claim the status of 'mature' research to sit alongside more established ways of tackling a subject. For example, in a different major discipline, engineering, Allen Cheng and Timothy Lu (2012) have studied the emergence of 'synthetic biology', which challenges entrenched disciplinary boundaries by reaching out to biology, offering a quite different perspective on what it means to 'do' both biology and engineering.

So, we have established the argument that the natural sciences are fragmented and have different 'wings' to them, representing their subdisciplinary specialisms. Nevertheless, there is usually quite a robust consensus among biologists, chemists, physicists and engineers on essential aspects of their work: on their object of study (the problem to be solved by a given wing of the discipline), on how to study that problem (the methods of experimentation), on what qualifies as vouchsafe evidence, and on when theories or explanations for a given phenomenon have become obsolete. Martin Hollis and Steve Smith describe this model of 'doing' natural science as follows: 'the broad idea is that events are governed by laws of nature which apply whenever similar events occur in similar conditions. Science progresses by learning which similarities are key to which sequences' (Hollis and Smith 1991: 3). Nicholas Onuf likewise insinuates that the idea of modern science is 'institutionalized through general acceptance of the procedural rules (*the scientific method*) for checking theoretical models (*models stipulating causal relations*) against evidence (*the findings from different experiments*) taken to represent some feature of "the real world" and refining these models accordingly' (Onuf 2009: 187, my emphasis).

This process of disciplinary development is shown in Figure 1, which assumes that the wheels of a discipline turn when scholars come to agree on: (1) the object/phenomenon/event/process to be studied; (2) how to study the object/phenomenon/event/process; (3) what qualifies as evidence about the object/phenomenon/event/process; and (4) when theories about the object/phenomenon/event/process have been disproved, or proven so untenable that new theories are needed to provide more adequate explanations.

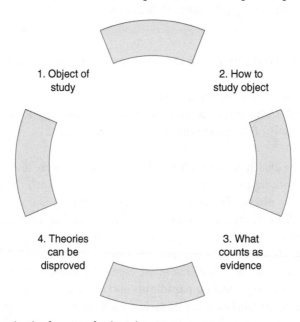

Figure 1   How the wheels of a scientific discipline turn

Having established what the disciplinary wheel looks likes for natural scientists, the question for students of IR is: can, we replicate this approach for disciplines in the social sciences? I am not sure we can, for the very simple reason that the subject matter of IR is **essentially contested** – there is no agreement on what constitutes the basic subject matter of IR. From this vexed issue, many other problems flow.

> As you progress through your IRT course make a list of all the essentially contested concepts, objects and ideas you come across. Why are they essentially contested? What has that contestation meant for how we study them in IR?

In the natural sciences, the objects we study tend to be physical things we can pick up, pin down, observe and measure, either with our own eyes or with the help of measuring devices such as blood pressure gauges for medics or speedometers for automotive engineers. A chemist can don a pair of safety goggles and drop a chunk of potassium into a basin of water to observe the furious reaction. A physicist can monitor the impact of temperature on solids by heating a strip of metal and watching the atoms vibrate faster and faster under a microscope. A biologist can test the impact of light on plant growth by measuring the relative speed of growth of the same plant in lighter and darker conditions. A medical doctor in an Emergency Room can hold up an X-ray to the light to see whether or not a bone is broken. Hence, as Kal Holsti rightly observes (1985: 7), 'To develop theory, before we can discuss technique, there must be some consensus on what we want to examine.'

In the natural sciences the tangibility of the subject matter helps researchers agree on the problem or object to be studied, on how to study it, on what counts as evidence and, finally, to agree on when theories have become flawed or obsolete. The disciplinary wheel turns smoothly without too much friction that might be generated by in-depth speculation on metatheoretical questions about ontology, epistemology and **methodology**. Natural scientists can put things that interest them under a microscope and study their properties and behaviour in order to generate theories. If they are unable to 'see' what interests them at first hand (the speed of light, for example) they have developed instruments that can measure them accurately in the absence of the visual evidence itself.

Importantly, all such measures come to be validated over time through consensus building in the scientific community. Experiments can be replicated by other scientists who can confirm the accuracy of the results and share ideas on what to study next. This process of **falsification** relies on each scientist's work being constantly tested and challenged by other scientists. This process is made easier by the existence of the physical objects that form the basis for experimentation in the natural sciences in different laboratories around the globe. We could say in very simple terms, therefore, that natural scientists generate knowledge the **empiricist** way. Like David Attenborough studying the behaviour of tree frogs in the Amazonian rainforest, natural scientists rely on having direct access to a 'real world' which they move through with the help of scientific instruments that help them see, measure and interpret the world around them.

To put it in formal terms, knowledge in the natural sciences is held to be accurate and reliable when it:

- has a grounded ontology – theory connected with the things, properties and events that exist in the world; what is held to be 'out there' and in need of investigation.
- is rooted in empiricist epistemology – theory about how we know things and what is regarded as valid/reliable/legitimate knowledge in a given discipline.
- flows from a robust methodology – rules and guidelines on how to set up experiments and interpret and record the data collected.
- is subject to falsification – a statement, theory or explanation might never be proved undoubtedly true but should be rejected when predictions derived from it turn out to be false.

Empirical scientific investigation tends to be the benchmark by which our claim to produce hard and fast knowledge about the world is judged. Do you think it is fair to judge social scientific knowledge production in this way? Studying IRT will give you lots of ground on which to come to a judgement.

We can now add these formal labels to the disciplinary wheel in Figure 2.

By now you will have twigged why I asked the question 'what is the world of international relations?' It is because the discipline of IR is centrally concerned with investigating relationships between events and processes in the world, yet there is no agreement amongst theorists on what precisely it is that the discipline should study, on how to study it, on what qualifies as evidence, and on when theories have been proved false. This is why

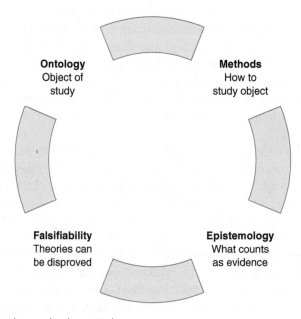

Ontology
Object of
study

Methods
How to
study object

Falsifiability
Theories can
be disproved

Epistemology
What counts
as evidence

Figure 2   The disciplinary wheel revisited

courses in IRT cover so many theories. None of their authors ever admit they are wrong because evidence can always be found to support a rejigged version of the theory, or supposedly established historical facts can be put through new interpretive lenses to generate new insights.

> Think about the differences between disciplines that study 'tangible' things and those that study 'intangible' ones. What does this imply for the reliability of the theories developed in each field, and what steps do you think we can take to develop more accurate methods for explaining the relationships between intangible things?

Unlike in the natural sciences where we can pick things up, put them down, throw them up in the air and see what happens, how can we possibly do this with 'the world', which is what scholars of IR necessarily try to do? In the following section we will start to see how this problem of the subject plays out in the study of IRT by exploring competing definitions of 'international relations'.

WHAT ARE 'INTERNATIONAL RELATIONS'?

At the start of his book *Understanding International Relations*, Chris Brown (2001: 1) explains why it is important to identify the scope of the field:

> The reason definitions matter in this way is because 'international relations' do not have some kind of essential existence in the real world of the sort that could define an academic discipline. Instead, there is a continual interplay between the 'real world' and the world of knowledge.

Brown adopts the same approach to the problem of the subject in IR that we did in the last section. His logic goes as follows:

- The development of academic disciplines is predicated upon there being a well-defined subject matter which organizes and focuses enquiry – for scholars researching it and students learning about it (maybe in time to become scholars themselves).
- IR theorists engage with a subject matter that does not necessarily exist in the 'real world' of observable (physical) things. We cannot pick 'states' up and slide them under a microscope to see how they interact. Nor do many of us get to 'see' states doing **diplomacy** at first hand because of the restricted access to policy communities.
- The subject matter of IR is made doubly hard to pin down because it is so bound up with contemporary developments in global politics and the *study* of global affairs.
- To put it another way: the world which scholars of IR are studying is constantly in a state of flux.
- Therefore, the subject matter of IR is in dispute.

COMMON PITFALL

In essays and exams, you will be expected to be able to summarize key ideas in the field of IR. Too often students do not show the patience to explain the interpretations that writers arrive at, or why. Introducing scholars as 'renowned Professor of IR' is irrelevant. Telling readers how they interpret IR is the crux. Note in the above how we have taken Brown's argument apart step by step by examining his assumptions and the conclusions he derives from them.

Brown (2001: 1) goes on to suggest that the field of IR encompasses the study of some or all of the following:

1. Diplomatic-strategic relations between **nation-states** – with a focus on war and peace, conflict and cooperation. This was the 'classical' subject matter of the discipline, also well described by Holsti (1985: 10): 'the consequence of a world made up of states, each possessing the capacity to make war against each other. Alan James is another person who equates IR with the study of 'inter-state relations', saying that we should only account for the influence of non-state actors as and when they impinge on what goes on between states (James 1993: 270).
2. Cross-border transactions of all kinds – meaning the whole gamut of political, economic and social exchanges between states.
3. Globalization – of economies, communications, transport and financial systems, **multinational corporations** and so on.

You can see from this all-embracing definition that, when looking at international relations, we are potentially looking at anything and everything that happens anywhere in the world. It is as difficult nailing down the subject matter of IR as it is nailing jelly to a wall: 'more keenly in some periods than others, almost every aspect of the study of international politics has been contested' (Burchill and Linklater 2013: 5).

As you progress through your course reading, think carefully about the particular focus of the texts you read because this will help you understand the way authors approach the 'problem of the subject' in IR.

Burchill and Linklater's inclusive approach is now quite common. To take another example, in their *Handbook of International Relations*, Walter Carlsnaes, Thomas Risse and Beth Simmons (2012) split their work into three parts. Part I is on 'historical, philosophical and theoretical issues'. Part II is on 'concepts and context', including chapters on state **sovereignty**, power, diplomacy, bargaining and negotiation, **interdependence** and the interactivity between domestic politics and international relations. Part III is on the substantive issues Brown majors on and which Burchill and Linklater incorporate into their list of themes and issues in IR.

The upshot of all this is that there is no agreement on what constitutes either the subject area of IR, or how to study this subject. Potentially, it 'encompasses all phases of human experience because its scope is global and its foci as diverse as the values, pre-occupations, and practices of people everywhere' (Rosenau 2002: 545). Grayson Kirk's 1947 comment on the state of the discipline is as relevant now as it was then (quoted in Schmidt 2006: 3):

> the study of international relations is still in a condition of considerable confusion. The scope of the field, the methods of analysis and synthesis to be followed, the proper administrative arrangements to be made in college curricula, the organization of research – all these are matters of continuing controversy.

 TAKING IT FURTHER

International Relations or World Politics?

In their textbook *The Globalization of World Politics*, John Baylis, Steve Smith and Patricia Owens (2014a: 2–3) begin by outlining why they use the term 'World Politics' rather than 'International Politics' or 'International Relations' in their book title (see also Viotti and Kauppi 2014: 1).

'World Politics', they say, suggests something 'more inclusive than either of the alternative terms. It is meant to signal the fact that our interest is in the politics and political patterns in the world and not only those between nation-states (as the terms internatiopnal relations or international politics imply)' (Baylis et al. 2008: 2). Their choice of title shows the power of language and labels, and why it is important for us to take both seriously when studying at university level. Let us break down their argument into its constituent parts:

- 'International Relations' implies the study of relations between nation-states. For greater accuracy we might rewrite it 'Inter-national Relations'.
- 'International Politics' is similarly limited: 'Inter-national Politics'.
- Neither signifier does justice to what Baylis, Smith and Owens consider to be the essence of the field, which is both wider and deeper than the relations between nation-states.
- IR for Baylis, Smith and Owens is about the study of *politics* and *political patterns* in the world. They are interested in explaining the web of connections and *relationships* between *all* actors in the world.
- Nation-states undoubtedly retain an immensely important place in the study of IR, but they do not play the only or even the most decisive part in global politics today. 'World politics' is more comprehensive and a more apt description of the realities of contemporary global political interactions, which involve states, institutions, international organizations, trans-national actors such as terrorist networks, regional actors and **sub-nationalactors**.

Other textbooks that opt for 'World Politics' indicate the stretch in meaning the term implies. For example, Jeffrey Haynes et al.'s (2011) *World Politics* begins with theories

(Continued)

(Continued)

and moves on to a number of themes and issues in IR such as democratization, 'new wars' and terrorism. Karen Mingst and Jack Snyder's (2011) *Essential Readings in World Politics* includes some specifically theoretical interventions but many more which talk to the 'themes and issues' agenda. Shawn Smallman and Kimberley Brown's (2011) *Introduction to International and Global Studies* is broader still. Theory is conspicuous by its absence with the emphasis firmly on the origins and evolution of contemporary global problems such as war, energy security and global underdevelopment. As with the Baylis, Smith and Owens book, nation-states are nowhere near as central to the presentation of IR in these books. The emerging consensus is well put by Peter Sutch and Juanita Elias (2007: 2) who write that the study of international relations 'does not tell us very much about our subject' because 'the agents of international relations that make up the political landscape of our subject area, are not nations at all'. You pay your money, you take your chances!

. . . .

SOME GOOD NEWS FOR IRT STUDENTS EVERYWHERE

Happily, to succeed at a course in IRT you do not need to become a fervent historian of the discipline. Nor do you have to develop a particularly expert knowledge of the ways in which writers and teachers carve up the discipline for their students. However, it is useful for you to be aware of debates arising from the 'problem of the subject' because they will shape the theories you encounter on your course and how those theories generate and apply knowledge about the 'real world'. Ask yourself why it is that some actors and methods have conventionally been 'held largely silent' by the discipline, while others have flourished and come to dominate the agenda (Watson 2006: 237). Forming an opinion on this question will help you in three ways. First of all, it will help you understand the theories you do cover. Second, it will help you analyse the strengths and weaknesses of these theories' claims to produce hard and fast knowledge about the world of international|relations. Third, it will help you make sense of the way in which IR has dealt with state-centric theories on the one hand, and those theories on the other hand that deal with the host of non-state actors that operate above, below and across state borders (a good example being Davis 2009).

QUESTIONS TO PONDER

'Can social scientists claim to produce the same kind of knowledge as natural scientists? Should they try?'

The first thing to do with this question is to consider definitional issues: how do we define 'natural' and 'social' sciences? Give examples of fields or disciplines you consider to belong in each category. Maybe even include a small two-column table listing 'social' or 'soft' sciences on the left and 'natural' sciences on the right. Think about defining the 'kind of knowledge' produced by each set of scholars: what are the similarities and differences? Is one more 'grounded', more certain, more reliable than the other, and if so why? A simple way to introduce the differences would be to use ideas about the 'problem of the subject' in IR and the 'tangible/intangible' divide explored in this chapter. If we can't pick up a piece of evidence up and throw it against a wall to test its properties, then it is probably not amenable to methods of investigation used by natural scientists. Ideas, practices and behaviours all fall into the latter category.

Your second task is to come up with some way of judging the implications of what you say in the first part. Assuming social sciences do produce different forms of knowledge, do you think this is a good thing or a bad thing – and what do you mean by 'good' and 'bad'? Do you think the social sciences should try to emulate the natural sciences at all? Certainly many social scientists would claim to produce 'objective' and non-biased knowledge – is that the same as being 'scientific', and how do they validate their approaches? The better students might throw into doubt the whole idea of the natural sciences being a paragon of virtue as far as scientific knowledge production is concerned.

COMMON PITFALL

When a question has two parts to it, students sometimes forget to answer the second part, especially when under pressure in exams. In the above, the second question 'should they try?' invites you to consider the knock-on (ethical) implications of your answer to the first part. Not bothering with the evaluative element of the question component will severely limit the mark you obtain, however good your answer to the first part. It's the second part of this question where most of the marks for being 'critical' (analytical) are to be gained.

'Why is the subject matter of IR essentially contested?'

This is slightly harder to structure than the first answer because it is open ended, inviting you to consider any and every reason why writers disagree about the most appropriate focus for IR. You have to be absolutely focused on narrowing your essay to just a few points, framed at the outset by the use of a simple, clear argument that outlines what you go on to say in the rest of the answer. Given that you are inevitably working to a time limit (in an exam) or a word limit (in an essay), one useful approach is to list all the reasons you can think of and then concentrate on, say, the three or four that you consider the most compelling. You can then structure your answer around each of the points in turn. A possible list might include:

- Labels: 'Inter-national Relations' (narrower remit) or 'World Politics' (wider remit)?
- Which actors?
- What is 'the world' in which these actors operate – which theme in IR are you explaining?
- The subject is ever-changing because the world is constantly changing.
- Events or issues seen as important in one era will not necessarily seem so in another.

REFERENCES TO MORE INFORMATION

Generally, on the problems of studying Politics and IR:

Shimko, K.L. (2011) *International Relations: Perspectives, Controversies and Readings*, 4th edn. Boston, MA: Houghton Mifflin Company.
A good introductory text which shows you where theory fits into the wider study of IR.

Bleiker, R. (1997) 'Forget IR Theory', *Alternatives*, 22(1): 57–85.
Critical evaluation of the methods, practices and limitations of orthodox IR.

Halliday, F. (1995) 'International Relations: Is there a New Agenda?', *Millennium*, 20(1): 57–72.
Examines the interplay between the global political agenda and how developments in the 'real world' of international relations affect the academic study of IR.

Walt, S.M. (1998) 'International Relations: One World, Many Theories', *Foreign Policy*, 110, Special Edition: Frontiers of Knowledge: 29–46.
Reviews the impact of the end of the Cold War on theorizing in IR.

Hoffman, S. (2001) 'An American Social Science: International Relations', in R.M.A. Crawford and D.S.L. Jarvis (eds) *International Relations: Still an American Social Science?: Towards Diversity in International Thought*. Albany, NY: State University of New York Press, pp. 27–51.

Goodwin, G.L. and Linklater, A. (1975) 'Introduction', in G.L. Goodwin and A. Linklater (eds) *New Dimensions of World Politics*. London: Croom Helm.
Has some useful words at the start on the distinction between 'International Relations' and 'World Politics'.

Jackson, N. and Tansey, S.D. (2015) *Politics: The Basics*, 5th edn. Abingdon: Routledge.

More advanced texts on the nature and role of theory:

Hollis, M. and Smith, S. (1991) *Explaining and Understanding International Relations*. Oxford: Clarendon Press.
Very good on **empiricism** and its implications for theoretical development.

Buzan, B. (1995) 'The Level of Analysis Problem in International Relations Reconsidered', in K. Booth and S. Smith (eds) *International Relations Theory Today*. Cambridge: Polity Press, pp. 198–216.

Singer, J.D. (1961) 'The Levels of Analysis Problem in International Relations', *World Politics*, 14(1): 77–92.

Martin, M. and Mcintyre, L.C. (eds) (1994) *Readings in the Philosophy of Social Science*. Cambridge, MA: MIT Press.
A series of excerpts from key writings in the field. Particularly recommended are Chapter 6 by Scriven, Chapter 9 by McIntyre, Chapter 18 by Lukes and Chapter 27 by Durkheim.

Herrman, R.K. (2006) 'Linking Theory to Evidence in International Relations', in W. Carlsnaes, T. Risse and B.A. Simmons (eds) *Handbook of International Relations*. London: Sage, pp. 119–36.
A defence of positivist thinking in IR together with a consideration of other approaches to connecting theory with evidence.

More general issues raised in this chapter:

Becher, T. and Trowler, P.R. (2001) *Academic Tribes and Territories*, 2nd edn. Buckingham: Society for Research into Higher Education and Open University Press.
See Chapter 3 for an account of how academics from across disciplines view their work and how this helps us define the concept of a 'discipline'.

Kuhn, T.S. (1996) *The Structure of Scientific Revolutions*, 3rd edn. Chicago, IL: University of Chicago Press.
Ostensibly about the natural sciences, this path-breaking book boasts a wealth of information about the positioned foundations of all academic knowledge – good for the second 'Question to Ponder' above.

Neuman, W.L. (2013) *Basics of Social Research: Qualitative and Quantitative Approaches*, 3rd edn. Harlow: Pearson Education.
In Chapter 1, Neuman argues that knowledge generated by 'scientific' research is more reliable than knowledge gained by other means.

Barnett, M. and Duvall, R. (2005) 'Power in International Politics', *International Organization*, 59(1): 39–75.
Gives you an idea of how to map disagreements between different IR traditions and explains the causes of some of their disputes.

2

INTERNATIONAL RELATIONS THEORY

[W]e are all theoreticians and the only issue is what kinds of theories should we adopt to guide us in our attempts to understand the subject matter. (Joynt and Corbett 1978: 102)

What is theory? Why do we have to bother with theory – can't we study IR on its own terms? Why not just look at the facts? These are just some of the questions you might legitimately be asking yourself as you embark on your journey through your IR studies. I want to answer them now by way of introduction, and then in Chapter 3 we will return to some of the core issues raised and develop them using the language and conceptual tools as they will appear in your course lectures, seminars and assignments.

WHAT IS THEORY?

Theories have to rely on some principles of selection to narrow their scope of inquiry; they discriminate between actors, relationships, empirical issues and so forth which they judge most important or regard as trivial. (Burchill and Linklater 2013: 14)

The previous chapter explored the consequences of the subject matter of IR being essentially contested: all scholars bring to the field conflicting yet sometimes overlapping opinions on what constitutes the 'essence' of IR. Disputes run even deeper than that, however. Not only do experts disagree on what to study, but they also differ on how to study IR and what qualifies as appropriate evidence to support their claims. With all this complexity and dispute in mind, it seems logical for **rational** human beings (assuming that's what academics are!) to seek to navigate some sort of logical path through this mire of uncertainty. This is where theory comes in.

Think about previous occasions when you encountered a theory or theories in your studies at school or college. What was the purpose of those theories? What did theorists try and achieve by developing them? Did they help you understand more about the subject and how? What were their strengths and weaknesses?

Burchill and Linklater's neat summary, above, of the part theory plays in the study of IR will be the starting point for our consideration of what theory actually is. The telling words they use are 'principles of selection'. Theories take complexity and try to simplify it. How theorists do this, and the success they have trying, are less important to us at this stage than recognizing the goals theorists set themselves (see Jørgensen 2010: 8–9 for a useful text box called 'Ten perspectives on the function of theory'). Let us take a range of opinions from leading thinkers in the discipline and to see how they treat theory:

- **Martin Wight** (1995: 15): 'By "international theory" is meant a tradition of speculation about relations between states.' You can see here how Wight solves the problem of the subject by taking a popular line on the appropriate subject matter of IR, reflecting its original date of publication (1966): it is nothing more, nothing less than a study of relations between states.
- **Hans Morgenthau** (1985: 3): Theories 'bring order and meaning to a mass of phenomena which without it would remain disconnected and unintelligible'. This is theory presented as a simplifying device to make sense of complexity.
- **Kenneth Waltz** (2010) 'Theories explain laws,' making them parallel 'to the definition of the term in the natural sciences'. Laws illustrate associations between variables, while theories explain the causal connections. Popular in American IR scholarship, the natural science rendering of theory (see previous chapter) is as follows (Rosato 2003: 585): a theory comprises a **hypothesis** stipulating an association between an independent and a dependent variable and a causal logic that explains the connection between them. The hypothesis is supported if it can be demonstrated experimentally that A (independent variable) causes B (dependent variable) because A causes x, which causes y, which causes B.
- **Martin Hollis and Steve Smith** (1991: 62–3): Theories perform three functions. First, theories abstract (group together events, situations or objects which are not identical). Second, they generalize (identify what these things which are not identical have in common by virtue of analysis of the available facts). And third, theories connect (identify cause and effect). This definition starts to move us away from considerations of how 'scientific' theory should or should not be and into the realm of how we put them to work. Abstraction, generalization and connection are, for Hollis and Smith, the basic prerequisites of theory in any academic discipline.
- **James Rosenau and Rosemary Durfee** (1995: 2): 'it is through theorizing that we can hope to tease meaningful patterns out of the endless details and inordinate complexities that sustain world politics'.
- **Barry Buzan** (2004: 24): Picks up regional dimensions to how we comprehend the nature and purpose of theory by writing that: 'Many Europeans use the term theory for anything that organizes a field systematically, structures questions and establishes a coherent and rigorous set of interrelated concepts and categories. Many Americans [see Waltz and Rosato above], however, often demand that a theory strictly explains and that it contains – or is able to generate – testable hypotheses of a causal nature.'
- **Liesbet Hooghe and Gary Marks** (2008: 2): These scholars from a different field, European Studies, show that you can find speculation about the nature of theory across the social sciences and humanities, and that you can be creative about where you look for this kind of material. They suggest that: 'Every theory is grounded on a set of

assumptions – intellectual short cuts – that reduce complexity and direct our attention to causally powerful factors.' It is reminiscent of the next authors' use of the term ...

- **Yale H. Ferguson and Richard W. Mansbach** (1996: 21): 'Theory purports to tell us what to look at and, by inference, what can be safely ignored. By simplifying reality, theory helps us organize our beliefs about an ever-changing world and offers an intellectual foundation for policies. Bad theory almost inevitably means bad policies.'
- **John Baylis, Steve Smith and Patricia Owens** (2014a: 3): 'a kind of simplifying device that allows you to decide which facts matter and which do not'. This definition undermines those who believe processes of theorizing in IR can or should mimic processes of theorizing in the natural sciences. Theory, they assert, is not simply 'some grand formal model with hypotheses and assumptions' (Baylis et al. 2014a: 3). Instead, we should be modest about what we can expect theory to deliver, and more aware of the presuppositions and biases we bring to the study of the social world.
- **Robert Jackson and Georg Sørensen** (2015: 55): 'We always look at the world, consciously or not, through a specific set of lenses; we may think of those lenses as theory.' Theory, according to this interpretation, forms a fundamental part of the world we live in; it makes the world and helps construct it for us whether we realize it or not.
- **Cynthia Weber** (2010: 2): 'IR theory makes organizing generalizations about international politics. IR theory is a collection of stories about the world of international politics. And in telling stories about international politics, IR theory doesn't just present what is going on in the world out there. IR theory also imposes its own vision of what the world out there looks like.' Weber pulls us even further from the realms of IR theory as natural science. Look at the language in that quotation. Words like 'story' imply imagined and imaginative elements to theories developed in the field of IR. Weber is in accordance with writers such as Baylis, Smith and Owens when she collapses the distinction between a 'world' of IR and a separate 'world' of the observer.

So, we encounter an array of perspectives on theory: what it is, what it should be, and how we should 'do' it. From the formal natural science model outlined by Waltz and Hollis and Smith to Weber's view that we are ourselves parts of the theories we devise, no two IR authors quite agree on what IR theory is or should be. In Chapter 3 we will revisit the debate about the impact of these debates on the nature of theory. For now, all you need to have clear in your mind is that these differences exist and they materially influence the work that goes on in the field of IR. In the next section we will take a step back and consider an even more basic question: why bother with theory in the first place?

Whenever you come across a definition of 'theory' make a note of it in a theory checklist as I have done above. It will provide you with a comprehensive list of writers and their respective viewpoints from which you can get lots of mileage in essays and exam answers.

WHY BOTHER WITH THEORY?

You are not alone if you doubt the 'value added' theory brings to the study of academic subjects. In this section we will review both sides of the argument by looking first of all at the positions taken by those writers who doubt the utility of theory. We then consider those writers who trumpet the value of theory – not just because they believe it is intrinsically useful to us but because it is inescapably everywhere, always shaping our study of the world whether we care to acknowledge its relevance or not. Several IR textbooks (for instance, Mansbach and Rafferty 2008) include reflections on the nature and uses of theory, so you can fruitfully consult these before moving to the detailed research.

The 'take it or leave it' approach to theory

In the discipline of History there is a book by Keith Windschuttle (1996) called *The Killing of History: How Literary Critics and Social Theorists are Murdering Our Past*. In the book, Windschuttle describes how History, as he sees it, concerned with the factually based narration of events in the past using archival documents and other remnants from the period in question, 'is now suffering a potentially mortal attack from the rise to academic prominence of a relatively new array of literary and social theories' which question traditional historical practices and the knowledge produced by them (Windschuttle 1996: 10). There is 'history', Windschuttle implies, and there is 'theory', and it is dangerous for the two to get mixed up because the former deals with the real world – the events and personalities that existed in the past – while the latter throws up needless conjecture about the reliability of all this knowledge. Too much concern with theory, Windschuttle argues, is dangerous. 'The central point upon which history was founded no longer holds: there is no fundamental distinction any more between history and myth' (ibid. 1996: 10).

Windschuttle's opinion is that we can have facts or we can have theory. We do not profit from mixing the two. In IR this 'take it or leave it' approach to theory can be exemplified using Raymond Aron's sceptical stance on theory. He said that theorizing international politics was more arduous than theorizing economics for a list of reasons that include the following: the international system is affected by happenings inside and outside states; states are not unitary actors possessing one single aim (i.e. different arms of the diplomatic machine may think about the same issue quite differently in terms of policy priorities); identifying the dependent and independent variables is impossible; supposed equilibria at the systemic level are inherently unstable; and prediction is impossible (Aron's position summarized in Waltz 1990: 25. For an excellent overview of Aron's contribution to international theory more generally, see Hoffman 1985).

As Rosenau describes this position (2003: 7–8): 'Frequent are the comments that theories are wasted effort and misleading, if not downright erroneous. "Come off your high theoretical perch," say the critics, "come down where the action is and get your hands dirty with real world data"'. This is something we can imagine Windschuttle saying, given his perspective above. Rosenau identifies three types of critic of 'theory' from within IR. First, there are people in government circles (the 'doers' as it were) who believe 'theory' is removed from the 'real' day-to-day public policy problems that need to be confronted. Second are journalists who echo Windschuttle by saying that theoretical language is gobbledygook ('Why don't they write in plain English?'). The third group is some academics who propound the notion that theory-based teaching is insufficiently policy-relevant (Rosenau 2003: 7–8).

William Wallace (a UK academic and politician all in one) put the latter view that IRT had become too detached from practice in a 1996 article on 'Truth and Power'. Having warned against the perils of 'scholasticism' and what he saw as IR scholars' increasing tendency to speak to each other rather than the outside world, Wallace opened fire on the 'flippancy' of the postmodernist 'celebration of theory at the expense of empirical work' (Wallace 1996: 311). Scholastic word games, he argued, are all very well. However, theory 'for its own sake' does nothing to contribute to public debate and certainly will not catch the ear of policy-makers (ibid.: 314). Wallace took the line that IRT needed to re-engage with the policy-driven agenda that made it such a fruitful approach to international affairs in its early years. Wallace did not suggest we 'leave' theory in quite the same fashion as Windschuttle, but he certainly gave the discipline cause to reflect on the uses of IRT. His opinion is an exemplar within IR of the view that we should treat theory with a degree of caution.

The 'theory is inescapable' approach

Many writers disagree with the view that we can 'take or leave' theory, like the dessert course on a restaurant menu. Writers subscribing to the interpretation that 'theory is inescapable' push the idea that theory is everywhere, and therefore that understanding theory is not an option but is rather forced on us by the conditions of our human existence. This is a very different understanding of theory and requires careful thought as you embark on your studies in IR.

A review of the literature in this area reveals two interconnected propositions about the role and value of theory. The first and arguably best known is associated with writers such as Steve Smith and Ken Booth, and features in some form in all their books and articles on IRT. The clearest rejection of the 'take it or leave it' line comes in Baylis, Smith and Owens' Introduction to *The Globalization of World Politics*:

> It is not as if you can say that you do not want to bother with a theory; all you want to do is to look at the 'facts'. We believe that this is simply impossible, since the only way in which you can decide which of the millions of possible facts to look at is by adhering to some simplifying device which tells you which ones matter the most. (Baylis et al. 2014a: 3)

Another writer who has long taken this position is James Rosenau:

> Being theoretical is unavoidable! Why? Because the very process of engaging in observation requires sorting out some of the observed phenomena as important and dismissing others as trivial. There is no alternative. The details of situations do not speak for themselves. Patterns are not self-evident. Observers must give them meaning through the theories they bring to bear. They must, to repeat, select out from everything they observe those aspects that seem significant and discard those they deem as inconsequential. (2003: 8)

Writing with Rosemary Durfee (Rosenau and Durfee 1995: 2), Rosenau had earlier made the point that 'inevitably we engage in a form of theorizing whenever we observe world affairs' because we are always involved – self-consciously or not – in a process of selection and abstraction when we try to make sense of goings on in the world around us. As they surmised, 'we are continuously impelled to treat any observation we make as partly a product of our premises about the way things work in world politics' (Rosenau and Durfee 1995: 3). Fred Halliday agrees, contending that theory performs three functions with respect to facts. First, theory helps us decide which facts are significant and which are not. Second, theory helps us explain how the same fact can be interpreted differently. Third, theory helps bring to the fore questions of ethics and morality which cannot be decided by an appeal to the facts alone. Whether you are an under-pressure member of a government, a busy journalist, or a lecture-worn academic you will use theory daily to come to a view on pressing political matters. Whenever we ask the question, 'of what is this an instance?' we are using theory to help determine the answer (Rosenau and Durfee 1995: 4).

When watching television, listening to the radio and sifting through news stories on social media think about the number of times you hear the words 'fact'. Why are the 'facts' of a story prized so highly? What is it about 'facts' that makes them so important to us? What, at root, *are* 'facts'?

Why do these writers see a world in which theory is inescapably everywhere? The answer lies in a second assumption about the role theory has played, unwittingly or not, in the actual conduct of international relations. As Stephen Walt explains:

> Even policymakers who are contemptuous of 'theory' must rely on their own (often unstated) ideas about how the world works in order to decide what to do. It is hard to make good policy if one's basic organizing principles are flawed, just as it is hard to construct good theories without knowing a lot about the real world. (1998: 29)

In this view, scholars engage in theoretical speculation (a very well-known fact), but so do policy-makers (a less well-known fact). It is only by knowing theory that we can improve practice and, by the same token, theoretical sophistication comes from knowing about the world policy-makers inhabit. As Martin Wight observed: 'The political philosophy of international relations is the fully-conscious formulated theory, illustrations of which you may find in the conduct of some statesmen, [Woodrow] Wilson, probably [Winston] Churchill, perhaps [Jawaharlal] Nehru' (Wight 1987: 221).

Our goal here is not to evaluate the persuasiveness of this argument (I leave that to you as you progress through this book and your IR studies), but rather to set out a range of opinions you might find interesting as points of departure. Steve Smith (1995: 3) puts the theory–practice overlap in its sharpest relief by writing that 'international theory has tended to be a **discourse** accepting of, and complicit in, the creation and recreation of international practices that threaten, discipline and do violence to others'. He points to the role that theoretical assumptions associated with the Realist tradition (explored in Chapter 5 of this book) played in moulding superpower foreign policies during the Cold War from 1945 to 1989, particularly in terms of the nuclear arms race. Playing an active part in the development of aggressive American and Russian foreign policies, this suggests, Realist IRT can be held partially accountable for some of the many horrors and (near) catastrophes the world witnessed during that period. Smith has therefore entered into dialogue with William Wallace (see above) over the alleged 'theory–policy' divide, which he sees as a misnomer. Theory and practice are not separate spheres of activity, Smith argues: 'theory is already implicated in practice, and practice is unavoidably theoretical'; the world is theoretical 'all the way down' (1997: 515).

Tim Dunne and Brian Schmidt agree that policy and theory intertwine, especially as far as Realism goes: 'From 1939 to the present, leading theorists and policymakers have continued to view the world through realist lenses' (2008: 92). Francis Fukuyama likewise suggests that Realism has provided 'the dominant framework for understanding international relations and shapes the thinking of virtually every foreign policy professional today in the United States and much of the rest of the world' (quoted in Little 1995: 71). Robert Jervis (2008: 575) cautions that this might be too simplistic a view: 'I suspect that this argument, taken too literally, excessively flatters us: can any instructor who has read final examinations really believe that our students have listened that carefully?' However, he continues (ibid.), there is something to recommend this interpretation, for 'it is certainly possible that many general precepts have crept into the minds of those who make foreign policy'. Recent research supports this view, showing how Realist 'pessimism' remains a widely used framework for analysis of USA–China relations (Zheng 2016). We come back to the principles of Realism in Chapter 5. For now, Martin Hollis and Steve Smith give us an excellent summary of the 'theory is inescapable' approach:

> [M]any International Relations scholars are directly involved in the US foreign and defence policy community. They try to use their theories to improve policy-making and they search for theories which will be relevant and useful for this purpose … Hence the truth of International Relations theories has something to do with which theories are known and applied in the process they purport to analyse. (1991: 70–1)

The salient point is that Realism is the theory most frequently cited by writers seeking examples of the theory–practice overlap.

Is it just coincidence that Realism is so often used as an illustration of the interplay between the theory and practice of international relations? As you go through your course see if you can find other examples from the literature where writers cite a direct connection between theory (any theory) and practice in international relations.

In sum, contrary to the 'take it or leave it' approach, writers in the 'theory is inescapable' school are very clear about the pervasiveness, the 'everywhere-ness' of theory. For them, there is no such thing as choosing to use a theory or not, because it is a fundamental part of life. And if that is not enough, they argue, look at the reasons why IR was founded as an academic discipline (explored further in Chapter 3 below). It was set up in the aftermath of the First World War (1914–18) to help us understand and explain (theorize) the relations between states, so that the futile carnage of the Great War could be avoided in the future.

The theory–practice overlap has not just come about by chance, but by design. As Burchill and Linklater (2013: 7) explain: 'The purpose of theory in the early years of the discipline was to change the world for the better by removing the blight of war. A close connection existed between theory and practice: theory was not disconnected from the actual world of international politics.' Jervis (2008: 573) argues that although this Liberal leaning has been severely questioned over the years, IR's founding intent is just as powerful today: 'even if they are not advising governments or writing op-eds, most students of international politics and foreign policy do wish to make the world safer and better'. If we accept the 'theory is inescapable' approach in general, then in the field of IR its ramifications are doubly important because it is a discipline and a practice that deals directly with war, conflict, death and destruction.

· ·

 TAKING IT FURTHER

Ray Winstone on facts and theory

In 2009 a UK advertisement for a breakfast cereal ran on television and in the cinema, featuring British actor Ray Winstone. In the advert Winstone complained that: 'When it comes to food there's a bit of a nanny culture thing going on. Don't do this. Don't do that. That is very bad for you. This is for your own good.' He argued that we should be free to choose for ourselves how we live and what we do to our bodies – the state should butt out. 'We're old enough and wise enough to just be given the facts, so this is a new cereal called Optivita. It contains oatbran which can help actively reduce cholesterol. Now, it's up to you to reduce cholesterol – or not.' In the final scene Winstone made clear he was not trying to bully us into making a decision. 'Well don't look at me: I'm not gonna tell you what to do.' The decision, it seems, was ours – to eat Optivita or not to eat Optivita.

There are many interesting points about this advert, not least the idea that you might choose to ignore the advice of a well-known 'hard man' such as Winstone. But the crucial point for us lies in the moves the advert made to convince us to buy this product. Winstone tells us that there is a 'bit of a nanny culture thing going on' when it comes to food. This is asserted as the truth (a 'fact' if you like). However, the nature of that 'nanny culture' was neither defined nor elaborated upon – as if every viewer would instantly plug into what he is talking about. There is an extensive British libertarian tradition of railing against an overweening 'nanny state' which unnecessarily interferes in the daily lives of 'ordinary people'. The advert was broadcast at a time when the then British Prime Minister Tony Blair was promoting the idea of 'social marketing'. This relied on food companies giving the public more information on health and diet because Blair felt that consumers were more likely to believe companies than the government and untrustworthy politicians (Wainwright and Carvel 2006). The 'fact' of the matter was that Britain was becoming less of a 'nanny state' just when this advert told us it was becoming more of one.

Thus, the 'nanny culture thing' was not a fact about the world, but a perspective relying on one reading of events. It was one interpretation or 'take' on the government's policy to promote corporate and social responsibility for healthy living. If we did not accept the theory of the nanny state as far as healthy eating went, then the rationale for both the cereal and the advert went out of the window. The idea that there are theory-free 'facts' about the world might not be as accurate as we might wish to believe.

Can you think of other advertisements which rely on theories about how the world works presented as straightforward facts about how the world works?

· ·

INTERNATIONAL RELATIONS THEORY ON FILM

To put more flesh on the bones of the argument that 'theory is everywhere' we can look to work that illustrates how we can see IRT in popular films. Scholars of IR are not alone in debating the value – or otherwise – of theory, and in doing so they show how deeply interconnected IR as a discipline is with the wider cultural context within which scholarship is practised and disseminated. If we take seriously this view that approaches to IR transcend the discipline, it has potentially radical consequences both for where we look to understand the theories, and how we can critique them in an academic sense. Gone in this account are the days of the lonely scholar sat in an ivory tower amidst a morass of papers and books, writing huge tomes which only get read by a handful of other scholars working in the same field, but of marginal importance to society as a whole.

> There is a popular phrase, 'It's only academic', used to refer to something that has theoretical relevance but no practical relevance. In the study of IR is it feasible to say that the books and articles we read are ever only of 'academic' relevance?

Two writers who make this point very effectively are Cynthia Weber (2013) and Dan Drezner (2011), who show us how we can use popular films and characters to understand and critique key IR theories. Other works operating in a similar vein include the book *Harry Potter and International Relations* edited by Daniel Nexon and Iver Neumann (2013) and Stephen Dyson's (2015) book using *Star Trek*, *Game of Thrones* and *Battlestar Galactica* to illustrate theories and issues in IR. At first sight this might seem a strange thing to do. Is not IR a distinct discipline of study with its own language, ideas, set of concepts, and 'great debates'? Is it not the case that early IR theorists and their successors today pride themselves on working in a separable, if not separate, social scientific discipline which they have worked for years to demarcate from history, law, philosophy, politics and economics (see Chapter 3)? What can Weber's films and Drezner's zombies tell us about a theoretical, sometimes abstract subject like IR?

How you answer this question depends on your view of what makes an academic discipline and what makes for a valid approach to studying IRT. Let us take a look at the reasons why Weber believes that it is enlightening to study IR through film using two quotes from her book:

> IR theory can be studied as a site of cultural practice. IR theory is an 'ensemble of stories' told about the world it studies, which is the world of international politics. Studying IR theory as a site of cultural practice means being attentive to how IR theory makes sense of the world of international politics. (Weber 2010: 4)
>
> Popular films provide students with answers to the question, How does an IR myth appear to be true? In so doing, popular films point to how politics, power, and ideology are culturally constructed, and how the culture of IR theory might be politically reconstructed. (Ibid.: 20)

The points that Weber and these other writers make are very thought provoking.

First of all, like Holsti (1985), she argues that the development of IRT reveals a good deal about the wider cultures and systems of thought within which those theories have been developed, particularly the 'Western' bias within the discipline. IR is assumed to be a site of 'cultural practice' which reveals theorists' unspoken assumptions about how the world operates and the unwritten agendas driving their work. Postcolonial IR (covered in Chapter 13 of this book) is particularly good on the subject of scholarship and the reproduction of entrenched power hierarchies: 'With few exceptions, the accounts of world politics that serve as the ground for IR theory-building and empirical analysis are Eurocentric, taking the perspective of the most powerful states in the international system' (Laffey and Weldes 2008: 556). Second, the 'stories' that IR theorists tell us about the world rely on the same plot lines, or narratives, we find in 'stories' told to us by novelists and filmmakers: beginnings, middles and ends are fictions created by us to make sense of a series of events chronologically.

As Dyson explains it (2015: 3): 'Real history fires the imagination of fantasy and sci-fi authors. And the study of international relations is, by necessity as speculative and imaginative as a lot of sci-fi.' This is not intended to be disparaging, Dyson continues (p. 3): 'the imagined notions are not incorrect – but they are of necessity hypothesized and unobservable'. He goes on to show that the central concept in the study of Politics and IR, power, is not tangible being defined in very different ways by different writers. In taking this approach, Dyson is picking up on the 'problem of the subject' we explored in the previous chapter of this book. Third, theories have to rely on hidden assumptions to make them 'work'. They are 'mythical' in the sense that they purport to describe aspects of the 'real world' whilst simultaneously constructing aspects of that 'real world' for us (this is what goes on in the Ray Winstone advert in the 'Taking it further' section above). Finally, since IR, like novels and films, is composed of 'stories' about international politics, uncovering the assumptions and ideologies behind the narratives IR tells enables us to rethink the basis of IRT itself.

This strategy for studying IRT is enlightening because:

- It helps us better understand the theories by making a difficult set of ideas and technical language more accessible to us as students.
- It helps us critique the theories as well us understanding them. Being able to critique theories will be a vital part of the assessments you undertake on your course in IRT, particularly in your final two years of study when the evaluative and judgmental skills (weighing up the pros and cons of different traditions of IRT) are being tested. Criticizing a theory in an academic way is not undertaken with a view to saying it is 'wrong'. Instead, critique involves: unpacking theoretical assumptions (explicit or implicit), empathizing with the evidence used by different theorists, and reading down into the theory to expose its explanatory and/or factual/evidential limitations.
- It provides us with a new dimension to the 'facts versus theory' debate. By arguing that theory is everywhere, even in Hollywood blockbusters such as *Independence Day* and zombie gore-fests, these scholars encourage us to think about theory's role in our efforts to explain international relations today.

You might be lucky enough on your course to spend time exploring how Weber and others use film and television to deconstruct IR theory in timetabled sessions. If not, you can still get full value for money by watching them in your own time and seeing how these writers make use of them in their work. You could incorporate the films as case studies in assessed work on the respective theories, themes and issues in IR they consider.

QUESTIONS TO PONDER

'Why do we need theories about international relations when we can look at the facts?'

There are two promising ways to approach this question. The first is to think about it in 'for and against' terms. You would begin by setting out the case 'against' theory and 'for' facts, looking at writers who question the utility of theory. You should mainly concentrate on writers from within the discipline of IR who posit the 'take it or leave it' approach to theory: Wallace would be a good case study and we explored his views above. Read his original article for the full detail of his arguments. You might show knowledge of the wider social scientific debates by referring to writers from outside the discipline, such as historians like Windschuttle who question the value or utility of theory – we also covered him above. In the second part of the essay you would consider the case 'against' facts and 'for' theory, using any of the points about the 'everywhere-ness' of theory raised by writers such as Steve Smith, Cynthia Weber and those who explain themes and issues in IR using film and television characters and plotlines. All this would be framed by your own view on which body of writing you find most persuasive – taking a stand in the debate is where you will accrue critical marks.

A second approach would be to present a structured list of reasons why you believe we should bother with theory and deal with each in turn in a 'fat paragraph' (of approximately 250 words). Taking this route makes it slightly harder to achieve balance in the essay because your tutor would presumably want to see some consideration of the 'take it or leave it' approach and you would have to think hard about where and how far to explore that interpretation. It might, for example, be useful to have a long introduction setting out the rationale for the assertion made in the question, and then arguing that you intend to knock it down by exploring a series of points from the literature on the value of IRT.

'How do IR theorists make sense of the world?'

Vague or open-ended questions can be both a curse and a blessing. To put it another way, they can be deceptively difficult to answer despite on the surface appearing to be fairly straightforward. The place to start is to try and pin down for your tutor what you take the different bits of the question to mean: Which IR theorists? Can they all be lumped together? Do all of them understand the word 'theory' in the same way? Are there differences between, say, a Realist and a Constructivist take on theory, and if so, how is this expressed in writers' ontological, epistemological and methods of studying IR?

Then think about the following: What does 'make sense of the world' mean in the question? It seems fair to take it to mean 'how do the theorists you have chosen study the world of IR?' That is, how do they make it intelligible to us as fellow students of international affairs? Here we get into issues raised in the previous chapter about how different IR theorists define their object of study.

One thing you might then do is choose a case study which exemplifies how academics from obviously different theoretical traditions 'make sense' of 'their world' of IR and draw conclusions from that. Weber's films, Drezner's zombies and Dyson's television shows could be used here, amongst other works.

> The use of case studies can provide you with valuable ways of comparing and contrasting different theoretical approaches to IR. Always make it clear why you choose particular cases and make sure to tell the reader after presenting case study material what conclusions you draw from it. Do not expect your tutor miraculously to be able to infer from your case studies why you chose them: make it explicit in the essay.

REFERENCES TO MORE INFORMATION

George, A. (1993) *Bridging the Gap: Theory and Practice in Foreign Policy*. Washington, DC: United States of Peace Press.

Lepgold, J. (1998) 'Is Anyone Listening? International Relations Theory and the Problem of Policy Relevance', *Political Science Quarterly*, 113(1): 48–62.

Prichard, A. (2011) 'What Can the Absence of Anarchism Tell us about the History and Purpose of International Relations?', *Review of International Studies*, 37(4): 1647–69.

Booth, K. (1997) 'Discussion: A Reply to Wallace', *Review of International Studies*, 23(3): 371–7.
He backs Steve Smith (1997) in his counter-attack on William Wallace's article on theory and practice discussed in this chapter.

Reus-Smit, C. (2012) 'International Relations, Irrelevant? Don't Blame Theory', *Millennium: Journal of International Studies*, 40(3): 525–40.

Carr, E.H. (1990) *What is History?* Harmondsworth: Penguin.
There are various reprints of the 1961 original. Especially thought-provoking is the opening chapter which rethinks the idea of 'facts' as value-free.

Goldstein, J.S. and Pevehouse, J.C. (2010) *International Relations*, 9th edn. New York: Pearson Education.
Usefully from a student point of view, the book is liberally sprinkled with 'thinking theoretically' text boxes which help you think through theoretical explanations for different outcomes in the cases covered.

Hay, C. (2002) *Political Analysis: A Critical Introduction*. Basingstoke: Palgrave.
The opening two chapters introduce you to the problems of defining the field of Political
Science (including the subfield of IR) and to the problems we encounter in trying to
study this subject 'scientifically'.

Burnham, P., Gilland Lutz, K., Grant, W. and Layton-Henry, Z. (2008) *Research Methods
   in Politics*, 2nd edn. Basingstoke: Palgrave Macmillan.
Chapter 1 outlines big debates about how to study Politics which filter into discussions
about how to study IR.

Axford, B., Browning, G.K., Huggins, R. and Rosamond, B. (2006) *Politics: An Introduction*,
   2nd edn. London: Routledge.
Chapter 14 by Rosamond introduces ways of thinking about IR and shows how the borders between domestic and international politics are in the process of dissolving.

Sterling-Folker, J. (2013) *Making Sense of International Relations Theory*, 2nd edn. Boulder,
   CO: Lynne Rienner.
This first chapter of the above book introduces you to the main contours of the debates
about 'theory' and shows how the book works by using different theoretical takes on the
same case: the Kosovo intervention of 1999.

Jabri, V. (2000) 'Reflections on the Study of International Relations', in T.C. Salmon (ed.)
   Issues in International Relations. London: Routledge, pp. 289–313.
Good on the nature of theory and the problems of defining the scope of IR as a subject area.

Hall, I. (2006) *The International Thought of Martin Wight*. Basingstoke: Palgrave
   Macmillan.

Neuman, W.L. (2014) *Basics of Social Research: Qualitative and Quantitative Approaches*,
   3rd edn. Harlow: Pearson Education Limited.
Chapter 2 covers general issues to do with the nature of theory.

Harding, S. and Hintikka, M.B. (eds) (2012) *Discovering Reality: Feminist Perspectives
   on Epistemology, Metaphysics, Methodology, and the Philosophy of Social Science*, 2nd edn.
   Dordrecht: Kluwer Academic Publishers.
See especially the chapters by Eve Keller on **gender** and science.

Roskin, M.G., Cord, R.L., Madeiros, J.A. and Jones, W.S. (2016) *Political Science: An
   Introduction*, 14th edn. Harlow: Pearson.
Good on the 'science' debate and introduces basic concepts useful for the study of domestic
and international politics.

3

THEORETICAL DEBATES

In this chapter we deepen our understanding of the theoretical debates that have dominated the academic study of IR. In Chapter 2 we began by trying to define the problematic term 'theory' and discovered that scholars do not necessarily view the nature and purposes of theory in the same way. If that did not make life difficult enough, we then encountered the debate that takes place between those scholars who question the utility of theory in explaining political affairs (as part of human affairs in general) and those scholars who laud the achievements of theoretical perspectives in making sense of a complex world. We labelled the former the 'take it or leave it' approach to theory and the latter the 'theory is inescapable' approach.

In this chapter I want to pick up a few loose ends I left dangling in that chapter. In particular, I want to take these general debates about the nature, value and role of theory and show you how they have played out in the study of IR. In order to do this, we will first consider the origins of IR as an academic discipline, to give you some context to the emergence of IRT as a mode of thinking about international affairs. Next, we will investigate a fundamental issue IR theorists argue about: the causes and consequences of anarchy in the international system. The third section will discuss how far we can tell a 'story' about the evolution of theoretical debates in IR. The fourth section reflects on standards by which we can 'judge' different theories so that you are aware of the complexities involved in this process. The final section considers how you can begin to think like an IR theorist, to help you with your studies.

ORIGINS OF IR AS AN ACADEMIC DISCIPLINE

The menu of theoretical approaches currently on offer in the study of IR is quite extensive – well into double figures. However, this was not always the case. Theories have been developed to account for a range of events and occurrences in the 'real world' of international politics: wars, diplomacy, conflict, crises, the rise and fall of powers in the international system, along with lower level or routine interactions of all kinds (economically and culturally) have all proved important stimuli in the development of new theories and the refinement of existing theories. To give just one example, look at the way in which the deep recessions/depressions around the world since the 2008 global financial crisis hit home have prompted a burgeoning of interest in Marxist understandings of the crisis of capitalism (see Chapter 9 of this book). In this view academics are not divorced from the world of international politics they attempt to theorize. Instead they are reacting to – and playing catch up with – events and processes that unfold sometimes quite rapidly and in unexpected directions. Thus, if we want to make a deep philosophical point that has important ramifications for your own study of IR, it can be argued that IRT is a dialogue with, and about, global history itself. How we understand the past has an important effect on how we interpret contemporary issues. We do not need to ponder this point in detail now. However, as a student new to the study of IRT it is important to understand when the discipline evolved, its core concerns, and how theorizing has evolved in a series of 'great debates'.

The study of IR as a separate academic discipline began after the First World War (1914–18). Until that time, scholars from various disciplinary backgrounds had reflected on the dynamics of international politics, and particularly on the conduct of diplomatic relations between states. Lawyers, historians, economists, philosophers and former diplomats themselves all had an input from their own 'outside' (academic) or 'inside' (policy-maker) vantage points. But there was no discipline devoted exclusively to the study of inter-state affairs.

This all changed after the mass death, destruction and devastation of the First World War. As the centenary commemorations around the world in 2014 rightly demonstrated, the Great War remains one of the touchstone eras for thinking about the horrendous human consequences that occur when power politics between states goes wrong. It seemed more important than ever after 1918 to try and find answers to three questions: Why do wars begin? What do wars achieve? What lessons can we learn from past wars to prevent future ones? When IR was founded as an academic discipline it was specifically tasked to generate answers to those tricky questions and drew on approaches, ideas and evidence from those other disciplines that had previously studied international diplomacy and conflict (Figure 3). The first Chair of IR was established in 1919 at the then University College of Wales, Aberystwyth, creating the modern discipline of IR. It was followed by a succession of similar posts in UK universities and elsewhere (Rosenberg 2016: 127).

IR thus shares an intellectual affinity with many neighbouring disciplines: its borders are quite porous. Pick up any IR journal today and you will see a proliferation of approaches, themes, issues and debates. This is a legacy of both its positioning in the academic marketplace and a reflection of changing times, bringing new issues onto the international political agenda. Of course, the world has moved on since 1918. To mention just a few of the epochal events that have moulded international relations in practice and theory, there

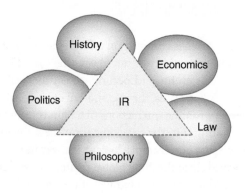

Figure 3   IR's creation as a discipline

was the Second World War, 1939–45; the Cold War, 1945–89; the collapse of the USSR and the reunification of Germany; and the Iraq invasion of 2003. Explaining the causes of war remains important in IR, but it now sits alongside a panoply of other themes and issues in 'high' and 'low' politics. One axiomatic concept recurs throughout this work, however, and that is 'anarchy'.

ANARCHY IN IR

> Domestic systems are centralized and hierarchic. International systems are decentralized and anarchic. (Kenneth Waltz, quoted in Onuf 2009: 186)

What do IR theorists argue about, animating research in the discipline? This question has partly been answered in Chapter 2 where we considered the 'problem of the subject'. The fact that IR tries to explain anything and everything that might come under the general headings 'international relations' and 'world politics' means there is little consensus within the discipline on what the subject matter of IR is, or what it should be. The sheer breadth of the discipline today, however, obscures the fact that in the early years of the discipline there was a bit more agreement on what IR scholars and students should study: it was all about how to manage inter-state relations to prevent war(s) between states. Everything else was secondary, if it was on people's radars at all. It seems fair to suggest, therefore, that in its formative years as a discipline, and right up to the end of the Cold War in fact, the 'agenda' of IR was more limited than it is today.

This had a very significant influence on the discipline: it placed the study of the condition of anarchy right at its heart, as *the* bone of contention between theorists. As Richard Ashley has observed (1995: 94–5, original emphasis), the obsession with anarchy brought three questions to the fore: 'How can there be [international] governance *in the absence of government*? How can order be constructed *in the absence of an orderer*? How can cooperation be facilitated *under a condition of anarchy*?' Part II of this book details how different theoretical traditions deal with each question. Justin Rosenberg explains it very well too (2001: 4): 'Exploring this logic of anarchy is held to be the distinctive task of IR theory – a task which must be kept more or less rigidly separate from the study of domestic politics which is governed by fundamentally different principles'.

For now, we need to clarify what 'anarchy' is and why it is foundational to the study of IR.

> If you want to get into the heads of different IR theorists, try thinking about how they define anarchy and how they view its consequences for international relations. Is it central to their work, and why or why not?

If you asked 10 friends down the corridor in your hall of residence to define 'anarchy', they would probably give you a range of familiar themes: lawlessness, chaos, disruption, violence, and opposition to 'the system' or 'the powers that be' might all feature in some combination in their answers. 'Anarchy' in its IR context has affinities with some of these themes. However, there is no getting away from the fact that it is a highly technical term when used by IR theorists and is part of the basic 'language' of IR as a whole. To get to grips with its meaning we will explore its **etymology** before showing how IR theorists have used it and defined it in their work.

Etymology

The word 'anarchy' comes from Greek and is a compound of two components:

1. The prefix An- means 'without', 'not' or 'lacking' (Dictionary.com 2016a).
2. The suffix -archos (Dictionary.com 2016b) comes from the word archon, meaning: one of the nine principal ruling magistrates of ancient Athens, or more generally an authoritative figure, a high official, or a ruler.

Putting the two parts of the word together we find that the literal meaning of anarchy can be any or all of the following:

*   No ruler.
*   Without a high official.
*   Lacking an authority.

In the study of IR this is key because the central unit of analysis was traditionally the sovereign state. Sovereignty is another word that can cause problems because of the various layers of meaning it has acquired over the years.

Sovereignty is a politically charged term. UK students will probably know it best from debates about the advisability of British involvement in the European Union (EU), and it made many appearances during the debates leading to the Brexit referendum of June 2016. For those opposed to Britain's membership of the EU, the EU detracted from British sovereignty (political, legal, economic) because EU laws take precedence over British laws (for more on sovereignty see UK in a Changing Europe 2016). There is another 'layer' of government above the British government that limits its room for manoeuvre – London shared its sovereignty with a different and, fatally for Eurosceptics, a less legitimate decision-making body.

In IR terms, sovereignty means that different states in the international system are independent, territorially defined and able to determine their own destinies. State sovereignty has internal and external dimensions. A state is internally sovereign 'when it exercises supreme authority over the affairs and people within its territory'. A state is externally sovereign 'when it is recognized as such by the international community', that is, when both its internal sovereignty and territorial integrity are respected and upheld by other powers in the system (Jackson and Sørensen 2015: 313). In sum, sovereignty, says Ben Rosamond, is 'about the power to make laws and the ability to rule effectively' (Axford et al. 2006: 485). Sovereignty, democracy and governance are often wrapped up tightly together. Nation-state sovereignty might be harder to define these days, but in a very real sense it remains an important feature of national foreign policy practices. Significantly, national leaders retain faith in sovereignty as a guide to decision-making, even in an era of globalization (for a forceful statement of this position see Mann 1993). Even in the era of complex globalization, the role of the state has not diminished even if it radically has been remoulded (very well covered in Scholte 1997).

We now have definitions of two key terms in IR: anarchy and sovereignty. Why are they fundamental to students in the discipline? Well, it all comes down to the potential problems of having all these sovereign states existing together side by side in the 'international system'. If each state is sovereign, who or what has the power/influence/authority/means to shape their behaviour so they can live peaceably together? What if one state, or a group of states, chooses to attack another state or group of states? What if one state or a group of states chooses *not* to recognize the domestic government or territorial integrity of another state? We have seen 'coalitions of the willing' undertaking all sorts of military and other interventions short of force at the international level throughout history. Moreover, what if the leader of one state turns on his own people and subjects them to crimes against humanity, or if a bloody civil war breaks out in a failed or failing state? Whose responsibility is it to help out? In the final reckoning, therefore, *who regulates state behaviour in an anarchic international system?*

IR scholars take the literal meaning of anarchy identified above and emerge with the following formulations in their work, which all focus on the 'ordering principle' of a system which exists in a condition of anarchy:

- **Booth and Wheeler** (2008: 2): 'Under anarchy, the last word rests with governments whose primary responsibility is to promote the interests, and especially the security interests of their own state.'
- **Hollis and Smith** (1991: 7): Argue that by calling the international system 'anarchic' we are suggesting 'not that it is chaotic [as in general usage] but simply that there is no government above the states which comprise it'.
- **Brown** (2001: 4): Likewise suggests that anarchy, in its IR context, 'does not necessarily mean lawlessness and chaos; rather it means the absence of a formal system of government'.
- **Donnelly** (1996: 87): 'Anarchy does *not* imply chaos or the complete absence of order. Rather, anarchy is the absence of political rule, of a "hierarchical" political order based on formal subordination and authority.'
- **Mearsheimer** (2001: 30): 'That the international system is anarchic … does not mean that it is chaotic or riven by disorder … it is an ordering principle, which says that the system comprises independent states that have no central authority above them.'
- **Waltz** (2010): 'Among states, the state of nature is a state of war'; the anarchic ordering principle entails 'each state deciding for itself whether or not to use force.'
- **Glaser** (1994–5: 50): Follows Waltz and the structural (Neo)realists (see Chapter 6) by defining anarchy as: 'the lack of an international authority capable of enforcing agreements'.
- For **Weber** (2010: 14): Anarchy 'denotes *lack of an orderer*' (her emphasis) – there is no one or nothing to impose order on the behaviour of states in a top-down way.
- **Holsti** (1985: 34): 'The absence of a universal authority'.
- **Nye and Welch** (2011: 4): Sum it up by writing that international politics is 'politics in the absence of a common sovereign – politics among entities with no ruler above them. International politics is a self-help system'.

'Anarchy' is a foundational term in IRT that will feature throughout your studies. Find a succinct definition from an established IR scholar which you can use as your definition at the beginning of essays and exam answers. Any of the above would serve you well – there will be dozens of others on offer in your course reading.

As we move through the various theories in Part II of the book you will see how anarchy and sovereignty play out in the various traditions we explore. For now, all you need to bear in mind is that these are not neutral concepts: they are loaded with meaning, and their implications for IR are constantly in dispute. The theorization of anarchy is what marks IR apart from Political Science more generally: 'the IR discipline had to insist that there was a significant difference between domestic and international politics. The notion of "anarchy" satisfied this quest' (Guzzini and Leander 2006: 75). The next section explains how IR theorizing has evolved to account for the study of international affairs in a condition of anarchy, and how changing times have brought new themes and issues to the fore.

· ·

 TAKING IT FURTHER

Anarchy personified: the Joker in Batman

The 2008 Batman movie *The Dark Knight* tracks the Heath Ledger characterization of the Joker as he moves through a relatively ordered society in Gotham City wreaking havoc on his physical surroundings and the city's inhabitants. He does not do this because he is working to some master plan: that's for the mafia, the police, the politicians, 'the schemers', as he calls them. He does it without any real thought for the consequences at all. He just enjoys causing trouble for the establishment, who with their 'plans' are trying to manage everything. He rails against a world of control and organization. 'Look what I did to this city with a few drums of gas and a couple of bullets,' he boasts. 'Introduce a little anarchy ...,' he continues, taking a revolver from his pocket, 'upset the established order, and everything becomes chaos. So, I am an agent of chaos. Oh, and you know the thing about chaos? It's fair' (see the movie clip on YouTube at Joker Scene 2008).

The Joker could be considered the personification of anarchy, its physical manifestation on Earth, the ultimate challenge to the hierarchical relations that, it is supposed, domestic systems and international systems require if they are to function 'normally'. The plot of *The DarkKnight* shows how fragile Liberal notions of order, cooperation and justice can be when society shifts from hierarchic to anarchic **structures**. Unfortunately, in IRT, it is the condition of anarchy not hierarchy that is said to prevail. Truces can only ever be temporary. We live in a state of fear and have to look after ourselves first and foremost, because others do not have the same incentives to do so.

· ·

THEORIZING IR

Telling the history of IR is complicated, to put it mildly, because of the difficulties we encounter in answering the following questions: Who are the key actors? What are the key dates and events? How do we track and describe the comings and goings of academic debates over time? Which themes and issues have dominated the agenda and (how) has our study of them changed over time? It is safe to say that a definitive disciplinary history is more or less impossible. It will inevitably contain gaps, distortions and simplifications because:

> the academic context itself often works as an incentive for over-rationalizing selected **ideational** threads that, once put together, allow for the orderly presentation of 'doctrines' that can be taught. An artificial coherence is thus manufactured and projected into quite diverse intellectual sources. (Guilhot 2011: 2–3)

The obstacles to writing definitive disciplinary history have not stopped IR scholars from trying – for instance, Alker and Biersteker (1995) tried to map the discipline in the 1980s. In the literature you read on your course you will find many books and articles telling the history of IR as having unfolded around a series of so-called 'great debates'. These serve as what novelist Tom McCarthy (2015: 1) would call its 'foundation myths', an 'imprint of year zero, a bolt that secures the scaffolding that in turn holds fast the entire architecture of reality, of time'.

Some textbooks, for example, Jackson and Sørensen (2015) still like to begin with the story of the 'great debates'. Others, for example Dunne et al. (2016), avoid this story until the very end. How does this affect their presentation of the 'story' of IR? What are the key fault lines these writers see running through the discipline today?

These 'great debates' have proved helpful in giving coherence to the discipline (Wæver 2016: 311; see also Viotti and Kauppi 2014: 2), by giving it focus and helping it regulate, categorize and 'place' scholarly writing within its borders. I will briefly review the gist of this story and then critique it using the work of Brian Schmidt (2006). From here we will develop a framework for understanding the nature of the theoretical disputes running through the discipline which it will help to have at the back of your mind when you begin your investigation of each theory, covered in Part II of this book.

IR's great debates

- **Great debate 1: 'Idealism' versus 'Realism'.** This controversy is said to have emerged in the formative years of the discipline between the First and Second World Wars, 1919–39, and continuing into the 1950s. It was a debate 'about the nature of international politics and the possibility of peaceful change' (Viotti and Kauppi 2014: 2). The 'winners' were the Realists who managed to depict the Idealists as head-in-the-clouds dreamers – utopians – who gullibly overlooked the true nature of power politics in the modern world. While liberal-minded politicians such as Woodrow Wilson (see Chapter 4) worked for global peace and security, the League of Nations collapsed around them and the world plunged into a disastrous second global war in the space of 25 years. It did not take too much effort to convince students and practitioners of IR that Realism 'was superior in its ability to rationally explain the persistent and ubiquitous struggle for power among nations' (Schmidt 2006: 11). After an early period of dominance, Liberalism was put firmly on the back foot, but was not killed off entirely.

- **Great debate 2: 'Behaviouralists' or 'scientists' versus 'Traditionalists'.** This was a debate about methodology that emerged in the 1960s – after the Realists had 'won' the first debate in and around the period of the Second World War. It pitted behaviouralists, especially in the USA, who believed that IR could best be studied using methods drawn from the natural sciences, especially quantitative statistics, against traditionalists 'who argued that the study of the social world was not amenable to the strict empirical methods of natural science' (Schmidt 2006: 11). It was a rehearsal, in fact, of the disputes about methodology that have impacted many social science disciplines in recent years, and which were covered in the previous part of this book. There was no clear 'victor', as in the first debate: methodological disputes have provided a constant source of debate and innovation in IR to this day.

- **Great debate 3: Neorealists versus the rest?** This is a far harder debate to describe, not least because we are not fully clear about who was involved or what they were arguing about! For Schmidt, the third debate developed out of a crisis within Realism in the 1970s, which found its theoretical assumptions being challenged by events 'on the ground' in international politics, especially by growing economic interdependence and the moves to create a New International Economic Order, a proposal adopted by the UN in May 1974 (UN 1974). Scholars increasingly attacked the state-centrism of Realism and noted that state relations were characterized as much by interdependence between states as by their independence from one another. Schmidt suggests that it was within the context of a focus on interdependence and economic relations between states that the subfield of International Political Economy (IPE) emerged (Schmidt 2006: 11). The third debate in IR therefore saw the growth to maturity of a range of new theories, notably those inspired by Marx (see Chapter 9) and the English School (see Chapter 7).

- **Great debate 4: 'Post-positivists' versus 'Positivists'.** I have called this the fourth debate, but for some writers (see Schmidt 2006: 12; Viotti and Kauppi 2014: 2), this is the *genuine* 'third debate'. The **post-positivists** came to prominence in the 1980s, and they were critical of all what to that point had been the dominant, mainstream approaches to IR (Lapid 1996). Feminists, Critical Theorists and postmodernists/poststructuralists (all of whom we explore in this book) critiqued the positivist approaches of the dominant theorists in the field. What they effectively said was that the alleged third debate was a non-debate because all the approaches identified above share the same commitments to doing IR the positivist way. This is much more of a divisive debate, therefore, because post-positivists interrogate central themes and issues in IR all the way down, including gaps and prejudices in IR scholars' approach to the subject matter itself (Smith 2004).

Having outlined the points of contention in the 'great debates' about IR, we can better see the problems of trying to write the history of the field. Everyone agrees that debates about IR have occurred and will continue to occur about all sorts of philosophical, theoretical and empirical questions. But no one can agree on how to capture the essence of these debates as they have arisen over time (Holden 2002). As soon as we try to put chronological boundaries or dividers between the debates, something of the complexity of the field gets lost – and this can present real problems when it comes to educating students about the contemporary study of IR and how it has reached its present state (as it were).

> When doing your IRT reading, make a note of all the different ways writers tell the story of the discipline. You might even think of different disciplinary histories as different theories about how to tell the story of IR. What does this tell you about the nature and value of theory?

From great debates to the positivist—normative distinction

Having told the story of IR's 'great debates', Schmidt sets about critiquing the idea that such a simple story can be told. Most damagingly, he writes, 'it is not evident that all of the three [or four] debates actually took place'. Second, he questions whether our contemporaneous 'stylized' versions of the debates can do justice to the contours of the discussions that have been taking place around the global academic community – it seems very much like a 'Western' account of IRT. Third, by focusing on the 'great' debates, he says we ignore other equally important and interesting disciplinary controversies that were taking place at the same time. And, finally, by telling the history of the field as a story of 'this happened then that' we risk giving chronological coherence to it where in fact none was evident (Schmidt 2006: 12).

In this light, is there a framework for studying IR theory within which we might explore key points of contestation amongst its scholars, and which makes it intelligible, but which does not claim to tell a simple chronological history of the field? Any such framework will be open to criticism, but one way I have found useful is to present the story of the discipline as an argument between two ways of acquiring academic knowledge: 'positivist' approaches on the one hand, and 'normative' approaches on the other. This de-centres great debates 1 and 3, above (too centred on specific theories) and brings to the fore the metatheoretical issues germane to debates 2 and 4 (for this distinction applied to the work of the IR theorist Karl Deutsch, see Ruzicka 2014). Let us look first of all at what these terms mean and then think about how we might categorize each of the theories you will cover on your course:

- **Kenneth Waltz** (quoted in Onuf 2009: 186): Cleaves to a positivist view of theory: 'A theory, while related to the world about which explanations are wanted, always remains distinct from that world. Theories are not descriptions of the real world; they are instruments that we design in order to apprehend some part of it. "Reality" will therefore be congruent neither with a theory nor with a model that may represent it [theory].'

- **Anthony Langlois** (2007: 152): Theory-building aims at explanation and occurs on the back of worldviews which are 'frames through which we see and understand the world. ... they circumscribe what we can see, and thus they give grounds for a particular interpretation of international politics'. Moreover, we see the world not untainted through frames of our own making but usually through frames which have been set for us by other people – communities of scholars and policy-makers. All theory therefore has normative and ethical implications (see also Griffiths 2011: 6–8).

- **Richard Devetak** (2013a: 165): Uses Max Horkheimer's categorization between traditional (positivist) and critical (normative) theory. In traditional theory the theorist is removed from the object of analysis; it assumes an external world 'out there'; and achieves objectivity by withdrawing the theorist him/herself from the object of study by leaving behind ideology, beliefs and values that would invalidate the inquiry (see Waltz's definition above). Critical theories, by contrast, are always embedded in social and political life; they 'allow for an examination of the purposes and functions served by particular theories'. In other words, normative theorists combine conventional theory (a study of an event/process/issue) with metatheory (theory about theory).

- **Jim George** (quoted in Zalewski and Enloe 1995: 299): Describes positivism as assuming 'a cognitive reaction to reality' rather than it 'being integral to its construction'. In other words, theory 'takes place after the fact'. For normative theorists, by contrast, 'theory does not take place after the fact. Theories, instead, play a large part in constructing and defining what the facts are'.

- **Steve Smith** (2004: 504): 'scholarship cannot be neutral; it is unavoidably partial, is unavoidably political, and unavoidably has ethical consequences. Crucially, this is the case whether or not the scholar is explicit about these ramifications.'

- **Kimberley Hutchings** (1999: xiii and 1–2): 'the theorist does not operate in abstraction from the object of analysis' (positivism); normative theories are 'concerned with how to criticize, change and improve the world as it is'.

- **Edward Said** (cited in Ramakrishnan 1999: 136; original emphasis): 'there is never interpretation, understanding, and then knowledge where there is no *interest*'. Theory for Said always masks a particular interest or is reflective of a particular set of power relations.

- **Paul Viotti and Mark Kauppi** (2014: 3): 'specifically endorses the use of formal hypothesis testing or causal modelling as *methodologies* – modes of research and analysis or a set of rules for the actual practice of investigating IR'. These methods can be quantitative (statistics and equations) or qualitative (in-depth case studies presented in narrative form) to test our hypotheses about IR.

- **Robert Jervis** (2008: 573): 'Even if we can logically distinguish between facts and values, it is hard to believe that we can ever succeed in being fully objective, especially when the topics under investigation are highly charged and the evidence is ambiguous. Would we really expect a scholar who deeply believes that the American interest is best served by a liberal internationalist policy to explain events in the same way that an isolationist or a unilateralist would?' Claiming objectivity is one thing; practicing it effectively (and knowing when it has been achieved) is an entirely different matter.

- **Benno Teschke** (Teschke and Cemgil 2014: 606): Post-positivism 'conceives of the scholar not as a disinterested, neutral, and autonomous observer outside politics, but as the situated subject of knowledge-production in a concrete socio-political context'.

Taking these definitions together we can summarize the distinction between positivist and normative approaches in Table 1.

Table 1   The positivist-normative distinction

Positivism	Normative
Also known as explanatory or traditional theory	Also known as constitutive or normative theory
A contested term	A contested term
Empiricist epistemology: the theory that knowledge is derived only or primarily from sensory experience	Focuses on: the *ought* as well as the *is*, privileging 'the moral or ethical dimension of activities in the international sphere (Neething 2004 : 11)
Naturalist: Social scientists can emulate methods of natural scientists to study society (domestic and international)	Critiques positivist belief in naturalism
There is a distinction between facts and values	Collapses fact/value distinction

Can we use this distinction between positivist and normative approaches to map IR theories according to their methodological, epistemological and ontological leanings? Quite possibly, if we sketch things as in Figure 4.

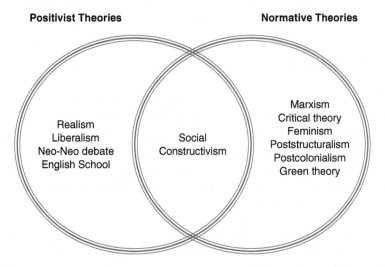

Figure 4   Mapping theories of IR

Reflections on the theory map

The merits of this framework are as follows:

- **Avoids history** – Moving away from the history of 'great debates' means we do not have to worry about whether or not we can tell a neatly packaged chronology of the discipline. As Schmidt argues, this approach does a disservice, a violence even, both to the range and the nature of the disciplinary debates in the field at any given moment in the past or present.
- **Freedom to choose** – The binary positivist–normative distinction gives students scope to make up their own minds about the evolution (the 'story') of the discipline. Rather than us lecturers and professors telling you the story you have more freedom using this model to place the theories (and their different 'wings') where you see fit. This is my sense of where the theories are placed, but you may disagree.
- **Nature of history** – If you do believe there is a story to be told about IR, then how important in your story is the positivist–normative dispute? Or do you think that the great debates capture the story well enough?

At the beginning of your IRT studies try starting off with my map in mind, and as you go through the course try and identify writers within each theoretical tradition who might not fit my classification so easily. Use the map as a living document and move individual theorists around within it as you go. You might find some writers appearing in both circles or in the overlapping area. What does this tell you about the 'map' of IRT today?

Two further questions arise from a consideration of the evolution over time of IRT. First, how do we judge the quality of competing theories? Second, how do IR theorists 'think', and how as a student new to the subject can we begin to think like these IR theorists? The next two sections of this chapter will attempt to answer these questions.

HOW DO WE EVALUATE IR THEORIES?

Should IR theorists be able to predict the timing and nature of seismic systemic international political events such as the end of the Cold War in 1989, or state actions such as the Russian invasion of Ukraine in 2014? Or should we have more limited expectations about what theories can offer us by way of predictive capacity? Scholars such as Burchill and Linklater (2013: 26) suggest we should have modest aspirations for theory: 'We probably should not expect too much from any empirical theory'. Rosenau and Durfee (1995: 2) concur that humility is the best way forward:

> If we can remain in awe of the complexities and changes at work in the world, ever ready to concede confusion and always reminding ourselves that our conclusions must perforce be tentative, then it should be possible to avoid excessive simplicity and intellectual paralysis.

Given the contingent nature of social affairs, it seems that this might be the wisest option. Nevertheless, it seems hard-wired in us to judge social theory in the same way we treat natural science theories. Even if prediction per se might not be the ultimate ambition, there is certainly a marked preference in IR to develop theories that explain something meaningful about the workings of the international system.

Take Kenneth Waltz's view. He argued that 'no one in any field is able to generate theories easily or even to say how to go about creating them'. That said, the more successful theories depict 'the organization of a realm and the connections among its parts' (Waltz 1997: 913). He uses Charles Darwin's theory of evolution in biology as an example: it is very good at explaining evolution but does not predict anything in particular – but it is no less significant and useful for it. This is a frequently put question in IR: can and should we measure the social sciences by the same criteria we measure the natural sciences? If the answer is yes, we are more likely to have higher benchmarks for judging theoretical contributions. Their explanatory capacity will be highest on the list. *How and what* they explain (including their 'fit' to the 'real world' of international politics) then becomes the focus for debate and discussion.

From here flows the point that comparing the relative strengths and weaknesses of theories is challenging. Theories are responses to particular issues, the identification of new 'causes', and they are the product of different intellectual traditions. If all theoretical perspectives emphasize different facets of the world, centre their attention on different actors (in short, 'see' different worlds, or 'read' the world differently), then our preference for one theory over another or others is taken from the world of facts and evidence and into the realm of **aesthetics**. Choosing between theories comes down to a question of the tastes of the person making the selection because there is nothing inherent in the theories themselves that can result in objective comparisons.

When evaluating the maze of theories you will encounter on your studies in IRT, it is important to bear in mind the debates the writers above are engaged in, about the standards for selection and choice-making in IRT. Were theory simply putting a mirror up to reality, there would not be much point in devising the theory in the first place because 'reality' would be coming to us unvarnished, requiring no technical expertise or formal training to access. Ask yourself, therefore, what do I expect of theory? How much evidence is enough to prove or disprove this theory? Can I draw the conclusion that this or that theory is 'true' or 'false'? Pondering such questions while you work through each theory will make you a critical and insightful student of IRT. All in all, it helps if you think like an IR theorist, and that is the theme of the next section.

THINKING LIKE AN IR THEORIST

Having explored various debates about the purpose and nature of theory, the chapter concludes with some reflections on how to think like an IR theorist. In essence, we are asking, What do IR theorists *do*? When approaching a new programme of study, it is important to grasp as early as you can what it is the scholars who have preceded you in the discipline are trying to achieve:

- IR theorists have, historically, been interested in explaining the interactions between states in the international system. This dates back to the origins of the discipline as a formal inquiry into the causes and consequences of global wars between sovereign nation-states.
- IR theorists have become increasingly interested in the practices of other actors in the international system which operate across, or transcend, state borders. They include supranational organizations such as the EU, multinational corporations such as Shell or Nike, loose transnational networks such as Al Qaeda or Islamic State in the Levant (ISIL), and transnational pressure groups such as Greenpeace, Human Rights Watch or Médecins Sans Frontières.
- Over time, IR academics have devised a variety of theories to explain the particular interaction or set of interactions that interest them the most, and which they feel best explain the 'international relations' they deem to be important.
- IR theorists use evidence, logic and reasoned argument to build their theories, test those theories and refine them over time. Different groups of IR scholar put their faith in different types of data-as-evidence. Some are statistically minded and build elaborate models to test associations and relationships between 'variables' in the international system. Others prefer qualitative data and the study of beliefs and meanings as they affect international practicies. There is no 'right' way to 'do' IR, but there are better and worse ways of applying the different methods, whether quantitative or qualitative.
- IR theorists use case studies from the 'real world' of politics, economics, history and law to ground their interpretations in the realm of 'facts'. Case studies can be used as testing grounds for the range of theories, and case study evidence needs to be justified as exemplifying something relevant and, ideally, generalizable. Exceptions to the 'norm' can also be illustrative because they flag up resistances and deviations to hegemonic practices in IR.
- Different IR theories can explain or interpret the same event or process in different ways. IR theorists might agree on some aspects of international affairs but not others. IR theorists can be quite 'tribal' as a result. Where you stand in a debate can often be a product of where you sit theoretically – but not always. Theories evolve over time to account for perceived anomalies or new evidence that challenges existing interpretations.

It is vital that you try and learn to think like an IR theorist. Courses in IRT are likely to test a lot more than simply your knowledge about the individual theories themselves. They will also look to see you engaging with debates about the role and value of theorizing international relations. The experts whose works you read on this course have to grapple with these difficult questions every day, so if you can show that you comprehend their predicament you are likely to succeed at your course.

Appreciating what IR theorists do on a day-to-day basis helps you understand a bit more about the academic enterprise itself. Every academic discipline has its own terminology, shared language and concepts that sometimes unite a field, and sometimes cause disagreements between scholars. Academic disciplines and sub-disciplines such as IRT have, over time, generated an array of expectations about what counts as knowledge and intellectual progress. It is a bit like taking part in a sport you have not played before. What you do is useless unless you understand the following: first, the basic rules and laws of the game; second, the spirit in which these rules and laws are to be implemented during play (the unfolding norms of the sport); third, who is supposed to do what within your team, if it is a team sport – everything from tactical positioning to strategic aims for the team; and finally, the shared meanings behind the actions of the various players in the game, in particular the designation of 'winners' and 'losers' (or runners up). When you have mastered the rules of the game, and everything implied by them, you will 'get' how to play the sport. The best players become those who practice the hardest and who are most dedicated to improving their skills. Success will not always be instant, but it does come over time.

In football (soccer), for example, it is only when you understand how the offside rule works that you can appreciate why the referee blows his or her whistle and the players stop the game when the linesperson raises his/her flag. Learning skills is one thing, but acquiring knowledge of the tactics and techniques for keeping onside is a key part of being a successful footballer. So it is in the academic world: the best students tend to be the ones who most quickly understand the 'rules of the game' and have the patience to spend time getting into the mindset of the experts they read and for whom they write essays and exam answers. Familiarity with conventions enhances comprehension and speeds adaptation to the expectations on you as a student. This book will give you advice on how to get to grips with IRT and help you express your thoughts with authority, using the 'voice' of the IR theorist. In short, it will help you to better understand the rules of the game in IRT – what it is that IR theorists do when they go to work every morning.

On your course you are likely to be assessed on two main grounds: (1) your understanding of each of the theories you cover on the curriculum; and (2) your ability to critique each of those theories.

QUESTIONS TO PONDER

'Can we tell the history of IR as an academic discipline?'

This question invites one of three responses. First, you might think we can tell a story about the evolution of the discipline. Second, you might argue that we cannot do this. Or third, you might think we can tell several stories, in which case your answer is both yes and no. Yes and no answers are not fence-sitting, they are often the best way of setting up academic answers, even if you come down slightly more towards one side than the other. When the world is not black and white but shades of grey it makes sense to survey as many of those shades as is realistically possible in an answer.

If you make either of the first two arguments, it is easy just to concentrate on one side of the argument: but do not forget to include analysis of the counter-arguments.

Knocking them down can you help make your case more convincing. More importantly, it will show your tutor that you have read around the subject and that you are aware of the broad sweep of the debate. Structuring an essay should not be too difficult because you can theme the opening part around the evidence to support your view; the second part will then be a **deconstruction** of the counter-arguments. The third answer (yes/no) is slightly harder to structure because you potentially have more to cover in the essay. Simply listing all the different types of story we could tell (great debates/positivism versus normative approaches) will take a lot of words and could become merely a description of those stories. Think carefully about how you can fit in a serious engagement with the arguments of writers who challenge the idea of a neat story about the discipline.

Across all three types of response, the better student will show an appreciation of the importance of key words in the question, notably the idea of telling linear history with a neat beginning, middle and end. Without getting too philosophical, these 'points' in time are often imposed by us retrospectively rather than pre-existing in the past itself, which was a much messier collection of beliefs and practices. If you subscribe to that view, the idea of a linear disciplinary history is harder to justify.

'How do you think we should judge the quality of different theories of IR?'

The key word in this question is 'quality'. Does it mean accuracy, scope, predictive capacity or empirical soundness? The question invites you to identify how *you* would go about judging such attributes, but do not feel compelled to devise a brand new set of criteria. You can happily draw on existing writers to make your case.

The obvious place to start is with writers such as Burchill/Linklater and Waltz who cover the evaluation of theories in their work as discussed above. You might either or also (depending on the word limit and/or time in an exam) explore what practising IR theorists say about the nature and strength of their theories, as well as analysing their critiques of other theoretical traditions. Theorists who cleave to a **naturalist** understanding of theory tend to have quite forceful appreciations about the quality of theory. More openly normative theorists who discuss the ways in which we are interminably 'inside' the theories we devise tend to be more modest about what theories can hope to achieve.

REFERENCES TO MORE INFORMATION

Wight, G. and Porter, B. (eds) (1992) *International Theory: The Three Traditions.* Leicester: Leicester University Press.

Booth, K. and Smith, S. (eds) (1995) *International Relations Theory Today.* Cambridge: Polity Press.
Contains a thorough analysis (pp. 8–29) of the various ways in which we might tell the story of the discipline.

Kubálková, V. (1998) 'The Twenty Years' Catharsis: E.H. Carr and IR', in V. Kubálková, N. Onuf and P. Kowert (eds) *International Relations in a Constructed World.* Armonk, NY: M.E. Sharpe, pp. 25–57.

Includes a useful diagram (pp. 42–3) which attempts to map the discipline and considers the problems with doing this.

Morgenthau, H.J. (1972) *Science: Servant or Master?* New York: W.W. Norton.
Explores the tensions between the worlds of academia (science, the pursuit of truth) and practice (the pursuit of power).

Buzan, B. and Little, R. (2000) *International Systems in World History: Remaking the Study of International Relations*. Oxford: Oxford University Press.
Thoroughgoing case for bringing history to the study of IR with an English School emphasis on how we theorize IR as interacting 'international systems' (see Chapter 7 of this book for coverage of the English School and Chapter 8 for how Marxist readings of world history have been inspired by this text).

Review of International Studies (2002) Interview with Kal Holsti by A. Jones, 28(3): 619–33.
Holsti bemoans the fragmentation of the discipline of IR and as such acts as a counter-point to the views of Steve Smith and others who see theoretical diversity as a source of empowerment.

Dingli, S. (2015) 'We Need to Talk about Silence: Re-Examining Silence in International Relations Theory', *European Journal of International Relations*, 21(4): 721–42.

Reiter, D. (2015) 'Should we Leave Behind the Subfield of International Relations?', *Annual Review of Political Science*, 18: 481–99.

Tauber, A.I. (ed.) (1997) *Science and the Quest for Reality*. Basingstoke: Macmillan.
See especially the editor's introduction and the chapters by Larry Laudan (on theories of scientific knowledge) and Hilary Putnam (on facts and values).

van der Pijl, K. (2010) 'Historicizing the International: Modes of Foreign Relations and Political Economy', *Historical Materialism*, 18(2): 3–34.
A Marxist perspective on the origins of the discipline of IR, so excellent grounding for the material covered in Chapters 9 and 10 of this book.

Henry, J. (2002) *The Scientific Revolution and the Origins of Modern Science*, 2nd edn. Basingstoke: Palgrave.

Lebow, R.N. (2014) 'What Can International Relations Theory Learn from the Origins of World War One?', *International Relations*, 28(4): 387–410.

Russell, B. (1948) *Sceptical Essays*. London: George Allen and Unwin.
A work of philosophy which deals with, amongst other things, the value of taking a scep-tical attitude to knowledge, 'dreams and facts', the superstitions of science, rationality and the psychology of politics. Particularly useful if you have never read a 'straight' work of philosophy because it helps you think about big issues in the human pursuit of knowledge.

Olson, W.C. and Groom, A.J.R. (1991) *International Relations Then and Now: Origins and Trends in Interpretation*. London: HarperCollins.

Blaikie, N. (2007) *Approaches to Social Inquiry*, 2nd edn. Cambridge: Polity.

Written for a general social science audience, the second chapter is excellent on whether social scientists can or should borrow methods and approaches from natural scientists.

Zima, P.V. (2007) *What is Theory? The Concept of Theory in the Social and Cultural Sciences.* London: Continuum.
An advanced text exploring different understandings of 'theory', including positivist, constructivist and poststructuralist approaches.

Wight, C. (2006) 'Philosophy of Social Science and International Relations', in W. Carlsnaes, T. Risse and B.A. Simmons (eds) *Handbook of International Relations.* London: Sage, pp. 22–51.
A study of the sometimes uneasy status of philosophical questions within the field of IR.

Waltz, K.N. (1979) *Theory of International Politics*, 1st edn. Boston, MA: McGraw-Hill.
See especially the opening chapter on the nature of theories and how we test them.

PART II

THEORIES OF IR

Part I of this book introduced the big debates that have shaped the study of IR over its years as a discipline of academic inquiry. These range from the philosophical (the kinds of knowledge we think we can produce about IR) to the empirical (the themes and issues IR scholars study and IR students are taught). Part II surveys the main IR theories that knit together in the contemporary discipline. Feel free to dip in and out as you see fit and do not be afraid of looking into theories you do not cover directly on your course. There are generally more theories available than there is time to study them all in detail. The more widely you can read around the subject, however, the better equipped you will be to appreciate the debates these writers are engaged in. In turn, the better able you will be to explore the disagreements between them succinctly and accurately in coursework essays and exam answers.

A word of warning: each chapter below tries to summarize in a couple of thousand words theories about which millions of words have been written. I put forward my interpretation of each tradition in the knowledge that it can easily be contested, and in fact that has been part of the challenge for me when writing this book. I have had to answer two central questions you as students will face when putting together your essays and exam answers. How do we define the essence – the absolute crux – of each theoretical tradition? What do we leave out? So, I present my overview not just in the *expectation* that you will be able to challenge the story I tell you as your reading progresses, but in the *hope* that you might. Bear in mind that this book is as much about how to think about IRT as it is the detailed knowledge of each theory, and it is in that spirit that I have tackled each theory.

The chapters in Part II can only give you a very brief introduction to each theory; it is up to you to delve further into each theory. There is no better way than reading the landmark texts. These give you a real insight into the hopes and ambitions for each theory set out by their leading exponents. Textbooks are useful guides to theories, but you will only truly develop your critical faculties by reading original theoretical work. This is especially important after the first year of study at university, when your ability to evaluate arguments is tested.

CORE AREAS

4

LIBERALISM

Key terms

- Anarchy
- Cooperation
- Democracy
- Democratic Peace Theory
- Functionalist integration theory
- Institutions

- Interdependence
- International Organization
- Peace
- Progress
- Security dilemma
- State

In this chapter we explore the founding theory of IR, Liberalism, which grew out of a much wider political theory of the state. We will put this theory in context by breaking it down into five parts: first, the historical context of the Liberal tradition; second, the impact of the First World War on thinking about IR; third, the Liberal resurgence after the Second World War; fourth, Liberal thinking on **international organizations** and institutions; and finally, the rise and fall (?) of Democratic Peace Theory from the end of the Cold War to the post-Iraq era.

THE LIBERAL TRADITION

> The liberal view of international politics and relations had a pervasive effect on the academic study of the field throughout the first four decades of [the twentieth] century. (Holsti 1985: 29)

Like many theories you will study on an IRT course, Liberalism traces its roots back way beyond 1919, when there was a drive to study IR as a separate field of study in universities. It draws on centuries' worth of political theory and political/economic thought, and applies them to the study of relations between states. Inspiration for Liberal IRT has come from various countries and periods and flows from the practice as well as the study of politics. Key Liberal thinkers and politicians you might hear about will include Erasmus (1466–1536), Hugo Grotius (1583–1635), John Locke (1632–1704), Adam Smith (1723–1790), David Ricardo (1772–1823), Immanuel Kant (1724–1804), Jeremy Bentham (1748–1832), Abraham Lincoln (1809–65) and

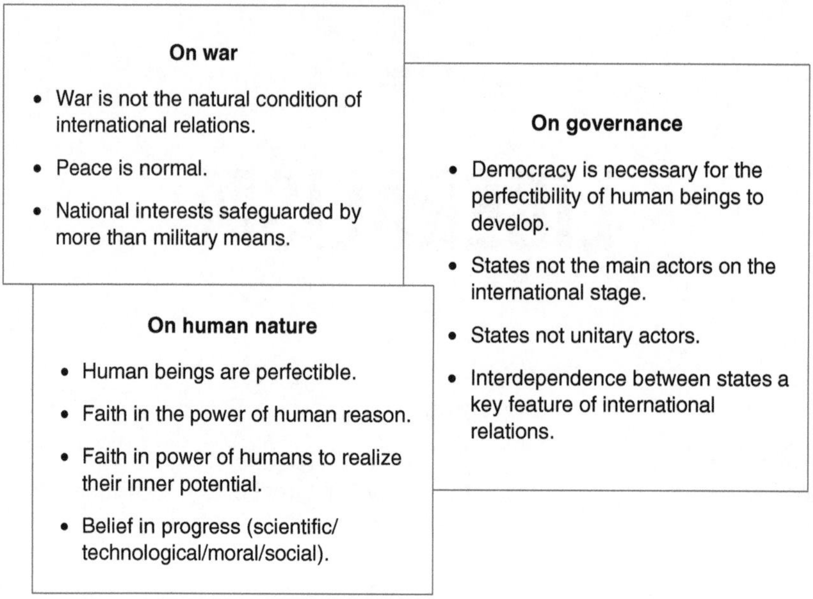

On war

- War is not the natural condition of international relations.
- Peace is normal.
- National interests safeguarded by more than military means.

On governance

- Democracy is necessary for the perfectibility of human beings to develop.
- States not the main actors on the international stage.
- States not unitary actors.
- Interdependence between states a key feature of international relations.

On human nature

- Human beings are perfectible.
- Faith in the power of human reason.
- Faith in power of humans to realize their inner potential.
- Belief in progress (scientific/technological/moral/social).

Figure 5   The Liberal tradition

Woodrow Wilson (1856–1924). A range of thinkers, scholars and policy-makers has helped shaped this diverse tradition.

Across the Liberal tradition identified in the works of the above individuals we see many themes intertwining and recurring over time. To help identify some of the most significant, we can break Liberal thought down into three categories (Figure 5). Having done that we will trace how Liberal ideas were moulded into a distinctive IRT in the aftermath of the First World War.

Justified or unjustified (see Haggard 2013), a popular way of framing the Liberal tradition in IR is that it is 'optimistic' about the prospect of international relations unfolding peaceably. Liberals suggest that human beings are, if not perfectible, then certainly capable of moral progress, particularly when given the opportunity to express their peaceable ambitions via democratic political structures. Liberals in IR extrapolate up from the domestic (state) level to the level of the international system. They treat states as individual units (like individual human beings living in national communities) and focus on the mechanisms by which states can and do choose to manage the worst excesses of the Realist **security dilemma** by regulating their interaction in international organizations (IOs) and institutions (for an extended treatment of the foundational IR concept of the security dilemma see Booth and Wheeler 2008). These can be established global actors such as the United Nations, its Security Council, the International Monetary Fund (IMF) or the World Bank, specialized agencies such as the International Labour Organization (ILO) or the European Bank of Reconstruction and Development, or newer organizations such as the Tribunal for the former Yugoslavia (for more see Abbott and Snidal 1998: 4).

. . . .

🌐 TAKING IT FURTHER
John Herz and the security dilemma

John Herz coined the term 'security dilemma' in the 1950s to explain the mutual fear and antagonism between the USA and Russia in the emerging Cold War. Like Herbert Butterfield, who developed the concept at around the same time (Wheeler 2008), Herz wanted to understand the dynamics of the nuclear arms race and, initially anyway, was quite optimistic that if both sides understood the security dilemma they would better be able to escape it. The concept has been studied, challenged, refined and reworked by, amongst others, Robert Jervis (1978, 2001) and Shiping Tang (2009). We will concentrate on Herz as one of the original proponents, but these later works provide superb factual and evaluative accounts of this central IR concept. All page references below are from Herz (1950).

Herz started from the assumption that sovereign states ('equal, free, and self-determining nationalities' – p. 160) live in a condition of anarchy, 'where groups live alongside each other without being organized into a higher unity'. This is a social condition, he stresses, and nothing to do with human aggression or peaceability (p. 157): 'conflicts caused by the security dilemma are bound to emerge among political units of power' (p. 158). After 1945, the rampant nationalism such as that which drove Germany under Hitler and Italy under Mussolini was on the back foot as states organized themselves according to Liberal ('Idealist') ideology (pp. 162–4). However, history shows that the Realist security dilemma consistently undermined Liberal, revolutionary and Marxist attempts to create harmonious global orders, famously after the Russian Revolution of 1917, which at the time forecast solidarity amongst the world's proletariat, well beyond Russia's borders (p. 170; we cover Marxist theory in Chapter 9).

After 1945 the Liberal project would, Herz argued, be beset by the same challenges: 'Faced with this growing interdependence but also with the security dilemma, their [sovereign states'] attempted way out is to expand their individual power, economically (in order to be self-sufficient in war), strategically (in order to safeguard its defense requirements), etc. This may be international provincialism, but it is hard to see how to escape it in a still anarchic international world' (p. 173). Political realism caused by insecurity combined with economic nationalism (contrary to the predictions of economic liberals discussed below in this chapter) would not quash the potential for imperialism and world war: 'Economic theory is cosmopolitan, but political fact is nationalistic' (p. 175, quoting Frank Graham). The struggle for economic resources becomes just one more source of division between states and nothing in the capitalist system mitigates this (pp. 176–7). Herz ended by calling for an approach based on 'Realist Liberalism': less utopian than Idealism, it must accept the Realist facts of international politics (pp. 178–9) and work towards a credible **balance of power** which stops the world slipping into another destructive all-out war.

. . . .

Economic liberalism is the counterpart and in some ways the precursor to Liberal thought on the conduct of international affairs in a condition of anarchy (see Part I of this book). Economic liberals (such as Adam Smith and David Ricardo) stress the beneficial effects of operating a free market at home and having free trade internationally, with minimal interference by the state. Peaceful economic relations between states are held in this view to underpin peaceful political relations between states. The **General Agreement on Tariffs and Trade (GATT)** is one of the most obvious contemporary manifestations of the idea that trade restrictions have a negative impact on the conduct of international relations. It embodies the Liberal view that: 'The greater the degree of economic interdependence that exists, the less likely states will be to enter into military conflict' (Smith et al. 2011: 12).

For Liberals, then, even though states exist in a condition of anarchy, progress and community spirit can be fashioned by creating formal and informal institutions of modernization – of economies, of technology, of human morality and of communication within and between states. Human beings, Liberals assert, possess the crucial power of reason 'and when they apply it to international affairs greater cooperation will be the end result' (Jackson and Sørensen 2015: 99). In this context, peace, progress and human advancement are all possible, even in a situation in which there are distinct entities known as states, each with their own languages, traditions, histories and political setups. *Difference* and *borders* in the Liberal account do not necessarily lead to *conflict*.

Jennifer Sterling-Folker (2006a: 56, original emphasis) describes it very well by writing that Liberal IR theorists take the same starting assumptions as Realist theorists (see Chapter 5) and investigate 'what *prevents* progress from being achieved, with the underlying assumption being that progress could be realized if we could uncover the barriers to collective action and promote their resolutions'. J.D. Bowen (2011) provides an equally instructive account of the Liberal approach to IRT: 'The international system creates opportunities for cooperation and conflict. It's up to the states and other actors in the international political system to either take advantage of those or not.' The world is not perfect, but Liberals argue that we (as individuals and states) can make the best of it, given certain preconditions that help build a sense of community. Moreover (and this lays the foundations for Constructivist IRT covered in Chapter 8 below), when we come to identify with others around the world, we are more likely to put trust in cooperative ventures (see Buchan et al. 2011). Liberals thus focus on the opportunities available to manage inter-state relations in a peaceful manner, whether bilaterally, regionally or in some cases as a global collective (pointing ahead to the **solidarist** elements of English School theory covered in Chapter 7 and the cosmopolitan strand to Green international theory covered in Chapter 14). As rational actors, they suggest, states are able to weigh up the costs and benefits of building, and remaining participants in, international institutions.

LIBERALISM AND IR AFTER THE FIRST WORLD WAR

The study of IR after its emergence as an academic discipline in 1919 coincided with a fertile period in Liberal thought about the relations between states in the aftermath of the Great War. What, everyone was asking, had been the ultimate value of that conflict to the states involved? How had they marched into such a disastrous war seemingly against their interests? Why had these same states persisted in sending thousand upon thousand of their citizens to their deaths for apparently minimal gains over the years 1914–18? Early scholars of IR set about trying to find answers to these questions. As William Wallace rightly suggests (1996: 302): 'International Relations as a discipline grew out of reflections on policy, and out of the desire to influence policy, or to improve the practice of policy.'

An influential person in helping Liberal theory become central to the early study of IR was Woodrow Wilson. He had been a political scientist and was President of the USA when in 1917 the country decided to intervene, decisively, in the First World War. In a speech to Congress in January 1918, Wilson declared that he wanted to make the world 'fit and safe to live in; and particularly that it be made safe for every peace-loving nation which, like our own, wishes to live its own life, determine its own institutions, be assured of justice and fair dealing by the other peoples of the world as against force and selfish aggression' (Wilson 1918). He proceeded to outline his 'Fourteen Point' programme. This is a long list to get through so we will just cover the most relevant ones here. They provide us with a vivid insight into how Liberals perceive international affairs. He demanded:

- **Point I: 'Open covenants of peace, openly arrived at'** – a call for open and honest diplomacy. This would help get around the problem of secret alliances which entangled states in war seemingly against their better judgement. Selecting a successful strategy for the conduct of international affairs is trickier when, as a state, you are bound to the decisions of other states as part of an alliance. This is particularly so when you are not quite sure which states are in alliance with which other states in the system, and when you are not sure with what degree of certainty they will back each other at a time of international crisis. This is why Liberal scholars focus on developing international institutions which set down rules, laws and guard the norms of international behaviour as prerequisites to achieving an open and honest 'game' of international relations.
- **Point III: Removal of economic barriers** – the establishment of free trade among all states consenting to the peace. The deeper the ties between states in trading terms, the less likely they will be to judge it financially attractive to wage war on their trading partners. This is the Smith and Ricardo approach to Liberal economics discussed above.
- **Points V–XIII: National self-determination** – interesting that this issue takes up well over half of the Fourteen Points. It includes the call to return invaded territories and to dismantle empires. While it was not named explicitly, it seems Wilson was a critic of the British Empire, which at that point spanned one quarter of the globe and which by definition was a barrier to the establishment of a global free trade regime. Backing all this was an emphasis on democratic governance as a force for good in global politics. In its contemporary form it can be seen in Michael Doyle's Democratic Peace Theory (see later in the chapter).
- **Point XIV: A 'general association of nations'** – to guarantee 'political independence' and 'territorial integrity' to 'great' and 'small' states alike (Wilson 1918) – the kernel of the League of Nations.

Liberal Internationalism is sometimes known as 'Idealism'. You might also find it called Classical Liberalism or Utopian Liberalism. Keep a note of all the different labels you come across and the characteristics writers ascribe to those various perspectives.

Through the elaboration of his Fourteen Points, Wilson became an influential advocate and architect of the League of Nations via the Paris Peace Conference of 1919.

The high contracting parties, in order to promote international co-operation and to achieve international peace and security

- by the acceptance of obligations not to resort to war
- by the prescription of open, just and honourable relations between nations
- by the firm establishment of the understandings of international law as the actual rule of conduct among Governments, and
- by the maintenance of justice and a scrupulous respect for all treaty obligations in the dealings of organised peoples with one another

Agree to this Covenant of the League of Nations.

Figure 6   Preamble to the Covenant of the League of Nations

Source: Yale Law School (2007)

He argued that there was no automatic harmony of interests between states. However, this did not have to lead to war. International order could be constructed with the help of international organizations, which would promote diplomacy, cooperation and the rule of law. The League of Nations is a concrete example of the widespread appeal and political influence of Liberal thought in the immediate aftermath of the First World War: note the Wilsonian leanings evident in Figure 6.

In Wilson's America, civil society and public opinion and exhausted nations globally: the League of Nations had a huge popular mandate when it was formed (Pedersen 2007). However, American support ebbed away over the ensuing years the League fell into disrepute, indicating that 'in practice states remained imprisoned by self-interest' (Dunne 2014: 118). It is a huge irony that for domestic reasons the USA decided not to join the institution it had created and the League quickly became a 'talking shop' shorn of real international political clout and legitimacy – for a thorough review of revisionist historical accounts of the League's work see Pedersen (2007). Adolf Hitler's aggressive diplomacy and Germany, Italy and Japan's military expansionism in the 1930s effectively exposed the League's weaknesses and, the story goes, 'dealt a fatal blow to idealism' (ibid.).

Note the connection between the rise of a theory and the international events occurring at the time it becomes popular. What does this tell you about the context within which theories of IR evolve?

LIBERALISM AFTER THE SECOND WORLD WAR

There is a parallel to be drawn between the real and lasting explosion in Liberal thought after the First World War and the resurgence of those same ideas after the Second World War. After 1945 there was another and this time more concerted push to create international organizations for the promotion of peace, prosperity and security at the regional and global levels. However, Liberals had learnt from the failure of the League of Nations, that they needed to be a bit more hard-headed about what they said and did to take account of the realities of power in international politics. After 1945, Liberals spoke a more 'pragmatic' language of IR (Dunne 2014: 118). We will briefly explore the origins and nature of two such bodies, the United Nations (UN) and the European Union (EU), before showing how these attempts to manage inter-state relations came from, and injected new lifeblood into, Liberal thought.

The United Nations

- **Origins.** Successor to the League of Nations which, as the official wisdom has it, 'ceased its activities after failing to prevent World War Two' (UN 2016a). The UN Charter was drawn up in 1945 by representatives of 50 countries. The UN officially came into existence on 24 October 1945 when the Charter was ratified by China, France, the Soviet Union, the United Kingdom, the United States and a majority of the other 50 signatories (UN 2016a). Compare the preamble to the Charter of the United Nations (Figure 7) to the preamble to the Covenant of the League of Nations (Figure 6).
- **Growth.** The number of states in the international arena has grown rapidly since 1945, helped by the decolonization of former Empires such as the British and the French, and the end of the Cold War in 1989. It began with 51 members in 1945. By 1975 there were 144 members. At the time the Cold War ended there were 159 members. With the accession of South Sudan in July 2011 the UN membership totalled some 193 states (UN 2016b).
- **Aims and activities.** The activities of the UN are guided by its initial aims (Figure 7) and they have expanded along with the number and diversity of the political, economic, social and cultural issues that have forced their way on to the global agenda since 1945. Altering the conduct of international affairs to prevent the recurrence of situations that led to the First and Second World Wars was key. Particularly prominent, and heading the UN's headline goals, was therefore its aim 'to save succeeding generations from the scourge of war, which twice in our lifetime has brought untold sorrow to mankind' (UN 2016c).

Take a look at the structure of the UN (2015) and you can see the sheer scale of its presence on the world stage at all sorts of levels and in relations to all sorts of issues, including the United Nations Children's Fund, World Food Programme, Office on Drugs and Crime, and its many specialized agencies. The UN deals with 'hard' security issues through the Security Council, but its approach to managing inter-state relations goes much wider and deeper than that.

We the people of the United Nations determined

• to save succeeding generations from the scourge of war, which twice in our lifetime has brought untold sorrow to mankind, and

• to reaffirm faith in fundamental human rights, in the dignity and worth of the human person, in the equal rights of men and women and of nations large and small, and

• to establish conditions under which justice and respect for the obligations arising from treaties and other sources of international law can be maintained, and

• to promote social progress and better standards of life in larger freedom …

Have resolved to combine our efforts to accomplish these aims.

Figure 7   Preamble to the Charter of the United Nations

Source: UN (2016c)

Media coverage of the UN's role in trying to resolve international disputes (for example, the question of the existence of Weapons of Mass Destruction in Iraq in 2001–3, or the Russian invasion of the Ukraine in 2014) can skew our impression of what the UN does. Using its website, make a list of some of the key economic, social and cultural programmes run by the UN and this will help you understand more about the breadth and scale of its activities.

The European Union

Britain's referendum of June 2016 on its membership of the European Union will lead to a major state leaving the EU for the first time in its history. Gloomy forecasters have suggested that this means the end of the EU, which will unravel as more and more member states hold similar referendums that result in leave votes. Whatever happens to the EU in the years during and after the Brexit negotiations (and this is not the book to deal with this issue), the EU, at least until the Eurozone crisis from 2008, stood out as a pioneering (but not perfect) form of regional integration which has helped inspire similar projects around the globe (Cameron 2010). It features here as an example of Liberalism in action in international relations, especially Liberal Institutionalism.

The EU was formally brought into being by the Maastricht Treaty in 1993. But European integration did not start then. Maastricht (and subsequent revisions such as

Amsterdam 1999 and the Lisbon Treaty 2008) extended and formalized processes of integration that had begun in the 1950s. It was this growth and development of institutions for European cooperation in the early post-war years that helped drive Liberal Institutionalism. We will briefly review these developments before summarizing what these two case studies tell us about this particular strand of Liberal thinking. Three key developments took place in terms of European cooperation in the 1950s:

1. **European Coal and Steel Community (ECSC)** – Based on the Schuman Plan of May 1950, in April 1951 six countries in western Europe (France, Germany, Italy, Belgium, the Netherlands and Luxembourg) announced that they were to pool their coal and steel resources and run those industries under common management. Its aim was to end 'the frequent and bloody wars between neighbours, which culminated in the Second World War' (Europa 2016a). This process took forward the Liberal economic principle that states enmeshed economically are unlikely to fall out diplomatically and politically, conducting more peaceable relations as a result. The ties that develop over time also build trust in cooperative ventures, states' calculations about the relative payoffs to be gleaned from engaging in conflictual and cooperative behaviour respectively, with the balance tilted toward the latter.

2. **European Defence Community (EDC)** – In June 1950 France announced a further plan to place military forces from consenting states in Europe under a single command. The EDC had regional and global security dimensions. Regionally it sought to ensure security in Europe by containing German forces within European as opposed to national military structures: it would help solve the 'German question'. On the global side the Cold War context was paramount. The EDC aimed to help defend Western Europe against possible attack from the Soviet Union by speeding up military rearmament in leading European nation-states. The EDC collapsed in 1954 when the French parliament, the National Assembly, failed to ratify the treaty. Prime amongst many concerns was the loss of French sovereignty or decision-making authority over its military forces (Ruane 2000). This shows that, ultimately, international organizations can only be as effective (indeed, can only come into existence) as states wish them to be.

3. **European Economic Community (EEC)** – Undeterred by the failure of the EDC, the six countries that developed the ECSC extended integration to many other sectors of their economies in 1957 with the Treaty of Rome. This saw the beginnings of the single market in Europe by enabling the free movement of people, goods and services across borders. As with the ECSC, the EEC used financial means to secure a political end: lasting peace and prosperity through economic cooperation. The EEC was renamed the EU in 1993 after the ratification of the Maastricht Treaty. As with the collapse of the EDC over half a century before, the Brexit referendum vote of 2016 is the latest proof that international relations conducted through international institutions are, ultimately, driven by the wishes of sovereign states, and that these are neither fixed nor necessarily permanent.

Liberal Institutionalism as a body of thought about IR grew directly out of the cooperative ventures embodied in the UN and the EU. The latter provided particularly fertile ground for theoretical innovation and has come to be associated with two writers in particular:

- **David Mitrany**: Developed **functionalist integration theory** after the First World War. 'Functionalism is concerned with the ways of creating ... a working peace system. It involves a diagnosis of the problems of disorder in international society, and a prescription for ways of shaping a better world' (Groom and Taylor 1975: 1). Mitrany argued (1933) that state authority in the modern era had been called into question as people sought out solutions to shared security, economic and political concerns across state borders, rather than working within the confines of those borders. Such efforts would increase as individuals saw the benefits of collective endeavours and this interdependence would then lead to peace and further integration across borders through what has become known as the 'spillover' effect of integration.

Functionalists assume (Groom and Taylor 1975: 3–4):

- Economic development promotes shared and recognizable values (Liberal economics).
- There is a need to develop mechanisms for the delivery of individual welfare across state borders.
- That states are not necessarily the best way of organizing society.
- Threats to individuals and states transcend national borders, rather than being confined within them: they are as often as not common threats and not unique to different states.

- **Ernst B. Haas**: Developed Mitrany's ideas after the Second World War. In *The Uniting of Europe* (2003, first published in 1958) and *Beyond the Nation-State* (1964), Haas argued that Mitrany had gone too far in theorizing integration at the global level. Integration at the regional level, however, could provide the kind of results Mitrany had predicted via spillover from lower levels of integration (economic/social) to higher levels (political). Such 'spillover' comes from two forces. One is functional, as cooperation in one lower level issue led to cooperation in a related area. The other is political, as the creation of supranational organizations such as the UN and EU propelled integration forward into newer, possibly more politically sensitive areas such as defence and security. The EDC might have gone too far in the 1950s, but look at the development of the Common Security and Defence Policy since its emergence in the 1990s, which has made the EU a key provider of security regionally and globally through civilian and military missions. Since 2003, the EU has been involved, amongst other things, in post-tsunami peace building in Indonesia, protecting refugees in Mali and the Central African Republic, and fighting piracy off Somalia and the Horn of Africa (Europa 2016b).

CONTEMPORARY LIBERAL IRT

The work on functionalism by Mitrany and Haas developed and applied Liberal assumptions to the post-1945 world of international relations. Their ideas and associated work in the realm of interdependence, international institutions and international governance (most famously Moravcsik 1998) draw on centuries-old Liberal ideas about human

nature, the organization of states, the causes of wars and how to manage inter-state relations in an anarchic international system. So what, in sum, are the main assumptions of
Liberal IRT and how does it make sense of contemporary international affairs? Studying
the work on international organizations and institutions, along with Democratic Peace
Theory, helps bring the story up to date.

Organizations and Institutions

Liberalism, at least until the 1970s, was popularized in parallel with the growth of international organizations (IOs). It assumed, first, that states were the main actors in the
international system because they were the locus for the key decisions affecting war and
peace. It assumed, second, that these states existed in the classic condition of systemic
anarchy. Liberal IR theorists assumed, third, that states were rational actors in the sense
that leaders could more or less accurately calculate the pay-offs to the state coming from
a range of diplomatic choices open to them. It assumed finally (this is the main departure
from Realism, which we cover in the next chapter) that the existence of international
organizations changed the nature of the calculations states make about war and peace.
Organizations create opportunities for wider and deeper strategic interactions between
states and they in turn inspire trust, build confidence and remove some of the element of
fear that characterizes relations between states in a self-help system.

Drawing on these assumptions, Kenneth Abbott and Duncan Snidal highlight three
principal functions of IOs (see also Keohane 1995: 291). First of all, they centralize collective activities 'through a concrete and stable organizational structure and a supportive
administrative apparatus'. For example, the World Health Organization (WHO) smallpox campaign is more effective as a centralized effort than a series of compartmentalized
state-led efforts 'because global scope avoids gaps in coverage' (Abbott and Snidal
1998: 4–5). Second, membership of IOs holds member states to account, avoids 'dupli-
cation and unproductive competition', and ensures that outputs are shared (ibid.: 14).
Finally, IOs can, especially when they do act and/or are perceived to act independently
from member state control, help manage inter-state conflicts and promote agreements
in the realms of both 'hard' and 'soft' security by providing information, confidence and
a degree of 'neutrality' in dealing with potentially divisive issues. To return to the WHO
smallpox campaign, the organization's structure and the 'reputation-staking effect of
membership' encourages wide participation. Free-riding problems (states signing up to
get the benefits without putting their fair share of money or resources into creating the
solutions) can be mitigated using the WHO's own resources (ibid.: 14). They conclude
as follows: 'Rational states will use or create a formal IO when the value of these functions outweighs the costs, notably the resulting limits on unilateral action' (ibid.: 5).

John Duffield (2007) has identified a considerable leap from the early Liberal
focus on organizations-as-rules to today's Liberal focus on institutions-as-norms.
This conceptual innovation is summarized in Table 2, below. As Abbott and Snidal
explain (1998: 8), 'the role of IOs is best understood through a synthesis of rationalist (including realist) and constructivist approaches', such that the gains from
cooperation feature alongside a consideration of the habits and norms of working in a
collective as motivations for state action. Why is this expansion of meaning important?

Table 2 Organizations and institutions

	Organizations	Institutions
Membership	States	States plus transnational actors
Actorliness	Sovereign	Negotiated/pooled sovereignty
Nature of relations	Regulative (rules and laws)	Constitutive (... plus norms and practices)
Behaviour	Constrained and ordered	Constraint by choice

Well, the first thing to say is that this change in conceptualization of the games states play globally has been seen in the development of regimes and Neoliberal IRT (considered in Chapter 5) as well as in some Constructivist and English School thought (Chapters 7 and 8), so you will read more about it later in the book (and see, for instance, James 1993: 271). Robert Keohane might be considered a pretty traditional theorist of IR, but even he wrestles with understandings of institutions that show the synergies between 'social scientific' and more **reflectivist** approaches to explaining cooperation in international politics (Keohane 1995: especially 285–92).

IOs, Duffield argues, keeps the focus on the 'game-playing' element of state-on-state interactions, with calculations about material gains to the state (in security and economic terms) paramount in leaders' minds. By giving them better information, a set of agreed rules and laws to abide by, and a better working knowledge of other states' intentions, membership of an organization helps a state measure more accurately the pay-off that making move X on the world stage might offer up in terms of reaching its economic, security or diplomatic objective Y. This long-held rationalist conception of institutions-as-organizations is of 'consciously constructed frameworks established by agents seeking to promote or protect their interests' (Duffield 2007: 5). States are still selfish utility-maximizers but they choose to limit their more assertive tendencies because they now perceive the incentives that a more pragmatic, diplomatic approach can bring them over the long term.

Duffield goes on to draw a distinction between an organization-centred understanding of formalized international cooperation and institution-centred work (see the table above). In institutions material gains still matter to states; they want to survive as states; they do not want to be attacked; and they seek to maximize their opportunities for economic growth. They are rational actors. However, underpinning the material is the 'ideational' connection that grows between them as they work alongside each other in international fora.

Hence, states in the Liberal view not only alter their behaviour in favour of cooperation because they are forced to through hard-headed calculations about the benefits to them of participating in international organizations. They also come to share values and other ways of 'being' in the world that imply their destinies are more and more tightly bound up with the fate of other states in the system. John Ruggie's definition of institutions is a telling one: 'persistent and connected sets of rules, formal and informal, that prescribe behavioural roles, constrain activity and shape expectations' (quoted in Onuf 2002: 226). In an institutional setting, states act not just because they have to (because they are 'ordered' to by being signed up to agreements) but because they want to. Emotion can come to accompany and underpin the rational interest-based account of international behaviour. Institutions are thus something broader and deeper than organizations, where identities as well as interests are in play. They are: 'relatively stable sets of related constitutive, regulative, and procedural norms and rules that pertain to the international system, the actors in the system (including states as well as non-state entities), and their activities' (Duffield 2007: 2).

So, the EU might have started life as an international organization but might now credibly be called an institution by virtue of its intention to create a 'zone of peace' across the continent of Europe and to lobby for the promotion of human rights and economic development around the globe. EU member states sign up to procedures and rules which shape their conduct (rules and laws or European Commission 'directives') and share in the promotion of the 'acquis Communautaire' – the Community 'way' of doing things. This has evolved as a norm over time, and which applicant member states have to accept when joining the club. The national law changes they make in line with the 'acquis' make them signatories to the Community method in spirit and practice. States retain the right – as did Britain in 2016 – to decide that they no longer share the values of this community, or to calculate that their interests are better served outside it. This aside, a positive view of the EU is that it has transcended state-on-state war (the founding rationale for its organizational dynamic) and is now busying itself with many other activities, with Brussels home to a lively range of lobbyists, pressure groups and so on.

An emphasis on 'stronger' Liberalism in the form of institutions perhaps better explains more about contemporary international relations than the 'weaker' organizational understanding. Thinking about Liberal IRT through institutional lenses changes the way we view international relations in three ways. First, it accents the cooperative as well as the conflictual elements of world politics. Second, it decentres the idea of states as rational utility-maximizers out to protect their own interests. Institutions shine a light on the shared values that can come to be important drivers of national decision-making in IR, alongside interests defined in security and economic terms. Third, it highlights the complexity of defining sovereignty in an era of complex interdependence. In English School and Constructivist theories, which we cover below, institutions have a yet more sociological content to them (see Buzan 2004: 167–204).

International organizations are said to differ from international institutions in important ways. Keep lists in your notes of how scholars conceptualise the two settings for state-on-state interactions, and how they identify the distinctions between them. Where are the organizations and institutions said to be similar and dissimilar, and do different theoretical traditions treat them differently?

DEMOCRATIC PEACE THEORY

Woodrow Wilson's belief that global history would vindicate the liberal democratic project never left international relations, even if it was rather overtaken by Realist pessimism during the Cold War (see the next chapter). Liberal IR scholars kept on with the view that there was something in the *character* of liberal states that predisposed them to conduct their international relations in a more pacific fashion than their illiberal counterparts (see, for instance, Babst 1964; Doyle 1983, 1986). The end of the Cold War did not, therefore, instigate but it surely helped popularize the interpretation that the 'victors' in the Cold War, the USA and its Western allies, had triumphed over an ideologically bankrupt and politically repressive Communist Soviet empire, in part because of the character of Liberal democracy (Owen 2011: 162). Confidence was high at the end of the Cold War that the Liberal vision could come to be shared the world over, enabled by technologies of globalization and backed by the spread of progressive norms within multilateral IOs and institutions (Fukuyama 1992). Democratic Peace Theory, as it came to be known, emerged as a popular research programme in the post-Cold War years. In this section we will briefly review the core tenets and metatheoretical persuasions of the theory, before reviewing some of the main criticisms that have been levelled against it.

An optimistic interpretation and a positivist research programme

Democratic Peace Theory (DPT) is, in a nutshell, 'the claim that democracies rarely fight one another because they share common norms of live-and-let-live and domestic institutions that constrain the recourse to war' (Rosato 2003: 585). As DPT has developed, the headline claim that democracies tend not to fight each other has been 'deepened to include the claim that "pairs of democracies are much less likely than other pairs of states to fight or to threaten each other in militarized disputes less violent than war"' (Russett and Oneal quoted in Macmillan 2003: 234). Look at the language of DPT. It does not deal in definitive statements (DPT is sometimes erroneously described as claiming that democracies *do not* fight one another) but in probabilistic statements (they *rarely* do so, or *tend* to do so less often). As Bruce Russett explains it (1995: 172): 'democracies are more likely to settle mutual conflicts of interest ... short of the threat or use of any military force'. However, the nuances of their arguments sometimes get lost in the translation to public debate and practitioner discourse, as in the simplified assertion that two countries with a Macdonald's in them have never been to war. Furthermore, many proponents of DPT have looked to positivist, mostly large-*n* (number) studies and rely on quantitative methods. DPT thus opens up interesting debates about how we *do* IR (Geis 2011: 166). In Jack Levy's words, the 'absence of war comes as close as anything we have to an empirical law in international relations' (Levy quoted in Hobson 2011a: 1905) – and this is what the subject is all about, right?

Why does DPT argue that democratic states rarely fight one another? A variety of factors are brought into play, including:

- The 'moral constraint' hypothesis (Friedman 2008). Democracies view other democratic states as more legitimate than non-democracies; fighting them is thus considered illegitimate.
- Publics – and states – act rationally on the basis of what is best for their state. The selfish protection of their own interests just happens to lead to peace more frequently than war: 'People want peace because they do not want to suffer the miseries and material losses of war, in contradistinction to them not wanting to impose miseries and losses on others' (ibid.: 552).

- Democracies are more responsive to lobby and interest groups, particularly economic interest groups who publicize the economic costs of war. This is the liberal economic dimension to DPT.
- This is all underpinned by the 'pacific-foreign-policymaking-public' hypothesis (ibid.). Democracies express the essentially pacifist tendencies of the populace, and because democratic states are more responsive to popular opinion, the chances of resorting to the use of force with other democracies are lower.
- The 'extension' hypothesis (ibid.). Good norms of internal behaviour become translated into good (pacific) norms of external action, building trust and cooperative tendencies. This is where the emotion comes in to support the initial rationalism driving democratic decision-making.
- The 'zone of peace' hypothesis: wars still occur against 'outsiders' existing on the fringes of the zone of peace. Democracies more often resort to war with non-democracies because 'the bond of moral solidarity that constrains power politics in inter-democracy relations is simply a priori absent in democracy-non-democracy relations' (ibid.: 550).

At heart, then, DPT uses a 'domestic analogy' to explain international relations. Walker (1995: 312) explains that a domestic analogy is 'the transfer of the philosophical and theoretical premises derived from the analysis of political community within states to the analysis of relations between states'.

The virtues of DPT are acknowledged by supporters and critics alike (for example, Smith 2011: 152). From the theoretical perspective that most interests us here, after years of being on the back foot in the battle of ideas in IR, DPT emerged to counter the Realist contention that states are condemned permanently to be insecure and threatened because of the anarchic structure of the international system. If 'zones of peace' can be observed between states sharing political structures, then Liberals could claim that state character, rather than the structure of the international system is a more persuasive explanatory factor in states' foreign policy decision-making (Rosato 2003: 585). At a stroke, Waltzian Neorealism (which we cover in Chapter 5) would be fatally weakened, if not destroyed altogether.

Key criticisms and questions

Theories of IR can be criticized on a number of grounds. Those levelled at DPT show the various ways in which academic debates occur as theories get developed, tested and refined over time:

1. **Empirical criticisms: How do we conceptualize 'democracy' and measure 'the history of war'?** Sebastian Rosato argues that the way DPT carves up the global history of wars and conflicts requires attention. This is an ontological criticism because it comes down to definitions of 'democracy' and 'war'. The crux is that the global history of conflict is not quite as easy to access as DPT seems to assume when official 'wars' are actually rare and 'democracy' is not an absolute but a relative term. Rosato's point (2003: 591) is that, during the Cold War, American

interventions (the USA did not declare war) were most often undertaken against democratic states such as Guatemala, Brazil and Chile. These governments were replaced by dictatorial regimes. How do these conflicts-short-of-war fit into DPT? Furthermore, DPT overlooks colonial wars which sought to reimpose autocratic governments favouring the imperial power (ibid.: 589). David Spiro adds that the central DPT finding is actually insignificant in the bigger scheme of things: 'Both wars and democracies are rare, and that is why there are not many wars between democracies' (Spiro 1995: 177). In the view of Rosato and Spiro there is insufficient evidence to prove a causal link between the character of a state and its propensity to engage in threatening or war-like behaviour.

2. **Metatheoretical criticisms:** These unpick the positivist underpinnings of the DPT research programme. As we saw in the previous part of the book, many writers say that the distinction between 'observer' and 'observed' is blurred – scholars are part of the world they are theorizing. They are constructing it at as they go instead of taking a microscope to the world of social affairs in pure detached or 'scientific' fashion. Thus writes Hobson (2011a: 1907): 'The Democratic Peace does not simply exist "out there", it only comes into existence through the categories used to identify and define it'. As agents respond to the publication of these supposedly objective empirical findings they shape their behaviour accordingly: 'their new behaviour is liable to alter or falsify the empirical observation which had been valid to that point'. No theory, DPT included, can stand apart from the world. This links to the normative, policy-focused criticisms.

3. **Normative criticisms:** These centre on the idea that DPT provided intellectual justification for the lengthy, ill-fated US-led invasion and occupation of Iraq from 2003. The widely negative opinions on the reasoning behind, and conduct of, the coalition's use of force have been wrapped in the idea that this was a 'fiasco' (Ricks 2006) for which blame needs attributing and accountability taken by the guilty parties. The governments of the USA under George W. Bush and UK under Tony Blair have been singled out for particular criticism, as the massive Chilcot Report on the UK decision-making that led to the Iraq invasion makes plain (The Report of the Iraq Inquiry 2016). What is at least as interesting about the Iraq story, however, is that scholars propounding DPT have been held to be, if not directly blameworthy, then morally responsible to some degree for over-stating the case for democracy promotion in the post-Cold War era: 'it [DPT] did play a role: one of a confluence of factors that brought about the mistaken choice to invade' (Hobson 2011b: 173). In overselling their claims, or not bothering to hedge them with due caution, writers such as Piki Ish-Shalom are quite adamant that DPT theorists helped market and legitimize the 'effort to democratize Iraq, supposedly servicing America's strategic interest of achieving a Middle East secured and stabilized as a zone of peace' (2011: 180).

These investigations into the ontology, epistemology and methods of research into DPT illustrate in one relatively self-contained sub-field of the discipline how theoretical debates unfold. It also highlights the huge overlap between theory and practice in IR and the influences of the one upon the other. We are left with a series of questions that DPT is now wrestling with since faith in the 'victory' of the West has been shaken after 9/11, the 'War on Terror', the costly and bloody invasions of Afghanistan and Iraq (from Hobson 2011a: 1918), and now the rise of Islamic State terrorism. The answers to these questions do not necessarily hinge on an acceptance of Liberal thought as set out in this chapter. What is the point of a zone of liberal peace if wars are still occurring on its fringes? How do democracies weigh up the benefits of peace against the costs of war with non-democracies? Is democracy promotion a viable way of spreading peace and security or is state sovereignty to be respected? Writers such as Gowa (2011) suggest that DPT may yet have theoretical and policy mileage in it, even if the high Wilsonian optimism of the early post-Cold War years has been sapped from the agenda. It is in need of refining to take better account of the changing character of war and conflict, as well as the contested concept of 'democracy' in the modern world.

QUESTIONS TO PONDER

'Why did the First World War provide such a strong impetus to the development of Liberal IR theory?'

There are a couple of promising approaches you might take when faced with this question. One is to use the literature on the origins of the discipline which we explored in Chapter 3, and expanded on above, to trace the overlap between the worlds of academia and practice which came together in 1919 to produce the discipline of IR we know today. From here you would study the early agenda of the discipline as being all about the promotion of peace, perhaps using a figure such as Woodrow Wilson as an exemplar of this early Liberal thinking. A second approach might be to home in on the Liberal agenda and key themes in Liberal IRT in the inter-war years. This is a reverse of the first approach because you begin with the theory and work back to the impact of war, rather than the other way around.

When answering questions containing references to momentous occurences like the First World War it is tempting to 'pad' the essay out with lots of details about the event in question, especially if you are already familiar with the history. In this example, the question does not ask for an account of the First World War, so only include as much detail as you need to make your point. You will get all your marks for demonstrating knowledge about Liberalism after World War I as opposed to the detail of the unfolding of the conflict. The question is about IRT not the First World War, so the balance must be very heavily towards the former not latter.

However you answer this question, you might also want to include elements of the Liberal agenda which predated the war (see Norman Angell's book in the 'References to more information' below), helping you to a sophisticated argument that the war accentuated aspects of Liberal thought but did not provide their 'origins' in any simple sense.

'Does the existence of the EU bear out the accuracy of Liberal IRT?'

This question invites you to consider the relationship between the theory and practice of IR as far as the formation of international organizations and institutions goes. As with the previous question, you will have to strike a balance between the detail you include on the history and development of the EU and the room you set aside for developing your response to the question. If you are ever in doubt about how much background material to put in an essay, a useful rule of thumb is: if in doubt, leave it out. Your tutor will not want a history of the EU and all its treaties from 1957 to the present day. Nor will he or she want to see potted arguments from the 2016 referendum debate, about sovereignty, peace and the cash states pay into the EU. You will lose marks if you debate the costs and benefits of the EU instead of answering the question set.

Your argument in the essay will depend on your 'reading' of IR – and the dynamics of European unity since 1945. Has the growth in the number and influence of international bodies like the EU stopped states from going to war once and for all? Or have they only helped reduce the likelihood, without changing basic features of the international states system? Whatever you choose to argue, make sure you set your main case out in the introduction and follow it through logically in the rest of the essay towards a conclusion (see Part III of this book on good essay-writing). The shift within Liberalism from organizations to institutions is a dimension you might tease out to give critical depth to your answer. The question talks about 'Liberal IRT', but as the Duffield article demonstrates there are many varieties of contemporary Liberalism which overlap with other theories such as Constructivism and the English School. 'Stronger' Liberalism (institutions) versus 'weaker' Liberalism (organizations) could be an organizing frame for your argument here.

NB, it is easier to answer this question when you know about Realist IRT, which we cover in Chapter 5. Realists criticize Liberals for placing too much emphasis on the power of international organizations to alter fundamental state interests flowing from concerns about their security and survival. For example, Britain's decision to exit the EU could be construed as a reassertion of national sovereignty against the organizational/institutional logic implied by Liberal integration theory. In an essay you would probably want to mention this element of the dispute between the two traditions as a way of framing your own argument and giving critical depth to your answer. But remember: the essay is not a debate about Brexit!

REFERENCES TO MORE INFORMATION

General PowerPoint overview:

Tey, R. (2008) 'Liberalism in International Relations', www.youtube.com/watch?v=5RfR-Co-QwIs&feature=fvwrel (accessed 26 July 2016).
Liberal thought before and between the First and Second World War:

Angell, N. (1909) *The Great Illusion*. London: Weidenfeld and Nicolson.
Argued against the then popular view that war was profitable for states by showing how, in fact, it undermined prosperity by disrupting or destroying commercial and political ties between states.

Woolf, L. (1933) *The Intelligent Man's Way to Prevent War*. London: Gollancz.
Encapsulates the essence of inter-war Liberalism. Note its gendered title (see Chapter 11 in this book).

Curry, W.B. (1939) *The Case for Federal Union*. Harmondsworth: Penguin.

Ashworth, L. (2006) 'Where are the Idealists in Interwar International Relations?', *Review of International Studies*, 32(3): 291–308.
Argues lucidly against ways in which the discipline of IR has defined the idealist tradition between the two World Wars.

For more historical context see also:

Sylvest, C. (2005) 'Continuity and Change in British Liberal Internationalism, *c.* 1900–1930', *Review of International Studies*, 31(2): 263–83.

Caedel, M. (2011) 'The Founding Text of International Relations? Norman Angell's Seminal yet Flawed *The Great Illusion* (1909–1938)', *Review of International Studies*, 37(4): 1671–93.

Overviews of the League of Nations, the UN and the EU:

Bickerton, C. (2016) *The European Union: A Citizen's Guide*. London: Penguin.
Kennedy, P. (2007) *The Parliament of Man: The United Nations and the Quest for World Government*. London: Allen Lane.
Knock, T.J. (1995) *To End All Wars: Woodrow Wilson and the Quest for a New World Order*. Princeton, NJ: Princeton University Press.
Ostrower, G.B. (1997) *The League of Nations: From 1919 to 1929*. Garden City Park, NY: Avery Publishing Group.
Pinder, J. and Usherwood, S. (2013) *The European Union: A Very Short Introduction*, 3rd edn. Oxford: Oxford University Press.

Bache, I. et al. (2011) *Politics in the European Union*, 3rd edn. Oxford: Oxford University Press.
See Part 1 on theories of integration and Part 2 on the history of the organization.

On Functionalism and Neofunctionalism:

Ghébali, V. (1975) 'The League of Nations and Functionalism', in A.J.R. Groom and P. Taylor, *Functionalism: Theory and Practice in International Relations*. London: University of London Press, pp. 141–61.

Haas, E.B. and Whiting, A.S. (1975) *Dynamics of International Relations*. Westport, CT: Greenwood Press.
Makes the case for the Liberal approach to IR; see especially Chapters 1–3.

Rosamond, B. (2000) *Theories of European Integration*. Basingstoke: Macmillan.
Overview of integration theories, including Functionalism and Neofunctionalism.

To get a flavour of the general themes in IR that exercise Liberals:

Franceschet, A. (2001) 'Sovereignty and Freedom: Immanuel Kant's Liberal Internationalist "Legacy"', *Review of International Studies*, 27(2): 209–28.

Mcgrew, A. (2002) 'Liberal Internationalism: Between Realism and Cosmopolitanism', in D. Held and A. McGrew (eds) *Governing Globalization: Power, Authority and Global Governance*. Cambridge: Polity, pp. 267–89.
Maps the Liberal tradition from the 1800s and unpicks its different strands.

Bertelsen J. (ed.) (1977) *Nonstate Nations in International Politics: Comparative Systems Analysis*. New York and London: Praeger.
A collection of essays on what are called in the book 'Non-State Nations': entities that operate as if they were nation-states but which are not confined to territorial borders, for example the Palestinian Arabs, the Zionist Movement and the Basques. Undermines the state-centricity of Realist IRT and therefore offers much food for thought.

Risse-Kappen, T. (1995) *Bringing Transnational Relations Back In: Non-State Actors, Domestic Structures and International Institutions*. Cambridge: Cambridge University Press.
Uses case studies in economics, about multinational corporations, security-building, and social and environmental movements to show that we cannot explain state behaviour without taking the cross-border activities of these non-state actors into account.

Axford, B., Browning, G.K., Huggins, R. and Rosamond, B. (2006) *Politics: An Introduction* 2nd edn. London: Routledge.
Chapter 15 by Axford gives you a succinct overview of the processes and impacts of globalization, as well as a short section on backlashes against it which help you begin thinking about Marxist IRT (Chapter 9 in this book).

On Democratic Peace Theory and its critics:

Brown, M. et al. (eds) (1997) *Debating the Democratic Peace*. Cambridge, MA: MIT Press.
Doyle, M.W. (2012) *Liberal Peace: Selected Essays*. London: Routledge.
Fearon, J.D. (1994) 'Domestic Political Audiences and the Escalation of International Disputes', *American Political Science Review*, 88(3): 577–92.
Knock, T. et al. (2009) *The Crisis in American Foreign Policy: Wilsoniasm in the 21st Century*. Princeton, NJ: Princeton University Press.
Maoz, Z. and Russett, B. (1993) 'Normative and Structural Causes of the Democratic Peace, 1946–86', *American Political Science Review*, 87(3): 624–38.

5

REALISM

Key terms

- Anarchy
- Human nature
- Interest

- Power
- Security dilemma
- State

Politics: it's knowing when to pull the trigger. (Don Lucchesi in *The Godfather Part III*)

We saw in the previous chapter that Liberal IR theorists are optimistic about the potential for some sort of peaceable order, however fragile, to emerge between states existing alongside each other in a condition of anarchy. For Liberals, the potential for conflict between states is diminished, but not ruled out altogether, by involving themselves in processes of cooperation undertaken in international organizations and institutions such as the UN and the EU. These act as forums for communication, building trust and confidence, for open diplomacy and the peaceful resolution of disputes. Organizations and institutions provide the bureaucratic settings in which states come together to agree on the laws and rules that they will all live by.

The first international organization, the International Telegraph Union (now the International Telecommunication Union, ITU), was founded in 1865; it is still going today, having expanded to take in mobile and satellite technologies on top of under-ocean cables and telegraphy. It is interesting that this organization brought together states and private stakeholders to increase global communication under the guise of liberal advancement (ITU 2016). Today, most major states are members of between 50 and 100 international organizations covering all aspects from politics, security and the economy, to culture and sport, such as the International Olympic Committee. The Central Intelligence Agency (CIA) has an online list of all organizations, including their history and membership, along with a country search tool that shows which organizations each member state is signed up to. It reveals that only the odd state, such as North Korea, is not part of this web of international organizations and institutions (CIA undated). For Liberals, international anarchy is a real and pressing concern, but it does not necessarily lead to states continually knocking against each other like balls on a snooker table.

Figure 8   Same startpoint, different endpoints

Realists acknowledge that these elements of the Liberal world of IR exist and that they have a meaningful impact on how sates interact. However, they do not put as much faith as do Liberals in the capacity of all these cross-border interactions to solve fundamental challenges to state security arising from the condition of anarchy. Realists 'are pessimistic about the prospects for international cooperation; they believe that competition between the major powers in the international system is the normal state of affairs' (Glaser 1994–5: 50). With a state's fingers perpetually 'on the trigger' in a self-help system, international security is a fragile notion (see Schweller 2011). The two traditions begin at the same place – explaining state behaviour in a condition of international anarchy. But the basic units of analysis and the central problem to be explained are the only things the two sets of theorists share. From here the two tradi-tions diverge dramatically over the consequences for international relations. Where Liberals see cooperation as the likely outcome, Realists see the perpetual threat of con-flict and war because they are trapped in a cycle of fear caused by lack of trust and/or a competition to dominate the system (Figure 8). Realism is the theory we most associate with the study of international affairs because it deals with the hard security concerns that directly affect the potential for human and state survival on the global stage. In John Herz's article on the security dilemma that we looked at in the previous chapter, he gives a great account of this distinction between the two theories (Herz 1950: 158):

> Realist thought is determined by an insight into the overpowering impact of the security factor and the ensuing power-political, oligarchic, authoritarian, and similar trends and tendencies in society and politics, whatever its ultimate conclu-sion and advocacy. Idealist thought, on the other hand, tends to concentrate on conditions and solutions which are supposed to overcome the egoistic instincts and attitudes of individuals and groups in favour of considerations beyond mere security and self-interest.

Why do the two theories share the same beginning but end up with two almost polar opposite views of IR? Exploring the basic tenets of Realist IRT will help us find out why. We will do this in four parts. The first part discusses Realist understandings of human nature. The second part examines Realist notions of power. The third part looks at the 'birth' of Realism in IR during the inter-war years 1919–39. The fourth part outlines the scale of the 'victory' of Realism over Liberalism after the Second World War.

REALISTS ON HUMAN NATURE

We saw in the previous chapter's account of the Liberal tradition that the essential goodness of human beings has been the touchstone of Liberal thought. In order to understand state-on-state relations, Liberals take this assumption about human nature from domestic polities and apply it to the level of the international system. They use the domestic analogy to explain international relations, with individual human agents in a national society replaced by states living in a condition of anarchy internationally. Liberals argue that people do not want to fight each other unnecessarily, especially if they do lots of trade with them. If peaceable public opinion can be voiced to government in a democratic political system, cooperation can and will occur at the international level through the medium of international organizations and institutions. But what if human beings are not essentially 'good' and peace-loving? What if they are aggressive, constantly expressing a lust for power and a will to dominate? There are many examples of individuals being seen as 'bad apples', Adolf Hitler being the most obvious. The mechanisms of law and order that constrain 'bad' individuals domestically are, if not lacking, then much less robust for states existing in a condition of anarchy. You cannot put a state in prison for committing illegal acts, as you can individuals within states. It is on this other side of the coin that Realist theory works its considerable magic over the discipline.

Hobbes and the state of nature

An excellent way to get to grips with the basics of Realist thought is to see how the English political and legal philosopher Thomas Hobbes (1588–1679) viewed the dynamics of politics. His 1651 work *Leviathan* contains an analysis of human nature which has become central to Realist IRT. Hobbes tried to think through what the world would be like in a 'state of nature' – a world in which men and women live together before the 'invention' of sovereign states.

In this world, humans revert to animalistic behaviour because no-one is safe from the potentially harmful behaviour of others. Trust on all sides is lacking; fear of others is pervasive: 'Fear, according to Hobbes, suffuses and shapes human life. … At once the principal causes of war and the principal means to peace, fear is the basis both of man's most urgent plight and his only possible means of escape' (Blits 1989: 417). In a state of nature there is nothing to regulate people's behaviour and no consequences for uncivilized behaviour towards others. This Hobbesian world of self-interested individuals looking to protect their safety and security produces a 'state of war' in which, as he famously puts it, life is 'solitary, poor, nasty, brutish, and short' (Hobbes 2007: Part 1, Book 13). It is the 'dog eat dog' approach to political and social relations.

· ·

🌍 TAKING IT FURTHER

Realism and human nature in *Shutter Island*

Based on the novel by Denis Lehane (2003) the 2010 film *ShutterIsland* tells the story of Teddy Daniels (played by Leonardo diCaprio), a confused individual seeking, but more often than not in conflict with, memories of his past. The story is set in and around Ashecliffe Hospital for the Criminally Insane, overseen by the sinister Dr Lester Sheehan (played by Ben Kingsley). This hospital is located on Shutter Island, with a geography reminiscent of the Alcatraz island prison off the coast of San Francisco. It is only reachable by boat. The film is about separation, madness, pain, control, escape, and the blurring of fiction and reality. In some regards it is much like the average lecture in IRT. Ashecliffe, apparently, is where bad things happen to people who have done bad things in their lives. The movie is full of fear, suspense, edginess and the constant threat of violence.

About two thirds of the way through the film, Teddy goes exploring the island, trying to uncover some information to piece together what is going on. He bumps into the warden who gives him (coerces him into) a lift back to the hospital. On the way the warden discusses his view of human nature. Violence, he remarks, is: 'God's gift ... God loves violence.' Teddy (standing in for the Liberal, optimistic approach to IRT) says he does not understand this position. 'Why else would there be so much of it?' asks the Warden. 'It's in us. It comes out of us. It is what we do more naturally than we breathe. We wage war. We burn sacrifices. We pillage and tear at the flesh of our brothers. We fill great fields with our stinking dead. And why? To show Him that we have learnt from His example.' With Teddy stunned into contemplative silence, the warden rams the message home. 'He gave us lust and fury and greed and our filthy hearts. So that we could wage war in His honor. There is no moral order as pure as this storm we've just seen. There is no moral order at all. There is only this – can my violence conquer yours?' (Lehane 2003: 244–5).

Lehane's warden should have been a Realist IR theorist. He is a pessimist who sees the worst in humans as the timeless product of Original Sin, destined to repeat the same mistakes over and over. Extrapolating up to the international level, Realists of this hue treat states as flawed entities clashing with each other because they are led by greedy, selfish, power-hungry humans.

· ·

Hobbes and the international state of nature

The Hobbesian world is not a nice one. Unfortunately, he argued, things do not get much better when people come together to try and get around the problems of living in this state of nature. In order to overcome their fear of each other, one approach is to create states within which men and women agree not to harm each other. These states are ruled by sovereign governments which have the 'absolute authority and credible power to protect them from both internal disorders and foreign enemies and threats' (Jackson and Sørensen 2015: 65). However, when different groups of men and women constitute themselves into distinct states to overcome their fear of each other, we then have the creation of a state of nature *between* all these different states. Where before it was people living in fear for their own livelihoods and security, it is now states experiencing this same fear. This is the classic Realist security dilemma: the enhancement of security at the domestic level (within states) goes hand in hand with the creation of insecurity at the international level. The agent or unit of analysis has altered from humans to states, treated as singular entities with given interests, but the central problem has not changed. Anarchy within states has been replaced by the hierarchy provided by a government. However, there is no credible way of getting around the existence of anarchy at the international level.

> Hobbes gave IR theorists two key concepts: self-help and the security dilemma. As you go through your course make a note of how each theorist you study uses (or not) these concepts. What do they mean by them and why are they more important in some theories than others?

Why is the situation different at the international level? Why can states not come together to resolve their mutual security issues as men and women living alongside each other within states can? The main reason is that the parties to the contract differ. Whereas individuals are happy to give up some of their independence to a state government in return for a resolution of their personal security dilemmas, states seem to have a much harder time making this move. There is a constant 'perception gap' whereby a state's military build-up as a defensive measure can, and is, all to easily interpreted as a potentially offensive move in the international game of diplomacy. Benign intentions can easily be misread as malign ambition. The key to understanding the security dilemma is, therefore, to appreciate the 'uncertainty that decision-makers can face in trying to determine others' intentions' (Roe 1999: 184). The rise of the security state is testament to the material means states have at their disposal to safeguard them against potential threats.

> Hobbesian or classical Realism attributes human characteristics to states: it is **reductionist**. How realistic do you think it is to explain state behaviour in the same way we explain human behaviour? What do the two have in common – or is the state of nature the guiding influence on the behaviour of both?

REALISTS ON POWER

If you are a human living in the original state of nature, or indeed a state existing in the international state of nature, it is obviously useful to have 'power' of some kind to help you out. Possession of 'power' will either help protect you from the aggression of other humans/states, or you can use your power to enable you to extract what you want from other humans/states. Power can coerce others; it can compel them to act in ways they might not otherwise; and power can deter others from attacking you. Possess power, possess more security. But how much security is enough?

· ·

 **TAKING IT FURTHER**

Power in David Mitchell's *The Bone Clocks*

Power is one of those words that features in all politics and IR theories at some point. In many ways the disciplines of Politics and IR are all about the definition of power, the identification of different forms of power, the legitimacy of power, and debates about the ways in which power can be exercised to achieve specified political objectives. In any set of social relations power is there if we look hard enough in the right places. Yes, it is exerted daily in the places we would expect: in governments, political parties and by militaries and defence forces. But power relations also exist in families, religions, in the lecture theatre, in sports governance, on quiz shows and in Hollywood.

Given that power is so pervasive in the conduct of human relations, it has been of endur-ing interest to novelists as well as academics. One such writer who reflects on power in a proto-academic sense is David Mitchell in his excellent novel *The Bone Clocks*. He has one of his characters (2015: 97–8), Hugo Lamb, a Cambridge University undergraduate majoring in Politics, reflect on power quite early on in the story: 'Power is the ability to make someone do what they otherwise wouldn't, or deter them from doing what they otherwise would.' This is a very standard definition of power as a form of force: compellence and deterrence. Lamb then expands, suggesting that power works: 'By coercion and reward. Carrots and sticks ... Coercion is predicated upon the fear of violence or suffering. "Obey or you'll regret it."... Reward works by promising "Obey and feel the benefit."' Here we have a very clear definition of power as it features in much IRT. Keep a note of all the different definitions you come across because it is a highly fluid term and one that requires careful unpacking in essays and exam answers. You can look both to IRT and wider sources such as novels to get ideas on how to define power.

Spoiler alert: Lamb ends up decanting the souls of human beings in an attempt to gain immortality. Perhaps his lust for power was showing up early in the book as a sign of what was to come?

· ·

Where does the interest in power come from and how does it feature in Realist IRT? We can find out how by looking at how three Realist writers, one classical and two modern, use power to inform their explanations of IR.

The 'timeless wisdom' of Thucydides

> The enduring anarchic character of international politics accounts for the striking sameness in the quality of international life through the millennia, a statement that will meet with wide assent. (Waltz 1979: 66)

Thucydides was a fifth-century Athenian general who wrote *History of the Peloponnesian War*, which documented the quarter-of-a-century conflict between Athens and Sparta in 431–404 BC (Thucydides 2004). This work of history has inspired many a Realist to cleave to a 'tragic vision of politics' (Lebow 2003: 35; Rosenau and Durfee 1995: 9–10). Claiming a timeless wisdom to Thucydides' work gives Realists a useful propaganda coup when it comes to attracting support for their explanations of international affairs, because they can portray them as being applicable far beyond 'any condition or attribute of the modern world ... but ... as a central feature of prior epochs as well' (Sterling-Folker 2006e: 15; see also Little 2005: 46). Alongside Thucydides we find Machiavelli, Hobbes, Spinoza and Rousseau marshalled together in the 'classical' Realist canon (Forde 1996). James Der Derian remarks that in identifying the 'eternal return of the ghost' of the classic such as Thucydides, writers such as Robert Gilpin (1984) can claim 'transhistorical power' for their actually historically situated and context-bound readings of the global past (Der Derian 1995: 383).

Thucydides told the story of an age of a few 'great powers' and many lesser powers, during which states' adaptation to circumstances they could do little to alter was an ineffable part of life; for an overview of Thucydides and his work see Nye and Welch 2011: 16–21). Thucydides' harsh dictum was that in order to survive and prosper states had to adapt to the reality they found themselves in, given their relative size compared to other states. Having established where they were in the international hierarchy of power they had to conduct themselves accordingly to stay safe and secure – from here you can trace a line to Hobbes' international state of nature. Thucydides opened the way for a discussion of morality and justice in the conduct of foreign policy that later Realists such as Hans Morgenthau would build upon. As Stanley Hoffman has observed (1995: 239–40): 'Much of the study of power in international affairs has been remarkably Athenian.'

Most IR treatments of Thucydides concentrate on the passage from the 'Melian dialogue' of 416 BC where he highlighted how power relations played out between the stronger Athenians and the weaker Melians. There was a recent history of conflict between them. The Athenians wanted to bring the Melians into their empire, to strengthen Athens against their principal regional rivals Sparta: 'by conquering you we shall increase not only the size but the security of our empire.' The Melians, in contrast, were interested in establishing the ideals of 'fair play and just dealing' and were worried about being brought into slavery to the Athenian empire. The Melians wanted to remain neutral and worried about the precedent the end of neutrality for them would set for other neutral states in the system: they claimed the invasion of Melos would increase rather than diminish the security dilemma. The Athenians disagreed: 'This is no fair fight ... It is rather a question of saving your lives and not resisting those who are far too strong for you.' If Melos was in the same position as Athens, claimed the Athenians, Melos would be acting in precisely the same way (all from Lygdamus.com undated: 2–4). The meeting between the Melians and Athenians ended in an agreement to disagree. Shortly afterwards, Thucydides explained, Athens besieged Melos, 'the Melians surrendered unconditionally to the Athenians, who put to death all the men of military age whom they took, and sold the women and children as slaves' (Lygdamus.com undated: 5).

The Melian Dialogue shows the exercise of power in its rawest form. This is power as coercion and violence: stick not carrot (see the Taking it Further box above). However, it is not merely what Thucydides said about power in international relations, but his whole approach to writing his history that should be of interest to you in terms of your understanding of the Realist tradition in IRT. Gregory Crane makes this point by writing that: 'Thucydides' *History* exhibits four characteristics common to many "realist" schools of thought – not only political, but literary, artistic, and scientific' (1998: Chapter 2).

Realism, like all IR theories you will cover, is much more than a list of foreign policy maxims. It is a way of seeing the world and of writing about it, so studying Thucydides can be doubly instructive. Let us take each of Crane's observations in turn:

1. **Procedural Realism.** Thucydides 'insisted upon a high level of observational accuracy', involving 'careful observation and precise reporting'. He castigated previous historians (such as Herodotus on the Persian wars) for inaccuracies. He located himself firmly in what we know as the positivist tradition of assuming a world external from him which he could experience and report on accurately. Thucydides did not just not rely on the merits of his account to speak for themselves, he knocked down rival approaches. IR theorists enjoy doing this too.

2. **Scientific Realism.** Follows from procedural realism. Thucydides was well aware of the methodological problems he encountered in trying to report accurately the evolution of the Peloponnesian War. Nevertheless, he was convinced such a task was possible. He wrote of examining 'the facts themselves' to get at the truth of this long conflict.

3. **Ideological Realism.** In setting his account against less faithful or accurate histories, Thucydides could claim that only he possessed 'a monopoly on truth'. He placed his work directly in opposition to 'idealism', which he took to mean 'the pursuit of an attractive, but ultimately ill-founded, vision of the world'. By stressing his emotional detachment, Thucydides could claim a special authority for his work that he denied to fanciful histories not rooted in observed facts. Unlike those imagined histories, Thucydides said he dealt with the 'real world'.

4. **Paradigmatic Realism.** Using a word popularized by the philosopher of science, Thomas Kuhn, Crane suggests we should see Thucydides' self-proclaimed advances towards objective history as a 'paradigm' shift (see also Holsti 1985). Thucydides set down a new method for history and established new benchmarks by which histories should be judged. But in doing so things got lost, some methods fell into abeyance, facts were overlooked. For example, Thucydides privileged military and political history: he ignored the role of women in Greek society and ethical questions around the conduct of the war. Thucydides' new paradigm claimed objectivity, completeness and impartiality, but can social scientific inquiry ever be impartial?

REALISM IN THE INTER-WAR YEARS

Echoes of both the style and substance of Thucydides' *History* are to be found in what would later become the tradition of Realist IRT. Two writers exemplify this very well indeed: E.H. Carr and Hans Morgenthau.

E.H. Carr

Carr's opinions on international relations were held in high regard because of his extensive policy and academic experience. He worked as a diplomat in the British Foreign Office between 1916 and 1936. As we have seen already (see Chapter 3) these were tragic decades encompassing the First World War and its volatile aftermath, as well as being

IR's formative years as a distinct discipline of academic study. In 1936, Carr resigned from the Foreign Office to take up a Chair (Professorship) in International Relations at what was then Aberystwyth University. While a student at Cambridge University, it is worth remarking that Carr had studied Herodotus' account of the Persian Wars and was clearly acquainted with the work of Thucydides (Carr 2001a: xi, 81 and 104).

A 'sustained critique of the way in which utopian thought had dominated international relations in the inter-war years' is how Martin Hollis and Steve Smith (1991: 21) have summarized E.H. Carr's *The Twenty Years' Crisis* (2001b), which was first published in 1939. What did Carr mean by 'utopian thought' and why did he attack it? Carr was dissatisfied with the main tenets of Liberal thought we identified in Chapter 4. He branded it 'utopian' in order to contrast it with an approach he deemed more 'realistic' – Realism. According to Carr, in utopian thought, human progress is achieved by essential human goodness being allowed to flourish in democratic states. These democratic processes are replicated and enhanced at the international level through international organizations and institutions, where disputes get resolved peaceably through dialogue between states. This gets around the insecurity and violence involved in Athens smashing Melos, as Thucydides recounted in the Peloponnesian War (see above).

For Carr, however, *willing* world peace was not the same as *achieving* world peace. Practical products of Liberal thought, such as the League of Nations, did not take into account realities that had to be dealt with in the world of foreign policy-making, such as the carrot and stick of power, cunning and subversion in diplomacy, and the use of force to settle disputes. Thus, Carr argued that Liberals had got everything the wrong way around. Instead of developing a theory (of human nature and IR) and trying to mould reality to fit the theory, Liberals should be looking at the reality out there and developing the theory to explain the patterns in it. Utopian thinking, he believed, had 'delayed the advent of social science' (Hoffman 1995: 215).

On your IR course you are more than likely to find Carr presented as a founding father of the classical Realist tradition in the UK and USA, so it is well worth looking at the 2001 version of *The Twenty Years' Crisis*. This contains an excellent introduction by Michael Cox that interrogates the easy assumption that Carr was a Realist thinker.

Carr's context: a Realist reality

The reality of the inter-war years in Carr's eyes was that international anarchy led to war and conflict in the international system. That his book was first published on the eve of the Second World War (1939–45) must have helped convince his audiences in the political and academic worlds that international reality in 1919–39 was best interpreted through Realist rather than Liberal lenses. He certainly appears to have been onto something and it was a conducive climate in which to sell new ideas about the conduct of power in international affairs.

Two issues in particular helped persuade Carr to this viewpoint. First, the collapse of the League of Nations undermined Liberalism's explanation of international relations. Established in accordance with Wilsonian principles in 1919 (see the previous chapter), the outbreak of the Second World War confirmed what many had feared for years previously:

the League did not have the diplomatic, political or military muscle to prevent inter-state wars. It was too much carrot and not enough stick. The rise and actions of the Axis powers, Germany, Italy and Japan, demonstrated in Carr's mind the truth of the Thucydidean principle that 'might is right' – the powerful do what they want, the weak do what they can. The Melian Dialogue seemed to have a timeless quality to it.

Second, the Great Depression in the USA, and the global recession that it produced, undermined the Liberal claim that free trade would promote harmonious international economic relations between states. Economic statistics from this period offer a glimpse of the scale of the depression. US unemployment rose from 3 per cent in 1929 to over 25 per cent in 1933 (Darby, cited in Schenk 1997–2006). Over the same four-year period, US Gross National Product halved from well over $100 billion per quarter to just over $50 billion per quarter (Moore, cited in Schenk 1997–2006). In Carr's view, inter-war international economic disorder on such a scale showed the frailty of the assumption that letting the free market do its work would promote global economic harmony. What was called for was new economic thinking, and this meant interventionist policies to promote full employment, equality and social justice. Carr was helped to this view by the success of the Russian five-year economic plans from 1929, which contrasted sharply with the downturn in the capitalist world over the same period. Thus, while Carr is now said to be an archetypal Realist he had elements of sympathy for more left-wing approaches to political organization.

. . . .

 **TAKING IT FURTHER**

From E.H. Carr to David Cameron: the Realist tradition in the present

It is argued that Realism has taken a firm hold in (especially but not exclusively) Western foreign policy circles since its popularization in the inter-war and post-1945 years. By this, we mean that for one reason or another (the transmission mechanisms are too complex to nail down precisely) core Realist tenets about international security and global order have become something of a default setting for many Western policy-makers. In the post-Cold War era they have been joined by elements of other IR theories to make foreign policy speeches very rich sources of evidence on which theory is doing best, practice-wise, at any given time.

Between them, David Cameron, British Prime Minister 2010–16, and William Hague, British Foreign Secretary 2010–14, developed an understanding of British foreign policy they called 'liberal Conservatism' (not so dissimilar from John Herz's Realist Liberalism outlined in Chapter 4). They spelt out its implications in a series of speeches, both men sticking to a tightly worded script. In the two quotations that follow the underlined words show Liberal themes, the *italics* show themes the English School might privilege (we come to the English School in Chapter 7, so refer back here at a later stage) and the **bold** font shows Realist themes.

David Cameron: 'I am a liberal conservative, rather than a neo-conservative. Liberal – because I support the aim of spreading freedom and democracy, and support *humanitarian intervention*. **Conservative** – because I recognise the **complexities of human nature**, and am **sceptical of grand schemes to remake the world**' (Cameron 2006).

William Hague: 'David Cameron and I have spoken in recent years of our approach to foreign affairs being based on 'Liberal **Conservatism**' in that we believe in freedom, human rights and democracy and want to see more of these things in other nations. But **Conservative**, because we believe strongly in the **continued relevance of the nation state** and are **sceptical of grand utopian schemes to re-make the world**' (Hague 2009).

This rough and ready piece of text analysis shows the place of Realism in contemporary foreign policy thought in the UK. The Cameron governments of 2010–16 came to the conclusion that foreign policy must be conducted with a 'conscience', hence the Libya intervention of 2011 and Hague's very personal interest in ending sexual violence in conflict which he put on the international agenda via action at the UN level (Daddow 2015). However, crusading democracy promotion à la Tony Blair in Iraq was not for Cameron or Hague. In Carr-esque fashion they believed the world will not be re-made easily or quickly; we have to work pragmatically with what we have (human nature and nation-states) and be cautious about what we can achieve by respecting cultural and religious differences. Their foreign policy outlook has Liberal–English School leanings but ultimately entails a critique of utopianism and takes British foreign policy towards a Realist understanding of international affairs. Realist IRT has proved remarkably durable both in terms of language and practice.

. . . .

REALISM AFTER THE SECOND WORLD WAR: MORGENTHAU

You gotta stop them at the beginning. Like they shoulda stopped Hitler at Munich, they should never have let him get away with that, they were just asking for big trouble when they let him get away with that. (Puzo 1991: 143)

So says Peter Clemenza, one of the hitmen in Mario Puzo's *The Godfather* novels, a man well used to fighting violence with violence. As we have seen earlier in this chapter, the deterrent and coercive effects of power are central to Realist thought, and they have emerged from a particular reading of global history in the twentieth century. As Rosenau and Durfee (1995: 10–11) describe this reasoning as it solidified during the twenty years' crisis between the World Wars:

Had the leaders of Britain, France, and the United States paid more attention to power and not imagined that good will and accommodation would be adopted by all, then actions to counter the aggressions of the 1930s might have prevented the outbreak of World War II.

Thus, as Robert Jervis has observed (1994: 855), 'the experience of Hitler was a greater sponsor of Realism than any written text could be'.

Carr went a long way to expounding the core principles of the Realist tradition. However, it was left to Hans Morgenthau to develop them in a rigorous 'scientific' fashion, one that would attract the US policy and academic communities into the Realist camp. Morgenthau was a German émigré to the USA who arrived there two years before the outbreak of the Second World War, having spent his early career teaching public law in Geneva and Madrid. His major IR-related books were written while he worked as a political scientist in various US universities (*Encyclopedia of World Biography* 2005–6). Morgenthau's *Politics Among Nations*, first published in 1948, responded directly to Carr's call for IR to be studied 'scientifically'. Morgenthau developed IR's appreciation of power and used this to inform his six principles of political realism. Hoffman (1995: 216–18) credits Morgenthau with being the true founder of the discipline of IR in the USA, using his work to inform US policy-makers deal with their new-found global power after the Second World War.

Morgenthau (1985) argued that a nation's power stems from many interconnected elements (see also the coverage in Rosenau and Durfee 1995: 16–17). First, its geography (size and position) can be important. For example, see how Britain's island status has shaped its outlook on everything from free trade to its place in Europe during the 2016 EU referendum debate. Second, power can come from a state's natural resources such as food and raw materials. Self-sufficiency is the ideal state because it diminishes the reliance on other nations for the basic means of survival – it lessens possible sources of insecurity to the state. Third, a state needs the industrial capacity to get the best out of its available natural resources. The Industrial Revolution might be an example of a state such as the UK meeting this recommendation. Fourth, there must be military preparedness to support the preferred foreign policy orientation of the nation. Fifth, the state's population must be able and prepared to apply the material implements of national power. This is only partly about population size. Sixth, 'national character' or the collective characteristics of a given people. Seventh, 'national morale' or the determination with which a nation supports the foreign policy of the government in peace and war. Eighth, and 'the most important factor', the quality of a nation's diplomacy. Ninth we can measure as a component of national power the quality of government in allocating resources and sustaining support for its policies at home.

The website Global Firepower (2016) might be considered a Realist way of measuring the national power of states. It uses a huge volume of statistical data to 'rank' 125 states in order of most to least powerful. The data cover: geography, military 'manpower' as a function of population size, resources, logistical issues such as road and railway coverage, lots on military kit and structure of the states' armed forces, and economics. In sum, 50 factors go into the assessment of the world's mightiest military powers and the list is searchable by country name, where you can drill down into the data. In 2016 the top 10 powers were, from 1 to 10: USA, Russia, China, India, France, UK, Japan, Turkey, Germany and Italy.

These elements of national power are all important. But they only make sense, Morgenthau contends (1985: 4–17), if we appreciate the following six principles:

1. **Politics has its roots in human nature.** As Jack Donnelly observes (1996: 86), 'Human nature is the starting point for realism. And the core of human nature, for realists, lies in the egoistic passions, which incline men and women to evil'. This nature is essentially as Thucydides and Hobbes described it, and it has not changed over thousands of years (Morgenthau elaborates on this in his third principle, below). If we take this as one of several 'objective laws' of politics, we 'must also believe in the possibility of developing a rational theory that reflects … these objective laws'. This possibility exists because we also assume that we can untangle 'truth' (deduced rationally from evidence) from 'opinion' (subjective judgement divorced from facts).

2. **Foreign policy-makers 'think and act in terms of interest defined as power'.** In international politics, power political considerations are everything. Ethics, morals, economics and religious prescriptions are all subservient to the exercise of power, as the Melian Dialogue made clear (see above). This assumption 'infuses rational order into

the subject matter of politics, and thus makes the theoretical understanding of politics possible'. We can only measure the quality of foreign policy decisions in terms of the extent to which they enhance a state's security, in other words, with regard to the extent to which they are 'rational' decisions. The language of ethics might be used to 'dress up' foreign policies for public consumption, but these policies should and will be all about preserving the national interest (is that what Cameron and Hague were doing in their speeches analysed above?). Writers such as Mark Curtis (2003) have made this point very strongly about recent British foreign policy.

3. Morgenthau's third element has two parts to it. **(i) Humans are basically self-interested, as are states.** Relations between humans and states play out via politics at the domestic and international levels respectively, and this is where their different interests are liable to collide. **(ii) A state's definition and use of power depend on the cultural and political context within which power is exercised.** Put broadly, power 'covers all social relationships which serve that end, from physical violence to the most subtle psychological ties by which one mind controls another'. Morgenthau here goes beyond power as 'stick', to take in power as 'carrot' and reward, with perception and psychology indispensable elements of it, and fundamental to it. Transforming the contemporary world means working with these enduring realities of international political life: interest and power.

4. **We can only judge the morality of a leader's actions on the basis of a careful examination of the choices open to him or her at a particular point in time.** There is no universal moral code by which we can judge such actions. Morgenthau endorses a 'situational ethics' whereby we judge actions according to a deep appreciation of what was possible under the prevailing circumstances at the time the decision(s) was/were made (Molloy 2008: 96).

5. **No nation has the right to claim its moral code as the world's moral code, or to impose its ideology onto others.** Such folly 'is liable to engender the distortion in judgment which, in the blindness of crusading frenzy, destroys nations and civilizations'. In fact, one test of morality is the extent to which we respect the decisions of others to live and act differently from ourselves. Here we see the Realist basis for criticizing crusading approaches to foreign policy that ignore local specificities. We saw earlier in the chapter how William Hague talked about British foreign policy using a mix of Realist and Liberal terminology. A further Realist element came through in his belief that 'it is important not to generalize too much … if we want them to work with us in our interest and to develop more of our values. We mustn't push them down their throats, we have to be careful about that' (cited in Gilmore 2014: 31). Hague's echo of Morgenthau's fifth principle of Realism was very marked indeed.

6. **Restatement of the autonomy of the political sphere with examples of how it works in practice.** 'The economist asks: "How does this policy affect the wealth of society, or a segment of it?" The lawyer asks: "Is this policy in accord with the rules of law?" The moralist asks: "Is this policy in accord with moral principles?" And the political realist asks: "How does this policy affect the power of the nation?" International politics is not for the faint of heart but we cannot wish human nature away.' Politics as the accrual and exercise of power is where Realism is at.

This chapter and the previous one have provided succinct overviews of the Realist and Liberal traditions in IR. These are two of the bedrocks of IRT. If you get to grips with them early on in your studies you will be able to make better sense of all the theories that have emerged later within the field. It is now up to you to generate a deeper understanding of these foundational theories by reading around them as widely as you can. Let us recap some of the key elements by way of summary. First, Realists and Liberals share several assumptions about IR (we will return to these in the next chapter). Second, they sometimes draw on the same case studies from the past for evidence, interpreting the 'meaning' of these historical episodes quite differently. Sometimes they just 'see' different worlds of international politics (indicating ontological differences, that is, what is 'out there' to be explained). This links to the third point: where Realists see conflict, insecurity and the perpetual threat of war between states, Liberals emphasize the possibilities for peace and human progress via cooperation in international organizations and institutions. Fourth, both theories make claims about how accurate/reliable they are based on appeals to history and tradition. Finally, neither theory is monolithic – they have different 'wings' to them. In the next chapter we will see how both theories have been updated in the forms of Neoliberalism and Neorealism.

> Realists tend to have a more pessimistic view of IR than Liberals. How would you describe your own view of IR: more optimistic or pessimistic? On what do you base this view?

QUESTIONS FOR DISCUSSION

'How relevant is Thucydides to the contemporary study of international relations?'

A good place to begin is to set out the claims on behalf of Thucydides made by Realist IR scholars. One way to do this is to make a note of all the writers who show direct knowledge of his work (E.H. Carr, for example) and they can form the basis of one side of the argument, that Thucydides *is* relevant. You might want to make the argument that a state's conduct in international relations is principally about the exercise of power in various forms. If so, you could use Thucydides' Melian Dialogue and trace its discourse on power and human nature through into the reflections on power in novels and the Realist thought of writers such as Carr and Morgenthau, as we have done above.

Equally, however, there will be writers who disagree. They question the utility of understanding contemporary international politics by looking at political relations between Greek city-states thousands of years ago. They attack some of Thucydidean/Realist assumptions about human nature, security, power, morality and the lust for violence. Here you can use Realism's traditional opponent, Liberalism, to make the case that it is not only Thucydides but the entire tradition inspired by him that misconstrues the nature of contemporary IR. Liberals question the definition of power and also the 'classical' Realist tendency to reduce international politics to a study of power. Many of the theories covered later in this book will help you critique Realism too.

David A. Welch has written an article entitled 'Why IR Theorists Should Stop Reading Thucydides' (2003). When you come across provocative articles like this, you should certainly read them – they provide you with a whole set of tools for challenging established theoretical positions.

Remember throughout the essay to make a central argument about 'relevance'. It is quite hard to set benchmarks, so one approach when planning your answer might be to give Thucydides a very simple score out of 10. If you think he's a 9/10: why? If you think he's a 2/10: why? Presumably if you are a Realist, your score will be higher than if you agree more with other IR theories.

'What role do ethical considerations play in Realist IR theory?'

This question invites you to consider the core assumptions and arguments about IR put forward by Realist theorists, and to gauge the place they give normative concerns around ethics and justice in the conduct of international politics. To begin with, you will have to specify what you mean by 'Realist', so explain which theorist or set of theorists you take to be representative of the tradition. In this chapter we have explored a few seminal writers but there are dozens to choose from.

You next need to highlight where morality features in the main writers you take to be representative of the Realist tradition. You could assess how they approach questions of morality in the international sphere in a number of ways. For instance, you could explore their views on private and public morality and explain that for writers such as Morgenthau there is no universal moral code – morality is to be judged in the context of particular decisions at particular times, and purely in the context of national interest.

You might also think laterally by comparing how the 'average' Realist writer treats morality compared to the 'average' Liberal writer, emerging with the conclusion that morality plays less of a role in this theoretical tradition than in others – or perhaps it is more accurate to say a more ambiguous role. The speeches by Cameron and Hague, explored above, highlight the awkward place ethics hold in much contemporary Western foreign policy thinking. Realist thought itself struggles to quieten a concern with normative issues: what 'ought' to be done can implicitly appear within supposedly impartial descriptions of what 'is' done. This kind of additional material might provide you with a case study to develop if you can track the overlooked ethical components of Realist thought, in Morgenthau for example.

REFERENCES TO MORE INFORMATION

For coverage of the general themes and issues pertinent to the Realist tradition:

Gilpin, R.G. (1984) 'The Richness of the Tradition of Political Realism', *International Organization*, 38(2): 287–304.

James, A. (1989) 'The Realism of Realism: The State and the Study of International Relations', *Review of International Studies*, 15(3): 222–6.

Jervis, R. (1978) 'Cooperation under the Security Dilemma', *World Politics*, 30(2): 167–214. Explication of the defensive Realist approach. These are Realists operating at the most optimistic end of the spectrum of Realist theory.

Wheeler, N.J. (2014) 'Interview with Robert Jervis', *International Relations*, 28(4): 479–504.
Wide-ranging interview, including early influences on his career, reflections on his key books and what Jervis sees as the crux of IR today.

Williamson, D. (2003) *War and Peace: International Relations, 1919–39*, 2nd edn. London: Hodder and Stoughton.

Herz, J.H. (1959) *International Relations in the Nuclear Age*. New York: Columbia University Press.
Shows the link between Realist thinking and events 'on the ground' during the formative years of the Cold War.

Hirst, P. (2001) *War and Power in the 21st Century*. Cambridge: Polity.
See Chapter 2 on the international system since 1648 and Chapter 4 debating possible futures for the international system.

On Thucydides and his legacy:

Chittick, W.O. and Freyberg-Inan, A. (2000) '"Chiefly for Fear, Next for Honour, and Lastly for Profit": An Analysis of Foreign Policy Motivation in the Peloponnesian War', *Review of International Studies*, 27(1): 69–90.

Bagby, L.M.J. (1994) 'The Use and Abuse of Thucydides in International Relations', *International Organization*, 48(1): 131–53.
Argues that Realists deploy Thucydides rather simplistically and offers alternative readings that are more useful, especially to foreign policy practitioners.

Monten, J. (2006) 'Thucydides and Modern Realism', *International Studies Quarterly*, 50(1): 3–26.
A further reassessment of Thucydides' Realist credentials.

Critical work on the Realist canon:

Beitz, C.R. (1979) *Political Theory and International Relations*. Princeton, NJ: Princeton University Press.
Elaborates the theory of cosmopolitanism through a critique of the state-centricity of Realism, especially its assumption that states exist in a Hobbesian self-help environment. Useful if you want to critique Realist theory.

Cozette, M. (2008) 'Reclaiming the Critical Dimension of Realism: Hans J. Morgenthau on the Ethics of Scholarship', *Review of International Studies*, 34(1): 5–27.

Reassesses Morgenthau's credentials as a critical thinker about IR through a close reading of his work on truth, power and the ethics of scholarship. Similar in intention to

Bain, W. (2000) 'Deconfusing Morgenthau: Moral Inquiry and Classical Realism Reconsidered', *Review of International Studies*, 26(3): 445–64.

Guzzini, S. (1998) *Realism in International Relations and International Political Economy: The Continuing Story of a Death Foretold*. London: Routledge.

Considers the theory, practices and crises in Realist thought as well as the Neorealist response to these crises in the theory (see the next chapter in this book).

Gilpin, R. (2002) 'A Realist Perspective on International Governance', in D. Held and A. McGrew (eds) *Governing Globalization: Power, Authority and Global Governance*. Cambridge: Polity, pp. 237–48.

Waltz, K.N. (2008) *Realism and International Politics*. New York: Routledge.

A collection of Waltz's essays from across his career. Part 1 on theory includes responses to critics and is particularly useful.

6

NEOREALISM AND NEOLIBERALISM

Key terms

- Anarchy
- Balance of power
- Political Economy
- Rationality

- Regimes
- State
- System

The debate between the Neorealists and the Neoliberals erupted in the 1970s and quickly developed into the major theoretical controversy within IR. Each body of writing is strongly rooted in the 'classical' variants of Realism and Liberalism we explored in the previous two chapters, taking touchstone assumptions and ideas from these traditions and developing them in new directions. With the emergence of the Neo-Neo debate, as it is sometimes called, we see how theoretical innovations in the field of IR continue to draw inspiration from changes on the 'real' international political, strategic and economic fronts. We begin this chapter by considering Kenneth Waltz and John Mearsheimer's Neorealism and move on to the Neoliberal reaction, which took a variety of forms, but which is largely associated with work on cooperation occurring in regimes and institutions.

NEOREALISM

In the previous chapter we identified key Realist assumptions and arguments by looking at the work of E.H. Carr and Hans Morgenthau. We saw that in the brand of Realist thought that emerged through the inter-war years and took hold of the discipline after the Second World War, explanations for war between states operated at two levels of analysis:

- **Level 1: Human nature.** Inspired by Hobbesian ideas about human insecurity in a state of nature, writers such as Morgenthau argued that if we understand the failings in human nature we understand most of the dynamics of international politics. Fear and mistrust of other agents 'out there' is exaggerated by a lust for power which can be a further cause of conflict.

- **Level 2: State interests in a condition of anarchy.** By transposing Hobbes' state of nature onto the realm of the international, we can explain international relations with reference to the quest for security on the part of self-interested and perpetually insecure states. Waltz developed Realist thinking via **'defensive' realism**, arguing that states generally want to survive and seek to enhance their security to the degree necessary to achieve this. Mearsheimer's **'offensive' realism**, also to be studied below, argues that states are as flawed as individual humans in a state of nature. Their ongoing quest for power and domination over the system causes perpetual instability even when a notional **balance of power** is in operation.

If you are truly to understand IRT you need to get to grips with the work of one of the, if not the single most, influential writers on the subject, Kenneth Waltz. Waltz published two important books, the gist of which he reflected on in many, many journal articles, which can also be good sources when you need to get to grips with what Waltz said at first hand. First, there was *Man, the State and War* (1959), which echoed Morgenthau and Carr's treatment of international relations as a never-ending series of conflicts among states trapped in a condition of anarchy. This book was pitched largely at the levels of analysis outlined above.

Twenty years later, Waltz went a stage further, publishing his *Theory of International Politics* in 1979, in which he sought to explain the causes of wars more systematically. 'It is not possible,' he wrote, 'to understand world politics simply by looking inside of states' (p. 65). That is, the 'goodness' or 'badness' of humans and/or states were insufficient explanations for the dynamics of international politics. He suggested that, to develop a viable theory of international relations, we need to focus on a third, higher, level. 'The repeated failure of attempts to explain international outcomes analytically – that is, through examination of interacting units [levels one and two] – *strongly signals the need for a systems approach*' (ibid.: 68, my emphasis). We do not explain international politics with reference to its principal actors – states – but with regard to observable phenomena at the system level. Investigating this new level 3 helps us account for the remarkably stable and predictable interactions between quite differently organized states over long periods of time, as well as their propensity to engage in war. We build level 3 theory by:

1. Conceiving international politics as a bounded realm, distinct from what goes on within states.
2. Discovering law-like regularities in international politics.
3. Explaining these observed regularities.

This process involves a set of further tasks:

4. Identifying the units in the system.
5. Specifying the comparative weight of systemic and sub-systemic causes of continuity (and change) in the system.
6. Showing how forces and effects change from one system to another.

Explaining IR via the behaviour of states took us some way towards a genuine theory, Waltz argued, but there was a missing dimension that inhibited theory development.

He observed that Capitalist USA and Communist USSR both sought out military power and influence and competed for strategic advantage, for example, by conducting 'proxy' wars in Latin America. The question that exercised him was *why* the similar behaviour, when the ideologies of each state were so different? If international anarchy exists, yet we cannot explain state behaviour using either of the two levels previously identified by Realist writers, then we need to search for an additional factor because these apparently very dissimilar states were behaving in markedly similar ways when it came to the big questions of war and peace. Waltz argued that the missing link could be provided by the structure of the international system itself, which compels states to preserve their security by constantly building up their power. Waltz's structural realism is captured in his concept of the 'balance of power' (very well explained in Rosenau and Durfee 1995: 21–4). This structures systemic level interactions between units in any given period and is 'defined by the arrangement of the system's parts and by the principle of that arrangement' (Waltz 1979: 80).

The balance of power and stability theory

'If there is any distinctively political theory of international politics, balance-of-power theory is it', wrote Waltz (ibid.: 117). Waltz assumed that states are unitary, rational actors; that they give priority to ensuring their own security; and that they exist in an international realm characterized by anarchy (Glaser 1994–5: 54). He said that to explain international relations the idea of the *system* is all important, defining a system as a set of interacting units exhibiting behavioural regularities and having an identity over time. In other words, a system and the changes in that system are both observable elements of international relations. States in balance of power theory help themselves in two main ways. On the one hand they use 'internal efforts', building up their economic strength, military prowess and 'develop clever strategies'. On the other hand, they use 'external strategies': alliance building and attempts to weaken opposing alliances (Waltz 1979: 118).

The system is where we need to focus our attention because its units – individual states – all do the same things in that system, regardless of where they are located, their prevailing ideology, culture, and so on. As described by Jervis (2010: 165), Waltz's position was that 'some crucial patterns in international politics do not change over time and that the international characteristics of states are relatively unimportant' (a position critiqued by Marxist approaches, covered in Chapter 9; see Rosenberg 2001; Teschke and Cemgil 2014). States only differ in terms of their relative capabilities and as these capabilities change so the system changes. A systematic change can come about by its ordering principle shifting from hierarchic. Or, change may occur 'as a result of a change in the distribution of capabilities among the units' (Hollis and Smith 2000: 866).

Waltz goes on to define two types of system, a:

- *Bipolar system* is one in which there are two major powers such as the USA and the USSR between 1945 and 1989.
- *Multipolar system* is akin to the international states system that preceded and followed the Cold War, where many powers co-exist.

What kind of international system prevails today? Do Waltz's categories have it covered or is it something altogether different? How many 'great powers' are there in the world today? On how to measure 'great power' status see Waltz (1979: 129–31) and Morris (2011).

In Waltz's view (1979: 161) 'few [states] are better than many' and bipolar systems are more stable than multipolar systems, albeit not *that* stable if the powers are great powers (p. 163). Nevertheless, in theory at least, 'with only two great powers, both can be expected to act to maintain the system' (p. 204) because it is in their respective interests to keep the status quo as it is. The rise of new powers represents a potential challenge to their long-term domination over global order. In a multipolar system there is less incentive for sates to act in this way. First, the potential for control is far less. Second, because calculating the outcome of state actions is far less certain when there are more actor responses to account for.

The latter observation reflects Garrett Hardin's insight that you cannot do merely one thing in a system (cited in Jervis 210: 168) – any action will have multiple and often unintended consequences. A benign intent could be perceived as malign, especially in a period of intense security competition or at a time of international flux. 'Each must choose a strategy with an eye to the strategies it expects others to follow. Furthermore, its behaviour must be guided by beliefs about the system dynamics that will unfold' (Jervis 2010: 170). None of this is straightforward. However, predicting the outcome of state actions is easier in bipolar systems and successfully imposing one or other great power's will on other actors in the system is easier too.

So what, in sum, are the continuities and changes between Realism and Neorealism?

- **Continuity** – Waltz assumes states are the key actors, that there is a condition of anarchy and that international relations are shaped by power politics. He contrasts the ordering principles of hierarchy which pertains at the domestic level with that of anarchy at the international level: 'National politics is the realm of authority, of administration, and of law. International politics is the realm of power, of struggle, and of accommodation' (1979: 113).
- **Continuity** – Waltz assumes states are trapped in an international state of nature, leading them to focus on security and survival in a self-help system.
- **Change** – Waltz does not root his explanation of international relations in Hobbesian theories of human nature, *à la* Morgenthau, although the echoes of levels 1 and 2 are rarely far from the surface of *Theory of International Politics*. For example, at one point he remarks that 'States, like people, are insecure in proportion to the extent of their freedom. If freedom is wanted, insecurity must be accepted' (Waltz 1979: 112).
- **Change** – Waltz's account gives far less room for state leaders to employ cunning and skilful diplomacy, although his 'develop clever strategies' could be interpreted as a nod to this tradition. The human facets of state to state diplomacy as a battle of ideas were qualities that Thucydides highlighted in his *History*, and which Morgenthau said could provide benchmarks for judging leaders' foreign policy decisions.

- **Change** – Waltz critiqued previous (Realist) theories of IR for paying insufficient attention to the systemic level. 'Blurring the distinction between the different levels of a system has, I believe, been the major impediment to the development of theories about international politics' (1979: 78). Neorealism is more like a 'proper' theory because it theorizes at the systems level as well as the unit level.

To summarize, we can use the words of Robert Keohane (1986a: 15–16): 'The Waltzian synthesis is referred to as neorealism, to indicate both its intellectual affinity with the classical realism of Morgenthau ... and its elements of originality and distinctiveness'.

Books such as Keohane's *Neorealism and its Critics* (1986b) are a great source of information: not only do they explain the nuts and bolts of each theory, they also include chapters by critics of the theory (and sometimes responses to the critics). It is like buying two books or more books for the price of one.

John J. Mearsheimer

The title of Mearsheimer's most famous book, *The Tragedy of Great Power Politics* (2001), sets him firmly in the Thucydidean camp. Mearsheimer is an offensive Realist (not literally) as opposed to a defensive Realist. Defensive Realists such as Waltz (see above) maintain that states are mainly interested in survival and above all 'they seek security'. There is a competition for power because it is the best means for survival in a condition of anarchy. However, such competition as there is does not flow from the search for power for its own sake (Mearsheimer 2001: 19). As Charles Glaser has suggested (1994–5), some Realists can be optimists too! Out of a strongly Realist self-help system can come the impulsion to cooperate.

Like Carr and Morgenthau, Mearsheimer has written many wide-ranging texts which are difficult to summarize in a few lines. However, his explication of the five 'bedrock assumptions' on which he theorizes offensive Realism serve as a great way into his thought (from Mearsheimer 2001: 30–2):

1. **The international system is anarchic.** This ordering principle means that states have no overarching authority above them, telling them what to do.
2. **Great powers possess military capability** which they can use to hurt and even destroy each other – nuclear weapons are the most obvious, but humans do not need such sophisticated weaponry to do damage to each other. 'After all,' writes Mearsheimer rather depressingly, 'for every neck, there are two hands to choke it'.
3. **States can never be certain about other states' intentions.** States do not always have hostile intentions towards each other. However, we can never be sure. Even supposedly benign states might be masking ulterior motives and their intentions can change quickly, perhaps with the election of a new leader. The possession of any offensive capability (including human beings themselves, as Mearsheimer assumes in assumption 2) creates the potential for conflict at any moment in history.

4. **Survival is the main goal for great powers.** They want to maintain their territorial integrity and the autonomy of their domestic political order. Security is their most important objective.
5. **Great powers are rational actors.** State leaders are aware of their external environment 'and they think strategically about how to survive in it'. They think about how their behaviour affects the behaviour of other states in an endless game of power politics. These last two in particular are very Waltzian assumptions.

From these foundations Mearsheimer goes on to build a theory of offensive Realism based on patterns of behaviour that cause states to act aggressively towards one another: fear, self-help and power maximization. The rest of the book analyses case studies of great power rivalry and expansion over the centuries. Mearsheimer highlights the recurring patterns in international relations (the *Tragedy* of his book title). The 1990s are highlighted as something of an anomaly to this general pattern. Growing competition between states in a multipolar twenty-first-century international system returned things to the Thucydidean 'norm': a world of recurring security competition between states.

Between them, Waltz on the defensive Realist side and Mearsheimer on the offensive Realist side have generated what they believe to be coherent and compelling theories about IR, because they are able to generalize about state behaviour irrespective of the character of the state in question. This structural approach to explaining IR accentuates the top-down pressures on national leaders. It makes such things as leader psychology, beliefs, dispositions, and a nation's foreign policy process play walk-on roles, at best (Jervis 2013). This is not the book to unpack this alternative, lower level, image of national foreign policy decision-making in IR, which you will get from courses on Foreign Policy Analysis and the like. Nevertheless, it is worth flagging up the fact that many theories that have hit IR from the 1990s attempt to redress the balance by bringing the human angle 'back in', as it were, in contradistinction to a focus abstract on the international system as the major force driving state decision-making. A few elements of this appeared in the major competitor to Neorealism that emerged in and around the 1970s: Neoliberal IRT.

NEOLIBERALISM

Just as Neorealism accepts the basic premises of Realism and pulls them in new directions, so Neoliberalism has the same relationship with the classical Liberal IRT (idealism) we considered in Chapter 4. Neoliberalism (used here as shorthand for Neoliberal institutionalism) can be considered an attempt to explain developments in the global political economy that gathered pace after 1945 (Keohane 1998: 83), with renewed attention to institutions and organizations in providing a certain degree of order to the turbulence that can sometimes be said to prevail in international politics. These groupings aim 'to create social orderings appropriate to [states'] pursuit of shared goals' (Abbott and Snidal 1998: 6).

Particularly influential in this tradition has been the work of Robert Keohane and Joseph Nye (Keohane and Nye 1977; Keohane 1982) and Stephen Krasner (1983).

The puzzle they wanted to solve was why do states trapped in a security dilemma, selfishly looking out for their own interests, choose to submit their authority and some decision-making autonomy to international bodies? Why, in essence, does cooperation occur in multilateral settings? Their ideas developed from the observation that there was relative stability in patterns of international economic cooperation despite the uneven distribution of international economic power around the globe. Such cooperation was all the more remarkable given the volatile nature of international relations in the 1970s brought about by such things as:

- In the global economy:
  - The collapse of the **Bretton Woods financial system** in 1971.
  - A quadrupling in the price of crude oil brought about by steep price hikes by the Organization of the Petroleum Exporting Countries (OPEC) in 1973 and 1979. The effect was comparable to that of the global financial crisis, banking collapse and sovereign debt crisis, especially in the Eurozone, that has massively heightened attention to the politics of international economic relations since 2008. The OPEC price hikes led to the formation of the International Energy Agency (IEA) 'to enable Western countries to deal cooperatively with the threat of future oil embargoes' (Keohane 1998: 85). In other words, the IEA was evidence of an institutional response to global economic crisis.

- In international politics and security:
  - The Yom Kippur War in the Middle East, 1973.
  - The Vietnam War between North Vietnam and American-supported South Vietnam, 1959–75.
  - The Soviet invasion of Afghanistan, 1979–88.
  - Ongoing talks between the USA and USSR over nuclear arms limitations.
  - The decline in US **hegemony** and the rise of powers such as Japan and blocs such as the EU (see Kratochwil and Ruggie 1986: 759).

The crucial advance these writers made on classical Liberalism was to introduce the concept of **international regimes** to the vocabulary of IRT, part of the drive to understand and explain the role of neoliberal institutions in global governance. 'International regimes have been defined as social institutions around which actor expectations converge in a given area of international relations' (Ruggie 1998a: 63). They are 'governing arrangements constructed by states to coordinate their expectations and organize aspects of international behaviour in various issue-areas. *They thus comprise a normative element, state practice, and organizational roles*' (Kratochwil and Ruggie 1986: 759, my emphasis). Regimes such as the General Agreement on Tariffs and Trade (GATT) and the Treaty on the Non-Proliferation of Nuclear Weapons (Keohane 1998: 84) were influential on the early regimes' literature (Kratochwil and Ruggie 1986: 769). The number of case studies has expanded dramatically as global governance has taken on new dimensions to cover all sorts of issues, from 'classic' trade and monetary relations to the environment, human rights and energy.

It is important before we get to the crux of this theory to point out that regime theory and much of the work on neoliberal institutions shares many Realist and Neorealist assumptions. It is a bit like Realism and Liberalism beginning at the same point but then diverging in their interpretations of what makes IR 'tick', so that their explanations end up looking quite different – see the previous chapter. As Keohane put it (1998: 86): 'scholars adopted the assumptions of realism, accepting that relative state power and competing interests were key factors in world politics, but at the same time drawing new conclusions about the influence of institutions on the process'. Neoliberal institutionalists assume that (adapted from Lamy 2014: 132–3; Viotti and Kauppi 2014: 146):

1. **States are the main actors in the international system** but not the only actors. 'With a disaggregated approach to authority structures, we can more meaningfully trace a middle position in which the nation-state is viewed as having declined in importance even as it still continues to be important' (Rosenau 1976: 14). However, state power must be taken seriously despite the depth of interdependence and the existence of many other actors in the international arena.

2. **States are rational actors interested in maximizing gains**. They are led by rational leaders who weigh up the potential costs and benefits of different courses of action and then select that course most likely to give them the highest net pay-off. 'International cooperation does not necessarily depend on altruism, idealism, personal honor, common purposes, internalized norms, or a shared belief in a set of values embedded in a culture' (Keohane 1995: 281).

3. States operate in a condition of **international anarchy** …

4. **… but cooperation is possible in an anarchic system** because states will 'shift loyalty and resources to institutions if these are seen as mutually beneficial and if they provide states with increasing opportunities to secure their international interests' (Lamy 2014: 133).

5. **The scope and depth of integration between states** is increasing at both the regional and global levels. This makes it possible to study behavioural regularities by states operating in different organizational settings.

6. **'Absolute' gains are more important to states than 'relative' gains.** 'Genuine cooperation improves the rewards of both players' (Keohane 1995: 281). This is counter to the Neorealist perspective of Waltz: 'When faced with the possibility of cooperating for mutual gain, states that feel insecure must ask how the gain will be divided. They are compelled to ask not "Will both of us gain?" but "Who will gain more?"' (Waltz 1979: 105).

7. **The tools of economic theory and economic modelling can be used to explain IR.** This is a metatheoretical point that echoes Waltz, who wanted to develop a theory of IR at the level of the international system. He used the idea of power distribution in the system to explain how decisions were made by states, akin to businesses in the economy looking at market conditions at given moments in time and varying their strategies accordingly.

Hence, there are certain affinities with Neorealism in terms of their assumptions and what is to be explained in a 'proper' theory of IR. Nevertheless, Neoliberal theorists argue that international organizations, regimes and conventions can radically alter state calculations and break what Realists and Neorealists take to be a 'necessary logical link between the condition of anarchy and war' (Viotti and Kauppi 2014: 146). In particular, these international bodies change state calculations about the relative *cost* of going to war, materially and ideationally – there is a Constructivist element we will come back to in Chapter 8. The gains element is vital.

TAKING IT FURTHER
Absolute versus relative gains

A fundamental distinction between Neoliberal and Neorealists is in their approach to state calculations about absolute and relative gains when they cooperate with each other in international settings. By 'gains' we mean 'benefits that accrue to participants that cooperate' (Jackson and Sørensen 2015: 121).

Neoliberals argue that international regimes (incorporating but going beyond organizations and institutions) facilitate cooperation by helping states make more rational choices about the potential outcomes of cooperation. Why is this? States involved in these institutions are both less likely and less able to cheat by reneging on commitments. So for example, State A, whose economy currently grows at an average of 1 per cent per year, will cooperate with other states in an international economic organization if it predicts that by doing so it will increase its growth rate to 5 per cent per year.

Neorealists argue it is more about the relative place of states within the international system. States will be wary of cooperating if they fear other states may benefit more than they do. If we take our example from above, Neorealists would propose that if another State B, with a current growth rate of 1 per cent, predicted a growth of 8 per cent per year by joining that international organization, then State A will be inhibited about cooperating because in *relative* terms it will be worse off inside the organization than outside it. It is the comparison/prediction element and the fear of lagging behind in relative 'power' terms that is key for Neorealists. 'A state worries about a division of possible gains that may favor others more than itself. That is the first way in which the structure of international politics limits the cooperation of states' (Waltz 1979: 106). For Neorealist critics of Neoliberalism, surmises Keohane, the condition of anarchy will always stymy cooperation: 'they [states] seek to protect their power and status and will resist even mutually beneficial cooperation if their partners are likely to benefit more than they are' (Keohane 1998: 88).

In Neorealist thought, states are 'concerned with preventing others from achieving advances in their relative capabilities' (Viotti and Kauppi 2014: 146). Neorealists depict a constant battle to 'keep the other states down' so that they cannot catch up or overtake your state in resource terms. The question for Neorealists is not 'do both or all states gain from an international agreement?' but 'who gains more?' This is very much a Cold War arms-race scenario and it flags up the centrality of the security dilemma to Realist thought more widely.

Neoliberals dispute that relative gains are the be-all and end-all for states. In time, they argue, the rational state can come to accept a relatively lower gain from international cooperation because other things come into play. Look at the EU, where economic integration clearly favours some states over others (ibid.); for example, see Germany versus Greece, Spain and Italy in the Eurozone crisis. The Neorealist perspective might be that the latter three countries would be better off in relative terms withdrawing from the

Eurozone and going back to their own currencies, over which they would have more control in exchange rate and other terms. However, they accept the idea of unevenly distributed economic gains in the Eurozone. Perhaps they fear the consequences of not having the Eurozone bailout safety net despite the stringent austerity programmes they are having to implement as a condition of receiving the bailouts.

The Neoliberal perspective would be slightly different. It would see the economics as part of a wider picture of multilateral relations that have built up over time in the EU. The argument would be that states have come to accept that there are some issues that cannot be tackled effectively by states acting unilaterally: war and peace are amongst them, but the environment and so on would also be examples. The EU could be said to be a forum where a state's selfish interests can be maximized because, for Neoliberals, institutions and regimes 'enable states to do things they otherwise *could not do*' (Viotti and Kauppi 2014: 147, emphasis in original). In a nutshell, Neorealists see institutions, organizations and regimes as constraining state behaviour whereas Neoliberals see them as permitting the realization of mutually beneficial outcomes. It is a more complex picture of what makes international politics 'tick'. Participation in cooperative ventures can both help states secure their existing interests and enable them to redefine their interests by helping them see what they share in common with other states.

States thus use international fora in a variety of ways (Kratochwil and Ruggie 1986: 796, quoting Krasner): first, to establish the principles of international behaviour ('beliefs of fact, causation, and rectitude'); second, to establish the norms of behaviour associated with the pursuit of those 'good' principles (the 'standards of behavior defined in terms of rights and obligations'); third, to agree on the rules the members of the club must abide by ('specific prescriptions and proscriptions for action'); and finally, on the decision-making procedures ('prevailing practices for making and implementing collective choice'). This is a form of hierarchy-creation by states that attempts to counter the seemingly all-pervasive effects of international anarchy. Some bodies such as the EU and UN have in place sanctions for 'bad' behaviour, such as sanctions and fines, in the EU's case overseen by the European Court of Justice, the ECJ. But it goes beyond that. States in the Neoliberal view come to stake their reputations on being seen to be 'good international citizens'. They also expect reciprocity, such that they will be treated as they act themselves. Obviously in this situation it is better for all states if their behaviour towards each other is positive and constructive rather than warlike and threatening, even at times of crisis or potential conflict (reputation and reciprocity are dealt with in Viotti and Kauppi 2014: 146–7). The key Neoliberal departure from Neorealism is, therefore, that states can be selfish interest maximizers but rely on regimes and organizations for the information and rules to enable them to achieve economic and national security.

CRITIQUING THE NEO-NEO AGENDA: OPENING UP IRT

Looking at the assumptions they made and the issues they studied, it is evident that there was minimal fuss for the writers explored in Chapters 4 and 5 in defining the subject matter of IR. It was all about the nature of state interactions when they found themselves in the security dilemma. Liberals and Neoliberals explained why states might cooperate in this anarchic world order, Realists and Neorealists explained why conflict would be an endemic feature of international life. As Holsti observed, 'States and the system of states – the essential actors and their behaviour, the units of analysis – remained the centerpieces of the study of international politics from the seventeenth century until the 1970s' (Holsti 1985: 23). Realists and Neorealists were much more pessimistic about the extent to which states could transcend the self-help system and give order to their interactions than their Liberal and Neoliberal counterparts. But while they disagreed in terms of outcomes, they shared a lot in terms of assumptions and procedures for investigating international relations.

Neorealism in particular has been attacked for its theoretical impoverishment and moral bankruptcy, not to mention its internal logical contradictions – most famously Ashley (1986), who amongst many pointed out that there is insufficient structural level analysis in Neorealism's supposedly structural analysis (see also Hollis and Smith 2000). These helped feed wider dissatisfaction with the 'state of the art' in IRT during the 1990s. The Cold War had now ended and the international order was being reshaped in quite dramatic and unexpected ways. There were progress calls for IRT to beyond what had become a rather sterile set of debates that had not kept pace with international realities of the time. One exemplar of this move to recast IRT was Steve Smith, who in 1995 had the following to say about the Neo-Neo debate: 'The debate is a Western, even North Atlantic one. It hardly begins to deal with the concerns of the vast majority of humanity, and very effectively silences those who do not fit into this US view of what international political is all about' (p. 24).

In 2001, Chris Brown echoed Smith's concerns about an increasingly narrow IR agenda centring on Neorealist and Neoliberal orthodoxies ('debate' might be pushing it, as one anonymous reviewer of the previous edition of this book helpfully pointed out). Brown pointed out that Neoliberal scholars such as Keohane accepted all the assumptions of Neorealism, merely interpreting differently the extent of the possibilities for cooperation in an anarchic international environment. He summarized the dispute between the two as follows: the challenge for Neoliberals is in maintaining cooperation, whereas Neorealists accent the challenges involved in getting cooperation going in the first place (Brown 2001: 49–50). They 'see' different worlds of IR and more often than not speak past each other.

The upshot for Smith and Brown was that the two sets of 'Neo' theories represented a dangerous narrowing of IR's disciplinary agenda. It had expunged from the agenda of IRT many of the most interesting events, themes and issues then being debated by policy-makers and in the global mass media. The critiques levelled at the Neo-Neo debate highlight the fact that there were other things going on in the discipline from the 1980s – new ways of defining and studying the problematic subject matter of IR. In the following chapters we consider a whole array of other theories that you are likely to encounter on your course. We begin with the English School.

QUESTIONS TO PONDER

'Do you think Waltz's Neorealist theory successfully created a "proper" theory of IR?'

For this one you will need to address three issues. The first is to identify what Waltzian Neorealism is. You can do this via a simple explanation of the key themes of his *Theory of*

International Politics, majoring on such concepts as the international system and the balance of power and his structural account of state interactions in a condition of anarchy. Even if you do not consult the original text (ideally you would), you should show familiarity with something relevant Waltz has written in Neorealism, perhaps in a journal article. Textbooks will take you some of the way but displaying knowledge of original Waltz would get you the most credit by far. Cutting and pasting a few lines from Wikipedia will not cut the mustard because the context provided by in-depth engagement with the theory is key to academic work.

Having demonstrated that you understand Waltz's theory, you then have the slightly more difficult task of explaining Waltz's claims about this being a 'proper' theory of IR. Why does he say this? On what grounds? It all comes down to his aim of generating a science of politics, and you can quote from his 1979 book and other publications to support you here, particularly his work on the system level and balance of power theory.

In light of all this, you then have to judge whether Waltz is right to present his theory as a 'proper' theory. What does 'proper' imply in the context of the question and how do we judge when a theory is 'proper' or not? The best answers will use this element of the question to investigate metatheoretical debates about the nature of theory and whether we can study IR as scientifically as Waltz suggests.

'Compare and contrast Neoliberal and Neorealist theories of IR'

It is tempting with questions such as this to fall into the trap of explaining one theory and then the other without addressing the core of the question: to compare and contrast them. Clearly you will have to demonstrate a robust working knowledge of each theory, but how much detail you include in this regard involves a judgement call on your part. Too much description will crowd out the space for analysis of the elements of overlap as well as the clear water between them. So one approach is to describe, first, Neoliberal theory, second, Neorealist theory and, third, weigh up where they overlap and where they differ. A possible problem here is that by leading off with a description of each theory you leave yourself insufficient time (in an exam) and space (in a coursework essay) to demonstrate to the marker that you can identify the similarities and differences between the two.

A second approach is to structure the essay in two parts. First, deal with the similarities and, second, the differences. This takes more planning, organization and knowledge of the respective traditions, but it will pay dividends because you will be getting to the heart of the matter right away. The very best answers will explain the similarities and dissimilarities and then go on to make some judgement about whether the one set outnumbers the other set. They may also take into account the metatheoretical critiques of the Neo-Neo debate by critics such as Richard Ashley, Steve Smith and Chris Brown who argue that, compared to the theories that 'hit' the discipline through the 1990s, these two theories share many unfavourable qualities in common.

REFERENCES TO MORE INFORMATION

Neorealism:

Berridge, G.R. (1997) *International Politics: States, Power and Conflict since 1945*, 3rd edn. New York: Prentice Hall.
On pp. 166–83, Berridge explores the Neorealist concept of the 'balance of power'. Ends the chapter with a good list of further reading.

Kreisler, H. (2003) 'Theory and International Politics: Conversation with Kenneth N. Waltz', Institute of International Studies, University of Berkeley, http://globetrotter. berkeley.edu/people3/Waltz/waltzcon0.html (accessed 25 August 2016).
Waltz talks about his educational influences, about being a political theorist and about the Neorealist vision of international politics. You can read the interview transcript, watch it as a webcast or listen as a podcast.

Mearsheimer, J.J. (1990) 'Back to the Future: Instability in Europe after the Cold War', *International Security*, 15(1): 5–56.
Updated Waltz's Neorealist balance of power thesis to predict trends in international relations after the end of the Cold War.

University of California Television (2002) 'Conversations with History: John J. Mearsheimer', 8 April, www.youtube.com/watch?v=AKFamUu6dGw (accessed 24 October 2016).
Discusses the Realist tradition and US foreign policy and relations with China.

University of California Television (2008) 'Conversations with Histor Stephen M. Walt', 3 November, www.youtube.com/watch?v=FSXZNm2jGVE (accessed 24 October 2016).
Discusses the balance of power and US hegemony in the international system.

Jervis, R. (1976) *Perception and Misperception in International Politics*. Chichester: Princeton University Press.
Discusses biases in the rational actor model of IR and as such is an excellent antidote to systems level explanations as set out in this chapter; a very powerful source of evidence to critique Waltz and Mearsheimer's Neorealism.

Ashley, R.K. (1986) 'The Poverty of Neorealism', in R.O. Keohane (ed.) *Neorealism and its Critics*. New York: Columbia University Press, pp. 1–26.
Review of International Studies (2004) 'Forum on the State as Person', 30(2): 255–316.

James, P. (1993) 'Neorealism as Research Enterprise: Toward Elaborated Structural Realism', *International Political Science Review*, 14(2): 123–48.

Lapid, Y. and Kratochwil, F. (1996) 'Revisiting the "National": Toward an Identity Agenda in Neorealism?', in Y. Lapid and F. Kratochwil (eds) *The Return of Culture and Identity in IR Theory*. London: Lynne Rienner Publishers, pp. 105–26.

Linklater, A. (1995) 'Neo-Realism: Theory and Practice', in K. Booth and S. Smith (eds) *International Relations Theory Today*. Cambridge: Polity Press, pp. 241–61.

Neoliberalism:

Goldstein, J. and Keohane, R.O. (eds) (2014) *Ideas and Foreign Policy: Beliefs, Institutions, and Political Change*. Ithaca, NY: Cornell University Press.

Keohane, R.O. (1984) *After Hegemony*. Princeton, NJ.: Princeton University Press.

Keohane, R.O. and Nye, J.S. (1977) *Power and Interdependence: World Politics in Transition*. Boston, MA: Little Brown and Co.

Clark, I. (1999) *Globalization and International Relations Theory*. Oxford: Oxford University Press.
Shows how globalization unsettles existing IR theoretical categories and helps us rethink both the concept of globalization and the framework of the discipline.

Mitrany, D. (1975) 'A Political Theory for the New Society', in A.J.R. Groom and P. Taylor (eds) *Functionalism: Theory and Practice in International Relations*. London: University of London Press, pp. 25–37.
See also the chapters in this collection by Nina Heathcote (Neofunctionalism), Michael Hodges and John Burton.

Nye, J.S. (1975) 'Transnational and Transgovernmental Relations', in G.L. Goodwin and A. Linklater (eds) *New Dimensions of World Politics*. London: Croom Helm, pp. 36–53.
Examines the actors in IR overlooked by state-centric theories and makes the case for integration theory and interdependence. See also the chapter by Richard Rosecrance.

Ruggie, J.G. (2000) *Constructing the World Polity: Essays on International Institutionalization*. Abingdon: Routledge.
Part 1 is particularly useful because it surveys dominant Neoliberal themes as well as meta-theoretical and methodological challenges.

7

THE ENGLISH SCHOOL

Key terms

- Justice
- Order
- Pluralism
- Rules

- Society
- Solidarism
- State
- System

English School thinking … provides social structural benchmarks for the evaluation of significant change in international orders; sets out a taxonomy that enables comparisons to be made across time and space; and provides some predictions and explanations of outcome. (Buzan 2004: 25).

You can open essays or exam answers with relevant quotes like this to focus your reader's attention on the central issue(s) you will raise in your work. They can be used to frame your central argument and, particularly if they are strongly worded, direct the reader's attention to the case you will be making in a vivid and memorable way. Make sure you refer to the quotation in the introduction to integrate it into your writing.

In this chapter and the next, we analyse two IR theories that are alike in some ways but very different in others: the English School and Constructivism. They straddle the positivist, science-like theories of Realism, Liberalism, Neorealism and Neoliberalism on the one hand, and the 'post-positivist' theories such as Critical Theory, feminism, Postcolonialism and Green International Theory on the other (for a useful overview of this distinction see Griffiths 2011: 11–12). Hence, when thinking about the 'place' they occupy in the canon of IR theories, you might see the English School and Constructivism as raising the profile of themes and issues which had previously been ignored or overlooked by earlier theorists. In so doing, they opened the door for a more radical reassessment of what IRT was all about.

INTRODUCTION TO THE ENGLISH SCHOOL

This theory is strangely named in that it was formed by scholars of varying nationalities. 'Contrary to what is implied by the name, the English School was never very English and is even less so today' (Dunne 2016: 108). A leading English School scholar has recently been led to comment that its title 'is a poor fit with what it represents' (Buzan 2014: 5). Nor does the English School offer a 'theory' clothed in the language of natural science that a Neorealist, for example, might find congenial. Rather, the English School gathers together a methodologically eclectic range of scholars writing empirically grounded accounts of world history. They identify and try to explain the progressive elements in international relations, which they often, but do not always, construe in terms of a 'society' of states, as opposed to a 'system' (Suganami 2005: 42). The 'society' element is fundamental and we return to it below.

As writers such as Renée Jeffery clearly demonstrate, and as has been well recognized by English School writers themselves (Buzan 1993: 328), the figure of the sixteenth–seventeenth-century Dutch lawyer and moral philosopher Hugo Grotius looms large in terms of influence over the English School. When you hear the phrase 'Grotian rationalism' it is Grotius to whom the reference is being made, and his thoughts on how to mitigate the most extreme effects of international conflict using international law. As Martin Wight described it: 'Rationalists are those who concentrate on, and believe in the value of, the element of international intercourse in a condition predominantly of international anarchy. They believe that man, although manifestly a sinful and bloodthirsty creature, is also rational' (cited in Jeffery 2006: 116). We will pick out Hedley Bull's version of rationalism below in our discussion of the concept of international society.

English School theorists therefore possess affinities with several of the theories you will usually cover on an IRT course, notably Realism, Liberalism and Constructivism, with some writers in this camp taking a recognizably 'genealogical' approach to international affairs that calls to mind more critically inclined poststructural theories (Reus-Smit 2002: 494). One might reasonably argue that the English School advances a broadly Liberal agenda whilst remaining cognizant of Realist international realities such as the international states system. Methodologically they use a wide variety of methods and look for inspiration as much to history, philosophy and international law as to 'political science' in its positivist guise (surveyed in Buzan 2014: 21–38). As canonical writers such as Hedley Bull have demonstrated, English School writers veer – sometimes in the same book or article – between Liberal optimism and Realist pessimism (Wheeler and Dunne 1996).

Given that the English School ranges so widely in terms of its subject matter (different international societies back through time) and in terms of its methodological instruments, it is not easy to pin down the writers that best represent the tradition as it has developed since the 1950s. Historically, English School work has been more popular outside US academic circles than inside, its name helping demarcate it from the heavier theoretical work of the post-1945 US scholars. There has always been something of a disconnect between the USA and 'the rest' of IR over questions of ontology, epistemology and methodology, and the English School approach throw this distinction into sharp relief. Among its early proponents, Martin Wight and Hedley Bull (both heavily accenting the Grotian analytical tradition), R.J. Vincent and Adam Watson are all central figures in the canon and worth seeking out; Charles Manning is a rather overlooked figure but Tanja Aalberts (2010) makes the case for including him as a seminal thinker who worked at the boundary where the English School today meets Constructivism. During the 1990s 'the English School was rejuvenated as a major "non-American" research programme' (Reus-Smit 2005: 82). Barry Buzan, Richard Little, Tim Dunne, Nicholas Wheeler, Alex Bellamy, Richard Jackson, John Williams and Robert Murray are amongst those who have developed English School theory in recent years. Andrew Linklater on cosmopolitanism (2010, 2016) and Adrian Gallagher's (2016) work theorizing the idea of 'humanity' itself both develop classical English School themes. This said, the English School remains rather an eclectic and elusive grouping (Jeffery 2006: 114). Looking across this diverse oeuvre it can be argued that despite some differences, 'the identity of the English School reveals itself ... as a historically constituted and evolving cluster of scholars with a number of plausible and inter-related stories to tell about [their similarities and differences]' (see Suganami 2005: 29). English School theorists speak to many pressing concerns in IR, such as sovereignty, intervention and the use of force and global governance. In short, as with all theories of IR, the English School is contested from within and without whilst retaining a certain consistency of approach that allows it to retain a separate identity from other 'movements' in the discipline.

One way to appreciate where English School 'fits' in IRT is to turn to one of its leading historians and practitioners, who judges that the English School avoids 'either/or' theorizing; it is a 'synthesis of different theories and concepts' combining 'theory *and* history, morality *and* power, **agency** *and* structure' (Dunne 2016: 108, original italics). Limited chapter space unfortunately precludes an in-depth examination of all the major English School theorists. However, we will explore the English School IR first by considering how Hedley Bull positioned it within prevailing IRT, and then unpacking its major concepts: state, system, society and order. We will then study the intra-theory debate between **pluralists** and solidarists to illustrate the different 'wings' of the theory as they have developed in the post-Cold War era.

HEDLEY BULL: *THE ANARCHICAL SOCIETY*

The title of Hedley Bull's definitive English School text (1977) gives us clues about where he was trying to take IRT. He fully accepted that states lived in a condition of anarchy in the international system, which is the familiar starting point for Realism, Liberalism and their 'Neo' variants surveyed in Chapters 4–6 of this book. By way of reminder, in an anarchic international system there is no 'chief' to regulate state behaviour at the international level, in the same way that governments (democratic or otherwise) do for their populaces at the domestic level. As we have seen, Realists such as Carr and Morgenthau held that without an orderer, the potential for conflict between self-interested states was ever-present. States, they suggested, are trapped in a security dilemma from which there is no easy means of escape.

Neorealists such as Waltz and Mearsheimer built their theories around the concept of the balance of power. They took the focus away from human nature and the decisions of national leaders to argue that the causes of conflict lay not so much with the actions of the units (states) but at the level of the system itself. For Neorealists the distribution of material power is what counts in IR. Liberal and Neoliberal theorists took the same assumption about the existence of anarchy but drew different conclusions. They argued that conflict did not have to be an endemic, permanent or necessary feature of international relations. Early Liberals eulogized the spread of democracy and good governance, themes that were resurrected in Democratic Peace Theory after the end of the Cold War. Liberal theorists after the Second World War concentrated on the growth of international organizations, institutions and regimes, showing how these could all affect the calculations that selfish, utility-maximizing states made about the positive benefits to them from cooperating in multilateral settings. How did Bull and the English School approach these issues?

It is probably fair to suggest that Bull's work was Realist in inspiration and Liberal in aspiration. It was Realist in inspiration because he wanted to open up dialogue about the implications of accepting the two founding assumptions of IR theory: that sovereign states are the main actors and that they exist in a condition of anarchy. As Richard Little (2005: 48) has argued: 'Bull's conception of the international system corresponds almost exactly with the one formulated by Waltz.' But from this Realist starting point he worked with distinctively Liberal ideas about what makes international politics 'tick'. We can see this by looking at his central case that 'a group of states, conscious of certain common interests and common values, forms a society in the sense that they conceive themselves to be bound by a set of rules in their relations with one another, and share in the working of common institutions' (Bull 1977: 13). A glance at some of the key terms in this statement reveals Bull's Liberal agenda:

- Common interests.
- Common values.
- Society.
- Rules.
- Sharing.
- Institutions.

The main distinction between Bull and Liberal/Neoliberal theorists was his effort to theorize the term 'society' into existence. His reading of global history led him to conclude that: 'order is part of the historical record of international relations; ... modern states have formed, and continue to form, not only a system of states but also an international society' (Bull 1977: 22–3). Or, as Alex Bellamy puts it, English School writers hold the Constructivist belief that 'states form an international society shaped by ideas, values, identities, and norms that are – to a greater or lesser extent – common to all' (Bellamy 2005: 2). An international system 'is logically the more basic, and prior, idea', wherein the interactions between states are rather limited and functional: 'war, diplomacy, trade, migration, and the movement of ideas' (Buzan 1993: 331).

> Bellamy's book *International Society and its Critics* (2005) is another of the 'two-for-one' style books you should find useful. It helps you both understand and critique English School theory.

Neorealists see stability as being produced by a settled balance of power. For Bull, however, states do not spend their entire time calculating their relative place in the hierarchy of international power rankings. Instrumental, rational calculations of this kind are accompanied, and in important ways displaced, by a sense of shared interests that develop in such settings as international institutions and regimes: 'stability and order are not a product of the anarchic international system, but the product of the common interests, institutions, rules, and values that characterize an international society' (Little 2005: 48).

They might only be two short words but Bull's notions of 'society' and 'order' were crucial to the development of English School thought. Let us now see how and why Bull worked so heavily with them, and how they informed his reading of global history.

FROM SYSTEM TO SOCIETY

Bull built his theory around four key words: state, system, society and order. He used these in specific ways to advance his argument that international relations are more ordered than Realists and Neorealists assume, and more like a society than Liberals and Neoliberals assume.

State

Bull defined 'state' in accordance with prevailing Realist, Liberal and Neo-Neo thought. A state, he argued, has three attributes. First, a state has sovereignty over a group of people. Second, a state has a clearly a defined territory. Third, a state has a government that orders the relations between its citizens. The *nature* of that government is less important than its existence and function in holding together the sovereign state. With this move, Bull helped expand the study of IR to take in Constructivist work which opens up the 'black box' of the state. Constructivists (to be studied in the next chapter) view IR as a social sphere, meaning that the beliefs held by people and organizations *within* states matter at the level of the international system because they influence materially state foreign and defence policies. International institutions and regimes can help in this process. Hence, Bull suggested that the flow of influence was not, as Waltz had it, top-down (from system to states) but involved more complex interactions in which state behaviour could also work upwards to affect the international system.

An interesting way to think through the differences between a 'system' and a 'society' is to play a simple word association game. Think of the first word or image that jumps into your head when you think of the word 'system'. Do the same for the word 'society'. Ask three friends to do the same. You should notice some patterns in the responses that help you understand what Bull was trying to get at by envisioning international relations in societal rather than systemic terms.

System

Bull's idea of a system at the international level was essentially Waltzian. The word 'system' implies functional cooperation between units without any sense of the shared purposes or interests that we find in an international society (see below). In the Solar System, for example, the planets all circle the Sun in predictable ways (once Isaac Newton and his successors made sense of their movements). But they circle the Sun not because they choose to, but because of gravitational pull on them from the Sun, by far the heaviest object in the Solar System. Systemic relations have none of the element of choice that characterizes societal relations. Given this, Bull argues that two or more states form a system when they 'have sufficient contact between them, and have sufficient impact on one other's decisions, to cause them to behave – at least in some measure – as parts of a whole' (1977: 9). Systemic interaction between states is thus fairly limited and comes down to state perceptions of their 'technical interest in manipulation and control as opposed to the practical interest in promoting diplomatic agreement and understanding' (Linklater 1995: 256).

Unlike Waltz, however, Bull put the concept of a system to different empirical and theoretical uses. He asked what the change from one system to another tells us about the possible existence of an international society over time. English School theorists have conventionally looked to history for evidence of what has characterized state systems in the past, notably 'the Western, the Greco-Roman, and the Chinese of the Warring States' (Watson 1990: 100). This helps English School theorists achieve perspective and context by getting beyond a Euro-centric or Cold War-heavy definition of the term 'system'. In turn, Watson suggests that we can carve up these different types of system along a spectrum of 'control' ranging across 'independence, hegemony, dominion and empire' (1990: 104–6). English School theory can therefore help us clarify what we mean by a system and to theorize change over time, between one type of system and another.

Society

We can see that the word 'system' has natural science-like connotations which helps us explain how things are ordered and how different parts or units in the system interact with each other to create and maintain a functioning whole. Think about those planets in the Solar System or, to take another example, the components in a computer system: system is a 'remarkable inanimate connotation, hinting, at least, at the functional and utilitarian' (James 1993: 282). Bull did not believe international relations could be classified in this rather abstract, cold way, with the units performing functions unthinkingly and unfeelingly without the capacity to exert agency on proceedings. After all, the relations between states and nations are conducted by, and reliant upon, the actions of the individuals within them. The idea of an international system overlooks the human element to diplomacy between states, and the even more funda-mental assumption about the 'innate sociability of humankind' (Jeffery 2006: 121).

An international society for Bull is more than a system, but is presupposed on the prior existence of a system (Jeffery 2006: 128). A society is, however, less than a civiliza-tion, in the sense that we might talk about the Greek or Roman civilizations in previous centuries, or, increasingly tenuously admittedly, 'Western' civilization today. A society might be something that comes about for more pragmatic reasons, less organically, we might say, than a civilization. But it is certainly a stage on in terms of understanding the depth and scale of inter-state transactions than Realists would have us believe when they talk about systems. 'International society', writes Justin Morris (2005: 206), 'does not, anymore than does domestic society, require unanimous acceptance of its under-pinning values and goals, but it does necessitate a sufficiently broad consensus among its membership to ensure that its existence can be preserved against the acts of recalci-trant states'. In its solidarist form (see below) international society 'is none other than mankind, encumbered and thwarted by an archaic fiction of an international society composed of sovereign states' (Wight 1987: 223). This classic IR paradox is considered in the movie *Arrival* (2016), when alien pods land simultaneously around the globe. Without an overarching coordinating mechanism (the UN is seemingly absent), sov-ereign states struggle to express their shared interest in finding out the reason for the landings and end up arguing with each other as much as the aliens. Societies emerge around agreed laws and rules that shape the conduct of states and connote what the term system is unable to: 'an associational relationship which lacks some kind of formal or holistic coherence' (James 1993: 284 and 279).

English School theorists have long grappled with three questions about the concept of an international society (Buzan 1993: 332). First, when do we know that a system has turned into a society? Second, who 'counts' as a member of international society at any given point in time? Third, is all or part of an international system necessarily incorporated in an emerging international society? Christian Reus-Smit (2005) has gone further, suggesting that the English School is incapable of proffering valuable interventions on the nature of contemporary international society and that it should be left to the more holistic approach of the Constructivists. Writers such as Richard Little (2005) do not go that far but have posed five searching questions about Bull's system/society distinction, which remained rather vague throughout his work (Buzan 1993: 332–6). First, how do we identify a society (global or regional?) and can apparently cohesive, values-based societies, such as 'European' and 'Chinese' co-exist? Second, what in fact separates a system from a society? Third, what are the boundaries between systems and societies and how do know when a transition has occurred or is occurring? Fourth, how and why do the notional 'boundaries' of international society alter over time? Finally, what is the relationship between a society and an Empire? This feeds into the Marxist perspective we cover in Chapter 9.

Adam Watson's work engages with these questions by tracing the evolution of international society from ancient times (the 'ancient states system') through 'European international society' and 'global international society' (Watson 2001). This shows the historical lineage of what might appear to be 'new' or unrecognizable developments in the international system today and tracks different types of society through global history (see also Buzan 2014: Part II). The detail of this work is interesting and insightful but a bit beyond what we can hope to cover in this chapter. The crucial point to take away is that English School IRT has blended together elements of earlier IR theories. Hard-headed Realist calculations about national interest combine with Liberal work on the social values and norms that develop in institutions and regimes to create a theory in which the anarchical international system creates the impetus for groups of states to work together to achieve common goals as part of an international society. Buzan's summary (1993: 336) of the two drivers behind the emergence of an international society provides much food for thought: 'There are thus two distinct ways for an international society to come into existence: what might be called the "civilizational" (*gemeinschaft*) and the "functional" (*gesellschaft*) models' (critiqued in Pasic 1996: 90–5). The 'civilizational' model implies a much deeper set of organic, identity-based ties than exist in the 'functional' model, which is more about the creation of order than the realisation of a community based on a shared identity, purpose or set of values. 'World society' is something deeper still and we return to that in our exploration of the pluralist–solidarist debate below.

Order

How does order in international relations evolve, and how is it maintained? For Bull, diplomacy and a respect for international law (as agreed in international institutions) are the foundations of international order and the prerequisite for the promotion of justice. This order, moreover, can be generated and maintained even among states with diverse, even *opposed* political, economic and social traditions. The key is that all states party to the agreements abide by those agreements and respect the rights of other states party to the agreements, irrespective of different ideologies and political organization internally.

Take the period of the Cold War, 1945–89, when two rival power-blocs, one led by the 'Communist' Soviet Union, the other by the 'Capitalist' USA, competed for economic/political/cultural hegemony over the international system. Even then, the threat of 'hot war' between the main protagonists was mitigated by their participation in common institutions such as the UN, which helped diffuse some but not all tensions between them. They had regular communication and could take decisions in tandem with other UN members in and outside the UN Security Council on events of global political, economic and strategic significance. It could be argued that this view largely depends on the 'theatre' we look at and that it ignores the 'proxy' wars that were fought out in continents such as South America. However, the point still holds, that here we had two states with very different ideological outlooks coming together in international organizations to realize what they had in common their obvious differences did not necessarily need to lead to war between them. They realized that they were a part of an international society even as they fought for global supremacy between 1945 and 1989.

· ·

TAKING IT FURTHER

Norms and Laws in Times of Conflict

When states engage in wars or, just as likely today, humanitarian interventions, these inter-ventions are, in theory at least, rule-bound exercises. It is not a case of 'anything goes' in times of conflict. Most states are signed up to the UN Hague Convention on the Law and Customs of War and the Geneva Convention which concentrates on 'the rights of individ-uals, combatants and noncombatants, during war'. It includes Conventions on Genocide and Torture and the treatment of prisoners of war (UN 1997). Over the past few years there has been a strong drive to codify international norms and law related 'to Preventing Sexual Violence in Conflict', which has resulted in action at UN level (UN 2013). By September 2013 this Declaration had been backed by two-thirds of states in the international community. In June 2014, London hosted a Global Summit to End Sexual Violence in Conflict (Gov.UK 2014), which has kept up pressure to secure greater rights for females in times of conflict, and more robust mechanisms for holding the perpetrators of these crimes to account. Even in times of 'hot' conflict, then, states order their interactions to such a degree that even something as apparently chaotic and violent as war demonstrates their shared commitment to sticking by the rules for the good of international society as a whole.

Perhaps this is why, today, the treatment of prisoners of war receives so much attention and why the abuse of Iraqi prisoners of war, such as in the Abu Ghraib detention camp during the US-led intervention from March 2003, were so widely vilified. The mistreatment led to a dwindling of support for an already controversial intervention. On top of that, the US military personnel involved were seen to be abusing the basic human rights of the Iraqi prisoners. Added to the alleged extraordinary rendition and torture of suspected terrorists (Gaskarth 2011), the Abu Ghraib detainees were said to be held in contravention of the laws of armed conflict, undermining both the official rules and unofficial norms underpinning the international society in which we live.

· ·

SOLIDARISM AND PLURALISM

[T]he disagreement between the two positions is to some extent an empirical one about how far, in the contemporary circumstances, it is possible to pursue higher goals such as the international protection of human rights without undermining the more basic goal of international order. (Suganami 2005: 39)

Since the end of the Cold War, states such as the USA, UK, Canada and Australia and international organizations such as the UN, EU and NATO have been engaged in increasingly intense discussions about whether and how to intervene in the affairs of another state for humanitarian or other security purposes. These debates have in large measure flowed from the increasing tendency by these states and organizations to sanction and lead military or other actions short of military intervention, such as economic sanctions. The years since 1989 have seen violence accompanying the fragmentation of states such as the former Yugoslavia into smaller, territorially bounded nation-states. Bosnia, Kosovo, Sierra Leone, East Timor and the civil wars in Libya and Syria have all shaped post-Cold War thought and practice on intervention, just as Iraq, Afghanistan, the 'War on Terror' and the rise of Islamic State have posed dilemmas about the way states safeguard international security.

The practice of intervening militarily or otherwise in the affairs of a state poses acute dilemmas for politicians and IR theorists because it strikes to the heart of one of the legal and ethical touchstones of the international state system: sovereignty. The practice of intervention, by definition, violates both the sovereignty and the territorial integrity of states and is therefore hotly contested. Should internal state matters remain internal state matters in a globalized world? When is a state in such disarray that external intervention is desirable? What is a 'grave humanitarian' crisis and how does it relate to genocide and humanitarian atrocities? Who decides when it is ethical to undertake an intervention? What types of intervention are ethical and effective? Do the supposedly ethical ends of an intervention justify the means? Which states or organizations are responsible for picking up the pieces after the 'intervention' phase is over?

English School theory has been well placed to consider these questions because it is attentive on the one hand to the human interactions that create 'international society' and 'world society' (Williams 2005), and on the other hand to the normative concerns emanating from the tension between human justice and international order: questions of human rights and intervention 'pose the conflict between order and justice at their starkest' (Wheeler and Dunne 1996: 92). The upsurge in modern humanitarianism 'reveals how commitments to the improvement of social arrangements transcend national frameworks' (Linklater 2010: 170–1). This is encapsulated in the intra-theory debate between the pluralists and the solidarists, which has 'further underlined the different the different enterprises that realism and the English School are engaged in' (Dunne 2005: 74). As Reus-Smit explains (2002: 490), 'scholars of the English School have consistently explored the potential for moral action in a world of sovereign states, fueling a debate between pluralists and solidarists'. Bull saw the potential for solidarity among states in an international society 'with respect to the enforcement of the law' (quoted in Wheeler and Dunne 1996: 95). This rather minimalist, legalistic appreciation has given way to stronger forms in recent years. For example, solidarists such as Nicholas Wheeler believe it to be 'the responsibility of the richer and more powerful states to take care of intolerable miseries experienced in less successful states' (Suganami 2005: 39). In this view, as long as interventions are the exception rather than the rule, order in the international system can be maintained. Solidarists are thus associated with the cosmopolitan tradition in English School theory and with 'world society' approaches (we come back to cosmopolitanism in Chapter 14).

Barry Buzan (1993: 337) suggests that 'international society' is the Realist wing of English School theory, with 'world society' being the Liberal idealist take on English School theory. International society focuses on relations between states (or whichever political units make up the international system). World society takes individuals, non-state actors and ultimately the global populace as the focus for global societal arrangements. Realism and Liberalism, pluralism and solidarism – you can see how getting to grips with the language of IRT is quite a challenge, requiring careful attention.

By contrast, pluralists such as Richard Jackson are more Realist inclined and associated with the 'international society' wing of English School thought. They have countered that interventions are 'likely to undermine international order and even that humanitarian intervention is a form of paternalism which is morally objectionable'. Pluralists do not rule out 'pacification, reconstruction, or development' of countries, but stress that they should only be undertaken with the consent of the host government (Suganami 2005: 39). Sovereign states are in a 'practical' association (in institutions and organizations) enabling them, in James Mayall's words, to 'rub along together'. The violation of this deeply entrenched 'norm' of international society can be destabilizing when imposed by the powerful on the weak as a new interventionist norm.

Barry Buzan points out that the pluralist perspective does not neglect ethics. By contrast, respect for diversity amongst different countries with different dispositions and ideologies is at the heart of this understanding of the relationship between order and justice in international affairs (Buzan 2014: 91). Hence: 'The conservative needs of order should be placed above the pursuit of justice should that pursuit conflict with the core tenets of international society' (Williams 2005: 23). The nub of the disagreement between solidarists and pluralists is therefore ontological. It concerns the location of moral responsibility in a sovereign states system. Solidarists believe humankind forms a unified moral community despite being artificially divided into states; pluralists see sovereign states as responsible for their own citizens' welfare (Suganami 2005: 40).

· ·

 **TAKING IT FURTHER**

Solidarism and pluralism in action: from the Blair Doctrine to R2P

Developments in IRT often reflect the practice of international relations as undertaken by states, international organizations and other actors in the international system, particularly when the practices are novel or unexpected (see, for example, the end of the Cold War and, just over a decade later, how the terrorist attacks of 9/11 shaped new thinking about order, identity and security in the twenty-first century). The solidarist–pluralist divide within English School theory closely parallels a debate on 'intervention' and the 'responsibility to protect' in the era of global interdependence (see Smith 2016). Tony Blair's 1999 Chicago speech, delivered during the Kosovo intervention by NATO forces, radically transformed thinking on intervention and sovereignty. It delivered a robust case for 'just war' at a moment of profound uncertainty in the international system. Talking of the 'unspeakable' things happening in Kosovo, 'ethnic cleansing, systematic rape, mass murder', Blair intoned that 'We cannot let the evil of ethnic cleansing stand', in Europe or on its borders. Why not? 'We are all inter-nationalists now whether we like it or not … We cannot turn our backs on conflicts and the violation of human rights within other countries if we want to be secure' (Blair 1999). Global interdependence, said Blair, brought the notion of a world society closer than ever before, meaning that we had to rethink the legitimacy of cleaving to outdated notions such as sovereignty if we are to safeguard basic human values of security, dignity and welfare (see also Blair 2001; for a reassessment of Blair's Chicago speech see Daddow 2009). It could be argued that Blair was putting a weak but characteristically *solidarist* case for intervention, albeit one in which nation-states remained significant actors on the global stage.

Blair's call to action came at a time of deliberation in the international community about how best to deal with the ethical concerns to which Blair had drawn attention. In 2001 the International Commission on Intervention and State Sovereignty (ICISS) published its report on responding to atrocities which, as then UN Secretary General Kofi Annan said, 'affect every precept of our common humanity' if, *contra* Blair, we believe that humanitarian intervention is an unacceptable assault on state sovereignty' (quoted in Evans 2004). The Responsibility to Protect (R2P), as it became known, challenges the doctrine of intervention in three ways (Evans 2004). First, it shifts the focus of attention from those planning to intervene to the needs of those needing support (the subjectivity of the Blair 'conditions' for intervention are well covered in Ralph 2011). Second, R2P acknowledges that it is the responsibility of individual states not to engage in mass killing or other atrocities within their borders and that intervention would only be considered if the state in question proved unable or unwilling to uphold its duties. Third, R2P incorporates the associated responsibilities to 'prevent' and 'rebuild', so is more comprehensive than the interventionist doctrine. Prevention, in particular, is the emphasis in R2P. By reasserting the essential inviolability of state sovereignty except in what would be exceptional circumstances, R2P would seem to have put the *pluralist* case for the circumstances of intervention and the responsibility of states before and after the breach of sovereignty entailed by intervention.

Looking at where the Blair doctrine landed Britain, the USA and their coalition of the willing in Iraq, could it be argued that the pluralists and proponents of R2P have a point?

. . . .

QUESTIONS TO PONDER

'Why did Hedley Bull posit the existence of an "international society"? Was he correct to do so?'

This question cues you to explain Bull's reasoning (show your knowledge of Bull's work), and then to tell the reader what you make of it (the marks for assessing/evaluating will be garnered here). An essay in two parts would be logical. Clearly it is sensible to concentrate mainly on Bull, but if you want to illustrate the English School's position with reference to other writers in the tradition, then that would be fine. Make sure to keep Bull's ideas to the forefront though.

In the first part you have to explain why and how Bull took IRT from considering systems, power and interests towards the idea that these relations constitute an international society. As such, you are being asked to summarize the key facets of Bull's thought, as they echo previous IRT (e.g. Realism and Neorealism) and where he departed from it. You can legitimately narrow your essay to focus on one seminal text (*Anarchical Society*), or you could pick ideas from across Bull's œuvre. The first option is probably the easier to sustain because it is a relatively self-contained work; you might tell the reader that Bull developed his ideas over time but that for the purposes of answering this particular question you are sticking to his first major foray into the subject. You could summarize *The Anarchical Society* chapter by chapter; but in order to remain within the recommended word limit for your essay you will surely be better off to take a thematic approach, using foundational quotes to illustrate your reading of Bull. The essential issue is to define what you think Bull meant by 'international society'.

In the second part you have to give your opinions on Bull's ideas about 'international society': how accurate and relevant do you think they are? Here you should demonstrate a familiarity with criticisms levelled at the concept (e.g. James 1993) and the follow-on questions asked of it (for example, Little's, explored above). These include: first, the vagueness of the distinction between 'system' on the one hand and 'society' on the other – when does the one become the other? Second, does 'international' in fact mean 'European', undermining the applicability of the theory to anything beyond the notional and rather limited borders of 'Europe' or the 'Western'? Third, did Bull's theory overlook the elements of a human 'world society' of values that exists among human beings as opposed to states; was he too state-centric? Realist theorists critique Bull for being insufficiently Realist; Liberals critique him for being too Realist, so you could couch your evaluation in these terms. What do you make of their attacks? You could answer this by considering what Bull would have said to his Realist and Liberal critics.

'How does English School theory differ from Realist and Liberal theories about IR? Which do you find most convincing and why?'

Whereas the last question concentrated on just one theory, this answer requires a good working knowledge of three, bringing with it a whole different set of challenges. That you have to cover so much ground makes your response harder to structure, so good planning and organization are vital. In an exam your time management will have to be rigorous so that you effectively address both parts of the question.

Let us deal with the first half of the question. On the surface it might be good to take each theory in turn, explaining their central tenets and then comparing and contrasting in a section at the end. The flaw in this approach is that it may be impossible to cram in all the information you need. Say you only have 2,500 words for your essay – how are you going to summarize three theories and then evaluate them in this limited space? And bearing in mind this is an English School-oriented question, it is worth showing your tutor you actually know a lot more about that theory than the other two. It may, then, be better to centre your analysis on English School theory, moving into the other two theories as and when necessary. You could, for instance, consider the use Bull and others make of Realist-inspired words like 'system' and 'interest' and Liberal words like 'institutions' and 'society'. The best answers might engage with the Constructivist leanings of much English School work as a way of playing the question at its own game (see the following chapter for a survey of Constructivism). This approach is harder to manage because it assumes a strong knowledge base, but it certainly should pay dividends in terms of demonstrating your ability to meet higher order learning objectives for the course.

In the second part you have to pick your favourite theory (assuming you have one). The marker will be looking for you to justify your choice with reference to either or both of two benchmarks. First, the coherence of the theory as *a theory*. Are its assumptions valid? Is it epistemologically grounded, i.e. does the knowledge it provides stack up effectively? Does it fit the 'facts' of international relations as understood by the theorist responsible? Second, you might consider the applicability of the theory today by asking: has it stood the test of time? Does it explain important facets of contemporary international relations? Making use of the pluralist–solidarist debate would help you show the development of the English School since the 1990s as a broad church for appreciating the historical dynamics of contemporary discussions about justice, order and national sovereignty.

REFERENCES TO MORE INFORMATION

Dunne, T. (1998) *Inventing International Society: A History of the English School.* Basingstoke: Macmillan.
The definitive history of the English School.

Wight, M. (1991) *International Theory: The Three Traditions.* Leicester: Leicester University Press.
A posthumously published collection of Wight's lectures at the LSE in the 1950s.

Bull, H. (1966) 'The Grotian Concept of International Society', in Herbert Butterfield and Martin Wight (eds) *Diplomatic Investigations: Essays on the Theory of International Politics.* London: George Allen and Unwin, pp. 51–73.

Bull, H. and Watson, A. (eds) (1985) *The Expansion of International Society.* Oxford: Oxford University Press.
Analysis of the growth and development of European and, increasingly, global 'society' from the sixteenth century onwards.

Manning, C.A.W. (1962) *The Nature of International Society.* London: London School of Economics.
This is unfortunately very difficult to find these days, so try these:

Murray, R.W. (ed.) (2015) *System, Society and the World: Exploring the English School of International Relations.* Bristol: E-IR Publishing.

Suganami, H. (2000) 'C.A.W. Manning and the Study of International Relations', *Review of International Studies,* 27(1): 91–107.

Robson, B.A. (ed.) (1998) *International Society and the Development of International Relations.* London: Cassell.
A collection of essays by leading English School writers assessing where they felt that the concept of 'international society' had taken IR to that point.

Brown, C. (2002) *Sovereignty, Rights and International Justice.* Cambridge: Polity Press.

Buzan, B. (2001) 'The English School: An Under-Exploited Resource in IR', *Review of International Studies,* 24(3): 471–88.
A forceful statement of the case that IR theorists neglect the English School at their peril.

Epp, R. (1998) 'The English School on the Frontiers of International Relations', *Review of International Studies,* 24(special issue): 47–63.

Finnemore, M. (1996) *National Interests in International Society.* Ithaca, NY: Cornell University Press.

Buzan, B. (2005) *From International to World Society? English School Theory and the Social Construction of Globalisation.* Cambridge: Cambridge University Press.
Chapters 1 and 2 are good on the weaknesses of English School theory and Chapter 6 on the institutions that constitute 'international society'.

Little, R. (2000) 'The English School's Contribution to the Study of International Relations', *European Journal of International Relations,* 6(3): 495–522.

Groom, A.J.R. (1975) 'Functionalism and World Society', in A.J.R. Groom and P. Taylor (eds) *Functionalism: Theory and Practice in International Relations.* London: University of London Press, pp. 93–111.
Shows the overlap between English School and Liberal thought.

Little, R. and Williams, J. (eds) (2006) *The Anarchical Society in a Globalized World.* Basingstoke: Palgrave.

Gong, G.W. (1984) *The Standard of 'Civilization' in International Relations.* Oxford: Clarendon Press.
A wealth of information on the changing faces of 'international society' through the ages by appreciating non-Western societies in China and Japan. Also useful as a precursor to Postcolonialism (Chapter 13 in this book).

Hoffman, S. (2000) *World Disorders: Troubled Peace in the Post-Cold War Era.* Lanham, MD: Rowman and Littlefield Publishers Ltd.
Chapter 2 covers Hedley Bull; Chapter 4 is on world order beyond Realist and Liberal perspectives.

Review of International Studies (2001) 'Forum on the English School', 27(3): 465–513.
A series of six short articles. See also the same journal's (2002) five-article section on the English School, 28(4).

Hjorth, R. (2011) 'Equality in the Theory of International Society: Kelsen, Rawls and the English School', *Review of International Studies,* 37(5): 2585–602.

Reus-Smit, C. (1997) 'The Constitutional Structure of International Society and the Nature of Fundamental Institutions', *Review of International Studies*, 51(4): 555–89.

Zhang, Y. (2003) 'The "English School" in China: A Travelogue of Ideas and their Diffusion', *European Journal of International Relations*, 9(1): 87–114.

Edkins, J. and Zehfuss, M. (2005) 'Generalising the International', *Review of International Studies*, 31(3): 451–72.
Poststructuralist reading of Bull's Anarchical Society, useful to read alongside Chapter 12 in this book.

On solidarism and pluralism:

Jackson, R. (2000) *The Global Covenant: Human Conduct in a World of States*. Oxford: Oxford University Press.

Linklater, A. (2009) 'Human Interconnectedness', *International Relations*, 23(3): 481–97.

Weinert, M.S. (2011) 'Reframing the Pluralist–Solidarist Debate', *Millennium: Journal of International Studies*, 40(1): 21–41.

Wheeler, N.J. (1992) 'Pluralist or Solidarist Conceptions of International Society: Bull and Vincent on Humanitarian Intervention', *Millennium: Journal of International Studies*, 21(3): 29–34.

Wheeler, N.J. (2000) *Saving Strangers: Humanitarian Intervention in International Society*. Oxford: Oxford University Press.

Williams, J. (2005) 'Pluralism, Solidarism and the Emergence of World Society in English School Theory', *International Relations*, 19(1): 19–38.

Williams, J. (2015) *Ethics, Diversity and World Politics: Saving Pluralism from Itself?* Oxford: Oxford University Press.

8
CONSTRUCTIVISM

Key terms

- Anarchy
- Identity
- Interest
- Norm

- Norm entrepreneurship
- Security dilemma
- State

> In giving form to the world, the mind makes the world real – *in our heads*. And yet the
> world *appears* to exist, more or less as we sense it, outside the mind. (Onuf 2009: 194,
> original emphasis)

At the time of writing this book I have a nephew who is seven years old and a niece who is five years old. Being the dutiful and generous uncle that I am, I have spent considerable money and time over the past few years purchasing various gifts for them. Last time out I wanted to buy them each a T-shirt for the summer, so off I went to the shops to see what I could find. I emerged with a mainly blue T-shirt for my nephew and a mainly pink one for my niece. My choice was made in part because of my preconceptions about what colours we associate with boys (blues) and girls (pinks). It also reflected the nature of the dominant colours in the boys' and girls' clothing sections in the shop. The girls' section contained lighter tones and more pinks and yellows, whereas the tones for boys' clothes were darker, with blues, blacks and browns more apparent.

As they grow up I have great fun choosing toys for them as well as clothes. There are many toys that both enjoy playing with, such as jigsaw puzzles and board games. But there are some toys I would give my nephew more readily than my niece, such as water pistols, Action Men and footballs. By the same token, my niece might prefer dolls, dressing up clothes and glitter make-up. For their sticker books, my nephew prefers gladiators, my niece the fairy princesses. It is not illegal or immoral to switch the gifts around, and the children would ultimately not care either way, one would think, especially at those ages. It is more that it would be considered unusual. You can probably see where this is heading. My gift ideas for my niece and nephew have, over the years, been shaped both by my own reading of what they might want, but more, no doubt, by my expectations of what they would want given *societal expectations* about what young boys and girls wear, and the toys younger people enjoy.

This intentionally simplified (and gendered – see Chapter 11) example indicates the intersubjective nature of social reality. The word intersubjectivity relates to the nature of shared meanings which are embedded in the language and other symbols we use to give meaning to the world around us. Intersubjective meanings 'derive from self-interpretation and self-definition, and the social practices in which they are embedded and which they constitute' (Kratochwil and Ruggie, quoted in Reus–Smit 2013: 231).

On a technical note, see the above quotation from Kratochwil and Ruggie. I found it in a book chapter written by Reus-Smit, which appears in a collection edited by two other scholars, Scott Burchill and Andrew Linklater. Reus-Smit provided the full Kratochwil and Ruggie reference in his chapter, so why did I not take that as my reference? In other words, why did I need to mention Reus-Smit at all if I have the original reference to work with? Because I did not actually read the Kratochwil and Ruggie article to find that quotation: Reus-Smit did. Through his efforts I was informed about the idea of 'intersubjective meaning' and it is therefore appropriate to credit him with being the original source of my information on that important point. Had I included the Kratochwil and Ruggie reference, including the page number of the quotation given to me by Reus-Smit, I would have been implying to you the reader that I had read the original article by Kratochwil and Ruggie. But I did not. The credit in this instance goes to Reus-Smit and we trust that, as a good honest scholar, he quoted accurately from the original.

The lesson: in essays and coursework assignments cite the **first**source from which you take your information. Do not duplicate references to Writer B from Writer A, if Writer A was where you located the evidence. This applies not just to direct quotations but to all evidence, arguments and interpretations that feature in scholarly work. If you could not be bothered to read original IRT but culled a few quotations from online summaries of books and articles, you still need to be *honest* about where you found this information. You risk being accused of bad academic practice if you do not reference honestly. See Part III of this book for more on study and writing skills, but this is such a common mistake I wanted to flag it up here too.

In the example above my actions were moulded by all sorts of decisions operating at different levels of consciousness. I was playing the role of 'good uncle' (my self-interpretation and self-definition) for children of a certain age (relying on societally constructed definitions of 'children' handed down through time). I was embedded in the social practice of 'gift buying' and this was in turn constituted by set of practices involving the exchange of money for material goods in various shops, which by definition limited/shaped my purchasing horizons by offering certain items that, intersubjectively thorough our purchasing decisions, the 'market' has come to see as being good sellers. Who would have thought that buying gifts would be so full of *meaning*?

Intersubjective meanings of this kind are everywhere in our daily lives: they can possess a taken-for-granted quality we do not even recognise. Take the examples of 'institutional facts' (Searle 2005) such as money, property rights, sovereignty, marriage, football and Valentine's Day (Ruggie 1998b: 856). Or from Stefano Guzzini and Anne Leander (2006: 79): 'If we watch a red light as a social scientist, we are not interested in the residual matter of electric circuits but, for instance, in the norms which the interpretation of this sign mobilizes.' The norm in this case is that, in most countries, the red light as part of a traffic warning system means 'stop'. There are sanctions for rule breakers and whole sets of legal practices can be brought to bear on offenders. The *meaning* of red traffic lights, invented in 1912 (Badon 2010) is now very well established, is taught to trainee drivers, and has a clear intersubjective meaning. It is a social convention or norm backed by rules that help keep it effective. Imagine the chaos that would ensue on our roads if, tomorrow, everyone stopped buying into the red–green light system of traffic signals. But they do not. Why? Because everyone subscribes to the idea that red–green signalling is part of what makes our roads 'tick'. People are safer and able to go about their daily lives more effectively on the basis of this simple intersubjective meaning, embedded in everyday practices millions of times the world over. This is Constructivism in action.

In IR, the Constructivist agenda – sometimes known as Social Constructivism – aims to 'interrogate defining concepts of the discipline and unravel alleged naturalness of concepts' (Aalberts 2010: 253). Or as Ruggie explains:

> The constructivist project has sought to open up the relatively narrow theoretical confines of the field – by pushing them back to problematize the interests and identities of actors; deeper to incorporate the intersubjective bases of social action and social order; and into the dimensions of space and time to establish the 'duality' of structure, in, [Anthony] Giddens's terms, at once constraining social action but also being (re) created and, therefore, potentially transformed by it. (1998b: 862)

This chapter will consider this wide-ranging approach to IR in four parts. The first part will provide some context and an overview of some core disciplinary understandings of Constructivism. The second part will survey the thought of a leading 'thin' Constructivist, Alexander Wendt. The third part will look at 'thick' Constructivism using work on norm entrepreneurship and the norm life cycle. The final part will analyse the Constuctivist idea of 'security communities'.

CONTEXT

Even if it's real, it's still a construct. (McCarthy 2015: 44)

Constructivism has been a long and productive intellectual movement within the social sciences. It made itself felt in the study of IR in and around the end of the Cold War. Where Neorealists and Neoliberals took a ready-made microeconomic theory to inform their appreciation of the games selfish states play in the international system, Constructivists have looked for inspiration to sociologists such as Emile Durkheim and Max Weber to inform their understanding of processes of socialization and the creation of intersubjective meanings in world politics that take on the character of 'the real'. Put another way, 'constructivism concerns the issue of human consciousness in international life' (Ruggie 1998b: 857 and 878). There is a crucial point here: 'For a constructivist, it is not the existence of a world independent of our thought that is at stake, but whether we can have unmediated access to it' (Guzzini and Leander 2006: 79). Constructivism is not an 'anything goes' relativism but an epistemologically-aware appreciation of how we interpret the world around us.

Constructivist international theory is, therefore, not a neat, self-contained entity or singularly identifiable 'theory'. It is a movement promoting a particular ontology of IR, spanning an array of methodological perspectives and epistemological commitments. 'Constructivism is not a theory of international politics,' more a 'sensibility' (Wendt 1999: 7). As two other exponents agree: 'Constructivism is a different kind of theory from realism, liberalism or marxism and operates at a different level of abstraction. Constructivism is not a substantive theory of politics. It is a social theory about the nature of social life and social change' (Finnemore and Sikkink 2001: 393).

Constructivism can be used to critique theoretical constructs in IR such as the notion of the 'national interest', 'anarchy', 'sovereignty' and the 'balance of power' (for example, Kratochwil 1982) as well as the discipline's modes of knowledge production more widely. In its 'thinner' guise (we are focusing on the iconic work of Wendt in this chapter) it retains strong connections to the state-centric approach of the Neorealists. In its 'thicker' manifestations it shares strong affinities with English School Liberal/ Neoliberal theories, as well as Critical Theory and some poststructural approaches to identity in IR. The multiple categorizations of this theory given in recent years say something about the complexity of agreeing on a one-size-fits-all definition, in particular as one approaches the 'thicker' end of Constructivism (for different ways of carving up constructivist work see Lupovici 2009: 198; Reus-Smit 2002: 493; Ruggie 1998b: 880–2). Constructivism is, therefore, quite hard to place because it deals directly with work that goes on in those 'neater' theoretical traditions, yet in another way it has enough of a distinctive epistemological and methodological agenda to mark it apart from them.

The normative turn

We have discussed previously in this book the social science debate between positivist and normative theorists. Positivists believe that the social world can be studied using methods drawn from the natural sciences; that facts can be disentangled from values; that regularities in the social world can be discovered in the same way that a natural scientist can discover regularities in the natural world; and that we judge truth claims on the basis of an appeal to our value-free facts (for more on the philosophy behind positivism, see Giddens 1974).

Normative theorists question each and every positivist assumption, and in so doing provide serious grounds for us to investigate both the epistemological status of positivist theory (its claims to produce accurate, testable and objective knowledge) and the methodological underpinnings of positivist research (its naturalist approach). First of all, normative theorists disagree that the study of the world should (could, even) be all about the way things are. They point out that this is a small 'c' conservative position which entrenches rather than challenges existing power arrangements. Second, normative theorists raise the question of the values inherent in all theory – even theory which claims to tell us simply the way things are. This opinion masks the fact that in telling 'the way things are' you are in fact telling *your version* of the way things are. It might not be my version, and almost certainly won't be the same as Victoria Beckham's, Rupert Murdoch's or Donald Trump's versions.

> Normative theorists doubt the existence of a single position from which we can either 'view' the reality of the social world or tell it in terms that are anything other than partial, skewed and relative to our own theories and preconceptions about the world and its workings.

Normative IRT

Normative theorists in IR raised awareness of their concerns about the positivist way of doing things by challenging some of the assumptions about how to 'do' IR theory which appeared in the most popular works in the field until the 1980s. You might, there-fore, usefully see Constructivism and the other normative theories we cover in the next few chapters as a reaction against Realism, Liberalism and their Neo-Neo offshoots. Constructivist writers work from the premise that IR is a far more complex field than those theorists had led us to believe (Onuf 1998). They point up the linguistic and com-municative bases of our apprehension of the world, accenting the compelling idea that:

> hardly anyone – even among the most ardent constructivists or pragmatists – doubts that the 'world' exists independent from our minds. The question is rather whether we can recognise it in a pure and direct fashion, i.e., without any 'description', or whether what we recognise is always already organised and formed by certain categorical and theoretical elements. (Kratochwil 2000: 91)

A variety of factors had led to dissatisfaction with the prevailing theoretical consensus in IRT. It encouraged new questions to be asked and new answers to be found using differ-ent methodological techniques:

- **The sudden fragility of Neorealism.** The end of the Cold War in 1989 undermined the Neorealist argument that the bipolar international system that had prevailed since the end of the Second World War would be an enduring feature of inter-national politics. 'Mainstream IR theory simply had difficulty explaining the end of the Cold War, or systemic change more generally' (Wendt 1999: 4). Suddenly, theorists wedded to explaining the 'facts' of the world as they saw them had to account for myriad new 'facts' about the Soviet Union and its satellite states, as well as wholesale systemic changes that were neither predicted nor well explained by prevailing Neorealist thought. As James Rosenau describes the situation (2003: 10): 'One would be hard pressed to find a textbook on International Relations (IR) of the 1980s that had a single paragraph, let alone a single sentence, in which allow-ance was made for the possibility of the Cold War and the Soviet Union coming to an end.' Renewed uncertainty about causes and motivators of change in the inter-national system animated Constructivists to ask: 'are structures *real* – really "out there" in the world?' (Onuf 2009: 184). Were Neorealists correct to impute so much causative influence to them in their explanations of international relations, and how should IR make sense of systemic change?

- **Globalization.** We could write a whole book on this phenomenon and still not explore each and every aspect of it. I take the word to mean increasing political, economic, technological and cultural interconnectedness between peoples and states around the world. For a more formal definition we could try: 'Globalization is the increasing integration and interdependence among countries resulting from the modern flow of people, trade, finance and ideas from one nation to another' (Bishop et al. 2011: 117). Until the 1980s IR theory was state-centric and not adept at explaining the rise and increasing influence of such non-state activity; by definition, such activity falls outside the scope of any theory which takes the state as the main unit of analysis. By the end of the 1980s, therefore, it was felt that many significant aspects of international activity were not being explained by core IR theories. In particular, the creation of state identities and their impact on the external behaviour of states were felt to be under-theorized (Lapid and Kratochwil 1996).

- **Ignoring other issues.** Globalization has not only increased the degree of interconnectedness between individuals, organizations and states around the world, it has intensified such connections and thereby increased our awareness of all sorts of issues and problems in the global arena. In Thomas Friedman's words, contemporary globalization goes 'farther, faster, cheaper and deeper' (quoted in Nye and Welch 2011: 258) than even interdependence theory catered for. IR theory by the 1980s was seen to be ignoring major cross-border politico-social movements such as the women's movement, human rights, environmentalism, terrorism, global inequality, oppression, exploitation and ethnicity as sources of identity creation and causes of conflict in the post-Cold War era. Constructivism, like other normative theories you will study, provided a way of plugging these and other gaps in IR's knowledge base.

Having explored the context within which Constructivist thought emerged, we can now outline how it 'came' to the discipline of IR. We do this first by looking at early or 'thin' Constructivism. We then move on to account for later or 'thick' Constructivism.

> Normative theories such as Constructivism, feminism and Green international theory have emerged to fill gaps scholars felt 'traditional' IR theorists left open. What does this tell you about the relationship between theory and practice in the field of IR?

'THIN' CONSTRUCTIVISM

In 1992, Alexander Wendt published an article in the major US academic journal *International Organization* called 'Anarchy is What States Make of It: The Social Construction of Power Politics' (Wendt 1992), a prelude to his book *Social Theory of International Politics* (1999). It helped raise the profile of what has become known as Constructivist theory of IR, adding to earlier works in this tradition including Kratochwil (1989) and Onuf (1989). Wendt admitted that 'there are many forms of constructivism' and that by the standards of other approaches in the field his is a 'moderate one' (Wendt 1999: 1). I have therefore called

Wendt's version of Constructivism 'thin' to denote that it does not so much seek to overturn Neorealist approaches to the study of IR as much as add the issue of 'identities' into the mix (for a critique of Wendt's under-theorization of 'identity' see Zehfuss 2006). 'Thin' Constructivism could equally be called 'Realist' Constructivism to highlight this agenda, because as Wendt himself argues, while his theory competes with Waltz's argument in some ways, 'it supports it in others' and he primarily tries 'to explain the latter's cultural conditions of possibility' (Wendt 1999: 15).

Wendt's article developed the Constructivist position (see also Wendt 1996) by ranging over the theory and practice of IR; so how to summarize? All references to page numbers below are to Wendt (1992).

Commitment to rationalism on the part of Neoliberals and Neorealists

Rationalism is a social theory which treats 'the identities and interests of agents as exogenously given' (i.e. given to them rather than being created by them). It therefore explains processes and institutions as impacting on behaviour rather than those identities and interests (pp. 391–2). Wendt wanted to give the constitution of identities and interests more of a say in the explanation for state behaviour and the outcomes that result from the interaction between states in the international arena.

Other theorists can help us bring identities and interests into the IR arena

Normative scholars, numbering amongst them feminists and poststructuralists – all of whom we study in this book – privilege identity and interest formation in their theories. These 'reflectivists' are also known as 'constructivists' and it is to these groups of scholars that Wendt turned for his ideas (p. 393).

Neorealists such as Waltz gave too much explanatory weight to systemic factors

They erroneously suggested that states operate in a self-help system mysteriously given to them 'by anarchic structure exogenously to process' (p. 394); it is as if states have no say over how they think and act. Wendt felt this structured view of IR was too **deterministic** because it ruled out the bottom-up effects on the international system that states could exert with, for example, a regime change or change in ideology (note the Constructivist debt to the end of the Cold War here).

Self-help and power politics are, for Wendt, not such fixed, unchanging certainties

They 'do not follow either logically or causally from anarchy' (p. 394); they 'are institutions, not essential features of anarchy' (p. 395). If states exist in a self-help world, it is because of processes they themselves have brought into existence. '*Anarchy is what states make of it*' (p. 395, italics in original).

The distribution of power is significant, but its effects are unpredictable

State calculations about how to 'be' and 'act' in IR are based on more than rational leaders' assessments of the absolute power of their state relative to the power and capabilities of other states in the system. Leaders are also concerned with perceptions of their own and other states' identities and possible future behaviour: on 'conceptions of self and other'. They might sometimes act for reasons other than the accrual of power or safeguarding national security. These identity perceptions are not given but dynamic, context-specific and relational to the actions of those other states (p. 397). Put another way, the international system is more fluid than systemic theories would have us believe, because states have a good deal of say over what goes on in the international arena.

Reifying anarchy prompts us to overlook uncertainties in international relations

To **reify** an abstract entity is to treat it as if it had human or living existence: 'the fallacy of treating social artefacts as self-constituted entities and vesting in them powers, attributes and dispositions' (Rosenberg 2013: 189). Wendt believed that IR scholars such as Waltz did this too readily with the abstract concept of anarchy. 'Actors do not have a "portfolio" of interests that they carry around independent of social context'; instead, they define their interests in the process of defining situations' (p. 398). Interests and identities are not given to states but are constructed by those states on the basis of learning from past experiences, their experience of very recent actions and their expectations about the future.

Underspecified nature of Waltz's definition of structure

A self-help international system is just one sort of system among several that can prevail. Wendt identifies three types of security systems: 'competitive' (Realist version), 'individualistic' (Neoliberal version) and 'cooperative' (Liberal version) (p. 400). He developed these in his book (Wendt 1999: Chapter 6) where they got labelled the Hobbesian, Lockean and Kantian versions respectively. If several types of security system have come and gone over the centuries, then how do we predict what type of system we might live in the future? For Wendt, Waltz cannot help us on this issue because his definition of structure overlooks identities and interests.

Arrival: An alien encounter

Wendt takes us back to the original 'state of nature' – remember Hobbes and his treatment in Realist theory (see Chapter 5). Wendt imagines a time when one state ('ego') first encounters another ('alter'), to illustrate his argument that there is nothing fixed about what the nature of this and future encounters will be (pp. 404–5). He proceeds by asking how we would react to being contacted by members of an alien civilization. Our response, he argues, would be highly context dependent and shaped by our 'reading' of their various gestures (words/actions) towards us (p. 405). It would also depend on whether we were able to interpret those gestures and their language effectively, as to what kinds of interactions would play out. Again, nothing about our response is determined in advance of this first encounter (pp. 404–7). The 2016 film *Arrival* tackles exactly this scenario too: it is a movie all about communication and problems of communicating intent when two parties do not even share the rudimentary basics of a common language system.

Theories of state behaviour to the 1980s ignored the question of authorship

An elaboration of the perils of reifying anarchy, which Wendt had addressed earlier in the article (see above). Wendt contended that Neorealists reified anarchy 'in the sense of treating it as something separate from the practices by which it is produced and sustained' (p. 410). Anarchy is taken to be something given to us, as existing out there, something not produced by human beings and the states they govern. Wendt's view is quite the reverse: that anarchy is authored by states and therefore a social construct – 'what states have made of themselves' (ibid.). Things could be very different. States do not have to operate in a condition of anarchy.

Case study material: institutional transformations of power politics

The title of part 2 of Wendt's article in which he examined sovereignty, cooperation and critical strategic thought. He highlights theoretical routes by which states might escape the supposedly all-conquering, all-structuring Hobbesian state of nature, and identifies how just such escapes have been put into practice in global politics since 1945 (pp. 410–21).

Variety of possibilities for systemic transformations

Using the example of Soviet President Mikhail Gorbachev's 'New Thinking', Wendt illustrated the capacity for state leaders to engage in critical, self-reflective learning which helps them change the nature of the world political 'game' they play. Action at the domestic and international level is needed to transform embedded attitudes, institutional practices and perceptions of identity of 'self' and 'other' (pp. 419–22).

> Wendt's use of the experience of Gorbachev's Soviet Union shows the context-specific nature of our theories about IR. Gorbachev's actions helped lead to the end of the Cold War and the demise of the bipolar international system. Academics, like politicians, were caught on the hop and started searching around for new explanations to replace theories such as Neorealism, which suddenly appeared empirically flawed, out of date and behind the times, being unable to account for change in IR.

International Relations theories are intimately connected to social theories

In conclusion, Wendt restated his position and added a few important caveats. Having spent an entire article trashing many assumptions and explanations put forward by Neo-Neo writers, Wendt took a step back from some of the potentially more radical aspects of his thought, as if he did not want to tread on 'poststructuralist' ground (see Chapter 12 in this book). Any of the possible transformations he talked about will, he says, have to be brought about and mediated by sovereign states. Ultimate responsibility for the nature of international relations will rest with them (p. 424). Wendt's article has been heralded as the cornerstone of Constructivist thinking in IRT. However, his parting remark that 'I am a statist and a Realist' (ibid.) has been used by critics to challenge his claim to have built a real and lasting bridge between positivism and normative theory, or rationalism and reflectivism as he put in the article.

'THICK' CONSTRUCTIVISM

Wendt's work was something of a game changer in IR because it made a conscious effort to theorize the social dimensions of state interactions at the international level. For some writers, however, Wendt did not go far enough, particularly on the identity side. We can call these 'thick' Constructivists who approach their research not through Neorealist lenses, as Wendt did, but with an eye on other sources of identity creation. They are interested in unpacking the ways in which identity informs the conduct of global politics not as an add-on to national interests, but as a motivation to international action away from, or prior to, interests.

We could equally call these Liberal Constructivists because they bring non-state actors into the equation and show how they can be as crucial as states at developing and spreading norms around the international system. In the process, the international system develops, if not into a world or even international society, but around the kernels of community within it. Different forms of community overlap in complex ways in and out of international organizations and institutions. These norms can come to influence state behaviour by moulding leaders' perceptions of how their state is seen on the world stage. This refined concept of rationality affects the balance of values and interests that come into play when leaders make their foreign policy decisions. For a good example of this approach in action, see Epstein (2008) on the rise of anti-whaling discourses and practice since 1945. We will tackle 'thick' Constructivism in two sections. The first will study norm entrepreneurship, the second will study the idea of 'security communities'.

Norm entrepreneurship

In an excellent article, Martha Finnemore and Kathryn Sikkink (1998: 888) used Neoliberal regime theory to generate some propositions about norms in IR: their origins, how they exercise influence and to specify the conditions under which they will be influential in global affairs. In effect they were asking how norms can be brought in to explain the workings of regulative (formally drawn up) and constitutive (informal, habitual) institutions, with reference to processes of socialization in international affairs. We can see the debt to Wendt and their ambition to go beyond him. 'Used carefully … norm language can help to steer scholars toward looking inside social institutions and considering the components of social institutions as well as the way these elements are renegotiated into new arrangements over time to create new patterns of politics' (Finnemore and Sikkink 1998: 891; see also Searle 2005).

Take the example of the EU, which we encountered previously in Chapter 4 on Liberalism. Functionalists saw the EU as a technocratic project which recalibrated state perceptions of the benefits to be gleaned from tighter cooperation through integration. Membership of the EU changed state calculations about the relative costs and benefits of cooperating with other states in this regional organization. When read through Constructivist lenses, however, functionalist theory looks slightly different – it is all about socialization and the build up of 'habits of trust' as a community of nations engaged in a shared project. At least this was how it seemed until the Eurozone crisis from 2008, compounded by Britain's eventual withdrawal from the EU after the 2016 Brexit referendum. However, back to the theory. As trust builds in an integrative venture (even between states which had been at war not much more than a decade earlier) it becomes 'internalized and internalized trust would, in turn, change affect among the participants. Changed affect meant changed identity and changed norms as empathy with others shifted' (Finnemore and Sikkink 1998: 905).

Hence, we can explain the EU with reference to changes in the calculations states make about the gains to be made from cooperation (a Realist/Neorealist approach). But we can tell an equally compelling story about the social processes involved, whereby states come to think and act 'European' because they have become conditioned to do so by regular and formal and informal interaction with other states building the European 'project'. Representatives of the states meet in all sort of institutional settings to share information, agree goals and make predictable their future behaviour by signing up to the rules and norms of European integration. Other international bodies such as the Association of East Asian Nations (ASEAN), the Gulf Cooperation Council (GCC) and African Union can be interpreted through the same, Constructivist, lenses. Norms can, however, develop around more discrete issues or themes in IR. To explain this process Finnemore and Sikkink developed the norm life cycle.

The norm life cycle

Using case study investigations into the women's rights movement and the spread of human rights, Finnemore and Sikkink use the norm life cycle to explain the origins, transmission of norms around the international system (all that follows below is from Finnemore and Sikkink 1998: 896–909, unless otherwise stated).

The first phase is 'norm emergence', which requires two elements. First 'norm entrepreneurs' spring up, pushing an issue onto the agenda. Norm entrepreneurs can be: individuals such as politicians; groupings such as political parties, pressure groups or think-tanks; lobbyists; international organizations or agencies thereof; or states themselves. Norm entrepreneurs need an organizational platform on which to build consensus around a proposed new norm. This could entail the creation of new platforms or the reorientation of existing platforms, imprinting new ideas on prevailing political discussions. Norm entrepreneurs 'create' issues by inventing language that names, interprets and dramatizes them: 'In order to develop, transmit, and promote norms, a force must be dedicated to changing the meaning ascribed to certain material practices within the relevant community'. Norm entrepreneurs achieve social change by: signalling commitment to change; creating coalitions; making defiance of norms seem costlier ('shaming') and making compliance with new norms seem more beneficial (Wexler 2003: 565; see also Finnemore and Sikkink 2001: 400–1). It is all about the social processes involved in shaping calculations about what is deemed to be appropriate behaviour in IR.

The second phase is norm cascade, which follows the creation of a tipping point. At this juncture one of two things will have happened in the international system. Either a critical mass of states has chosen to adopt the new norm (one third of the states in the system) and/or a sufficient number of 'critical' states with the capacity to influence the decisions of other states has accepted the new norm. 'Critical states' could be defined either by their leadership position within the system (the USA might be a good example) or their 'moral stature'. It is hard to generalize about which states have moral stature; it depends on the issue being discussed. Either way, their adoption of the norm by that state or group of states enhances the prospect of the norm being validated and legitimated for onward adoption by other states who might have been more reluctant at first.

An example of a tipping point being reached in contemporary international relations might prove to be the USA and China ratifying the November 2015 Paris climate change agreement. Indeed, the Paris deal only comes into force when countries representing 55 per cent of total greenhouse gas emissions and 55 per cent of the world's population are signed up (Phillips et al. 2016). The USA and China are the world's two largest economies; they are the biggest emitters of greenhouse gases (37 per cent between them); and historically, both countries have been proven reluctant to bind themselves into such agreements. Their material and ideational position in the global economy would appear to make their partnership on this contentious issue very significant and probably the only way the Paris agreement can come into force.

After the tipping point has been reached, the norm cascade is unleashed. The norm cascade is a dynamic process of 'international socialization intended to induce norm breakers to become norm followers'. States might want to adopt a new norm to be seen to be belonging to the international community, or conversely so that they are not deemed to be 'rogue' states. States like North Korea actively revel in this status: they are rejecting the notion of international society. States might also act out of 'peer pressure', to gain 'esteem' from other states, or because membership of international organizations and institutions encourages them to take the new norm seriously despite their previous inclination to reject it on cost, interest or ideological grounds.

The third phase is norm internalization: 'norms may become so widely accepted that they are internalized by actors and achieve a "taken-for-granted" quality that makes conformance with the norm almost automatic'. In this phase norm contestation has been replaced by norm acceptance (see the anti-slavery norm in contemporary IR, for example). What was an emergent norm at the beginning is now a dominant or hegemonic norm. 'Once norms are internalized, one abides by them not out of fear of the pending sanctions associated with them, but out of some inner conviction' (Ullmann-Margalit 1977: 172).

🌐 TAKING IT FURTHER

Failed norm entrepreneurship

Most of the work on norm entrepreneurship studies why and how norms succeed. The work accounts for the mechanisms by which norms are developed, accepted and internalized by states. What about rubbish norm entrepreneurs?! Sometimes consideration of an exception can help test and refine a theory (see, for example, Bailey 2008).

In my book on New Labour and the European Union (Daddow 2011: 66–76), I applied the norm life cycle framework to the case of the Tony Blair and Gordon Brown governments' attempts to 'sell' the idea of the EU to the British people between 1997 and 2010. I used discourse analysis, quite a popular method among Constructivist researchers. New Labour leaders perceived that the 'norm' (the dominant, instinctive, habitual appreciation) was for the British to be spoken about as (and to play the role of) the EU's 'awkward' or 'reluctant partner'. They wanted to develop and legitimate a 'pro-European' norm that could overthrow the pervasive discontent with the EU that put Britain at the lowest end of opinion polls in terms of support for the EU across the member states. Blair was the lead 'entrepreneur' and he used organizational platforms such as the Britain in Europe group as well as many set piece speeches on the subject to get his message across. Unfortunately, his powerful Chancellor of the Exchequer, Gordon Brown, was working somewhat at odds with his Prime Minister. He adopted some highly sceptical positions towards such touchstone integration ventures as the single currency. There was no real coordinated 'entrepreneurship' in the first place because both men feared a strong backlash from a vocal and influential Eurosceptical press, especially newspapers in the Rupert Murdoch stable such as the *Sun* and *The Times*. This finding went some way to supporting Finnemore and Sikkink's assertion that norm entrepreneurs sometimes need to risk their reputations and show strong-willed leadership to advance their cause: fear of failure can inhibit norm entrepreneurship.

New Labour never managed to reach a tipping point to cause a norm cascade, although it was possible to ascertain what that tipping point might have entailed. Extrapolating from the Finnemore and Sikkink model, a tipping point would have been reached in one of two ways. First, when a reasonable majority of the polled population expressed support for continued membership of the EU. Second, when a number of 'critical' newspapers – the most widely read titles – switched from Euroscepticism to a supportive line on the EU, or at least became more balanced in their coverage over a period of time (on the 'Murdoch effect' in this policy realm, see Daddow 2012). Arguably, achieving the first task was always conditional on achieving the second. In the course of the New Labour years, Euroscepticism in the press did not diminish; if anything it increased, as did the general Euroscepticism of the British people. As a result, New Labour's much vaunted push for Europe never resulted in the establishment of a new norm, albeit there were some decisive yet all too sporadic moves made to create and sell a new norm. In 2016, the British people voted to leave the EU, showing that their Euroscepticism was as entrenched after 13 years of New Labour government as it had been at the outset. The intervening Coalition and Conservative governments had done nothing to challenge the Eurosceptic norm.

This domestic (intra-state) case study tested the norm life cycle model and found that it travelled nicely to explain the social, cultural and psychological underpinnings of political decision-making. New Labour possessed one image of British identity and role in the world, the press and public quite another. Blair and Brown tried – so they claimed – to develop a new approach to British foreign policy, but they, in fact, fell prey to structural constraints (such as media ownership and ideology) only partly under their control or influence. Research into failed norms can help us unpack further the interplay of interests and identities that shape state behaviour, as well as helping us get to grips with the 'fear' that holds states back from creative and/or cooperative ventures on the world stage.

SECURITY COMMUNITIES

The idea of a security community originated in the 1950s in the work of Karl Deutsch and his collaborators from across the disciplines of Political Science and History (Deutsch 1957). They studied the North Atlantic security community that was, then, emerging after the Second World War, testing the Liberal hypothesis that in time such a community could lead to the elimination of war. Deutsch's project dovetailed synergistically with the work on functionalist integration we covered earlier in the book (see Chapter 4; see also Neoliberal institutionalism in Chapter 5). Deutsch's concept of the security community was later developed by Constructivist IR theorists including Emmanuel Adler and Michael Barnett, who expanded the empirical testing ground for the theory to new cases from around the globe (for example, Adler and Barnett 2008). Regional organizations and regional governance are now quite frequently treated from a security community perspective, the focus being on identity and norm-generation (for example, Lopez-Lucia 2015): the concept is in a constant process of definition and debate. It is important to point out that it has also been adapted for their own purposes by English School and Democratic Peace theorists, but for reasons of space they are not treated here (on which see Koschut 2014). We will focus on Adler's 'Imagined (Security) Communities' article to illustrate how the concept feeds from, and back into, 'thick' Constructivism in IR. All the page references below are to Adler (1997a) unless otherwise stated.

Adler, like other Constructivists studied in this chapter, was dissatisfied with Realist and other IRT that closed down a discussion of the social identity of states by boxing them off as bounded sovereign territories that possessed an interest in security, but little else, at the international level:

> I argue instead, from a constructivist perspective, that state social identities and interests are not fixed but evolve from the diffusion and convergence of causal and normative understandings across national boundaries, high levels of communication, economic interdependence, and cooperative practices. Furthermore, not only do identities and interests evolve, they also have the potential to converge. (p. 252)

In the Realist view, each state possesses a set of interests and an identity. However, the latter is actually a function of the former – a state's identity *is* its interest in security and nothing more, because they are security focused actors in the international system – and therefore identity is not considered fit for analysis. Adler wanted to turn this notion on its head by focusing on the active diffusion of state authority in such realms as 'security, economic welfare, and human justice (human rights)'. Following John Ruggie (1993), Adler argued that there are 'non-territorial spaces' in which states come together to conceptualize shared problems, define policy challenges, and coordinate responses (p. 252). That states have *chosen* to do this told him that something beyond Realist interests was shaping state policy preferences in the international area. This is the radical departure for IRT: it 'suggests an evolution towards socially constructed and spatially differentiated transnational *community-regions* which national, transnational and international elites and institutions, sometimes under the leadership of outstanding individuals, help to constitute'

(p. 253, original emphasis). These individuals and the groupings they help engender are the norm entrepreneurs of which Finnemore and Sikkink were writing at this time. In these community-regions three things go on. First, people willingly communicate across state borders. Second, they are actively involved in the political life of the region and engaged in regional purposes. Third, as citizens of states, they impel states in the region to act in the regional good and to think regionally as far as governance goes (p. 253).

The original idea of a security community referred to a community of states whose members agree to not fight each other physically, but to settle their disputes in some other way (p. 255). Deutsch proposed two types of security community:

- Amalgamated security community: two or more sovereign states formally merged into an expanded state.
- Pluralistic security community: the sovereign states retain their independence but are integrated to the point where the states 'entertain "dependable expectations of peaceful change"' (p. 255, quoting Deutsch).

The pluralistic community arises when members share a sense of togetherness or 'we-feeling' based on a mutual identity and sense of loyalty to each other. Adler and Barnett refined the idea of the pluralistic security community to mean: first, an absence of war between those states; second, an absence of significant preparations for war by some state or states against another state or states in the same community (Acharya 2014: 15).

These definitions and the refinements that have been made to them over time flag up the divide between Realists and Constructivists (especially on this Liberal wing of the tradition) about the nature and impact of the security dilemma on state behaviour. This is not some utopian fantasy land, because the security community idea does not deny that sovereign states will come into conflict. It is not the *absence of conflict* between states in a pluralistic community that is at stake, but the *will and mechanisms to manage such conflicts as do erupt peacefully* that distinguishes security communities from other types of security relationship. States in a security community come together to pursue common values and interests within the community context. It does not require the prior identification of an 'other' against which that community operates, and lacks a sense of how the community might respond to the emergence of any such external threat (ibid.: 15–16). In identity terms, the shared, positive, 'we' feeling is intrinsic to the idea of a security community.

Adler gave several examples of pluralistic security communities: the EU, in which states 'act as the local agents of a regional good' (p. 265; see also Hobolth, 2011), for discussion of the EU as a 'regional imagined community'); the North Atlantic Community (a looser non-geographically defined grouping that cuts across NATO, the EU and the Council of Europe); Scandinavia; and the USA–Canada. He predicted that in time ASEAN and other groupings might develop into security communities (p. 256). The Organization for Security and Cooperation in Europe (OSCE), previously the Conference on Security and Cooperation in Europe (CSCE), was the nearest thing to the ideal-type security community, Adler argued, because it was founded on an inclusive not exclusive sense of identity and is open to 'all states that express a political will to live up to the standards and norms of the security community' (p. 257).

TAKING IT FURTHER

The OSCE as security community

The Organization for Security and Cooperation in Europe (OSCE) is an intergovernmental body dealing with early warning, conflict prevention, crisis management and post-conflict rehabilitation – the kinds of issues that military organizations such as NATO are ill-equipped to deal with. It was constituted by the 1975 Helsinki Act at the Conference on Security and Co-operation in Europe (CSCE). The OSCE originally sought to promote dialogue between states of the East and states of the West and established 10 basic 'principles of behaviour'. At the end of the Cold War the CSCE transitioned from 'an institutionalised diplomatic conference with no institutional structure' to 'a full international organisation' (Adler 1997a: 269). As the OSCE, it helped the newly independent states in central and eastern Europe make the transition to democracy and free market economies, as well as dealing with internal and external threats to their security and stability. This makes the OSCE the largest of the specifically security-focused international organizations. It has 57 members (as of May 2016) spanning three continents: North America, Europe and Asia (OSCE undated). Crucially also, it is the only organization outside the UN that brings the USA and Russia to the same table.

Adler described the OSCE as the security community *parexcellence*. It 'encourages the elites and peoples of its ... member states to imagine that they inhabit a shared cognitive region' (ibid.: 268). The organizational infrastructure is now mature, containing a Secretariat, Council of Foreign Ministers, the Conflict Prevention Center and what is now known as the Office for Democratic Institutions and Human Rights (p. 269). These fulfil seven community-building functions: (1) promoting political consultation and bilateral/multilateral agreements among members; (2) setting and monitoring liberal standards, for instance on human rights, within and between OSCE states; (3) attempting to prevent violent conflict before it occurs; (4) developing techniques for the peaceful settlement of disputes in the OSCE space; (5) building mutual trust by promoting military transparency and cooperation (in theory there is no 'guessing' about armaments levels, which can induce fear and arms racing); (6) supporting the building of democratic institutions and the smooth transition to market economies; and (7) assisting in re-establishing the rule of law and institutions after armed conflicts (p. 270).

All in all, the OSCE, for all the criticisms levelled at its weakness in supporting its principles and commitments in the face of acts of military aggression, such as the Russian invasion of Ukraine in 2014 (Permanent Mission of Ukraine 2016), the OSCE is said through these practices to have fostered 'positive and dynamic' interactions in and through its institutions. These have generated a palpable 'we-feeling' among its member states as well as a 'process of collective identity formation and trust which, in turn, drives dependable expectations of peaceful change' (Adler 1997a: 276–7).

Adler reflected that the socially constructed nature of security communities is key both to their identity and to the success of the Liberal project they manifest: they 'are dependent on communication, discourse and interpretation, as well as on material environments' (1997a: 258). Practical shared knowledge of how to settle disputes is fundamental to the enterprise. This needs to be 'institutionalised in some kind of rule of law or regulation structure that generates trust' (pp. 258–9). Institution-building is thus similarly crucial to the exercise, as Neoliberal institutionalists have long pointed out, because of their civilizing functions (pp. 259–60). The day-to-day work in these institutions and the civil society organizations that spring up around them to provide technical knowledge, support and advice, promotes the internalization of norms of behaviour that would in all likelihood be lacking without participation in the security community. Adler suggests that if a group of states who self-identify as 'democracies' band together in such a fashion, certain behaviours – such as a concern for human rights – become appropriate, while others – torture, for example – become inappropriate or illegitimate. 'Henceforth, the state follows democratic norms not just because its people believe in democracy, but because the category "democratic state" now defines, in part, their identity' (p. 264). Interests, in this account of a socially constructed community, are not the only or even the most important driver of a state's behaviour internationally. Identities are firmly in focus in Constructivist IR.

QUESTIONS TO PONDER

'Critically evaluate Wendt's judgement that "anarchy is what states make of it"'

Answering this question successfully relies on two things: first, a solid understanding of Wendt's 1992 article (and related work if you wish); second, a familiarity with some of the key critiques levelled at his work. Lower marks will go to students who show a bit of knowledge with Wendt's position but who do not bother critiquing his position. The average student will spend a good deal of time exploring the detail of Wendt's argument and then skip through a critique or two fairly briefly at the end of the essay. To achieve marks at the higher end of the spectrum, therefore, you should demonstrate an incisive understanding of Wendt's main position and then make sure you devote at least as much time exploring the critiques. The term 'critically evaluate' implies that you are not just setting out those critiques but weighing up their merits (just as those writers weigh up the strength of Wendt's article). To this end, you should be seeking out articles (for example, Wendt 2000) where writers including Wendt himself respond to the criticisms levelled at him. Using his own words is a good way of showing you have read around the subject and will reinforce your understanding of Wendt's position, as well as how he has modified it over time.

'How does a focus on norms help us explain state behaviour in the international system?'

Your emphasis in this essay can be on the use of norms by 'thick' Constructivist scholars. You can begin by assessing what you mean by 'norms', and how they have been theorized as part of the wider Constructivist project on identity and change in the international system. You can get a lot of mileage out of Finnemore and Sikkink's norm life cycle. It is probably worth pointing out that Constructivists did not 'invent' norms, but they developed Neoliberal work on regime theory to divert our attention to the social basis of international action. In the introduction to the answer you will need to be clear about what you think a study of norms can contribute. Whatever you argue be sure to structure the answer around advancing that case robustly and from an informed position rooted in a knowledge of the relevant theoretical literature. It sounds easy, but it isn't!

Having demonstrated that you are familiar with the concept of norms and how they have been put to work in Constructivist case studies, it is worth stepping back to compare and contrast the key moves 'thick' Constructivists have made with regard to 'thin' Constructivists such as Wendt and, ideally, Neorealists and their structuralist approach to explaining IR. There is a line to be drawn between Waltz and Wendt on the one hand and Finnemore and Sikkink on the other, in the sense that Waltz basically ignored identity as a cause of state action, Wendt took it seriously but did not fundamentally challenge the core tenets of Neorealism, whereas Finnemore and Sikkink challenge the state-centricity of both. In the dialogue between them we see the 'old' debate between Realists and Liberals playing out in a different form. Alongside it has come the development of new priorities within IR that have moulded the discipline into the twenty-first century in some decisive ways.

REFERENCES TO MORE INFORMATION

Gallemore, C. (2011) 'Theory in Action: Constructivism', www.youtube.com/watch?v=kYU9UfkV_XI&feature=relmfu, 10 June (accessed 7 August 2016).

General overview including analogy to the *Matrix* movie series:

Adler, E. (1997) 'Seizing the Middle Ground: Constructivism in World Politics', *European Journal of International Relations*, 3(3): 319–63.
Biersteker, T.J. and Weber, C. (eds) (1996) *State Sovereignty as a Social Construct*. Cambridge: Cambridge University Press.
Checkel, J.T. (1998) 'The Constructivist Turn in International Relations Theory', *World Politics*, 50(2): 324–48.
Gergen, K.J. (2003) *An Invitation to Social Construction*. London: Sage.
Hopf, T. (1998) 'The Promise of Constructivism in International Relations Theory', *International Security*, 23(1): 171–200.

Weldes, J. (1996) 'Constructing National Interests', *European Journal of International Relations*, 2(3): 275–318.

Theorizes the concept of 'national interest' using Wendt's brand of Constructivism and uses a case study from US foreign policy during the 1960s Cuban Missile Crisis to illustrate the applicability of this approach to IR.

Gaskarth, J. (2006) 'Discourses and Ethics: The Social Construction of British Foreign Policy', *Foreign Policy Analysis*, 2(4): 325–41.

Like Weldes, uses a case study to illustrate the applicability of Constructivism to the study of IR.

Katzenstein, P.J. (ed.) (1996) *The Culture of National Security: Norms and Identity in World Politics*. New York: Columbia University Press.

See Chapters 2 (co-authored by Wendt among others), 12 and 13, where the big theoretical questions are addressed.

Jepperson, R.L., Wendt, A. and Katzenstein, P.J. (1996) 'Norms, Identity, and Culture in National Security', in P. Katzenstein (ed.) *The Culture of National Security: Norms and Identity in World Politics*. New York: Columbia University Press, pp. 33–75.
Price, R.M. and Reus-Smit, C. (1998) 'Dangerous Liaisons: Critical International Theory and Constructivism', *European Journal of International Relations*, 4(3): 259–94.

Cederman, L. and Daase, C. (2006) 'Endogenizing Corporate Identities', in S. Guzzini and A. Leander (eds) *Constructivism and International Relations: Alexander Wendt and his Critics*. London: Routledge, pp. 118–39.

Fierke, K.M. and Jørgensen, K.E. (eds) (2001) *Constructing International Relations: The Next Generation*. Armonk, NY: M. E. Sharpe.

Smith, S. (2001) 'Foreign Policy is What States Make of It: Social Construction and International Relations Theory', in V. Kubálková (ed.) *Foreign Policy in a Constructed World*. Armonk, NY: M. E. Sharpe, pp. 38–55.

Sterling-Folker, J. (2000) 'Competing Paradigms or Birds of a Feather?: Constructivism and Neoliberal Institutionalism Compared', *International Studies Quarterly*, 44(1): 97–119.

Suganami, H. (2002) 'On Wendt's Philosophy: A Critique', *Review of International Studies*, 28(1): 23–37.

Zehfuss, M. (2002) *Constructivism in International Relations: The Politics of Reality*. Cambridge: Cambridge University Press.

Prügl, E. (1998) 'Feminist Struggle as Social Construction: Changing the Gendered Rules of Home-Based Work', in V. Kubálková, N. Onuf and P. Kowert (eds) *International Relations in a Constructed World*. Armonk, NY: M. E. Sharpe, pp. 123–46.
Introduces you to the constructedness of gender taken up in Chapter 11 of this book.

On norms and the norm life cycle:

Cortell, A.P. and Davis Jr., J.W. (2000) 'Understanding the Domestic Impact of International Norms: A Research Agenda', *International Studies Review*, 2(1): 65–87.

Keck, M.E. and Sikkink, K. (1998) *Activists Beyond Borders*. Ithaca, NY: Cornell University Press.

Klotz, A. (1995) *Norms in International Relations: The Struggle Against Apartheid*. Ithaca, NY: Cornell University Press.

Klotz, A. (2002) 'Transnational Activism and Global Transformations: The Anti-Apartheid and Abolitionist Experiences', *European Journal of International Relations*, 8(1): 49–76.

Legro, J.W. (1997) 'Which Norms Matter? Revisiting the "Failure" of Internationalism', *International Organization*, 51(1): 31–63.

Tarrow, S. (2003) *Power in Movement: Social Movements and Contentious Politics*, 2nd edn. Cambridge: Cambridge University Press.

Tarrow, S. (2007) *The New Transnational Activism*. Cambridge: Cambridge University Press.

Towns, A.E. (2012) 'Norms and Social Hierarchies: Understanding International Policy Diffusion "From Below"', *International Organization*, 66(2): 179–209.

Applied work on norms:

Goertz, G. and Diehl, P.F. (1992) 'Toward a Theory of International Norms: Some Conceptual and Measurement Issues', *Journal of Conflict Resolution*, 36(4): 634–64.

A state-centric, pre-Finnemore and Sikkink attempt to come to terms with norms using the case study of decolonization.

Bratberg, Ø. (2011) 'Ideas, Tradition and Norm Entrepreneurs: Retracing Guiding Principles of Foreign Policy in Blair and Chirac's Speeches on Iraq', *Review of International Studies*, 37(1): 327–48.

Krook, M.L. and True, J. (2012) 'Rethinking the Life Cycles of International Norms: The United Nations and the Global Promotion of Gender Equality', *European Journal of International Relations*, 18(1): 103–27.

Skarbek, D. (2012) 'Prison Gangs, Norms and Organizations', *Journal of Economic Behavior and Organization*, 82(1): 96–109.

Stevenson, H. (2011) 'India and International Norms of Climate Governance: A Constructivist Analysis of Normative Congruence Building', *Review of International Studies*, 37(3): 997–1019.

Wapner, P. (1996) *Environmental Activism and World Civic Culture*. Albany, NY: State University New York Press.

On security communities:

Deutsch, K. (1978) *The Analysis of International Relations*, 2nd edn. Englewood Cliffs, NJ: Princeton University Press.

Lebow, R.N. (2014) 'Karl Deutsch and International Relations', *International Relations*, 28(3): 288–95.

Mouritzen, H. (2001) 'Security Communities in the Baltic Sea Region: Real and Imagined', *Security Dialogue*, 32(3): 297–310.

Ruzicka, J. (2014) 'A Transformative Social Scientist: Karl Deutsch and the Discipline of International Relations', *International Relations*, 28(3): 277–87.

Ulusoy, H. (undated) 'Revisiting Security Communities after the Cold War: The Constructivist Perspective', http://sam.gov.tr/wp-content/uploads/2012/01/Hasan-Ulusoy3.pdf (accessed 6 August 2016).

9

MARXISM

Key terms

- Capitalism
- Class
- Historical materialism

- Imperialism
- Inequality
- World System

You know what capitalism is: getting fucked. (Tony Montana in *Scarface* 1983)

The theories we have covered so far in this book form what you might call the 'core' of the discipline. Ask someone in the street what they think makes the 'stuff' of international relations and their answers would probably include power politics, terrorism and security, diplomacy, interventions, war and conflict and the work of international organizations. The world they described to you would probably resonate with many of the theorists whose work we have studied in Chapters 4–7. Realists would identify with the war/conflict elements; Liberals would identify with the emphasis on negotiations, treaties and multilateral action; while the ears of English School writers would prick up at hearing your interviewees mention intervention.

In the last chapter we saw Constructivist writers wrestling with some of the themes left neglected by this rather conventional IR agenda. Constructivists tried to bring the study of 'identity' to the mainstream study of IR, but simultaneously, in its 'thin' form at least, they underscored the place of states in our understanding of who 'makes' IR by using these as the central units of analysis. In effect, we found early Constructivism alleging a departure from IR's mainstream but not making as decisive a contribution as promised. 'Thick' Constructivists went a lot further from mainstream issues by focusing on norms and security communities. Several other theoretical traditions have also attempted a more thoroughgoing break from the mainstream of IR. In this chapter and the next two we consider three of the best known of these: Marxism, Critical Theory and feminism.

This chapter opens with a discussion of where and how Marxism 'fits' in IRT. It moves on to consider Lenin's theory of capitalism, imperialism and exploitation, which lays the ground for an exposition of the Marxist take on globalization and imperialism. The third section studies development issues as they feature in World System Theory (WST). The fourth and final section studies a more recent theory, that of Uneven and Combined Development.

MARX AND MARXISM

> Neither Marx, Lenin nor Stalin made any systematic contribution to international theory. (Wight 1995: 24)

Karl Marx's key works were written well before the discipline of IR was founded, and as a result there has been something of an awkward relationship between the 'core' of the discipline and Marxist and neo-Marxist agendas (tracked in Holsti 1985: 61–80). Realists in particular have been dismissive of Marx for overlooking the *real* dynamics of international politics: the struggle for power and security between sovereign political entities. IR theorists such as Martin Wight (see the quotation above) shared this criticism of the ontological positioning of Marxist work. As he saw it, 'it was too preoccupied with the economic aspects of human affairs to be regarded as a serious contribution to the field (Linklater 2013: 113). Marx's ideas did, however, inspire a range of Critical Theory in the 1980s (see next chapter) and at the same time instigated a renewed focus on states and markets in shaping international politics, encapsulated in the political economy approach. The 'triumph' of capitalism at the end of the Cold War might have sounded the death knell for Marxism, but this was more a feature of American IR scholarship than that in Europe, where left-leaning academic research in IR has always featured more prominently (ibid.: 114). As a result, Marx retains a distinctive place within the discipline and is particularly well suited to a critical analysis of oppression and exploitation in the era of globalization.

The two main works by Marx you will probably have heard of were both published in the nineteenth century: *The Communist Manifesto*, co-authored with Friedrich Engels, appeared in 1848 (see Marx and Engels 1998). The three volumes of *Capital* appeared in 1867, 1885 and 1894, respectively (see Marx 2008). In *Capital* Marx sought to explain the evolution of the capitalist system of economic production and to diagnose its ills. His normative goal was to bring about revolutionary change by highlighting what he considered to be the exploitation of the masses (what he called the 'proletariat') by a privileged few (the 'bourgeoisie'). To grasp the triangular relationship between Marx, the writers inspired by him and IR, it is helpful to bear in mind four features of this body of work:

1. **Capitalism is a 'system' in its own right.** We have seen the word 'system' used before by IR theorists. For instance, Neorealists use system level explanations to account for inter-state relations in an anarchic international system; Constructivists suggest that the international system is not something that exists 'out there', it is more 'in our heads', albeit no less 'real' for that. Marx saw in capitalism a different type of system altogether. In the dynamics of global capitalism in particular, he saw forces structuring state interactions which Realists and Liberals totally ignored. Within this system, capabilities and interests are not defined in raw power terms, as in Realist and Neorealist theory, but in terms of whether you are a member of the bourgeoisie (owning the means of production and creaming off the profits) or a member of the proletariat (selling your labour but not receiving in terms of

payment the full value for the labour you give). World System Theory used this terminology to explain IR in economic structuralist terms (see below).

2. **Economics as politics.** Marx held a materialist conception of history, whereby economic development and the social relations governing such development were effectively the motor of history (Rupert 2016: 130). Advances in technology change the nature of the productive process. This in turn this prompts changes in the means of production as producers try to get on board with new technology and make the most of their enhanced productive capacity. The quest for greater profits, especially when there is intense competition between firms in a marketplace, means the search for greater efficiency in the productive process. This can lead either to a sidelining of human labour or a less central place for it in production processes, with man/woman replaced by machine. Marxist writers not only see economics and politics as intertwined, as the one *necessarily* affects the other, they go further in seeing economics 'as the driving force of world politics' (Sterling-Folker 2006c: 200). It is primarily developments in the economic realm shape that shape the social arrangements and configurations we observe in contemporary political life. For Marxist writers, economic relations determine the content and conduct of domestic and international political action.

Note how Marxist writers change our view of what makes the subject matter of IR: from politics and security in a condition of anarchy to economic relations in a global capitalist system. It represents a compelling shift of ontology and a new dimension to the 'problem of the subject'.

---

3. **Normative theory.** Marxist writers tend quite openly to blend elements of positivism with a normative agenda. In tracing the development of the capitalist system, Marx was also thinking through how that system could be changed. 'Marx was not an impartial commentator but hoped that by increasing our understanding of capitalism it would be easier ultimately to overthrow the system' (Smith et al. 2011: 17). He wanted to benefit the oppressed masses of workers whom he felt were not being paid sufficiently for the labour they sold to the owners of the factories where they worked. This was a view of security and insecurity pitched at a very local level: the level of individual humans themselves. Marxist writers are generally quite comfortable about putting forward agendas for change – they write with a purpose.

4. **Disciplinary development.** Marxist ideas became popular within the discipline during the 1970s, when even the domination over the system by the bipolar stand-off between 'East' and 'West' could not mask some highly divisive goings on at the systemic level. James Rosenau's 'International Studies in a Transnational World' provides an excellent illustration of the rather confused state of affairs at this time: 'Virtually each day's news seems filled with surprises, with a bewildering array of developments that do not seem to fit into any of the explanatory niches on which we have long relied' (1976: 2). Economic issues such as the Arab oil embargo and out-of-control levels of inflation were high on this list of systemically significant developments. Moreover, the international monetary system 'teetered near collapse', challenging the power of

governments to mobilize state resources and build alliances in the face of huge and unpredictable capital flows across national boundaries. The post-2008 global financial meltdown has come to be seen in exactly this light, as a stimulus to work in IRT that takes seriously the political consequences (for states and the 'system' of multilateral organizations) of the economic choices of influential non-state actors.

The key point is that Marx's economic focus is starkly at odds with the ideas and goals of mainstream IRT as I have presented its development after 1919. Conflict for Marxist writers is not principally the product of a security dilemma or other problems such as arms racing between states operating in an anarchic international arena; rather, it is the product of cross-state rivalry within the system of capitalism itself. Security of a quite different kind is at work – economic security. Capitalism entails an endless search for new markets and resources. Capitalist firms can inadvertently draw states into conflict as they trawl the globe looking for new ways to expand their profit margins. This was the theme of Lenin's work and it also has loud echoes in the Marxist interpretation of globalization. We will begin with Lenin.

Lenin on capitalism and imperialism

Vladimir Lenin was a politician and political theorist who led the Russian Republic and the Soviet Union, as it became, from 1917–24. This period saw the imposition of Communism on the Russian state in accordance with Lenin's Marxist ideological leanings. His writings from the time give an excellent insight into Marxist interpretations of capitalism and its failings. Lenin's novel spin was to link capitalism to imperialism, and our focus here is on the logic of his argument as presented in his 1916 book, *Imperialism: The Highest Stage of Capitalism*. All references in what follows are to Lenin (2010), unless otherwise stated.

The 'IR' element of this book is abundantly clear in the preface to the Russian edition, where Lenin explained his reasons for putting pen to paper:

> I trust that this pamphlet will help the reader to understand the fundamental economic question, *viz.*, the question of the economic essence of imperialism, for unless this is studied, it will be impossible to understand and appraise modern war and modern politics.

For Lenin the driver of international affairs was the economics of capitalism and imperialism, and he devoted his book to exegesis of this connection.

For Liberals writing in Lenin's time, global free trade was seen as a source of peace and stability in the international system. Realists at this time were very much on the back foot, as it were, because the conditions of the peace after the First World War had yet to be settled, and the international system had yet to start degenerating into the scenes that led to the Second World War. Lenin's 'vision' of IR was very, very different from both these 'Western' traditions, indicating that writers do tend to 'see' IR through different lenses for all sorts of reasons, not least geography and their formative political experiences.

Lenin began with an account of industrial growth and the concentration of production in the hands of fewer and fewer, and larger and larger, companies. His data was taken from economic statistics in the USA, Britain, Germany, France and the Netherlands. He called this concentration of production 'the rise of monopolies' and considered it 'a general and fundamental law of the present stage of development of capitalism' (p. 19). He dated this rise in monopoly capitalism to the beginning of the twentieth century, when: 'Cartels became one of the foundations of economic life. Capitalism has been transformed into imperialism' (p. 21). Note that at this stage Lenin was identifying the sources of domestic imperialism, that is to say, imperialism by capitalists operating within nation-state borders, as large firms squeeze out smaller competitors and hoover up their markets and customers. In the second chapter, Lenin charted the complicity of banks and bankers with this process, with financial institutions themselves starting to become concentrated monopolies: 'Thus, the beginning of the twentieth century marks the turning point from the old capitalism to the new, from the domination of capital in general to the domination of finance capital' (p. 53). At this point, however, capitalism was still entrenching its monopolistic tendencies *within* nation-states.

At this point Lenin shifted focus to the global arena, showing how, by 1910, four countries (the Britain, the USA, France and Germany, in that order) owned 80 per cent of the world's finance capital: 'Thus, in one way or another, nearly the whole world is more or less the debtor to and tributary of these four international banker countries, the "four pillars" of world finance capital' (p. 73). Chapter 4 linked the monopolistic tendencies of capital within nation-states to its export abroad, to begin to account for Western imperialism. The 'super-abundance' of capital, he suggested, needed an outlet beyond the restrictive confines of these countries' borders. There was also something in the nature of capital and the capitalistic enterprise that would restrict surplus value from being put to good use socially: 'As long as capital remains what it is, surplus capital will never be utilized for the purpose of raising the standard of the living of the masses.' Why not? Because 'this would mean a decline in profits for the capitalists'. Instead, 'it will be used for the purpose of increasing those profits by exporting capital abroad to the backward countries' (p. 75). In this way, Western capital began to infiltrate and grab a hold over other countries internationally, tying them into its vice-like grip: 'finance capital has also led to the *actual* division of the world' (p. 80; original emphasis).

In the fifth chapter Lenin outlined the division of the world by the 'core' capitalist countries (as they would later be termed in the World System model explained below). He refuted Liberal economic theory, that the internationalization of capital would 'give the hope of peace among nations under capitalism' as 'absurd' (p. 90). Instead, he quoted politicians such as Britain's Cecil Rhodes, a mining magnate active in South African politics and Prime Minister of the Cape Colony, 1890–96. In a speech in 1895, Rhodes declared that potential problems at home could be solved by looking abroad:

My cherished idea is for a solution to the social problem … we colonial statesmen must acquire new lands to settle the surplus population, to provide new markets for the goods produced by them in the factories and the mines. The Empire, as I have always said, is a bread and butter question. If you want to avoid a civil war you must become imperialists. (Rhodes, quoted by Lenin on p. 97)

Such was the link that Lenin drew between monopoly capitalism, the concentration of ownership of industry and the banks, and state-fostered imperialism. The later chapters of the books assessed how this system might rot from within: 'imperialism is leading to annexation, to increased national oppression, and, consequently, to increasing resistance' (p. 154). This was a powerful assessment of the drivers of international politics in and around the time of the First World War. Its echoes today are to be found in Marxist understandings of globalization, so we will deal with them next.

GLOBALIZATION OR IMPERIALISM?

Whole books and articles have been dedicated to trying to define the phenomenon of 'globalization', and we are still no nearer a definitive account (Scholte 2008). To give a further indication of the problems that surround the term, in 2004 a new journal was launched, *Globalizations*, the pluralization in the title being suggestive of the many complex interdisciplinary understandings and explosion of definitions that have developed around this signifier (Rosenau 2004). Some have pointed out the pitfalls of the generalizations implied by the term, especially in its singular form. For an excellent discussion of how the term has been dealt with – badly – by IR, written from a Marxist perspective, see the work of Rosenberg (2000: Part 1, and 2005). He has entered into a productive debate with Jan Scholte on the merits of globalization theory (see Scholte 2005). This is not the place to weigh up the arguments on each side of a very wide-ranging empirical and metatheoretical debate, but it is worth reflecting on the purchase the term has come to have, and how it has been 'read' by Marxist theorists.

Globalization has many dimensions: political, economic, technological, social and cultural are just the main ones that occur when we consider the ways in which the world is said to be shrinking under the effects of globalization. The term 'global village' has been coined to describe the cumulative effects of globalization (McLuhan and Powers 1989). The apparent paradox of combining reference to the entire globe with something as small as a village helps highlight the idea that today we know much more about events going on around the world than we did previously. We are more influenced by global events, we experience them more intensely, and have greater capacity for our actions and ideas to be carried around the globe. This is due to a lethal cocktail of: 24-hours-a-day news media; new technologies such as portable satellite systems and mobile phones which bring us pictures from trouble spots all over the globe; and internet and social media which encourage instant reaction to breaking stories.

In July 2010 it was found that, with some 500 million members, if Facebook was a nation it would have been the third largest in the world (*The Economist* 2010). Within five years, in January 2015, Facebook had grown to be the most populous 'nation', with 1.39 billion users logging on – more than the population of China, the largest country on Earth (*The Huffington Post* 2015). The microblogging site Twitter does not have anywhere near the same volume of users as Facebook, but it is growing fast. In 2010 it had 30 million active users per quarter. By the second quarter of 2016 the figure was well over 300 million: a tenfold increase in active user numbers (Statista 2016). It is rare, now, to go a whole day without hearing immediate Twitter reactions to political, cultural and sports stories from some elite, celebrity or member of the pubic, and their reactions can, in turn, shape the news agenda on particular issues. In the good old days, letters to opinion-forming newspapers such as *The Times* or *Washington Post* might have performed this function – much, much more slowly.

· ·

 TAKING IT FURTHER

Bankers and the global financial crisis

Why did the 2008 global financial crisis erupt? A very large share of the blame went to the bankers, along with the politicians who let them get away with light-touch regulation on their loan activities, and on how many liquid assets (hard cash) they held in reserve to fund losses. As the movie *The Big Short* (2015) so eloquently explained, a particular problem was mortgage lending to people who had bad credit histories, or who had borrowed way over what they could afford to repay if the debt was called in. The bundling-up of bad debts as financially viable new assets was what helped the contagion in this 'housing bubble' to spread around the system once the first payments defaulted. It led to the collapse of some banks, such as Lehman Brothers in the USA. Meanwhile countries such as the UK bailed out banks such as Northern Rock and Royal Bank of Scotland. Wrapped up in the blame-game came accusations that capitalism itself was at fault, as a series of huge, background structural factors ate away at the credibility of the system. Structuralist explanations of this kind only take us so far, however, for capitalism as a system, and the associated phenomenon of globalization, are human-made. They unfold on the back of decisions taken by humans as individuals, working in collectivities, whether these be in big corporations, states or international institutions. Capitalism and globalization came from somewhere; they were not 'given' to the world by some exogenous force.

An interesting take on the structure–agency debate in IR is provided by the debate that has emerged since the financial crisis about the role of individual bankers themselves in the disaster that befell the global economy. Clive Boddy wrote a short theoretical article, floating the hypothesis that there was a certain 'psychopathy' among individuals drawn to banking: 'Psychopaths are the 1% of people who have no conscience or empathy and who do not care for anyone other than themselves' (2011: 256). It follows that a corporate psychopath is someone who works and operates in an organization such as a bank. They are usually some combination of liar, cheat, bully 'and have a negative impact on many areas of organizational effectiveness' (ibid.: 256). They exert powerful agency but in negative ways. Boddy's Corporate Psychopaths Theory of the Global Financial Crisis is that a host of corporate psychopaths were able rise to power in big financial organizations: their 'single-minded pursuit of their own self-enrichment and self-aggrandizement to the exclusion of all other considerations has led to the abandonment of the old-fashioned concept of noblesse oblige, equality, fairness, or any real notion of corporate social responsibility' (ibid.: 257; we return to corporate social responsibility in Chapter 14 on Green International Theory). Enabled by globalization and light touch regulation and oversight, structural weaknesses in the system stopped holding these psychopaths in check, allowing 'greed unfettered by conscience' to turn into 'corporate fraud, financial misrepresentation, greed and misbehaviour' on a massive scale (ibid.: 258).

(Continued)

(Continued)

If proven, Boddy's theory would add an extremely novel dimension to the Marxist diagnosis of the ills of the capitalist system. The dystopian world Boddy depicts is of hyper-capitalism: capitalism gone (even) mad(der): an economic meltdown caused by a crisis of human values. Other writers such as André van Hoorn have put Boddy's theory to the test using a questionnaire designed to test financial workers' ethics and values, compared to people working in other sectors of the economy (van Hoorn 2015). His sober empirical assessment leads him to argue that there are only trivial differences between people in finance and other occupations, in terms of their ethics and values – the moral codes by which they live and work. Van Hoorn (ibid.: 266) concludes that, alluring as the narrative of the Corporate Psychopath Theory is, the global financial crisis was not caused by the dysfunctional values of people in finance. Nevertheless, they worked in sectors where the structures of regulation and accountability were too weak. It was the structures, not so much the agency, that help explain the financial crisis. Marxists can take much from this debate, as can all students of IR, because it picks up many important themes in IR: structure and agency, levels of analysis, behavioural norms, institutional set-ups, and how to study the decisions of the people who lead (and follow in) states, markets and foreign policy decision-making (see, for instance, Teschke and Cemgil 2014).

· ·

Thankfully we only need to consider here the economic implications of globalization (the different dimensions are debated in Sachs 1998). For some, globalization is an inevitability, a phenomenon that modern states have to adapt to and take advantage of, but also work *with*, to solve cross-border problems such as environmental degradation, the global financial crisis, international terrorism and cyber-terrorism. As former British Prime Minister Tony Blair put it in a speech to the Foreign Policy Centre in March 2006, 'the defining characteristic of today's world is its interdependence', but while economic globalization is now in its 'mature' phase the politics of globalization are lagging behind. 'Globalisation is a fact … This is the age of the inter-connected. We all recognise this when it comes to economics, communication and culture. But the same applies to politics' (Blair 2006). For Neoliberals such as Blair and Barack Obama, who subscribed to the same thesis, globalization exists, it is real, we can see and feel its effects and we can choose to embrace and work with them or ignore them. Obama said in a press conference in June 2016 that globalization is 'here' and 'done', meaning it is an unarguable fact of international life that we all must accept. All we can do is work with what we have been left with (Naylor 2016).

Globalization is one of those politics and IR buzzwords. In any essay or exam question where it features you will need to show knowledge of its essentially contested meaning. Hanging your hat on a definition from an established source is the way to go in that situation.

Marxist writers have quite a different take on globalization. Where Blair and Obama see it as an essentially benign force posing challenges, yes, but also offering the hope of solutions, for Marxist writers, globalization is not something that happens to us but something we have created – and it is not a wholly beneficial enterprise. In a highly Constructivist take on things, a Marxist might argue that globalization is something that we in the West, or in WST terms, the 'core', have *authored*. Globalization in its economic guise has been driven by the spread of multinational corporations and cross-border financial transactions, all supported by an international financial and regulatory regime led by international organizations such as the International Monetary Fund (IMF) and the World Bank.

Marxists and Critical Theorists (on the latter, see the next chapter) make the point that globalization has 'intensified the instances and possibilities of "transnational harm", rendering nation states incapable of providing citizens with their basic needs of justice, social and physical security'. Clearly, write Vijay Mishra and Bob Hodge (2005: 398), looked at from a Postcolonial point of view, '"postmodern" globalization incorporates new forms of colonization …, which build on past practices, deployed by the usual suspects'. They might disagree on the solution but they agree on the problem. Marxists are pessimists about globalization whereas Neoliberals are, broadly, optimistic about it. To illustrate this point, let us take a look at three examples of how a Marxist might respond to Blair's globalization thesis.

Globalization is not new

Hearing policy-makers talk of globalization, we might labour under the impression that there was a beginning to it – some year or event (never defined) that marked the beginning of the process. A Marxist would ask: can we pinpoint the 'start' of globalization? No, because as with the contemporary unfolding of any long-term process, locating its origins is problematic. This is key, because, whereas policy-makers believing in globalization theory might want to present the era of globalization as 'new' or 'different' from previous eras, Marxists can place globalization in their longer story about the evolution of modern capitalism going back hundreds of years. Furthermore, since globalization has become a driver of domestic and foreign policies in many states, globalization is being used as the rationale for diminishing workers' rights as states seek to help their national businesses stay competitive. Capitalism in this view is a race to the bottom in terms of wages and working conditions.

Globalization is a new form of imperialism ('Westernization' universalized)

Noam Chomsky presents a damning indictment of the Neoliberal consensus on globalization by suggesting it is no more than a rhetorical smokescreen by the conglomeration of states and institutions that make up the privileged 'West': 'It is only the Third World that is to be subjected to the destructive forces of free market capitalism, so that it can be more efficiently robbed and exploited by the powerful' (1991). Just as the British, French, Dutch and other European states conquered empires by force (the same states identified by Lenin in his book, explored above), a Marxist take on contemporary military interventions by leading Western powers would be that these are expressions of imperialist exploitation by a different name (an interpretation critiqued in Scholte 2008: 1476–8). Postcolonial writers (about whom see Chapter 13 below) often join in the condemnation of the exploitative practices of globalization. Graham Huggan and Helen Tiffin, for example, argue that formerly colonized countries remain locked into 'European or Euro-American world views' under globalization. 'Just as colonies once provided the raw materials for European industrialization, post-independence states now frequently find themselves exploited by multinational companies (sometimes in league with corrupt post-independence politicians' (Huggan and Tiffin 2008: 2).

Just as critics argue that economic free trade doctrines are masks for economic exploitation of the periphery by core states, so interventions (superficially/rhetorically) for humanitarian reasons or to promote democracy can be read in the same way. Work on, amongst others, the Kosovo intervention of 1999 (Cafruny 2006) has astutely pointed out that energy security (keeping open oil and gas pipelines and flows of these vital natural resources from Russia, Central Asia and the Middle East) surely played a part in the decision to intervene in these regions. In fact, argues Cafruny, the Kosovo intervention was partly predicated on a long-established supposition by US and European policymakers that they needed to diversify their sources of oil supply to counter the challenge from Middle Eastern exporters and 'ensure continued dominance of international oil markets' (2006: 217). The War on Terror can be interpreted in the same way, as an attempt by America to make the world safe for its penetration by American companies, the idea being that 'The business of war is profitable' (Weigley 2013).

Which account of these interventions do you believe? Do we have to choose? Can we combine elements of the Marxist take on them with elements of the policy-makers' justification to generate a multi-causal explanation?

International organizations entrench institutionalized inequalities between states

Ngaire Woods well captures the Marxist take on international institutions such as the UN, the World Bank and the IMF, stating:

> Existing multilateral organizations are still hierarchically arranged. Their authority and effectiveness depend on the will and actions of their most powerful members and, as the most powerful states balance up the advantages of stronger and more effective institutions against possible losses in their own control and sovereignty, they repeatedly come down on the side of the latter. (1999: 9)

While ostensibly these bodies work to reduce poverty and enhance the integration of less developed states into the global economy, a Marxist views them quite differently: as covert agents helping to enmesh these states further into the exploitative structures of the capitalist system. Postcolonial writers in IRT ally with Marxists to make the same claim, that these bodies 'overwhelmingly benefit the wealthy' (Vasquez 2002: 191). They are all interested in the concept of 'fairness' and how power relations work in the international system to alleviate or entrench 'fairness' in global economic institutions. The World Trade Organization is another such organization that receives this treatment (see Dunoff 2003).

Contrary to the popular idea that globalization exists and that it is a benign trans-formative force shaping the modern world, you can see that Marxists take a different view. They interpret economic, political and military interventions by core states in periphery states as starkly at odds with the high sounding moral rhetoric about pre-venting humanitarian disaster and advancing liberal democratic ideals about which we hear so much. The globalization thesis, in the Marxist view, is severely open to interpretation because it is a 'concept' not a 'fact'. Perhaps the best summary of this viewpoint from the 'real world' of international relations came in the 1974 Cocoyoc Declaration, about which more in the next section. This extensive quotation from near the end of the document (Cocoyoc Declaration 1974) perfectly captures the Marxist critique of the complicity of states, markets and international institutions in keeping the have-nots in a position of having nothing to benefit the wealthy states and peoples in the international system:

> There is an international power structure that will resist moves in this direction. Its methods are well known: the purposive maintenance of the built-in bias of the existing international market mechanisms, other forms of economic manipulation, withdraw-ing or withholding credits, embargoes, economic sanctions, subversive of intelligence agencies, repression including torture, counter-insurgency operations, even full-scale intervention. To those contemplating the use of such methods we say: 'Hands-off. Leave countries to find their own road to a fuller life for their citizens.' To those who are the – sometimes unwilling – tools of such designs – scholars, businessmen, police, soldiers and many others – we would say: 'Refuse to be used for purposes of denying another nation the right to develop itself.' To the natural and social scientists, who help design the instruments of oppression we would say: 'the world needs your talents for constructive purposes, to develop new technologies that benefit man and do not harm the environment'.

The next chapter deals with international organizations and institution as tools of 'hegemony', so we will return to this theme later. Now, it is important to consider the global economic picture as seen in Marxist approaches to international relations, and the economics of those relations in particular.

WORLD SYSTEM THEORY

In October 1974 a UN group met in Cocoyoc, Mexico, to discuss economic development and the environment.

The concept of development is another essentially contested term that deserves careful unpacking. It usually comes with Liberal connotations of states moving in linear fashion to some satisfactory economic destination. However, there are definitions that alight on the human and social dimensions of development, including the distribution of power. These are informing current practices at UN level downward. For an overview of the definitional challenge see Myrdal (1974).

The resulting document, the Cocoyoc Declaration, is now drawn upon in histories of international action on sustainable development (and so is of relevance to the Green International Theory chapter later in this book). However, many of the passages in the document were given over to the need to create a more level international playing field for less developed nations in the context of a critique of Liberal development theory (defended in Stiglitz 1998). The Cocoyoc Declaration thus stands out as a great example of the fusion of international practices and academic debates: it drew attention to themes and issues that then become theorized by IR scholars around the world. All the references in the next two paragraphs are from the Cocoyoc Declaration (1974).

The global economic challenge was identified at the outset: 'The problem today is not primarily one of absolute physical shortage but of economic and social maldistribution and misuse; mankind's predicament is rooted primarily in economic and social structures and behaviour within and between countries.' It was not the quantity of available resources that was the issue, but the way in which those resources were *distributed* globally, and the social *structures* that shaped economic relations between some groups of states and other groups of states in the system. Uneven distribution, the Declaration continued, had been ingrained in the system during five centuries of colonial control, 'which concentrated economic power so overwhelmingly in the hands of a small group of nations'. Free market mechanisms and liberal free trade practices were doing nothing to remedy the problem of the allocation of resources to where they were most needed: some sort of redistribution mechanism was required. Moreover, the richer, more powerful nations were buying up poorer nations' raw materials, manufacturing goods with them, and selling the finished products back to those poorer nations at inflated prices. Marx and Lenin's theory of the surplus value of capital being used to create more profits for the rich was evidently in operation.

The Cocoyoc group observed a 'world market system which has continuously operated to increase the power and wealth of the rich and the relative deprivation of the poor'. However, this situation was not permanent. It was not a natural occurrence or an international given that would structure international relationships for time immemorial. It was made by humans and could be un-made by humans, being 'rooted not in unchangeable physical circumstance but in political relationships which can, of their very nature, undergo profound reversals and transformations'. The Declaration went on to explore three areas that needed rethinking if the planet's resources were to be used more effectively to cater for basic human needs: development; diverse challenges facing different states; and greater capacity for states, weaker and stronger, to determine their own futures. The Declaration followed with a series of proposals to remedy these ills.

We can easily spot the differences between the Cocoyoc Declaration and the work of scholars modelling unequal relations in the international system at this time. The most famous of these, arguably, is World System Theory (WST). Inspired by work on development theory and under-development in peripheral countries regions of the globe (Puntigliano and Appleqvist 2011), WST developed around the work of Immanuel Wallerstein, particularly his three-volume *The Modern World System* (Wallerstein 1974, 1980, 1989). Wallerstein put a new spin on the idea that state interactions are shaped by unseen systemic forces, his argument being that the system is not shaped by relative levels of material power but by the workings of the global capitalist economy. A state's

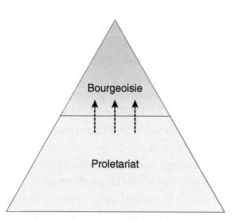

Figure 9   Marx's class system

behaviour in WST is shaped by the position it occupies in the global capitalist system, and it is this position that affects that state's 'capabilities, identities and interests' (Freyberg-Inan 2006: 225).

Remember Marx's idea that political life within states is defined by the fraught relations between the bourgeoisie (exploiters) and the proletariat (exploited masses) (Figure 9). In Marx's vision, wealth creation in the capitalist system flows from the proletariat to the bourgeoisie. In Figure 9, the darker the shade the wealthier the class, so here we see wealth concentrated in the hands of very few capitalists. It is also noteworthy that capital tends to reside in the hands of few in society at the expense of many, hence the pyramidal structure. Moving from the level of domestic society to the international level of the global capitalist system, states can be grouped into three categories which broadly map onto the class division Marx identified in the domestic arena (Figure 10).

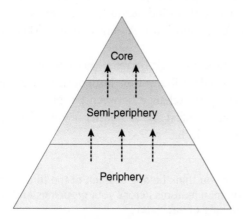

Figure 10   Marx's class system at the international level

In WST the classic Marx model has been adapted so that 'bourgeoisie' equates to 'core' states and 'proletariat' with 'periphery' states. The crucial difference, however, is the existence of a group of countries called the 'semi-periphery' which sits between the two others:

- **Core states** – These states are the most advanced in economic terms. They combine consumerist, mass market industries and technologically advanced agricultural production, the ownership of which resides in the hands of an 'indigenous bourgeoisie'. You might have heard these countries go by the name 'First World' – in economic terms they are 'the most prosperous and powerful' states in the international arena (Sterling-Folker 2006c: 202). The USA is the best example of a 'core' state today. As the leading Latin American development economist, Raúl Prebisch, put it: 'Indeed, the now advanced countries were, and have continued to be, centripetal [meaning things being attracted or sucked towards a centre] in the historical development process, with the periphery playing a subsidiary dependent role' (1981: 434). Prebisch's claim echoes the work on the structural inequalities built into international economic organizations described above, and presaged the Theory of Uneven and Combined Development to be covered below.

> It is important to note that the WST core–periphery model is dynamic: states can move between categories depending on changes to their political and economic structures over time.

- **Periphery states** – At the other end of the spectrum, we find states which export raw materials, defined as any unprocessed product used in the manufacturing process. Periphery states also sell unskilled labour to core producers (Sterling-Folker 2006c: 202). Core states manufacture goods using raw materials from the periphery and sell back the finished products to consumers in periphery states. The irony for periphery countries – what used to go by the name of the 'Third World' – is that they buy from core states goods made from the labour and materials they provided. Not only that, they buy them back at marked-up prices which are far in excess of what it would have cost to manufacture them indigenously, had they developed the capacity to do so. Poorer states in Africa and Latin America, such as Malawi, might today be considered periphery states.
- **Semi-periphery** – These states sit between the core and periphery, combining economic, political and social attributes from both of them (Sterling-Folker 2006c: 202). In the process of unequal exchange between periphery and core states, the semi-periphery states act out a crucial role as a buffer or zone. Today, semi-periphery states might include Brazil and India.

> Make a list of countries you think belong to each of the three categories set down in WST. What are the common features across your groupings and can you find statistics to support your positioning of each state?

In sum, WST provides us with a structuralist account of economic exploitation in the global arena. It helps us identify the position of various states within the system and theorizes the processes by which they have come to find themselves in that position.

WST offers a neat model of the workings of the global economic order often ignored or overlooked by even those theorists, such as Neoliberal institutionalists, who take seriously the economics of international relations. Marxist-inspired writers more often than not have a malign rather than benign view of ongoing developments in the international political economy, and this is well illustrated by the Marxist take on the phenomenon of 'globalization', as we saw earlier in the chapter.

TAKING IT FURTHER

The exploitation of child labour in periphery states

The term 'sweatshop' has come to mean a factory where unskilled labourers are paid a pittance for their labour, and where they are treated appallingly in terms of pay, hours, working conditions and rights (for example, to form unions). We often associate the term with multinational corporations that have their headquarters in core states but which profit from the cheap resources and labour located in periphery states (see, for example, Fuller 2006). The UN's International Labour Organization (ILO) counts sweatshops amongst its research into 'forced labour', which is defined as the situation that exists when someone is trapped in a job by coercion or deception, and which they cannot leave. The ILO judged in 2012 that there were some 21 million people in forced labour; over half of those are in the Asia-Pacific with Africa and Latin America also high on the list. Of these 21 million forced labourers, 18.7 million (90 per cent) were in forced labour in the private economy. This figure broke down as follows: sexual exploitation (4.5 million), with 14.2 million in economic activities such as agriculture, construction, manufacturing or domestic work (sometimes slavery). The remaining 2.2 million were in state-imposed forced labour, for example in prisons, or in work imposed by the state's military or rebel armed forces (ILO 2012).

Writers in the Marxist tradition are inspired by these harrowing statistics and stories supplied by agencies monitoring forced, exploitative, unfair or cheap labour to pen theory with purpose. They use them to help advance our understanding of the subtle and sometimes not so subtle forms of coercion of the poor and weak by the wealthy and strong. This is economic power operating within and across state borders. The existence of sweatshops and 'invisible' global networks such as human trafficking challenge the state-centric approach to IR at the 'core' of the discipline. Meanwhile, indicators of economic inequality and the like would seem to provide support for the WST understanding of IR: they are empirically visible manifestations of the core exploiting the periphery.

Addendum: sweatshops in the West?

In July 2016, a UK Parliament investigation into conditions facing workers at Sports Direct factories around the UK reported a 'disturbing picture'. The owner, Mike Ashley, admitted that workers had been paid below the national minimum wage, later agreeing to compensate the workers affected. The investigation also unearthed harrowing stories of worker mistreatment, including staff being penalized for taking short breaks to drink water and for taking time off work when ill. 'Allegations also surfaced of some workers being promised permanent contracts in exchange for sexual favours.' There were serious health and safety breaches, including one instance of a woman giving birth in a toilet (all from Commons Select

(Continued)

(Continued)

Committee 2016, which includes a link to the full report). Marxist and feminist scholars (see Chapter 11 below) would both be able to use this case study to highlight forms of economic and gender-based inequality and oppression. In the era of advanced globalization and the speedy movement of people and capital, one wonders how many similar cases may now come to light.

· ·

THE THEORY OF UNEVEN AND COMBINED DEVELOPMENT

The Theory of Uneven and Combined Development (U&CD) is an attempt by Marxist writers to theorize 'the international' using sociological accounts of human development and world history. It therefore attempts to go beyond 'classic' World System Theory and is also a powerful critique of Realist understandings of the international system. U&CD is also in dialogue with the historical sociology of the English School, with writers such as Barry Buzan and Richard Little name-checked throughout the writings of the leading U&CD theorist, Justin Rosenberg (2010). U&CD is complex and alluring; this section will try outline Rosenberg's international theory, which brings classic Marxist themes right back into focus for the student of IR.

U&CD attempts to answer a series of questions that test all theoretical traditions in IR: 'why *are* there many societies?' What feature(s) of social development account for this outcome and, therefore, all the phenomena we construe as 'international'? (Rosenberg 2010: 166, original emphasis, and 2013: 191). Marxist theories have had a go at this, remarks Rosenberg, but none has yet satisfactorily come up with a convincing answer. To address this deficiency Rosenberg (2010) has developed a multi-level model of development and international relations, finding that the weaknesses in Marxist arguments at levels 1 and 2 necessitate the theorization of a new level 3:

1. **Level 1 – External factors:** 'Dynamics of political multiplicity over-determine processes of uneven and combined development *from without*' (Rosenberg 2010: 167, his emphasis). This is Leon Trotsky's investigation of the historical spread of capitalist industrialization. Trotsky's case study was nineteenth-century Russian development. Trotsky asked why Russia had apparently taken a different path economically and politically, post-industrialization, from countries such as England, France and Germany (ibid. 2013: 195–201). He pointed to factors such as levels of development, types of society, size of territory, population and historical experience as having moulded countries' interactions in a world of separate powers. 'At no point, however, does this fact of political multiplicity itself become the object of analysis: it is not itself being explained by unnevenness' (ibid. 2010: 168). This process of theorizing begins at Level 2.
2. **Level 2 – Intrinsic factors:** 'Political multiplicity, being perennial, is an internal (but untheorized) *aspect* of uneven and combined development' (ibid.: 167, his emphasis). At this level, political multiplicity is not so much an external influence on uneven development but a property of it. It is well established that human

societies have always developed at uneven rates. This is the case *within* societies as well as *between* them, yet multiplicity within societies does not always lead to their fragmentation. What is it that links uneven development and multiplicity *among* societies? (ibid.: 169–70). Delving deeper, into level 3, might well provide the answer.

3. **Level 3 – Emergent factors:** 'Political multiplicity *arises from* the uneven and combined quality of social development' (ibid.: 167, his emphasis). This level has turned the level 1 explanation on its head: different rates of development are now the prior explanation for political separation among the units – states – in the international system. It also gets beyond the level 2 assumption that political multiplicity is a permanent feature of uneven development, but one that is left unexplained.

At this point Rosenberg turns to the work of Buzan and Little to elaborate level 3. They argue that uneven development has manifold implications for our understanding of IR and global history. It means that international systems will contain differentiated units; it is a stock feature of world economies; it is bound up with centre–periphery process formations; and it is a more general feature of the historical process: 'History does not move at the same speed all across the planet' (Rosenberg 2010: 172, summarizing and then quoting Buzan and Little). However, instead of attributing political multiplicity to uneven development – as does Rosenberg – Buzan and Little swing the other way and explain it via social differentiation. As human societies transitioned from small hunter-gathering bands into stratified communities structured by hierarchical power relations, accompanied by greater self-reliance and the acquisition of stable or relatively stable territories, so the basic need to interact with other communities diminished. The acquisition of material power and security also became more commonplace (Rosenberg 2010: 174). Thus, greater vertical stratification within societies seemed to explain the growing divisions between them, when these low level political units formed into states. Given this convincing depiction of the emergence of political multiplicity in the international system, what scope is left to bring Uneven and Combined Development into the picture?

The first step is to redefine the concept of development in Marxist terms. Rosenberg reminds us that Marx described humans' relationship with nature as foundational: it initially provides the means of subsistence for humans and in turn nature ends up put to the service of human needs (initially basic needs; in many cases, later, capitalist consumer wants) as societies develop new technologies of production. Human history unfolds in this view as a series of generations inheriting and taking on social and natural relations from the past. Each generation widens and deepens 'the productive interaction with nature' in the name of mobilizing social power (Rosenberg 2010: 179).

The second step is to recognize that the natural world, in those early years as humanity spreads out from its original home in East Africa, is 'the largest single source of uneven development': climate, topography and ecology all pay a part in this variability globally. The process of peopling the Earth was intrinsically founded on various forms of adaptation to social and ecological conditions. The 'combined' element refers to the trading and human relationships that developed between the different groups of humans, with adaptation to unevenly distributed resources being the motor of these exchanges (ibid.: 180).

The third step is to show how the theory of U&CD can explain political multiplicity better than Realist and English School formulations. If so, it would be a true theory of international politics in which the realm of the international is defined sociologically as 'that dimension of social reality which arises specifically from the co-existence within it of more than one society' (Rosenberg 2013: 185). Rosenberg stresses that uneven development alone cannot explain political multiplicity. The crucial addition in the construction of the international is that of the 'combined' element of geopolitical pressure (ibid.: 196): U&CD becomes both enduring feature and source of 'the international' (ibid. 2010: 186–7). In making this move Rosenberg sets down a uniquely Marxist take on anarchy as the product both of Neorealism's geopolitics and classical Marxism's take on the the dynamics of social and human development (ibid. 2013: 187): the nature of society becomes the grounding explanation for the existence of 'the international' as a social fact (ibid.: 193).

Rosenberg goes on to demonstrate how we can use the theoretical tools of U&CD to explain big issues in IR, a good example being his examination of the First World War (ibid.: 205–24). He first of all suggests that the century prior to the outbreak of war in 1914 'was heavily shaped by the historical unevenness of capitalist industrialization as a global process'; second, that the history of Germany in this period was shaped by the challenges resulting from Trotsky's 'combined development'; and third, that the proximate causes of the Great War lay in 'German fears and ambitions' that arose 'organically within the process of U&CD we have been reconstructing' (ibid.: 207–8). This same theory could 'travel' to other cases of war and conflict, and thus presents a distinctly Marxist theory of war in IR that accounts for system *and* unit level features of what makes things 'tick' in the realm of the 'international'. At a time when IR is, apparently, going through a period of crisis or uncertainty about its goals and methods of study, Rosenberg (2016) believes that U&CD could breathe new life into the discipline. It can remove it from the straight jacket of Political Science *and* provide it with a 'big idea' that travels beyond its borders.

QUESTIONS TO PONDER

'Can Marxist texts provide a valid theoretical intervention in IR when they are so obviously "positioned"?'

The fundamental issue raised by this question is one of theoretical validity, which we discussed in Part I of this book. There are many ways to judge the quality of a theory: it needs to be reliable, to be evidentially sound, to be testable and subject to falsification, and perhaps to have predictive capabilities. One way to think through this question might therefore be to set out the basic Marxist position with reference to key exponents such as those discussed above, or others you read about on your course. The better answers will challenge the assumption that there is one coherent 'Marxist' tradition by making clear the variety of agendas pursued by different writers influenced by Marxist thought: some are more positivist and attempt to be more 'scientific' than others. Wide reading and preparation will alert you to the competing styles within this broad church.

The question is also cueing you to think about the word 'positioned'. Any word in quotation marks in an essay or exam question needs careful attention somewhere in your response. Think about what it means to say that a theory is 'positioned' – do you think a theory can ever be anything other than 'positioned'? However much we might aim to be scientific and objective, can we really be so? If Marx and writers inspired by him openly admit to wanting to overthrow (or challenge) the 'established order' does that make them any more positioned than theorists who claim not to be positioned and just to be looking at 'the facts'?

'Is Rosenberg's theory of Uneven and Combined Development a genuine theory of "the international"?'

Rosenberg's work is a novel addition to IRT and contains within it a lot of food for thought, empirically, theoretically and metatheoretically. His 2016 article is particularly strong on the latter because it has been written to address the perceived crisis in IR as a discipline of inquiry, and to question the view of writers such as Dan Reiter (2015), who suggests that we could leave IR behind as a subfield of Political Science.

Your first task is to explain the theory of U&CD. Familiarity with Rosenberg's work will obviously be essential. You could theme your discussion around the ideas of 'uneven' and 'combined development' separately so that the marker is clear you have understood what Rosenberg is getting at. If you can summarize his work in the context of Marxist readings of the social basis of world history – and the effects of capitalist industrialization on societies – then you will confirm that you appreciate the theoretical tradition within which Rosenberg works.

This is a metatheoretical question and requires metatheoretical speculation in your answer. Rosenberg set his theory up as a refinement of, and challenge to, the work of Neorealists such as Kenneth Waltz. Hence, you need to pay special attention to the portions of his books and articles dealing with the requirements of a genuine theory of the 'international', and how U&CD meets those requirements. In several places in his oeuvre, Rosenberg explains the deficiencies of Neorealist theory and how U&CD can fill in the gaps. He reflects at length on the novelties provided by U&CD and how it meets Waltz's criteria for a 'proper' theory of IR. You will need to run your answer through with a central argument, by taking and defending a position on whether or not you think U&CD does indeed meet these criteria.

REFERENCES TO MORE INFORMATION

Marx, K. (2008) *Capital: A New Abridgement*. Oxford: Oxford University Press.
Marx's works have been published and reprinted many times over and you can find books containing the full text and abridged versions. The first volume of *Capital* is probably the best known, so the above text is very useful, containing almost all of Volume 1 and extracts from Volume 3.

Di Marco, L.E. (ed.) (1972) *International Economics and Development: Essays in Honour of Raúl Prebisch*. New York: Academic Press.

Cox, R.W. (1987) *Production, Power and World Order: Social Forces in the Making of History*. New York: Columbia University Press.
We visit Cox's work in the Critical Theory chapter, next in this book.

Teschke, B. (2009) *The Myth of 1648: Class, Geopolitics, and the Making of Modern International Relations*, 2nd edn. London: Verso.
Argues that the modern states system was moulded by more than national rivalry; we can only account for it successfully if we include class conflict and economic development. It thus compliments the Theory of U&CD covered in this chapter.

Burbach, R. (2001) *Globalization and Postmodern Politics: From Zapatistas to High-Tech Robber Barons*. London: Pluto Press.
Part 1 is especially recommended because it sets out Neo-Marxist interpretations and responses to globalization.

Bieler, A. and Morton, A.D. 'Poststructuralism and the Randomisation of History', in C. Moore and C. Farrands (eds) *International Relations and Philosophy: Interpretive Dialogues*. London: Routledge, pp. 157–71.
Callinicos, A. (2002) 'Marxism and Global Governance', in D. Held and A. McGrew (eds) *Governing Globalization: Power, Authority and Global Governance*. Cambridge: Polity, pp. 249–66.
Davidson N. (2016) *Nation-States: Consciousness and Competition*. London: Haymarket Books.
Kubálková, V. and Cruickshank, A.A. (1980) *Marxism–Leninism and the Theory of International Relations*. London: Routledge.
Obama, B. (2008) Speech on globalization, www.youtube.com/watch?v=7owMXrLu2d8 (accessed 9 August 2016).
van der Pijl, K. (1998) *Transnational Classes and International Relations*. London: Routledge.

Bush, R., Johnston, G. and Coates, D. (eds) (1987) *The World Order: Socialist Perspectives*. Cambridge: Polity.
See the chapter by Ankie Hoogvelt, which gives empirical support to claims for the existence of a 'world capitalist system'. Hoogvelt expanded and updated this thesis in A. Hoogvelt (1997) *Globalisation and the Postcolonial World*. London: Macmillan.

Aronowitz, A. and Gauntney, H. (eds) (2003) *Implicating Empire: Globalization and Resistance in the 21st Century World Order*. New York: Center for the Study of Culture, Technology and Work, Graduate School and University Center of the City University New York.
Gill, S. (ed.) (2015) *Critical Perspectives on the Crisis of Global Governance: Reimagining the Future*. Basingstoke: Palgrave Macmillan.

On Dependency Theory and World System Theory:

Sens, A. (2012) 'Dependency Theory', www.youtube.com/watch?v=JN6LlMY2ApQ& feature=related (accessed 9 August 2016).
A good overview with reference to World System Theory and Neo-Marxism.

Kontext TV (2015) Interview, 'Immanuel Wallerstein: The Global Systemic Crisis and the Struggle for a Post-Capitalist World', 8 June, www.youtube.com/watch?v=riK3dl-gusrI (accessed 9 August 2016).

Wallerstein, I. (2004) *World-Systems Analysis: An Introduction*. Durham, NC: Duke University Press.
An updated version of WST, giving you the nuts and bolts of the theory and its application today. Will save you ploughing through the lengthy and densely written historical material in the original three volumes!

Chang, H. (2003) 'Kicking Away the Ladder – Globalization and Economic Development in Historical Perspective', in J. Michie (ed.) *The Handbook of Globalization*. Cheltenham: Edward Elgar, pp. 385–94.

Dykema, E.R. (1986) 'No View without a Viewpoint: Gunnar Myrdal', *World Development*, 14(2): 147–63.
On the thoughts of one of the foremost development economists, also explores metatheoretical issues.

Axford, B. (1995) *The Global System: Economics, Politics and Culture*. Cambridge: Polity.
See Chapter 2 on Marxism, Imperialism and Wallerstein's World System Theory.

Jenkins, R. (1970) *Exploitation: The World Power Structure and the Inequality of Nations*. London: MacGibbon and Kee.

On Uneven and Combined Development:

D'Costa, A.P. (2003) 'Uneven and Combined Development: Understanding India's Software Exports', *World Development*, 31(1): 211–26.
Fouad, M. (2015) 'Reframing Development Theory: The Significance of the Idea of Uneven and Combined Development', *Theory and Society*, 44(5): 471–97.
Glenn, J. (2012) 'Uneven and Combined Development: A Fusion of Marxism and Structural Realism', *Cambridge Review of International Affairs*, 25(1): 75–95.
Green, J. (2012) 'Uneven and Combined Development and the Anglo-German Prelude to World War I', *European Journal of International Relations*, 18(2): 345–68.
Kiely, R. (2012) 'Spatial Hierarchy and/or Contemporary Geopolitics: What Can and Can't Uneven and Combined Development Explain?', *Cambridge Review of International Affairs*, 25(2): 231–48.

10

CRITICAL THEORY

Key terms

- Capitalism
- Communicative action
- Emancipation
- Hegemony

- History
- Legitimacy
- Order
- State

Critical Theory (CT) is closely allied to the Marxist approaches we explored in the previous chapter. It is also interesting in that it has an affinity with some of the poststructuralist approaches we study later in the book, as well as the Constructivist sensibility we covered in Chapter 8. All in all, CT is difficult to 'place' as a self-contained theory about IR, because in both its scope and its methods it transcends many of the other theories of IR. Here is a flavour of the problems IR theorists have experienced 'placing' CT:

- Mark Rupert identifies CT so strongly with Marxism that they are covered in the same book chapter (Rupert 2007).
- Sterling-Folker (2006d) puts CT nearer the poststructuralist end of the spectrum and includes it in a chapter with that approach to IR.
- Hutchings (1999: 88) helpfully suggests that we use CT in the singular to refer to the Marxist and/or neo-Marxist variant explored in this chapter, but reminds us that it can be used to cover any 'non-orthodox' theoretical perspective. This is why CT also goes by the name 'International Political Theory' because its methods can be used to study international politics and social and political theory (that is, theory of the state) more generally.

Summing up, Hutchings observes that that the terminology used to refer to this array of critical perspectives 'can be somewhat confusing' (1999: 88, note 3). You will have to be careful in essays and exam answers to state exactly what you mean by CT and how you see it relating to other positivist and normative theories of IR.

This chapter begins by introducing you to the origins of CT. For simplicity I have labelled this 'First-generation' CT. We then study 'Second-generation' CT in the form of Jürgen Habermas. Finally, the chapter discusses 'Third-generation' CT in the work of Robert Cox and Andrew Linklater. This band of writers has drawn core ideas and approaches from those First- and Second-generation thinkers into IR in a much more thoroughgoing way.

INTRODUCTION TO CT

To use the terminology we have been working with throughout this book, CT embodies an activist approach to the study of social affairs – it has a purpose to it. As Christopher Hobson writes (2011a: 1919): 'There is an onus to acknowledge the normative and political dimensions of our work, and to seriously consider how it may impact the world being studied.' Richard Devetak, quoting J. Maclean in the process, describes this impetus as follows: 'Behind critical international theory lies the conviction that "international relations could be other than it is at both the theoretical and practical levels"' (2001: 145). Here we see Constructivist thought shining through in the sentiment that things could be different if we think and act in ways that go against custom, convention and social norms. Like Marxism, feminism and poststructuralism, Devetak writes later in the chapter, CT concentrates on the concept of exclusions: how to spot them and how to overcome them. It 'sets itself the task of understanding the conditions under which emancipation in world politics is possible' (ibid.: 166).

First-generation CT

First-generation CT emerged in the years between the First and Second World Wars in Germany among the so-called Frankfurt School, which included diverse thinkers such as Max Horkheimer, Theodore Adorno, Walter Benjamin, Herbert Marcuse, Erich Fromm and Leo Lowenthal (see Peoples 2009: 7–18).

> Note how CT emerged in Germany at exactly the same time as E.H. Carr and others were expounding the virtues of Realist thought over Liberal thought in the UK. Why do you think CT took so long to make itself felt within the discipline of IR?

The aim of these writers was 'to salvage Marxist thought from its orthodox, political manifestations' (Sterling-Folker 2006d: 158), which restricted its emancipatory potential by centring the debate almost exclusively on economic relations. The concern for the Frankfurt School was, rather, 'to comprehend the central features of contemporary society by understanding its historical and social development and tracing contradictions in the present which may open up the possibility of transcending contemporary society and its in-built pathologies and forms of domination' (Devetak 2001: 146). Production, they argued, is more than a function of economic relations, it is inherently constructed and rooted societal relations. The echoes of this are to be found in Rosenberg's *Theory of Uneven and Combined Development*, which we discussed in the previous chapter. Ideas, intersubjective meanings, norms, institutions and social practices all influence the where, when and how of the production of material goods (Sinclair 1996: 9). In other words, the Frankfurt School wanted to use Marxist ideals, building upon them in new ways to challenge the view that the state was the natural or normal basis on which societies should be organized. In short, they interrogated how we have come to *think* about states as embodiments of social practice.

Second-generation CT: Habermas

Second-generation CT is associated with the work on 'legitimacy' by Jürgen Habermas. His logic is as follows (all from Lynch 2006: 183–4, unless otherwise stated):

1. There are two types of action: 'strategic' and 'communicative'.
2. Strategic action is undertaken to manipulate another person or state via 'threats, incentives or rhetoric'. For example, states use strategic action when they use military force to coerce (force an opponent to do something they might not otherwise do) or deter (prevent an opponent from doing something they might otherwise do). It is about 'influencing the other through the threat of sanctions or the prospect of gratification' (Crawford 2009: 188).
3. Communicative action occurs 'when actors set aside their self-interest, their relative power, and even their identities in order to seek truth – or at least consensus about the right course of action'. Communicative action 'is oriented to reaching understanding' and is more about consensus building than threats and promises (Neal 2009: 188). International institutions are the embodiment of communicative action in IR because they put the onus on understanding and reconciliation over recourse to war, aggression or the threat or use of force to settle international disputes.
4. Strategic action produces only temporary agreement because it is imposed by one actor on another. Communicative action, by contrast, is more legitimate because both actors have engaged in rational argument in an environment in which 'all affected actors are effectively able to speak and be heard'. When fully functioning, communicative action effected through international institutions can alter not only state calculations about their interests, but – in a Constructivist vein – their identities as international actors.

For Habermas, legitimacy for a specific action in the international arena only accrues if there has previously been a full and frank discussion by all actors likely to be affected by that course of action, for example a military intervention. In this forum it is not Realist power or force that wins the day, but 'the rationally more convincing argument' (Sterling-Folker 2006d: 164). According to Habermas, such 'ideal speech acts' are possible. They should in addition set the benchmark by which we judge states' behaviour because these should be based on *how* they reach decisions as well as what those decisions are. Habermas' work on communicative action is wide-ranging and complex.

It is a form of social theory that mixes philosophy, ethics, politics and linguistics to help us see the potential for a genuinely international public sphere to emerge. Critical Theorists do not just want to explain the world but to critique it and contribute to human betterment by encouraging open and equal exchanges between states and peoples about matters of contemporary importance. We shall now see how these variants of CT have been applied within IRT using the work of Cox and Linklater: our Third-generation thinkers.

CRITICAL THEORY IN IR: THIRD-GENERATION THINKERS

In different ways, both First- and Second-generation work has been felt within the study of IR for at least two decades. We will use the work of two scholars to illustrate this impact: first, Robert Cox, whose major intellectual debt is to Marxism, and, second, Andrew Linklater, who draws more on Habermas' theory of communicative action to chart the possibilities for us to transcend the Realist logic of the state system (Hutchings 1999: 66, 70).

Cox on societies, states and order

As described by Timothy Sinclair, Cox's research programme has two elements to it. On the one hand, he wants to understand how a relationship, institution or process operates on a day-to-day basis. On the other hand, Cox wants to understand the wider ramifications of the processes by which these things work, 'the contradictions and conflicts inherent in a social structure … and the nature and extent of structural change that is feasible' (Sinclair 1996: 8).

> Note here how Cox combines positivism (explaining the nature of a relationship/institution/ process) with a normative agenda (how can we alter that relationship/institution/process in the future?)

CT is all about understanding aspects of the prevailing order, but also takes a much broader perspective which sees that initially contemplated part as 'just one component' and seeks 'to understand the processes of change in which both parts and whole are involved'. It is a guide to 'strategic action for bringing about an alternative order' rather than a 'guide to tactical actions' that sustain the existing order (Cox 1996a: 89–90).

In his article 'Social Forces, States and World Order', published in 1981, Cox rethought what he saw as a narrow and overly deterministic Marxist conception of 'structure'. A structure, he suggests, does not wholly determine individual actions; people have more room for manoeuvre than that. Sure, individuals cannot ignore structures but they can resist and oppose them in ways that may bring about structural change. This is the

Constructivist element to Cox's thinking. What is a 'structure'? For Cox, 'Three categories of forces' interact in a structure (all from Cox 1996a: 98–9), the direction and strength of the interaction being dependent on the particular case at hand:

1. **Material capabilities** – The Marxist element: 'technological and organizational capabilities', including natural resources and the wealth that commands them.
2. **Ideas** – Two kinds. To begin with, we have intersubjective meanings that shape our views of the world at a fundamental level. These are historically 'durable' ideas such as the idea that the world is made up of states, which has become something of a social institution in the practice and study of IR. Then we have ideas about the world held by different groups within societies. Whereas the first set of ideas are common throughout a particular historical structure, the competing sets of ideas held by people in society continually hold out the prospect for change through the establishment of new structures or the transformation of existing structures.
3. **Institutions** – Are used to stabilize and perpetuate a social and political order. They are the embodiment of all the power relations that prevail at their point of origin; 'are particular amalgams of ideas and material power which in turn influence the development of ideas and material capabilities'. Institutions have social, ideational and material dimensions.

Having identified the components of a structure, Cox then goes on to set out his method of understanding 'historical structures' (ibid.: 100–1). The undertaking is to establish the nature of the sphere of human activity from a 'study of the historical situation to which it relates', and then to look within it for rival structures 'expressing alternative possibilities of development'. This is effected on three interrelated levels:

1. **Social forces** – Flowing from the organization of production and the production process.
2. **Forms of state** – As derived from a study of the nature of state/society at the particular historical juncture.
3. **World orders** – The make-up of forces that shape the interactions between states.

The connections between levels means that developments in one realm affect developments in the other two. The task of the Critical Theorist is to capture the totality of the historical process that led to the present configuration of structures on each of these levels, and then to ascertain the possibilities for change in the future arising from possible structural change within each level, as well as at the 'macro' world order level itself. Adapting Cox's own diagrams (ibid.: 98 and 101), we can present the gamut of relationships between and within the levels as shown in Figure 11.

Below, we see the flows of influence between the three spheres of activity Cox suggests we uncover using the method of historical structures. Within each level its component structures (ideas, institutions and material capabilities) are constantly interacting with each other. Given the circulation of ideas, institutions and material capabilities between the levels as well as within them, the possibilities for transformations in human activity are endless.

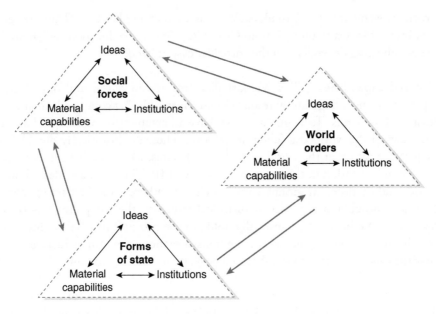

Figure 11   Cox's levels and their internal structures

Cox sets out an ambitious research programme which invites the student of IR to be a good positivist in order to be a good normative theorist. This raises interesting questions about the relationship between the two types of theory.

In the rest of the article, Cox shows how to apply his method of historical structures to understanding the global order prevailing under the **Pax Americana** (ibid.: 102–13). Rather than detail the moves he makes here I will leave you to read up on this and turn instead to his second key article, 'Gramsci, Hegemony and International Relations', first published in 1983, where he developed the concept of 'hegemony' in IR in two stages.

The first part of the article reconsidered the concept of hegemony using the work of Marxist thinker Antonio Gramsci (on whom see Gill 1993; Rupert 2009). Cox began by arguing that hegemony is not 'dominance of one country over others' or another word for 'imperialism' (1996b: 135). The first definition makes it too focused on state-on-state relations; the second is too far from the Gramscian meaning to make it relevant. The Gramscian reading of hegemony shifts our gaze from the 'power from above' approach of 'state power', which is rather naked, coercive and bluntly defined. Gramsci's approach to power sees it as 'bottom to top' dealing with the constructed consent, which 'the dominant group exercises through society'. Power in the Gramscian reading is evident in state actions but something more diffuse, operating at a superstructural level in 'civil society' (Gramsci, quoted in Ramakrishnan 1999: 143).

> Keep a list of different definitions of 'hegemony' as you come across them in your reading. They will be useful when it comes to writing essays and exam answers on global order and the manufacture of consent in the global political economy.

The only way we can understand the meaning of 'hegemony', Cox suggests, is to study when it is that periods of hegemony begin and end (and therefore when historical epochs can be called 'nonhegemonic'). He identified hegemony in international history as follows (1996b: 135–6):

- **1845–75:** *Hegemonic* – a world economy with Britain central and holding the balance of power in Europe (also see Milner 1998: 114).
- **1875–1945:** *Nonhegemonic* – reverse of Period 1. Many other powers such as Germany challenged British supremacy, two global wars erupted and global free trade collapsed.
- **1945–65:** *Hegemonic* – a world economy with the USA central to the promotion of order, but arguably not as stable as during Period 1 (see also Milner 1998: 114–15).
- **1965–83** (Cox's 'present' at the time he first published the article): *Nonhegemonic* – a fracturing of the US-centred period of hegemony after 1945.

The crux for Cox is that hegemonic periods are not based on naked exploitation or coercion of weak states by the strong, but are formed when the order created is 'universal in conception'. Moreover, hegemony is about more than state-on-state relations but about civil society operating 'on the world scale' (Cox 1996b: 136). The principal tool for the manufacturing of legitimacy behind the dominant mode of production is international organizations, which aid 'the process through which the institutions of hegemony and its ideology are developed' (ibid.: 137). International organizations facilitate hegemony in five ways (ibid.: 138–9):

1. **Rules** – International organizations make, enforce and change the rules, notably in areas of monetary policy and trade relations. The GATT, the IMF, the World Bank and the 'Big Four' global accountancy firms are such institutions operating today at the global level. At the regional level, the European Central Bank's (mis?)management of the Eurozone might be a further example.
2. **Products** – International organizations are generally set up by the state that establishes the hegemony, or at least they have its full support. This informal structure of influence might be seen in the role the USA plays in IMF decision-making and the role the Permanent-5 (the USA, Soviet Union, China, France and Britain) play in decision-making in the UN Security Council. In the IMF, for example, 61 per cent of the votes is held by 14 of the most powerful nations in the international system, while just 39 per cent of the votes are held by the remaining 172 members. Of those 14 most powerful members, the US share of the vote is a little under 20 per cent, the next most powerful members are Japan, Germany, the UK and France with 5–6 per cent each (BBC undated).

3. **Ideology** – International organizations set the parameters for policy discussions, legitimating the approaches and practices of the 'dominant social and economic forces'. The neoliberal agenda at the IMF could be one example of the ideological legitimation function performed by this organization, linking to Marxist critiques of international institutions noted in Chapter 9.
4. **Elites** – Sometimes also brought in from periphery states, they may wish to change the ideological *status quo* but end up co-opted by it. Thus, writes Cox (1996b: 139), 'Hegemony is like a pillow: it absorbs blows and sooner or later the would-be assailant will find it comfortable to rest upon.' Part of the process of creating a social class that transcends state borders, making the world safe for the spread of global capital.
5. **Absorption of counter-hegemonic ideas** – A bit like the co-option of elites, in that new ideas or approaches can be sucked into the organizational machinery and regurgitated as hegemony-supporting policies which say one thing but actually achieve another.

Try and bring Cox's model up to the present day by pinpointing periods of hegemony/nonhegemony since 1983. Where would the end of the Cold War fit in? How would you define the world today: hegemonic or nonhegemonic? Which state(s) or supra-state actor(s) are responsible (by accident or design) for promoting international order?

Through his work on social forces, order and hegemony, Cox invites us to get inside the workings of states in order to better understand their internal dynamics and, from an IR perspective, the interactions between them. Using his method of 'historical structures', Cox hopes to show that many of the things we take for granted as existing 'out there' in the world, like states themselves, are not social 'facts' but things we build ourselves. Even though Cox's greatest debt is to Marxism, we can see a strongly Constructivist turn to his thinking.

BEYOND REALISM AND MARXISM: LINKLATER

Linklater set out to write 'a critical international theory which endeavours to incorporate and yet to supersede the main achievements of realism and Marxism' (1990: 7). His rationale was that the three dominant traditions in IR at his time of writing had taken the discipline so far. However, none in isolation had really solved the conundrum of explaining interactions between states and the system(s) within which they operate. For Linklater (ibid.: 10–27) the flaws in each tradition were obvious:

- **Realism.** Focuses on the causes and consequences of war within an anarchical system but overlooks other important webs of relations between states, such as their economic relations. Lacks any sort of emancipatory agenda, seeing a system that perpetually reproduces itself in the context of power relations, from Thucydides to the present.
- **The English School (using the language of the time, Linklater referred to this as Rationalism).** Incorporates the best features of Realism in a larger framework that

accounts for order as well as conflict. In English School theory, world politics is driven by more than 'strategic competition' between states because solidarity can be engendered through states believing themselves to be members of an international society (ibid.: 15; see Chapter 7 in this book on pluralism and solidarism). However, it is Western-centric and ignores the possibility that global values and other sources of order and disorder might exist.

- **Marxism (or Revolutionism in the language of the day).** Sees conflict in the international system not as the outcome of nation-state insecurities but as the product of tensions within the international system of capitalist economic production which cuts across state borders. Revolutionism underplays military insecurity and non-economic sources of conflict – taking us back to the merits of Realism. Plus, it was dealt a huge blow by the end of the Cold War, which undermined the possibility of forming a 'socialist' world state system.

Having surveyed the state of the discipline, Linklater's conclusion was that elements of the first and the third approaches (from Realism: geopolitics; from Marxism: capitalism) are vital to a comprehensive understanding of IR. However, in isolation, neither tradition is sufficiently attentive to the fabric of global history to possess the explanatory force their proponents claim for them. As he put it, 'a critical theory of international relations can only be developed by moving beyond the realist and Marxist perspectives' (ibid.: 165).

> The 'world' Linklater sees is neither that of the Marxist nor the Realist. It is a more complex one in which states share the world stage with all sorts of other social forces that cut across state boundaries.

For Linklater, the 'critical' element of CT comes from its extension to our understanding of 'community' through a reinvigorated Marxism. This refined Marxism takes into account all the drivers of human norms and relations between societies rather than just class struggle (ibid.: 171). His broad concept of IR chimes in nicely with the general drive behind CT identified in this chapter. It takes old concepts and looks at them afresh; it invites us to de-naturalize things about the world we take for granted; and it holds out hopes for a new international ethics which would work for all in the world rather than a privileged few.

QUESTIONS TO PONDER

'Are we living in a period of US hegemony? Answer with reference to Cox's work on world order.'

There are at least two steps you will have to take to devise a convincing answer to this question. First of all, you have to define 'hegemony'. Knowledge of the two articles by Cox explored in this chapter will be important, but you can refer to any of his books/articles as long as they are relevant to the question set. Cox does a lot of the work for you in both dismissing populist definitions of 'hegemony' and then setting out his preferred definition.

The better answers will supplement Cox's work with a range of competing definitions of 'hegemony', particularly as it features in Realism. If you have made a checklist of these definitions, your task here should be fairly easy. Reading up on Gramsci and his followers would show sound acquaintance with the most nuanced theoretical formulation of 'hegemony' as 'informed consent': hegemony by stealth, as it were.

Having explained Cox's understanding of 'hegemony' you then have to judge whether the world today is hegemonic: and if so, who or what is the hegemon? You could do this in one of two ways. On the one hand, you could use Cox's analysis of the features that have made for hegemonic periods in history and those that have made for non-hegemonic periods, weighing up how the world today looks compared to these ideal type periods. On the other hand, you could avoid the past comparisons and go straight for analysis of the social/material/ideational/institutional forces you see prevalent in the world today and how far these constitute a form of hegemony. The danger is that you pick and choose the 'facts' to suit your argument, so pay attention to: the starting point of your selected period, its ideological underpinnings and the organizational fabric as expressed in networks of political and economic practices in international affairs. The best answers will stay close to Cox's idea that hegemony rests on consent more than coercion/force, so avoid offering accounts that major on US military action around the globe. Hegemony is a product of states, to a degree, but is something altogether more elusive than that in its Gramscian guise, with institutions and organizations co-opted to the cause.

'Do the differences between Critical Theorists undermine our ability to call it a "theory" of IR?'

This is a tricky question which invites you to reflect on the nature of CT as a form of inquiry into IR, and to investigate the nature of 'theory' more generally. Early on in the answer you will therefore have to scope your answer by paring it down to some basics. On CT, you might pick two or three writers as exemplary of the kinds of debates these theorists have among themselves. The same goes for theory: there are many perspectives on what this term means, so ground your work in a definition of theory that reflects what theory/ies should 'do' (the functions they should fulfil) in IR.

In terms of structure you could go for a yes/no approach. First of all, present the contention that fragmentation within a theoretical tradition undermines its claim to posit a coherent or unified approach to the study of IR (Neorealism is perhaps the most unified theory, to give one possible benchmark). Then look at the converse view that writers in the CT tradition share enough in common to mark them out from other theoretical traditions in IR. For instance, they are all inspired by Marx; they all look at non-state as well as state actors in IR; they take issue with Realism. The best answers will allude to the fact that all theoretical traditions have different wings to them and interplay with other theories. (See the debates about how to categorize Constructivist approaches and how they overlap, for example, with the English School. The same can be said for post-structuralism, Postcolonialism and feminism.) Overall, therefore, your argument will turn on your opinion of how much unity we can expect within *any* theory of IR. You could easily put the argument that many of what are called theories in IRT textbooks are not in fact theories at all but 'sensibilities' – loosely connected sets of propositions about what to study in IR (ontologically speaking) and how (methodologically). If you advance this perspective you will need to debate the conceptual relationship between words such as 'theory', 'tradition' and 'sensibility/mindset', so be prepared to work the grey cells using engagements with the philosophy of international theory.

REFERENCES TO MORE INFORMATION

Generally on CT:

Stanford Encyclopedia of Philosophy (2005) 'Critical Theory', http://plato.stanford.edu/ entries/criticaltheory/ (accessed 17 August 2016).
Excellent overview of CT together with an insight into the divisions between writers in this tradition.

Giddens, A. (1985) *A Contemporary Critique of Historical Materialism*, Vol. 2: *The Nation-State and Violence*. Cambridge: Polity.

Held, D. (1980) *Introduction to Critical Theory: Horkheimer to Habermas*. Berkeley, CA: University of California Press.

On CT in IRT:

Ashley, R.K. (1981) 'Political Realism and Human Interest', *International Studies Quarterly*, 25(2): 204–36.

Mittelman, J.H. (2004) 'What is Critical Globalization Studies?', *International Studies Perspectives*, 5(3): 219–30.

Neufeld, M. (1995) *The Restructuring of International Relations Theory*. Cambridge: Cambridge University Press.

Keyman, E.F. (1997) *Globalization, State, Identity/Difference: Toward a Critical Social Theory of International Relations*. Atlantic Highlands, NJ: Humanities Press.
Applies CT to the study of globalization and points ahead to the chapters in this book on feminism, postmodernism and Postcolonialism.

Wyn Jones, R. (ed.) (2001) *Critical Theory and World Politics*. Boulder, CO: Lynne Rienner.
A comprehensive collection that showcases the work of both Marxist and more Habermas-inclined theorists.

Worth, O. (2011) 'Recasting Gramsci in International Politics', *Review of International Studies*, 37(1): 373–92.

Review of International Studies (2005) 'Forum on Habermas', 31(1): 127–209.
Includes articles on the Frankfurt School as well as on Feminist Critical Theory.

Review of International Studies (2007) 'Critical International Relations Theory after 25 Years', Special Issue, 33.

YouTube (2007) 'Jürgen Habermas interview', 1 February, www.youtube.com/watch? v=jBl6ALNh18Q (accessed 17 August 2016).
Short piece in which Habermas sums up the key themes of his research and how they relate to contemporary world affairs.

11

FEMINISM

Key terms

- Gender
- Masculine/feminine
- Patriarchy

- Rationality
- Security
- Sovereignty

> [F]eminism defies premature attempts at closure. There are the political-theoretical versions: radical, Marxist, liberal, psychoanalytic feminisms and there are more abstract conceptual visions or versions including a feminist variant on structuralism, world systems theory, feminist standpoint theory … as well as feminist post-modern theories. (Elshtain 1995: 342–3)

Feminist scholarship came to the discipline of IR in and around the 1980s and 1990s. As with other normative theories we have covered in the last few chapters in this book, it was not IR that produced feminist scholarship. Feminists, rather, came into conversation with IRT as part of a wider social and intellectual movement from the 1960s that has had – and continues to have – a major impact across politics, academia and society (Young 2016: 3). In IR, feminist scholars have added a vital new term to the language of IR: gender. This has gone hand in hand, in many but not all cases, with a thoroughgoing reassessment of the ways in which IR scholars try to make sense of their subject matter, including such disciplinary fundamentals as war, security and anarchy. Feminist scholarship can also be referred to as gender theory.

Feminist scholars have therefore achieved two significant things in IRT. First, they have 'added' women where previously they were overlooked or invisible in the study of international affairs. But much more than this, second, they have reassessed definitions and re-thought methods of studying central IR concepts such as the state, security and sovereignty. As such, critical branches of feminism share affinities with 'thick' constructivism and poststructuralism in that they seek to go beyond hackneyed ways of defining and studying IR to lay bare the power relations in 'doing' IR a certain way. Meanwhile, Postcolonial feminists accent the experiences of 'non-Western' females and other subjects left out, or marginalized by, European and North American accounts of global politics and history. This chapter will begin by introducing the concept of gender and move on to highlight the different varieties of feminist scholarship you might encounter on your course in IRT.

As you read around feminism make a note of the similarities and differences between feminism and some of the earlier theories such as Realism and Liberalism in terms of: subject matter, methods, and the kind of knowledge the traditions produce about IR.

GENDER

Of all the keywords in feminist scholarship, 'gender' is the one you need most urgently to get to grips with. Understand the theoretical foundations of 'gender' and you will be a long way on the road to appreciating feminist scholarship. When we are filling out forms to get passports and student cards, or during opinion surveys and so on, we are asked to tick one of the two 'gender' boxes: male or female. It is easy to tick the correct box because we all know what the differences between men and women are: men are 'male' and women are 'female', right? But what is it, beyond biological differences, that distinguishes masculinity from femininity? It is precisely this question that feminist scholars seek to answer through analysis of the constructions of each category and their day-to-day ramifications in the practice and theory of IR.

Feminists argue that IR has excluded/marginalized women empirically (by not seeing them as valid subjects for study) and theoretically (by constructing the conceptual building blocks of the discipline on concepts associated with masculinity).

Here are two of many definitions of gender that unpack this essential concept:

- **V. Spike Peterson** (1992: 8): 'the socially constructed dichotomy of masculine–feminine (man–woman, maleness–femaleness) shaped only in part by biologically construed male–female dimensions'.
- **J. Ann Tickner and Laura Sjoberg** (2016: 180): 'a set of socially constructed characteristics describing what men and women ought to be'. Masculinity is associated with characteristics such as 'strength, rationality, independence, protector and public' and femininity with 'weakness, emotionality, relational, protected and private'.

Note how Peterson, Tickner and Sjoberg all unstitch the constructedness of the gender categories we commonly take to be givens or 'natural' parts of our worldview. Feminist scholarship tries to highlight the artificiality of these supposed givens and also shows how the masculine characteristics have been privileged or looked more favourably upon within IR than feminine characteristics – how international relations operates a **patriarchal** system that works for men at the expense (literally in financial and security terms) of women. As Daryl Jarvis puts it (2001: 105), gender is 'an indispensable ingredient in the study of international politics, a means of understanding not just the systemic basis of the international system, but of the power structures embedded in those relations'.

In the introduction to her edited collection, *Gendered States*, Peterson (1992: 9–10) elaborates four reasons why it is useful to 'gender' IR:

1. **Decentres biological explanations** – Conceptions of maleness and femaleness are not fixed through time (as demonstrated by history) or across national boundaries at the same point in time. Taking gender constructions as 'given' rather than 'made' obstructs our understanding of the subtle yet powerful part they play in the practice and study of IR. Charlotte Hooper explains this point: 'historical and anthropological research suggests that there is no single "masculinity" or "femininity" and that both are subject to numerous and fairly fast changing historical and cultural variations' (2006: 377).

2. **Interdependence of key words** – Peterson looks at the interrelationship of the terms 'masculine' and 'feminine' and their associated characteristics such as 'rationality' (masculine) versus 'emotionality' (feminine). They are not mutually exclusive but interdependent, she argues, meaning that our understanding of the one is necessarily dependent on the characteristics we attribute to the other. Usually, feminine characteristics are valued less than masculine ones; this highlights the power *in* language to degrade the feminine at the expense of the masculine. An exploration of the power relations at work in representing a notional 'Other' to help define one's 'Self' identity is one of the main ways in which poststructuralist approaches have been put to work in IRT, whether by gender or Postcolonial theorists.

> Feminism is not just about women or women's concerns. It feeds into social theory and questions about our ways of 'being' in the world, male or female.

3. **Structure and agency** – Feminist scholarship is comfortable working with questions about the 'subjective, everyday' and relating these to historical or structural contexts within which these day-to-day experiences are felt. There is no privileging of one level of analysis as we have, for example, in Neorealist theory, which emphasizes the structural determinants of state behaviour over the decisions made at unit level (by national leaders, for instance). Downplaying the identity/beliefs/idiosyncrasies of the states themselves means Neorealists ignore the human, social and ideational aspects of IR that theorists from the English School, Constructivism, Critical Theory and the 'post-' approaches find interesting.

4. **Diversity** – Feminists pursue an inclusive approach to the subject matter of IR by speaking to all of the following issues: power, identity, security, diplomacy, culture, sexual relations, discourse, the international division of labour, poverty and militarism. This wide agenda gives feminists a distinctive handle on all of the big ontological, epistemological and methodological questions about IR as a discipline, covered in Chapter 3 of this book. See Cynthia Enloe (2001) for a good example of the eclectic range of subjects to which this theory speaks.

FEMINIST PERSPECTIVES

By saying that there are different strands to feminist thought, we are not saying that they are mutually exclusive or that they are somehow in opposition to each other. However, there are distinctive approaches to feminist IR that are worth noting. They highlight the porous nature of the boundaries between the theories covered in this book and the capacity for one theoretical tradition to house a diverse array of perspectives. Something of this complexity is captured in Figure 12.

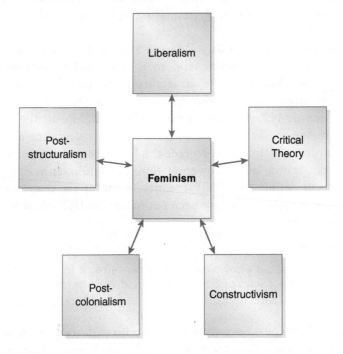

Figure 12   Feminism in IRT

Feminist scholars develop aspects of wider work both in IR and the social sciences more generally. Here we will follow the work of Tickner and Sjoberg (2016: 182-87), who give a breakdown of how these myriad influences show themselves in feminist scholarship. However, the take-home point is the overlap between the various theoretical traditions and this is as good a place as any to seek them out.

That writers cannot agree on how best to capture the field of feminist scholarship says something about the breadth and depth of its concerns. Keep a note of all the variations for use in essays/exams where you have to define 'feminism' or 'gender theory'.

Liberal feminism

Liberal feminists basically accept the conventional framework of IR by looking to add women and women's issues to the IR agenda as it currently stands. This 'add women and stir' approach takes existing subject matters methods and introduces women where previously they were either invisible, forgotten about or glossed over. They do this by documenting 'various aspects of women's sub-ordination' (Tickner and Sjoberg 2016: 182) in economic, political, legal, social and health terms (the extent of physical and mental abuse compared to men, for example). Liberal feminists seek out women's contributions to society and shine a light on them to make a call for greater equality and fairer treatment. International organizations like the UN and pressure groups such as Human Rights Watch have collected vast amounts of data, statistics and reports on gender (in)equality and women's human rights around the world, which can be mined for information to help the Liberal feminist cause (UN 1997–2010; Human Rights Watch 2012). A selection of stories from the Human Rights Watch website in August 2016 shows the myriad themes discussed in this context: Saudi Arabian female participation in the Rio Olympic Games; the abuse and exploitation of migrant workers in Oman; violence against indigenous women in Canada; female sex trafficking in Lebanon; domestic violence in Russia; and gang rapes in Burundi.

Critical feminism

Critical feminists want to go beyond adding and stirring women into existing IR practices and scholarship. Taking inspiration from the work of Marxists and Critical Theorists such as Robert Cox (see Chapter 10 of this book), they stress the part perceptions of the key word 'gender' have played in moulding social and state relations in the international system. Gender in the Critical perspective is another structure that shapes (often unwittingly) how men and women interact, and how social relations of all kinds and at all levels of national and international society are infused with power inequalities. Critical feminists show how all this plays out in the form of material (economic) inequalities and the maltreatment and exploitation of women. After highlighting these structural iniquities, Critical- and Marxist-inspired theorists hope that they can be changed in the future, giving their work an emancipatory edge, or in Kimberley Hutchings' words, 'a productive impact on how international politics are to be understood and judged' (1999: 83). 'Gender' in this perspective is another of those unseen 'structures' that shape the conduct of international affairs without making any impact in theories such as Neorealism. Gender in this view is nothing less than a social institution possessing culturally relative meanings around the globe and changing across time: but it is ever-present if we know how and where to look for its impact on international relations.

TAKING IT FURTHER
Gender and film

In a blog post from November 2014, Soraya Chemaly discussed the findings of a study by the Geena Davis Institute on Gender in Media. The study looked at the role of women in film, assessing 120 films from 10 of the most profitable film markets globally (all the references below are to Chemaly 2014). The findings, argues Chemaly, show up the 'status and

(Continued)

(Continued)

mainstream cultural assumptions about social roles and of power', particularly the relative 'invisibility' of women in the movies – both in acting roles and the behind-the-scenes jobs that bring movies to our screens in the first place. 'With very small changes', she concludes, 'the ratio of men to women in film has remained fundamentally unchanged since 1946.' This study tells us a lot about gender roles in contemporary society and supports the liberal feminist case in IR and elsewhere.

Some of the headline statistics on women in film are as follows: globally, there are 2.24 male characters to every 1 female character; of all the speaking or named characters only one third was female – this went for children's' movies as well; under a quarter of the movies surveyed had a female lead; about one-fifth of film makers were female; females constitute 7 per cent of directors, just under 20 per cent of writers, and 22 per cent of producers; and France has the worst gender ratio, nearly 10:1 in favour of men. The negative impression conveyed by the blunt statistics is exaggerated by the *roles* assigned to women in the movies. For example: female characters are more than twice as likely than male characters to be wearing sexy or sexualizing clothes; female characters are more than twice as likely to be skinny; female characters are almost twice as likely to be naked or partially naked; there was a clear imbalance in the job roles assigned to males and females in the movies, with males disproportionately depicted as lawyers, judges, academics and doctors. Just three women were depicted as political leaders with power: 'One didn't speak. One was an elephant. The last was Margaret Thatcher.'

● ●

Constructivist feminism

Following the Constructivists explored in Chapter 8 of this book, feminist scholars interested in the social construction of reality focus on the ideational rather than the material aspects of global politics. They 'focus on the way that ideas about gender shape and are shaped by global politics' (Tickner and Sjoberg 2016: 184). They are interested in discovering the nature of the beliefs that shape our gendered world, as well as the language through which these beliefs impact upon international practices. Constructivist feminists work at de-naturalizing divisions between the genders by investigating the ideas that lie behind these constructions and asking: where have our ideas about gender come from; are they just; and how might they be altered?

● ●

 TAKING IT FURTHER

Female representation in national parliaments: the case of Rwanda

The previous Taking it Further box discussed the negative statistics on women in the movies. This box appraises women in politics, seen from an international perspective. Although the picture is not uniformly positive there are signs of a more progressive story to be told, with the case study of Rwanda a shining example.

UN statistics on female representation in national parliaments around the world give a damning picture of the limited inputs females continue to have into elite level political decision-making (see UN Women 2016). The UK now has its second female Prime Minister, Theresa May, and the USA nearly – but not quite – elected its first female President, Hillary Clinton, in 2016. Although they are high profile figures, leadership positions in politics remain disproportionately elusive for many females. On the plus side, the number of women in parliaments nearly doubled between 1995 and 2015. However, as of August 2015: only 22 per cent of national parliamentarians were female; there were 11 female Heads of State and 10 female Heads of Government; there were 37 states in which women accounted for under 10 per cent of parliamentarians in the lower houses, with several chambers having no female representation at all. There were distinct regional variations: the Nordic countries averaged over 40 per cent female representation, the Americas 25 per cent, Europe excluding the Nordic countries just under 25 per cent, sub-Saharan Africa 23 per cent, Asia 18 per cent, the Middle East and North Africa 17 per cent, and the Pacific just over 15 per cent. To give some select nations on female representation in the lower house from the 2016 census (Women in National Parliaments 2016): the USA was 98th in the world (19.4 per cent), the UK 48th (29.4 per cent), China 71st (23.6 per cent), Germany 26th (36.5 per cent) and Japan 155th (9.5 per cent). Haiti, Micronesia, Palau, Qatar Tonga, Vanuatu and Yemen all had no female representation in the lower house. The top five scoring nations in 2016, in reverse order, were Sweden (43.6 per cent), Seychelles (43.8 per cent), Cuba (48.9 per cent), Bolivia (53.1 per cent) and Rwanda (63.8 per cent). The remarkable case of Rwanda is worth dwelling on.

Rwanda has made female participation in decision-making, and the life of the nation more widely, a firm political priority. Why has there been such a drive to inculcate gender equality so strongly in Rwandan politics? Juliana Kantengwa (2013) links it to the devastating genocide of the early 1990s, during which one million Rwandans lost their lives. The genocide 'was the result of a divisive and destructive culture that had pervaded our society'. Kantengwa argues that inclusiveness and equality were at the heart of the national reconstruction process. In other words, liberal themes were uppermost in people's minds as Rwanda rebuilt its internal politics and civic society. This process included: quotas on female representation in parliament (24 seats of the 80 are reserved for women, but voters consistently vote in many more than this); physical tasks for women in rebuilding the nation; peace-building in times of insurgence; and female involvement in truth and reconciliation, and justice and government programmes. Longer-term issues such as education and low levels of literacy among women compared to men were also addressed. Two decades later, writes Kantengwa, 'gender roles had changed'.

This is an excellent example of feminism in action, as well as a case study into the impact on gender roles of such things as a nation's culture, history, politics and security environment. Changing hegemonic constructions of what it 'means' to be a woman in Rwanda has led to the emergence of a different type of politics: Rwanda has seen nothing less than a new construction of its gender politics.

. . . .

Poststructural feminism

This is the widest, most thoroughgoing feminist perspective that questions how we apprehend the world through language, our theories about the world, and our 'scientific' ways of studying IR. It works from the idea that 'women have generally been outsiders, excluded from historical processes that have framed contemporary political and economic life, as well as from the development of knowledge that has interpreted those processes' (Tickner 1996: 148). It concentrates on unpacking the latter exclusion by investigating the identities implicit in different gender constructions. We have seen above how gender divisions are constructed and play out around the interdependence of terms such as 'masculine' and 'feminine'. These terms are hooked onto arrays of characteristics we associate with each gender. We further noted that these categories and characteristics are imbued with power relations in that masculine characteristics tend to be looked upon as the standard for the rest of humanity to live up to. Things masculine tend to be privileged over things feminine.

Poststructural feminists use the 'gender as power' idea in two important ways:

1. They rethink the basis of the supposedly objective knowledge claims made by Western science. As Peterson points out (1992: 12–13), Western philosophy has tended to be the preserve of Western elite males, in which men's experiences are said to be representative of all human experiences (i.e. they are universalized); supposed gender differences have been institutionalized in the academy and policy practice; and the Western phallocentric order privileges masculine qualities over feminine ones (for example, masculine 'reason' is elevated above feminine 'passion').

> One of the most famous feminist reworkings of practices in conventional IRT was J. Ann Tickner's (1988) reformulation of Morgenthau's six principles of 'political realism'. Tickner suggests that 'it is a partial description of international politics because it is based on assumptions about human nature that are partial and privilege masculinity' (Tickner 1988: 431). Work through her line of thought to see the depth of the critique poststructural feminists have of IR in its positivist Realist-Liberal guise.

2. Poststructuralist feminists apply this reasoning to IR by rethinking the ways in which the language of IR sets up artificial binaries between, for instance, 'civilized/uncivilized, order/anarchy, and developed/underdeveloped' (Tickner and Sjoberg 2016: 185). Also consider how often terms such as 'good/evil', 'state/failed state', 'secure/insecure', 'terrorist/freedom fighter' feature in the practice and study of IR. Poststructural feminists invite us to see the real-world implications of what are in fact artificial binary distinctions which implicitly privilege one of these terms over the other. What is more, they 'seek to expose and deconstruct these hierarchies' (ibid.: 185).

> Can you think of other artificial binaries commonly used in the practice and study of IR? Which of the two terms is privileged? What are the consequences in theory and/or practice?

Postcolonial feminism

This branch of feminism makes two broad contributions to the study of IR. The first has an affinity with poststructural feminism and the Postcolonial movement more generally (see Chapter 13). It highlights the structured nature of the oppression and/or invisibility of women in former colonial states. Even in states which have formally declared their independence from their former 'masters' (note the gendered terminology), Postcolonial feminists argue that colonial constructions of 'self' and 'other' linger on and denigrate the 'other' as inferior (ibid.: 186). Like constructivist and poststructural feminists, they highlight the importance of binary categories and therefore see language as a significant site of oppression and dominance.

The second contribution is to have a critical debate with other feminists. Postcolonial feminists unpick the fabric of the feminist movement. They argue that feminism has tended to be the preserve of elite Western women, who have made their concerns stand in for the concerns of all women around the globe: they criticize the universalizing tendency of some Western feminism. Just as feminists criticize the tendency for men's experiences to be held up as representative of humanity as a whole, so Postcolonialist feminists take issue with feminist scholarship that confuses Western women's concerns with those of women from other parts of the world. There is, they say, no universal understanding of women's needs and we need to be aware of cultural, religious and ethnic divergences (ibid.: 186).

Where Liberal feminists tend to add to the existing IR agenda, their Critical, constructivist, poststructuralist and Postcolonialist counterparts point to major iniquities not only within the world of IR as *practice* but in IR as *theory*. Feminism is not just about raising the profile of women in IR but about raising awareness of the gender-biased nature of IR as an academic discipline. Work on the philosophy of science, on the constructedness of gender and the discrimination in the very language we use to think about IRT force us to rethink what it is that IR is all about. We have further cause to rethink these disciplinary practices in our encounter with poststructuralism in the next chapter.

QUESTIONS TO PONDER

'Can "gender" concerns be added to the existing IR agenda? Answer with reference to at least two feminist scholars you have studied on your course in IRT.'

Your first mission with this question is to scope it by defining the key terms 'gender' and 'existing IR agenda'. With the former you need to give some sense of the constructedness feminists see in the term. Using definitions from key writers studied above – and others – you can pull out the implications of treating gender as a construction, as we did in this chapter. This is a good tactic for two reasons. The first is that it shows your wide knowledge of the literature and that you know the meaning of *the* key term in feminist IRT. The second reason is that you will immediately produce the names of at least two scholars as directed by the question. Moving on to the other key term in the question, it is arguably trickier to define the 'existing IR agenda'. It is open to you to define it how you wish, and one good way is to use the conception of IR prevalent in feminist critiques of its limitations as a discipline. In other words, come at the existing IR agenda through the eyes of feminist critics of IRT. Instead, or in addition, you might also go back to writers such as Holsti and/or Constructivist writers who present views of a disciplinary 'core' of Neorealism and Neoliberalism which was dominant until the early 1990s.

Having established the conceptual and definitional framework for the essay, you need to come up with a response. Your argument will depend upon what *you* see as the mainstream IR agenda, and how feminist theory fits with this. You should ideally try and show that you are aware of arguments that gender and/or women are more than 'variables' which can simply be stirred into IR as part of an ever widening agenda (Liberal feminism).

Reference to the more critically inclined variants of feminism will help you establish the argument that gender actually subsumes IR by providing a critique of Western philosophy of science as we conventionally understand it. An 'it depends' answer might therefore work well. The debates within feminism point to its slightly fragmented nature as a cohesive 'theory' and some sense of a loose but identifiable feminist 'sensibility' might usefully feature in your answer.

'"Gender hierarchy is not coincidental to but in a significant sense constitutive of Western philosophy's objectivist metaphysics" (Peterson). Discuss the implications of this statement for IRT.'

It is perennially difficult to structure answers to 'Discuss' questions. Some students fall into the trap of writing everything they know about some of the major terms raised in the question. To get past this erroneous approach try and think through why Peterson wrote what she did and how her ideas have been received by other feminists and critics alike.

Your first job is to summarize Peterson's argument: untangle the thrust of her case for your reader in a few hundred words. Ideally you would know where this quote comes from (Peterson 1992) and some of the kinder IR lecturers will give you the source in the question, if they are in a good mood. But if not – and they are not obliged to be in a good mood – you should have read enough of Peterson's work to be able to capture the essence of her argument. The implications of this statement are many and varied, so the amount you include will naturally depend on the word and/or time limit you have. Normally at undergraduate level you will not be able to cover more than four or five points in depth in the body of an essay or exam answer. You want to try and showcase the point of view that takes 'conventional' IR theory as a sub-set of the positivist, objectivist view of science, and therefore that it can be critiqued on a number of grounds.

Any of the following broad issues could be included and they would need breaking down: 'gender' and science (science as 'masculine'); feminism as a philosophy of social science; gender and power of/in language; IR theory as a masculine pursuit (by men, about men, for men); IR, the public sphere of the international and the neglect of the private (women's realm); is 'gender' a variable? The best answers will do more than explore Peterson's intervention, they will pay some homage to writers who see gender either as irrelevant to, or a pointless distraction from, the core concerns of IR as a discipline, so finding critics of the feminist approach in your course readings will help you out here.

REFERENCES TO MORE INFORMATION

On gender in IRT:

Chong, Y.W. (2012) 'Beyond the Gender Binary', talk at TEDxRainier, Seattle, November, www.youtube.com/watch?v=-Lm4vxZrAig (accessed 22 August 2016).

Steans, J. (2013) *Gender and International Relations*, 3rd edn. Cambridge: Polity.

True, J. (2001) 'Feminism', in S. Burchill and A. Linklater (eds) *Theories of International Relations*, 5th edn. Basingstoke: Palgrave, pp. 241–65.
Excellent overview of the contours of feminism and the contribution it has made to IR theory.

Elshtain, J.B. (2006) 'Reflections on War and Political Discourse: Realism, Just War and Feminism in a Nuclear Age', in R. Little and M. Smith (eds) *Perspectives on World Politics*. Abingdon: Routledge, pp. 368–75.
A feminist deconstruction of the language and assumptions of Realist theory.

Enloe, C. (2009) 'Picking Up the Pieces: Making Feminist Sense of the Iraq War', Lecture at Quinnipiac University, 24 September, www.youtube.com/watch?v=WTFaxobkVps&feature=related (accessed 19 August 2016).

Whitworth, S. (1989) 'Gender and International Relations: Beyond the Inter-Paradigm Debate', *Millennium: Journal of International Studies*, 18(2): 265–72.
One of the landmark works in feminist IR scholarship.

Whitworth, S. (2005) 'Militarized Masculinities and the Politics of Peacekeeping', in K. Booth (ed.) *Critical Security Studies and World Politics*. Boulder, CO: Lynne Rienner Publishers, pp. 89–106.
Case study of Canadian peacekeeping, illustrating how feminist concerns are central to the study of military values and practices.

Tickner, J.A. (1988) 'Hans Morgenthau's Principles of Political Realism: A Feminist Reformulation', *Millennium: Journal of International Studies*, 17(3): 429–40.
Classic 'standpoint' feminist study which rewrites Morgenthau's work from the perspective of women and in doing so shows the gender bias in this supposedly objective Realist account of IR. Textbooks in IR often feature Tickner's work, so it is useful to have read the original.

Tickner, J.A. (2006) 'Feminist Perspectives in International Relations', in W. Carlsnaes, T. Risse and B.A. Simmons (eds) *Handbook of International Relations*. London: Sage, pp. 275–91.

Blanchard, E.M. (2011) 'Why is there no Gender in the English School?', *Review of International Studies*, 37(2): 855–79.

Zalewski, M. (2011) '"I Don't Even Know What Gender Is": A Discussion of the Connections between Gender, Gender Mainstreaming and Feminist Theory', *Review of International Studies*, 36(1): 3–27.

On feminism and gender studies more generally:

Keller, E.F. (1985) *Reflections on Gender and Science*. New Haven, CT: Yale University Press.
Critique of the Enlightenment scientific project which equates 'objectivity' with 'masculinity'.

Krause, J. (1995) 'The International Dimension of Gender Inequality and Feminist Politics: A "New Direction" for International Political Economy?', in J. Macmillan and A. Linklater (eds) *Boundaries in Question: New Directions in International Relations*. London: Pinter, pp. 128–43.

Lloyd, M. (2005) *Beyond Identity Politics: Feminism, Power and Politics*. London: Sage.

Lange, L. (2003) 'Woman is Not a Rational Animal: On Aristotle's Biology of Reproduction', in S. Harding and M.B. Hintikka (eds) *Discovering Reality: Feminist Perspectives on Epistemology, Metaphysics, Methodology, and the Philosophy of Social Science*, 2nd edn. Dordrecht: Kluwer Academic Publishers, pp. 1–16.
Demonstrates how an appreciation of gender helps us think critically about the big questions in the philosophy of science and IR. Good for the second question to ponder above too.

Butler, J. (1999) *Gender Trouble: Feminism and the Subversion of Identity*. London: Routledge.

Spender, D. (ed.) (1981) *Men's Studies Modified: The Impact of Feminism on the Academic Disciplines*. Oxford: Pergamon.

Butler, J. (2011) 'Judith Butler: Your Behaviour Creates Your Gender', www.youtube.com/watch?v=Bo7o2LYATDc (accessed 19 August 2016).
Snappy introduction to the concept of gender.

Braunstein, E. (2003) 'Gender and Foreign Direct Investment', in J. Michie (ed.) *The Handbook of Globalization*. Cheltenham: Edward Elgar, pp. 165–75.

Chinkin, C. (1999) 'Gender Inequality and International Human Rights Law', in A. Hurrell and N. Woods, *Order, Globalization, and Inequality in World Politics*. Oxford: Oxford University Press, pp. 95–121.

Review of International Studies (2007) 'Forum: Women and Human Rights', 33(1): 5–103.

Steans, J. (2002) 'Global Governance: A Feminist Perspective', in D. Held and A. McGrew (eds) *Governing Globalization: Power, Authority and Global Governance*. Cambridge: Polity, pp. 87–108.

12
POSTSTRUCTURALISM

Key terms

- Deconstruction
- Discourse
- Genealogy
- Identity

- Power/knowledge
- Sovereignty
- Statecraft

> The postmodern vantage point is one of critique. Its aim is to unsettle, to jar, to challenge, and to subject our most fundamental beliefs and principles to intense critical scrutiny. (Shinko 2006: 168)

> Postmodernist theory calls for a radical re-thinking of how we think. (Hutchings 1999: 82)

A loose and wide-ranging intellectual movement, poststructuralism swept through the social sciences from the 1970s onward. Some scholars jumped on board, liberated by the critical tools it offered them; others have been left confused about what it all means; some are actively hostile to anything to do with the 'p'-word. Critics of poststructuralism from within IR have variously called it 'evil', 'dangerous', 'bad IR', 'meta-babble' (Krasner and Halliday, cited in Campbell 2016: 203). They have, further, questioned the 'novelty of the arguments developed by the proponents of these allegedly new paradigms' (Navon 2001: 612). James Der Derian notes that French/'continental' philosophy in general has not gone down well in the Anglophone core of the discipline, and this has affected the reception of leading poststructuralist writers such as Michel Foucault: 'The dual imperative of protecting the state and IR theory from any sudden change has always placed a premium on traditional approaches ... Taking on many of the shibboleths of IR led to charges of blasphemy' (2009: 70). Bruce Russett's dismissive take on postmodernism (another word for poststructuralism, often used interchangeably with it) is illustrative of this tendency: '"Post-modernism" may have a place in art museums but it should be kept out of the study of international relations' (1995: 176).

Keep a record of the reasons why different writers you study are supportive of, apathetic about, or hostile to some of the 'newer' IR theories like poststructuralism. What informs their views and what does this reveal about the nature of debates about IRT?

The main thing poststructuralism has in common with the other theories covered in this book is that calling it 'theory' might cause more problems than it solves. There are many variants of poststructuralism, just as there are many strands to Realism, Liberalism and the English School. Moreover, poststructuralism is like Marxism, feminism and Postcolonialism in being a broad social and intellectual movement that cuts across disciplines. Some feminists might class themselves as poststructuralists, but not all; some Marxists might see themselves as poststructuralists, but not all; Postcolonialist writers are renowned for their transgression of all these notional theoretical boundaries. Like Constructivism, it is difficult to bracket poststructuralism as a theory: in its ontological and epistemological positioning it is something more like a 'sensibility'. IR is just one site for poststructuralist work among many.

Poststructuralist works come under many names. On your IRT course you might find it called 'postmodernism' or 'post-positivism' because scholars are not always clear on the distinctions between them. Either that, or they find the term too loose or inapplicable in the context of IRT (Campbell 2016: 204–5). Postmodernism tends to be more associated with literary theory as opposed to social theory – but not always (van der Ree 2014). The distinctions between the terms are therefore quite arbitrary and there is a lot of slippage between them.

> I have chosen to use the label 'poststructuralist' in its broadly accepted IR sense to encompass postmodern and post-positivist works, even if some authors might take issue with being labelled poststructuralists.

The first two categories are self-explanatory, the third is more problematic. How do we identify a 'post-' text or do we just know one when we see it? Sterling-Folker goes some way to making this point when she writes: 'The postmodern IR scholar also focuses on what the positivist would consider trivial or unrelated to IR, such as the spy novel, football, defense manuals, *Star Trek*, and popular culture' (Sterling-Folker 2006d: 162). It is not only the subject matter that defines poststructuralism, however. Poststructuralists draw upon an eclectic array of sources, ideas and practices to challenge ontological, epistemological and methodological conventions in IR. In this process, 'readings of Derrida and Foucault have been particularly important' (Hutchings 1999: 77).

As the two quotes at the start of this chapter make clear, then, works written in the 'post-' tradition want to critique things we take for granted in IR, like the idea of the state. In this respect they help us reassess not just the world as we see it, but the ways in which we think we see the world. While it has obvious affinities with Critical Theory and 'thicker' varieties of Constructivism, as well as an emancipatory agenda that chimes with other openly normative IR theories, poststructuralism brings concepts and ideas all of its own to the IR table.

> If you find poststructuralism challenging, difficult and unsettling then do not fear! 'Post-' approaches to the social sciences and IRT jolt us out of cozy, established ways of thinking and invite us to think the unthinkable: 'Poststructuralism contends that a focus on the autonomous agent [the basis of Western philosophy and political theory] needs to be "deconstructed", contested and troubled' (Namaste 1994: 221).

In this chapter we can only introduce you to some of the most influential ways in which poststructuralism has been felt within IRT. We will do this, first, by introducing the key concepts and methods associated with poststructuralism. Second, we will take you step-by-step through a poststructuralist study of statecraft by Devetak (1995). By the end of the chapter you should be able to grasp the meaning of basic 'post-' terms and be able to spot poststructuralist IR texts when you see them.

POSTSTRUCTURALIST IDEAS, CONCEPTS AND APPROACHES

Works of IR written in a poststructuralist vein are built on one, some or all of the following ideas, concepts or approaches inspired by the work of the French philosophers Michel Foucault (1926–84) and Jacques Derrida (1930–2004). They share a Marxist and Critical Theory interest in emancipation, through the exposure of arbitrary 'closures' in the knowledge we are fed daily by elites such as politicians, journalists and, yes, academics. However, a key point of difference between poststructuralists and Critical Theorists is that the former are much more sceptical about our ability to access a 'truth' that could function as a corrective to these gaps, biases and prejudices in all forms of knowledge. Poststructuralists are, therefore, suspicious of the totalizing potential for replacing one metanarrative with another, as if that will wipe out the narrative problem altogether (van der Ree 2014). By definition, this is an impossibility – we are always 'trapped' in a linguistic or narrative cage. We will unpack the poststructuralist approach by looking its toolkit of deconstruction, power/knowledge, representation and discourse.

Deconstruction

Inspired by the philosophy of Jacques Derrida, 'deconstruction' is another of those widely used and abused terms in the social sciences. According to Devetak, it 'defies definition' but 'can be understood as a strategy of interpretation and criticism directed at concepts which attempt closure or totalization' (Devetak 1995: 20). According to Mishra and Hodge, what deconstruction does best is: 'interrupting, intervening, opening up the discourses of the dominant, restoring plurality and tension' (Mishra and Hodge 2005: 386). Poststructuralists want to jar 'the whole edifice of common-sense notions' (Devetak 1995: 20), sharing the emancipatory agenda common to Critical Theory, explored in Chapter 10 of this book, as well as Marxism, covered in Chapter 9.

Poststructuralists take it a stage further, however, by using deconstruction in a variety of ways, the technique of 'double reading' being especially popular (see the next section). Claudia Aradau summarizes it by suggesting that in IR, 'a deconstructive perspective has challenged taken-for-granted "truths" about what the international is and how it functions. Deconstruction has helped IR scholars destabilize both hegemonic texts and dominant understandings of the subject.' Especially important has been its unsettling of dichotomies and breaking down the supposed barriers between inside and outside, domestic and international, and self and other (Aradau 2010: 107–8), along with a reassessment of practices of power in the international system.

Maja Zehfuss (2009: 141–2) uses the example of 'gender' to illustrate the concept of deconstruction and how it works as a tool of critical IR, arguing that we can use it to overturn the privileging of supposedly masculine characteristics over supposedly feminine characteristics. Zehfuss asserts that it is possible to argue that 'the (putatively masculine) ability to rationally and objectively assess various options is not as good as the (putatively feminine) ability to take feelings into account'. However, this critique merely reproduces part of the thinking it allegedly overturns, by accepting that 'feminine' can be distinguished from 'masculine'. In being accepting of this artificial distinction: 'The original hierarchy remains possible and can therefore reassert itself'. A second move is necessary to displace this system of thought altogether: Derrida's 'displacement'. A displacement would involve investigating whether 'masculine' can be thought of as separate from and antithetical to 'feminine'. Derrida invites us to reconsider our structures of thought, believing that the dichotomies on which our thought patterns are based are artificial, biased and 'do not work'.

Power/knowledge

Added to the tool of deconstruction, poststructuralists investigate the ways in which power is generated by putting artificial closures or limitations on our understanding of the world. Following on from that, they analyse how the exercise of power is deeply inter-twined with the production and transmission of knowledge around societies.

The focus on power/knowledge comes directly from Foucault's understanding of power, which is quite different from the definition of 'power' many IR scholars work with. To use the IR terminology, the conventional meaning of power is essentially repressive. It is associated with state power, whether manifested physically in the form of guns, bullets and nuclear warheads, or ideationally in terms of the persuasive power of a political speech or media reportage, for instance. Repressive power 'from above' involves the imposition of limits or constraints on our thought and actions. It often aims, bluntly, at telling us what to do. This is power as threat, control and coercion. Foucault – like Gramsci (see the Critical Theory chapter, above) – sees power as being more produc-tive than a negative, repressive instrument of control.

By contrast the power of which Foucault speaks is the power to define and impose those limitations in the first place. How, he asks, is language used to limit our thinking about what is normal, legitimate and proper in the world? Who is it that gets to circumscribe our social 'truths'? Productive power shapes things, builds things, describes and categorizes them. Naked power from above might be contrasted both with feminist renderings of the term (for example, Elshtain 1995: 354–6) and a similarly nuanced Foucauldian notion of power from below. 'It is not simply a means of repression or coercion, but rather it flows throughout society in networks'; it is 'not simply possessed but practiced' (Neal 2009: 163). Foucault worked on topics such as discipline and punishment in prisons (Foucault 1995, 2001) and sexuality (ibid. 1998a–c), particularly the production of meaning in sexuality and homosexuality. He also wrote more expansive texts on discourse and orders of knowl-edge (Foucault 2002). Central to all of his work was the idea that 'social identities are effects of the ways in which knowledge is organized' (Namaste 1994: 221–2).

The television show *The X-Files* gave us the positivist motto, 'The truth is out there'. For Foucault, things were much more complicated. 'Truth is a thing of this world: it is produced only by virtue of multiple forms of constraint. And it includes regular effects of power. Each society has its regime of truth' (1991: 72–3). James Keeley summarizes Foucault's appreciation of regimes as intrinsic to the discourse by which they are constituted:

> a regime gives specific definition and order to a public space or realm of action. It specifies a phenomenon and an issue-area deemed of public interest and in this sense 'politicizes' them. It identifies the relevant qualities of the occupants of that space. It defines the relations within which they see and are seen by each other and in terms of which they conduct the public business with respect to that issue-area. (quoted in Ramakrishnan 1999: 142)

This is a quite different 'regime' from the more or less formal and institutionalized cooperative regimes we see at work in Neoliberal theory (see Chapter 6 in this book). Foucault gets behind the facade of language to ask what sources of power societies have erected under truth, behind truth and around truth to give it authority and legitimacy: to make truth be seen to *function* as truth, and to support socially constituted regimes of truth? How does an always *partial* truth about the world come to parade as *the* truth – to make truth appear to hold fast across time and space?

Representation

Foucault's interest in discovering 'regimes' of truth led him to engage with issues of representation: how different regimes of truth call the world to mind the world for us through language. In doing so, Foucault was building on the work of structural linguistics by the Swiss philosopher Ferdinand Saussure – hence the name post-structuralism (see the 'Animating Poststructuralism' clip on YouTube by Christopher Bolton (2012), referenced at the end of this chapter).

So how do we understand 'representation'? We are forever using words in the place of things. In the context of IR, terms such as 'globalization', 'War on Terror', 'freedom', 'international system', even 'humanity', by necessity, relate to objects, people and clusters of things that have a 'real world' existence. Think of the names of countries too: 'the USA', 'Britain', 'China', 'Australia': these are 'imagined communities' to use Benedict Anderson's famous terminology (Anderson 2006). However, these IR 'things' such as wars, interventions and even nations themselves are social constructions rarely *directly* known in their totality, 'even if previously visited by policy makers or currently described to them by others – including diplomats in the field or CNN reporters' (Henrikson 2002: 438; see also Buzan 1993). Country names conjure very different meanings at different points in time (think Germany in 1943 and Germany today), and have very different meanings to different individuals and groups at the same point in time (see how Hillary Clinton and Donald Trump constructed Mexico as an object of US foreign policy in their 2016 presidential campaign speeches). Country names are contested and slippery terms, but the reasons for that contestation and slipperiness are not often exposed to debate and discussion. Country names, like words-as-representations more widely, have taken-for-granted qualities that flag up the lack of fixity in language (see Campbell 1996: 166–9). The point for Foucault, therefore, is that our words can only ever *stand in* for, they represent, these social facts; words can never *be* those things. Individual words in this interpretation are more like concepts: always slippery and prone to manipulation and misapplication.

Discourse

To summarize Foucault's line of thinking so far: we have all these words in our respective languages which are used to represent – or stand in for – the things they are meant objectively to be describing. In the process, this makes the meanings of words slippery and prone to ambiguity. But he does not stop at identifying the gap between the units of language (signifying words) and the essentially unknowable things they represent (for example, 'globalization' or 'Madagascar'). Foucault takes this problem with the units of language and applies it to the systemic level of our sentences and paragraphs, to demonstrate that, at this level, the problems of language relating to things become even more acute. It is at this level of discourse that, Foucault suggests, we see the productive power of language.

The study of discourse has become 'a means of gathering the things said and written on a particular subject in a particular context by a particular group of people (often but not always political elites), in order to try to interpret what is being done politically through such statements' (Neal 2009: 166). Campbell (2007: 216) describes discourse as 'a specific series of representations and practices through which meanings are produced, identities constituted, social relations established, and political and ethical outcomes made more or less possible'. Discourses do not simply describe the world, they produce meanings, constitute identities, establish social and political relations and help make possible different political and ethical outcomes (Campbell 2016: 208; see also the selection of definitions on offer in Ramakrishnan 1999: 137) – that in a nutshell is the productive power of discourse. For Der Derian (2009: 71): 'Discursive practices mediate and often dominate IR by establishing what can be said and who can say it with authority.'

> The study of discourse is popular among 'Post-' scholars and 'thick' Constructivists, illustrating the blurred boundaries between these heavily overlapping schools of thought in IRT.

We can have a discourse about anything. It will necessarily be positioned (relying on a web of slippery words-as-signifying representations, as demonstrated above), as well as being imbued with power relations. For Miguel Cabrera, discourse is 'the coherent body of categories, concepts and principles by means of which individuals apprehend and conceptualize reality … and through which they implement their practice in a given historical situation' (2005: 22–3). In representing and giving meaning to social action, discourses are inherently performative. In other words, discourses can offer up the power relations that lie behind them for critical scrutiny but they can just as easily mask them from view and make us believe that certain things or ways of 'being' in the world are natural, timeless or universal when in fact they are not. 'A discourse provides a set of possible statements about a given area, and organizes and gives structure to the manner in which a practice, topic, object, process is talked about. In that it provides descriptions, rules, permissions and prohibitions of social and individual actions' (Kress, quoted in Fowler 1992: 42). There are discourses of terrorism, security, human rights, international community, climate change and the state. Each discourse relies on an architecture – or facade – of language which 'creates' the field. Each and every one of these fields can be read 'against the grain' to expose its limits as well as its meaning-making processes.

 TAKING IT FURTHER

David Campbell: *Writing Security*

David Campbell's book *Writing Security* starts with the premise that: 'Danger is not an objective condition ... that exists independently of those to whom it may become a threat' (1998: 1). Danger, he continues, 'is an effect of interpretation' rather than an objective quality of a given event or set of events (ibid.: 2). Threats to a state's national security are constructed out of the interplay between conceptions of national identity and interpretations of what is, or is not, perceived to pose a threat to the values bound up with that sense of identity: 'the boundaries of a state's identity are secured by the representation of danger integral to foreign policy' (ibid.: 3). The rest of the book is an extended engagement with the principles and assumptions of two prominent theories of foreign policy action in IR: Realism and Marxism. Both readings, Campbell asserts, are flawed because they 'maintain that there are material causes to which events and actions can be reduced'. For Realists, foreign policy activity is guided by material power considerations. For Marxists, foreign policy activity is guided by economic calculations. In both theories state interests are paramount. To advance a different perspective – 'dissent' – Campbell draws on the work of Foucault to interpret how key terms such as 'danger', 'threat' and 'power' have 'historically functioned within discourse' on US foreign and security policy from the end of the Cold War through to the mid-1990s (ibid.: 5–6). Campbell's particular reference is to 'moments' in contemporary US military history such as the Iraqi invasion of Kuwait in August 1990.

Campbell's book treats recent US foreign policy as the product of a series of 'texts' about US identity and its global mission since the end of the Cold War. Policy documents, speeches and the US citizenship test are all mined for insight into the practices of identity creation that have gone into making US foreign policy. Foundational IR texts such as Thomas Hobbes' *Leviathan* are deconstructed or 'read against the grain' to make the argument that foreign policies do not emerge *after* the creation of states, but are 'integral to their constitution' (ibid.: 60). Conjoining 'inside' with 'outside', Campbell echoes writers such as R.B.J. Walker (1993), who challenge the conceptually hegemonic appreciation of the practice of international relations which makes possible the study of IR. The assumption is of a domestic, private realm internal to states standing prior to – and separate from – a public, anarchic realm of the international 'out there' beyond neatly constructed state borders. This poststructuralist reading of the problem of the subject in IR makes the ways IR theorists have come to know the world (rather than the world itself) the object for critical discussion. As Walker summarizes this approach, 'Theories of international relations are more interesting as aspects of contemporary world politics that need explaining than as explanations of contemporary world politics' (1993: 6). Campbell's *Writing Security* is an excellent case study of poststructuralism in action in IRT.

Genealogy

In light of the overwhelming power, influence and everywhere-ness of the discourses through which we make sense of the world, Foucault invites us to write not histories but **genealogies**, which highlight power-knowledge relations. Genealogy is not history of the beginning–middle–end variety based on a neat chronological story about how things turned out as they did. A genealogy brings to our attention the contextualized nature of all knowledge and shows up the many ways in which that knowledge interplays with power to construct identities at all levels: for us as individuals, the countries we live in, and the political and social institutions in which we participate. For Jens Bartelson genealogy 'is strategically aimed at that which looks unproblematic and is held to be timeless; its task is to explain how these present traits, in all their vigour and truth, were formed out of the past' (quoted in Reus-Smit 2002: 494).

Steve Smith argues that it is important to apply a genealogical attitude to a discipline like IR because 'international theory has tended to be a discourse accepting of, and complicit in, the creation and re-creation of international practices that threaten, discipline and do violence to others' (Smith 1995: 3; see also Smith 2004). A genealogy of IR, says Richard Ashley (1986), tallies with the Critical Theory approach in being a form of metatheory. It exposes the link between the practice of IR and its discourses. It asks how things came to be this way in the discipline and inquires into the politics behind the production and dissemination of academic knowledge about IR. Genealogies investigate how dominant discourses such as Realism emerged and rose to prominence within the discipline, how IR scholars have created the subject matter, and the techniques on which scholars rely to claim that their theory or interpretation is the most valid or truthful (covered in Smith 1995: 4–7). In the work of those writers who investigate the genealogy we can clearly see an interest in taking IR beyond issues of ontology, epistemology and methodology and into a discussion of power and authority: IR narratives in this view 'are struggles to impose authoritative interpretations of international relations' (Devetak 2013b: 4). There is a clear emancipatory agenda on the cards.

> That genealogists seek out the positioned nature of knowledge about IR perhaps explains why some scholars in IR are nervous about the advent of poststructuralism within the discipline. It radically challenges claims to scientific 'objectivity'.

To give an example, take Maha Zehfuss' article on the terrorist attacks of 9/11, which when I first read it reminded me very much of Jean Baudrillard's superb (1995) writings gathered together in the book *The Gulf War Did Not Take Place*. In this work on the 1990–1 Gulf War that followed Iraq's invasion of Kuwait, Baudrillard investigated how those events have come to be represented in our 'hyperreal' postmodern age, and how they fed the creation of a US-led New World Order after Saddam Hussein's troops were beaten back within their national borders. It is a classic work that questions our experience of and access to, 'reality'. I was teaching military students when I first came across this book and I remember much consternation about the book's title. Of course the Gulf War happened, they said, we were there in tanks and aeroplanes!

The poststructuralist sensibility jolts us into thinking about the nature of reality in very different ways than we have been taught to.

Zehfuss' piece does something similar for 9/11, exploring the politics of memory and the use of the attacks in the USA as a platform for a range of repressive Western responses to terrorism at home and abroad. 'Killing civilians in Afghanistan, arguably violating the human rights of those detained by US forces, curbing our civil liberties, this is all justified because of the events of September 11. Remember. You saw it. Thousands dead' (Zehfuss 2003: 514; all page references in this section are from this article, unless otherwise stated). This is memory construction, Zehfuss argues, used in the service of a variety of practices constituting the 'War on Terror' and this, she continues, is highly problematic. We might, as the title of the article suggests, actually be better forgetting September 11 altogether.

Zehfuss defends this claim by questioning whether this was in fact an 'act of war' on the USA and/or 'the West' by Al Qaeda. And if it was, was a military response to safeguarding security the appropriate response? Moreover, was the sense of vulnerability engendered by the attack over-inflated? (pp. 515–16). A dose of Realist IRT would not go amiss, Zehfuss argues, because it would caution us to work with the prevailing forces in world politics instead of trying to overturn them in the search 'even more aggressively for an elusive security'. For instance, in many nations such as Germany – along with the USA, the other country case study in her article – strong measures on surveillance and the curtailment of civil liberties were rushed through after the attacks, leading to a 'new quality of intrusion into the individual's privacy by the state in the name of preventing crime and terrorism' (p. 517). These measures were all put in place because the facts of 9/11 were constructed 'as something exceptional' (p. 518), and an exceptional act demands an exceptional response, right?

In President George W. Bush's post-9/11 discourse, Zehfuss perceives a 'crude form of othering' (p. 519) of 'them' – the barbaric terrorists – who attacked 'us', the innocent, heroic civilian victims. She goes further than that by arguing that the same Western identity Bush and his acolytes in the US government, Germany and elsewhere claimed to be defending through their actions, were in fact undermining core features of that identity – a postmodern irony. A further issue concerns how the attacks fit into our historical narratives of the Western battle against terrorism. If 9/11 is taken as a unique event and a 'start point' for our thinking about the 'new' nature of global terrorism, it legitimates a wider set of responses than if it is depicted as 'just another terrorist attack' or 'crime' in a series of unfolding actions in which the USA *already possessed agency and responsibility*. To unpack this complex account of identity and history, Zehfuss turns to Derrida and Friedrich Nietzsche to investigate the difficulty of proposing 9/11 to have been '"an uncaused" cause' (see pp. 521–2).

Zehfuss' work on 9/11 echoes Baudrillard's on the Gulf War. Think again, they suggest, about the conditions of possibility and the discursive moves made to justify these conflicts. Poststructuralism, in this vein, investigates the normative basis of supposedly common sense givens about the world, often delivered to us by elites in the form of authoritative political narratives and associated sets of practices, parroted by the media. National identity, history, war and security: they are all imbued with a politics of representation in elite discourse, and wrapped in an aura of 'truth' (the 'reality effect' of discourse). The Holocaust, the two World Wars, the Vietnam War and the Kosovo intervention can all be treated in this way (see Edkins 2003). Even the idea of the 'state' can be destabilized, as the next section will demonstrate (see also Edkins and Zehfuss 2005).

CASE STUDY: DECONSTRUCTING 'STATES'

Devetak's (1995) book chapter 'Incomplete States' helps us appreciate the impact of the poststructuralist turn in IR in two ways. First, it shows the similarities but, more importantly, the ruptures between poststructuralist theory and other post-positivist theories covered in this book. Second, the chapter casts light on the artificiality of IR's disciplinary discourses about the state. The steps Devetak takes are as follows:

1. **Identifies the problem area.** At the beginning of the chapter Devetak notes a paradox: *'there is statecraft, but there is no completed state'* (1995: 19, his emphasis). This sensibility echoes 'thick' Constructivist and 'post-' forms of thinking in IR by questioning 'our intuitive notion of fully formed, stable actors, producing and reproducing a predictably stable and invariant world' (Lapid 1997: 8).

2. **Defines statecraft.** Devetak introduces the writers on whom he draws for inspiration about his conception of statecraft as an ongoing effort to define the state rather than the result of the settled existence of states. His use of Machiavelli in tandem with Derrida is unsettling because the former is normally used by Realists to support their theories of state behaviour in a self-help system (Devetak 1995: 20–1).

3. **Challenges Neorealist and Neoliberal IRT.** Devetak identifies the theories against which he has developed his concept of statecraft – Neorealism and Neoliberalism – and explores Waltz's comfortable assumption that 'completed' states interact as fully fledged units in the international system. For Devetak, Waltz assumes too much: we cannot take states as completed entities at all.

4. **Introduces Critical Theoretical approaches.** The argument here is that to understand the 'inside' (states) we have to understand their 'outside': all the different institutions and settings that provide the realm of the 'international' in which states interact (Devetak, 1995: 25). State boundaries, Devetak writes, are built on social power as well as clearly defined territories. To overlook the former by only concentrating on the latter is to misconstrue the historically produced, 'temporary and provisional' nature of state boundaries (ibid.: 25–6). Hence, it is insufficient to look to 'sovereignty' as the arbiter of what is internal and external to states when that concept can be called into question (ibid.: 27–8).

5. **Poststructuralism and the state.** Here, Devetak uses Hegel to argue for the 'dynamic and ongoing' processes of state construction which we have to account for when we collapse the boundaries between 'inside' and 'outside' (ibid.: 29). It is by overturning the 'inside/outside' distinction that we move out of the realm of Critical Theory and into the realm of deconstruction. Using writers such as Campbell, Ashley and Foucault, Devetak shows how states are never completed entities. Foreign policy discourses, he argues, are practices that give shape to or help construct states; these discourses are not resorted to by states *'after* their full, completed constitution' (ibid.: 32).

Devetak's interpretation of the dynamics of statecraft is a superb example of poststructuralist IRT in action. It goes beyond Critical Theory by taking a genealogical approach to the subject matter of borders, sovereignty and the state. It also draws on a Constructivist sensibility, radically reworked to show the historically contingent nature of the discursive environment of IRT. The linguistic furniture currently popular in the discipline, suggest poststructuralists, may well not be up to the job of helping us appreciate the true complexity of international relations.

QUESTIONS TO PONDER

'How can taking a genealogical approach help illuminate the study of IR?'

This question cues you to weigh up the benefits and the costs of writing genealogies of IR. Clearly your first task is to summarize what 'taking a genealogical approach' means by using, ideally, the work of Foucault – or at least a summary of his views as presented, above, by writers such as Campbell, Smith or Ashley. There are many other potential suspects.

Having defined the essay's key term, you then have to set out what you think the benefits of genealogy are and can be for IR. All of the above writers (plus many 'thick' Constructivists) cover this issue in some detail, so you can structure this part of the essay around the three or four that in your opinion are the most illuminating. Make sure when you introduce new concepts (for instance, 'regime of truth') or use technical terms such as 'discourse' that you pause to define these terms for your reader. You could use a case study such as Devetak, above, to illustrate how the genealogical approach works in practice, along with the type of knowledge it can produce.

The most successful essays will not stop at the benefits. They will consider the 'backlash' against poststructuralist approaches to IR by exploring some of the arguments advanced by writers who think they are either jargon-filled mumbo-jumbo or a dangerous distraction from the 'real' concerns of IR: studying the causes of war, the potential for peace, international security, the environment and so on. Showing that you are familiar with all sides of a debate helps demonstrate your wide reading and your critical ability to weigh up competing positions among key writers. The fundamental point to bear in mind is that compare and contrast questions demand an evaluation on your part. Without taking a stand in the debate you will not be able to gain marks towards the upper end of the spectrum.

'Why do you think "poststructuralism" has been received with such hostility by some writers in the field of IR? Is their hostility justified?'

Answering this question first of all relies on a robust definition of 'poststructuralism', so you should find a writer or writers who define this difficult term and run with their ideas. You could perhaps include a brief analysis of other competing terms such as postmodernism and explain why you either do or do not choose to use the terms interchangeably. However you do it, you need to set off in the essay from a position where the marker knows precisely what you mean by the terminology.

Your next task is to demonstrate good knowledge of both poststructuralism (briefly so as not to waste too many words) and, most importantly, the criticisms levelled at it by some IR writers. In Campbell's textbook chapter (2007), he lists five writers who criticize poststructuralism, so it is not as if they are thin on the ground. You will need to know not just what they say but why they say it, so read their original works and summarize them. How many you can cover will depend on the word limit you have (for coursework) and time limit (for an exam answer). You could try grouping their critiques together themati-cally. They tend to focus on: questions about the relevance of poststructuralism to IR as a field of study; its ethical implications (the slide into various forms of relativism); and its relevance to the practice of international relations, including policy relevance – it is often argued that policy makers generally look upon abstract theorizing as a distraction from 'doing' things in international relations.

Having set out the criticisms, you are then invited to evaluate, or weigh up, how far they land punches on poststructuralist IR. Have they depicted the poststructuralist move-ment (as you understand it) accurately? Do the critics misunderstand the nature of IR by writing off this huge intellectual movement? What would writers such as Zehfuss and Devetak say to their concerns about poststructuralist interventions in IRT? At the start and end of the essay remember to set out your core argument: do you agree or disagree with the critics?

REFERENCES TO MORE INFORMATION

Before you read the original works of writers such as Foucault and Derrida it is worth checking out introductions to their thought:

Artese, B. (2010) 'An Introduction to Poststructuralism'. Comes in three 10-minute parts. Part 1 (31 March): www.youtube.com/watch?v=6d-7ReYQkUc. Part 2 (31 March): www.youtube.com/watch?v=bpcCmaxThsY. Part 3 (1 April): www.youtube.com/watch?v=EqOVlE0C64g (accessed 23 August 2016).

Hoy, D.C. (1986) *Foucault: A Critical Reader*. Oxford: Basil Blackwell.

The School of Life (2015) 'Philosophy: Michel Foucault', www.youtube.com/watch?v=B-BJTeNTZtGU (accessed 23 August 2016).

Danaher, G., Schirato, T. and Webb, J. (2000) *Understanding Foucault*. London: Sage. Especially Chapter 3 on discourses and institutions and Chapter 5 on power.

Andersen, N.A. (2003) *Discursive Analytical Strategies: Understanding Foucault, Koselleck, Laclau, Luhmann*. Bristol: The Policy Press.

Foucault, M. (1991) 'Truth and Power', in P. Rabinow (ed.) *The Foucault Reader: An Introduction to Foucault's Thought*. London: Penguin, pp. 51–75.

Foucault, M. (1977/2007) *Security, Territory, Population: Lectures at the Collége de France, 1977–78*, trans. G. Burchell. Basingstoke: Palgrave Macmillan.

Stocker, B. (2006) *Derrida on Deconstruction*. Abingdon: Routledge.

Baudrillard, J. (1994) *Simulacra and Simulation*, trans. S. Glaser. Ann Arbor, MI: University of Michigan Press.
The French sociologist's classic study of postmodernism.

Moi, T. (ed.) (1986) *The Kristeva Reader*. Oxford: Basil Blackwell.
Guides you through the writings of Julia Kristeva.

Barthes, R. (2009) *Mythologies*. London: Vintage Classics.
Poststructuralist work on representation and language. There are many versions of this classic text.

Vucetic, S. (2011) 'Genealogy as Research Tool in International Relations', *Review of International Studies*, 37(3): 1295–312.

Chomsky, N. and Foucault, M. (2007) 'Chomsky vs. Foucault', www.youtube.com/watch?v=kawGakdNoT0, 17 April (accessed 23 August 2016).
A debate on societal organization and the amorphous nature of 'power'.

Ransom, J.S. (1997) *Foucault's Discipline: The Politics of Subjectivity*. Durham, NC: Duke University Press.

Lloyd, M. and Thacker, A. (eds) (1997) *The Impact of Michel Foucault on the Social Sciences and Humanities*. Basingstoke: Macmillan.

On representation, discourse and deconstruction:

Bolton, C. (2012) 'Animating Poststructuralism', 9 November, www.youtube.com/watch?v=6a2dLVx8THA (accessed 23 August 2016).
Brilliantly explains structural linguistics, including the problems of words standing in for – representing – objects in language.

Bloom, H. et al. (1979) *Deconstruction and Criticism*. New York: The Seabury Press.
A collection of essays by five of the leading proponents of deconstruction.

Norris, C. (1993) *Deconstruction: Theory and Practice*. London: Routledge.
Thorough overview of the will to deconstruct evident in writings by Derrida, Nietzsche, Marx and Wittgenstein.

Nealon, J.T. (1993) *Double Reading: Postmodernism after Deconstruction*. Ithaca, NY: Cornell University Press.

Burnham, P., Gilland, K., Grant, W. and Layton-Henry, Z. (2008) *Research Methods in Politics*, 2nd edn. Basingstoke: Palgrave Macmillan.
See Chapter 10 for an introduction to discourse analysis.

Howarth, D. (1995) 'Discourse Theory', in D. Marsh and G. Stoker (eds) *Theory and Methods in Political Science*. Basingstoke: Macmillan, pp. 115–33.
In the second edition of this popular text, discourse theory is strangely absent.

Milliken, J. (1999) 'The Study of Discourse in International Relations', *European Journal of International Relations*, 5(2): 225–54.

Fairclough, N. (2000) *New Labour, New Language?* London: Routledge.
Dissects New Labour's domestic and foreign policy discourses from a critical linguistic perspective and shows you how their manifestos, legislative proposals and policy speeches made sense of the world for their audience.

Wodak, R., de Cillia, R., Reisigl, M. and Liebhart, K. (2003) *The Discursive Construction of National Identity*, trans. A. Hirsch and R. Mitten. Edinburgh: Edinburgh University Press.

Good on how to use methods of critical discourse analysis to investigate national identity construction and then applies that method to the case of Austria.

Edkins, J., Shapiro, M. and Pin-Fat, V. (2004) *Sovereign Lives: Power in Global Politics*. New York: Routledge.

More generally on poststructuralism and IRT/Politics see:

Hay, C. (2002) *Political Analysis: A Critical Introduction*. Basingstoke: Palgrave. See Chapter 7.

Keeley, J.F. (1990) 'Toward a Foucauldian Analysis of International Regimes', *International Organization*, 16(1): 83–105.

van der Ree, G. (2014) 'International Relations 10: Poststructuralism', www.youtube.com/watch?v=0IVSA2mETqM (accessed 23 August 2016).

Walker, R.B.J. (1995) 'International Relations and the Concept of the Political', in K. Booth and S. Smith (eds) *International Relations Theory Today*. Cambridge: Polity Press, pp. 306–27.
Deconstructs the 'inside/outside' binary in IR and therefore pulls the rug from under the feet of state-centric theory.

Munslow, A. (2007) *Narrative and History*. Basingstoke: Palgrave Macmillan.
Explores the mechanics of representation using Foucault and others to examine how history is made meaningful to us. Also reassesses the concept of 'facts', so useful for your wider readings into the philosophy of social science.

Renwick, N. and Krause, J. (eds) (1996) *Identities in International Relations*. Basingstoke: Macmillan.

Devetak, R. (2005) 'The Gothic Scene of International Relations: Ghosts, Monsters, Terror and the Sublime after September 11', *Review of International Studies*, 31(4): 621–45.
Highlights the importance of language, symbols and imagery in constructing IR as a field of thought and practice.

Ashley, R. (1988) 'Untying the Sovereign State: A Double Reading of the Anarchy Problematique', *Millennium: Journal of International Studies*, 17(2): 227–62.

Ashley, R. (1988) 'Living on Border Lines: Man, Poststructuralism, and War', in J. Der Derian and M. Shapiro (eds) *International/Intertextual Relations: Postmodern Readings of World Politics*. Lexington, MA: Lexington Books.

Der Derian, J. (1995) 'A Reinterpretation of Realism: Genealogy, Semiology, Dromology', in J. Der Derian (ed.) *International Theory: Critical Investigations*. Basingstoke: Macmillan, pp. 363–96.

13

POSTCOLONIALISM

Key Terms

- Discourse
- Empire
- Ethnicity
- Identity
- Knowledge
- Power
- Subaltern

> While the term postcolonial itself has been debated and contested, the crucial point of departure for the body of scholarship loosely categorized as postcolonial theory is to foreground the history and politics of **colonialism** in making sense of our present social reality. (Biswas 2016: 221)

Postcolonialism, like feminism and poststructuralism, has been another relative latecomer to the field of IRT, hitting the field in the late 1980s and 1990s onward. If you have read most or all of the preceding chapters in this book, covering each IR theory one by one, ask yourself whose voice or voices have we heard most from? There is an argument to be made that IR has – in the main – been developed, taught and practiced by (often privileged) white Western males. This is something very acutely evident in feminist scholarship, but not only there. Postcolonialism exposes the latent biases in existing IR renderings by reminding us of the discipline's blind spots, judged in terms both of subject matter and the epistemological claims of positivism. It highlights 'lingering colonial hierarchies of race, class and gender despite the winding down of the formal colonial period' (Sylvester 2014: 185). Ramakrishnan agrees: 'Postcolonialism is useful in understanding the realms of representation and perception. An exposition of postcolonialism is worthwhile as a project which unravels the language of global political economy of control, if not its process' (1999: 163). We can see that Postcolonialism has strong affinities with Marxism and poststructuralism as well as being in dialogue with (Western) feminism, as we shall see below.

Thus, feminist scholars ask: where are the women in IR? Marxists ask: where are the classes in IR? Postcolonialists inquire: where is the ethnic diversity and what forms of control from now absent Empires linger on, informally, in the world today? An interdisciplinary body of work, Postcolonialism explores the power relations that govern IR's ways of representing the world, highlighting race and ethnicity as global structures too long ignored by the core of the discipline: 'postmodernity and postcolonialism find themselves enmeshed in exploring the very meanings of emancipation and of the consequences, good or ill, that may accrue to it' (Kadir 1995: 20). Postcolonialists produce normatively inclined work that critiques both the formal and informal practices of colonialism that have given rise to exploitation, alienation and repression of large portions of the globe by a supposedly rational, enlightened European imperialist order. Postcolonialists are interested in identifying entrenched hierarchies and subjecting them to critique.

As with other 'post-' approaches that have come to the field of IRT, Postcolonialism also resists easy categorization (Abrahamsen 2007; Mishra and Hodge 2005: 379). As R.S. Sugirtharajah has written, 'postcolonialism is interdisciplinary in nature and pluralistic in outlook … it is attracted to all kinds of tools and disciplinary fields, as long as they probe injustices, produce new knowledge which problematizes well entrenched positions and enhance the life of the marginalized' (quoted in Kumar 2011: 654). Postcolonial writers take inspiration from literary theory, philosophy, history and new approaches to anthropology and ethnography. As with IR in general, Postcolonialism has a 'problem of the subject' all of its own because 'postcolonial theory is not concerned with a unified "problem"' (ibid.: 665). In general, however, it is activist. Whichever form it takes, it 'continues in a new way the anti-colonial struggles of the past' (Young, quoted in Huggan and Tiffin 2008: 8).

In this chapter we will consider the dynamics of Postcolonialism mainly using the work of Edward Said, but with the usual proviso that his work is one of hundreds we could use to illustrate this rich interdisciplinary tradition. Like all the other theories, Postcolonialism also has its critics as well as its proponents (for instance, Eagleton 1998). Mark Salter's pithy definition helps appreciate how Postcolonialism can be applied to IR: 'the set of inquiries into historical and contemporary colonial relations of power' (2010: 129). This is a useful platform on which to build our investigation of Postcolonialism in this chapter. It begins with discussion of Said's canonical text *Orientalism*, which illustrates the interplay of themes that make up the Postcolonial sensibility. The second section uses Said's work to address the issue of language, discourse and Postcolonialism. The third section looks at how Postcolonialism has made itself felt in IRT using some works that reassess 'big' issues in IR using the tools provided by Postcolonial thought.

EDWARD SAID'S GALVANIZING EFFECT: *ORIENTALISM*

In 1978, Edward Said published *Orientalism*, a book in which he traced how the 'West' had placed, used and directed the 'rest' of the world through a series of practices that furthered Western interests using the information it had gleaned about the 'rest'. In the Preface to his book, Said (2003: xii) explained his progressive reason for writing: 'History is made by men and women, just as it can also be unmade and re-written, always with various silences and elisions, always with shapes imposed and disfigurements tolerated, so that "our" East, "our" Orient becomes "ours" to possess and direct.'

In a book that has since become a touchstone work of Postcolonial thought, we see several key features of what would later emerge as Postcolonial IRT (see also his *Culture and Imperialism*, 1994):

- **Things can be different.** Constructivists promote the idea that structures in the international system that we take for granted, such as 'anarchy', are in fact made by states. Poststructuralists (see the section on 'statecraft' in the previous chapter in this book) take this further by arguing that the idea of the state is constantly being remade and refashioned in the international arena. Said reinforced our appreciation of the contingency of international life by noting that our accounts of history refer to a past 'back there', but that there are, in the final analysis, only representations of that past, not a resurrection of the past itself. The Marxist and poststructuralist element to this book is also very plain. Said treated written History as a representation, stressing 'the agential making of history' (Teschke and Cemgil 2014: 607). It is, he said, always part of a conversation and is always in an actual or potential state of flux because of the slippage between our signifiers (words) and the signifieds (personalities, events, themes, issues and other happenings) we write up as History (see also Daddow 2006). These events can be 'unmade and rewritten', just as all social norms can be, if we possess the means, the imagination and the will to do so. New sources coming to light, new conceptual lenses for grasping the 'meaning' of the past, and new ideological agendas: all of them contribute to the production of fresh interpretations of the past, and the meaning of that past in the present. When all is said and done, 'stories are but one-sided representations. There are always other sides to stories' (Teschke and Cemgil 2014: 622).

> Said used the term 'Orient' to apply to various regions of the world notably the Middle East and parts of Africa and Asia. The terminology is of its time. What do you think we mean by the 'West' and 'the rest' today? Are the supposed divisions down to geography, politics, economics, culture or identity?

- **'Ours' is not 'theirs'.** Postcolonialists investigate who it is that tells us about how the world works – what makes it 'tick'. For Said, the West had generally spoken for the 'rest' in that Western scholars dominated the study, categorization and education about global civilization during the past two centuries or so. In the process, Western voices dominated other voices in the world. Western representations of these 'other' indigenous peoples who had their own stories to tell were simply drowned out, if they were recorded anywhere at all. The stories that Westerners told about the character of these peoples and their politics and cultures arguably told us more about Western beliefs and prejudices than they reflected the reality of life in those other worlds.

> We noted in Chapter 11 that Postcolonial feminists criticized their Western counterparts for writing works that implied that feminists shared the same or similar concerns the world over. This debate within the feminist movement tells you a lot about the Postcolonial agenda: encouraging awareness of diversity.

- **Discourses are power.** Another indication of the affinities between Postcolonialism, Critical Theory and Poststructuralism. 'The relationship between Occident and Orient is a relationship of power, of domination, of varying degrees of a complex hegemony … a sign of European-Atlantic power over the Orient than it is a veridic discourse about the Orient' (Said 2003: 5–6). Said observed that within supposedly disinterested scientific discourses produced in the West about the rest of the world, resided complex mechanisms of domination and an imperialist mentality that did more than a disservice to the 'rest' being written about. This mentality did a gross series of injustices to the 'reality' of life in the non-Western world. Here we see the obvious debt to Foucault, studied in the previous chapter. The 'Orient' was constituted through a series of overlapping discourses and this dramatically affected the way it was 'experienced and dealt with' (Varadarajan 2009: 296).

TAKING IT FURTHER

'Power' in *Orientalism*

Near the beginning of *Orientalism*, Said (2003: 12) set out the different dimensions of power that infuse discourses about the 'Orient':

1. Power political: The establishment of colonial structures for governing foreign territories. The administrative elites from 'core' countries sent to 'peripheries' to arrange economic and social life in the interests of the core. This would count as the repressive power of imperial states to subjugate the workings of other states in the international system so that they functioned, principally, to help the economy, security and geostrategic ambitions of the imperialist states.
2. Power intellectual: The subjection of the Orient to study by linguists, historians, anthropologists, scientists and so on. Involves measuring, naming, ordering and placing the 'other' in relation to the West (see below).
3. Power cultural: Orthodoxies, canons of taste, texts and values. The exercise of 'soft' power in international relations.
4. Power moral: Ideas about who 'we' and 'they' are, as well as how 'we' and 'they' think. Implied in the language – the discourse – put in place to describe and evaluate the colonized peoples.

Said's concept of power was Foucauldian. IR in its formative years as a discipline concentrated on repressive power: the power, for example, of one state to compel another to do its will by the threat or actual use of force (Power Political). Power for Foucault and Said is more productive than that: it is the power that comes from being in a position to tell others the way the world works; the power that comes from knowledge. In the above typology, Said's first dimension of power is repressive, the remaining three are productive, and it is no coincidence that the vast bulk of *Orientalism* is given over to studying those dimensions.

LANGUAGE, DISCOURSE AND POSTCOLONIALISM

> And postcoloniality is the twisted grimace of an unrelenting colonialism whose perti-
> nacity clones itself with aberrant vehemence in new regimes of power. (Kadir 1995: 19)

Feminist scholars have implicated language directly in the patriarchal domination of
women by men, through history into the present. A large part of their critique involves
analysis of the binary oppositions within language used to compare masculine/feminine
characteristics. For example, look at the binaries 'rational/irrational', 'detachment/commitment'
and 'brutality/compassion'. In each case the former term is privileged and it is no coincidence
they are all associated with Western constructions of positive masculine qualities. The latter,
feminine qualities are not regarded as highly, so that the universal benchmark or standard for
humanity is essentially a masculine standard. This language infuses everything from scientific
methodologies to the attributes of states as unitary, security-seeking rational actors operating in
a self-help international system.

> When you spot different theorists using the same ways of defining or critiquing a
> particular aspect of IRT, make a note of it because it helps you see the similarities
> across apparently different theoretical traditions.

Bill Ashcroft, Gareth Griffiths and Helen Tiffin (1994: 7) remark that imperial
oppression came in part via the 'control over language' as 'the medium through which
a hierarchical structure of power is perpetuated, and the medium through which conceptions of "truth", "order", and "reality" become established'. Their book traces how
Postcolonialism has been stimulated by the reclaiming of English as language and writing by indigenous populations, resulting in innovative and new forms of literature. Just
as Marxism has inspired theoretical work as well as practical action in the form of the
anti-globalization movement (Gill 2008), so Postcolonial fiction, poetry, diaries and
other testimonials are 'sources of valuable information on the nature of colonialism and
post-colonialism' (Sylvester 2014: 185).

How has this control over language been exerted? Said (2003: 40) reported the binary
oppositions that Western speakers traditionally set up in their discourses used to frame
the characteristics of 'Europe' on the one hand (which historically could stand in for 'the
West') and the 'Orient' on the other. Despite saying nothing about Postcolonialism in the
original version of *Orientalism*, 'the work nevertheless provided scholars with many registers with which to address and interpret both Orientalist, self-serving, colonial discourses
(within which are embedded a European compulsion to confine the other) and the highly
adventurous, indeed agonistic, discourses of anticolonial struggles' (Mishra and Hodge
2005: 375). Table 3 shows Said's binaries in operation.

Said recommends that we pay attention to the language through which we represent ourselves and others because this process of identity construction has dangerous
implications if and when it is built on prejudice. As Gordon Pruett has remarked,

Table 3   Said's binaries

European	Oriental
Rational	Irrational
Virtuous	Depraved
Mature	Childlike
Normal	Different

'Western identity, and especially its sense of superiority, depends upon the denigration of that which is not itself. A single term for such a view when applied to persons is racism' (quoted in Ramakrishnan 1999: 156). In Orientalist discourses, the European characteristics are held up as positive, while Orientalist characteristics are criticized and/or undervalued. Perhaps even to portray them as above is to downplay the violence these hierarchies deliver to our representations of the Oriental. Maybe Table 3 should be formatted as shown in Figure 13, which illustrates how the attribution of *difference* is imbued with a set of *power* relations.

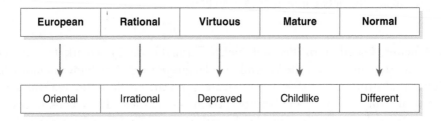

Figure 13   The practical effects of Said's binaries

Note in Figure 13 how the 'Oriental' is said to be 'irrational' – very much in the same way as feminine characteristics are looked down upon in gendered discourses of masculinity and femininity. Europeans are, it seems, 'better' than Orientals because they are more masculine.

What Said and the Postcolonialists question is the basis these supposedly time-less qualities have in 'reality', and the ethics of privileging one of the terms over its supposed opposite or antithesis. In Figure 13 we can see how the European characteristics are both stronger (bolder) and deemed to be of a higher order than their Oriental counterparts. They are deemed to be enlightened/Enlightened. This assumption, and the manifold subjugations and silences imposed on the rest of the world by linguistic practices and new forms of postmodern governance by 'the West', have been carefully picked apart and opened to critical scrutiny by Postcolonial writers.

POSTCOLONIAL IRT

So far in this chapter we have considered the interdisciplinary nature of Post-colonialism as an intellectual movement using Said's work on Orientalism. We homed in on the issue of language and discourse to demonstrate the affinities of Postcolonialism with poststructuralism, whilst also making the point that, in terms of its emancipatory agenda and points of critique, poststructuralism shares many things in common with Marxism, feminism and forms of Critical Theory. The question therefore arises, how have IR scholars made use of Postcolonial insights and methodological tools? We can answer a case study on Cuba's role in the Cuban Missile Crisis of October 1962.

Reassessing the Cuban Missile Crisis

Mark Laffey and Jutta Weldes' (2008) article on the Cuban Missile crisis demonstrates how Postcolonialism can be put to work in IRT. (All page references in this section are to this article, unless otherwise stated.) Laffey and Weldes begin by setting up the story of the Cuban Missile Crisis that will probably be familiar to all students of international politics and history. It is an account of a Cold War standoff between the USA and Russia in October 1962 over Russia's stationing of nuclear missiles in Cuba. The two countries were engaged in a tense period of crisis diplomacy that, the story goes, narrowly prevented global nuclear destruction. As you will note from the main actors in the story: 'Simply put, Cuba didn't matter in the Cuban missile crisis' (p. 555). However, this view was challenged in the 1990s, with scholars from the USA, Russia and Cuba brought together in a series of meetings in the three countries in 1989–91. The aim of the meetings was to generate oral histories that would help us understand the role that Cuba played in the unfolding crisis – especially the revolutionary leader Fidel Castro, a controversial figure whose death in November 2016 sparked wildly conflicting obituaries. The intention of the message was clear: 'The effort to produce a critical oral history constitutes a postcolonial intervention in the literature, enabling Cuban voices to challenge standard views of the crisis' (p. 556). How was this to be achieved?

Giving Cuba agency is what matters for Postcolonial treatments of the Cuban Missile Crisis. If you have been lucky enough to visit Havana – the capital of Cuba – and seen the numerous memorials and historical sites of interest relating to the country's role in the missile crisis, you will doubly appreciate the rationale of bringing Cuba into the story. In Cuba, the crisis is celebrated as a touchstone moment in the development of Cuba as a nation after the 1959 revolution, as well as an important event in the history of the Cold War. Cuba's interpretation of the crisis is rarely heard outside of the island, however.

Laffey and Weldes use their intervention to assess the ways in which IR scholarship has worked in tandem with – principally USA – policy-makers to marginalize Cuban voices in the telling of the Cuban Missile Crisis. This, they remark, is 'not an oversight but an effect of power' (p. 557). The USA, they continue, has often treated 'smaller coun-tries' as domains wherein the USA can pursue its interests militarily, economically and diplomatically, treating them as 'just a locale' or venue for different kinds of operation (Domínguéz, cited on p. 557). A good example from recent literature would be Marlon James' novel *A Brief History of Seven Killings* (2015). It depicts American CIA operatives and diplomats shuttling around the Caribbean trying to organize the islands' politics to suit Washington's interests in the region. Agency in that story is all with the Americans: the 'small' states are but pawns in its great global game.

In the first part of their article, Laffey and Weldes (2008) set the scene by discussing the 'Eurocentric' accounts that dominate scholarship in IR. These, they say, lead to a certain invisibility and/or silence on the part of many countries and regions around the globe – look at Africa, for example (p. 558). This prevailing structure of IR scholarship is reflected in accounts of the Cuban Missile Crisis, which imply that Cuba did not count as an actor worthy of study in the unfolding drama: 'Here as elsewhere, world politics was great power politics' (p. 558). When Cuba did feature, it only did so in US narratives to foreground the idea that Cuba was a Soviet puppet. Postcolonial scholarship, in contrast, sees the 'necessity of giving voice to those rendered invisible, mute, unintelligible, or mad' (p. 559). It is not just about the production of new facts (as with Liberal feminist scholarship in Chapter 11) but a creative process of reading old facts in new ways. This is the critical, poststructuralist element so key to Postcolonial scholarship, 'showing how dominant understandings and practices take on different meaning when viewed through **subaltern** eyes' (p. 560).

TAKING IT FURTHER
Cuba in international relations

In Chapter 11 on feminist IRT, Cuba made an appearance as one of the leading states in terms of the number of females in its national parliament. For a state about which not a great deal seems to be known in 'the West' (hence Postcolonial work on the Cuban Missile Crisis), and with what *is* known tending to be fed through the lenses of a battle between capitalist and communist political economy, this statistic might have come as a surprise to you – it did to me. Cuba is often written off as a cranky socialist-communist outpost with not much going for it other than nice beaches: 'a concentration camp [with] palm trees' (Vasquez 2002: 189). But there is a lot more to Cuba than meets the eye – if we can be bothered to look.

As one astute observer suggests (all page references are from Vasquez 2002), Cuba is an example of a country that questions 'the premises of neo-liberal globalization' and struggles against its impacts. Cuba might even provide a model for less developed countries encoun-tering a similar plight, particularly those in trouble with debt from Western-imposed structural adjustment programmes, which have had disproportionate effects on women, the working poor and the most marginalized portions of the population generally (p. 186). Vasquez finds many 'successes' for the Cuban alternative. First, it ranks very well on the provision of human services. It stands out above Latin American and Caribbean countries in several quality of life indicators such as life expectancy, infant mortality, access to safe water and literacy (p. 188). Second, Fidel Castro's health reforms after 1959 were remarkably successful at eradicating common diseases such as malaria, tetanus, diphtheria and policy (p. 194). Third, despite its own economic difficulties, Cuba has provided aid to at least 22 Third World countries. In 1985 Cuba had more medical doctors working abroad than the World Health Organization, and approximately one civilian aid worker for every 625 of its people. In the same period the USA had about one civilian aid worker per 34,700 of its people (p. 195). Third, education in Cuba has been successful at improving the attainment levels of its children so that its poorest students score on a par with the most advanced students of every Latin American country (p. 196).

These and other statistics would need to be brought up to date to test their contemporary relevance, and its record on human rights would require careful attention, to generate a balanced picture (Human Rights Watch 2016). However, they illustrate some very important components of Postcolonial IRT. As Marxist writers also remind us, there *are* alternatives to the Neoliberal model of capitalist consumerism, it is just that many in the privileged West do not experience or encounter them directly, if ever. We do not even know much about where alternatives are practised let alone how they work. Accounting for these alternative approaches helps us think again about many taken-for-granted 'realities' of IR, such as globalization, security, power, interdependence, hegemony, exploitation, capitalism and development. Postcolonial IRT also puts metatheoretical issues in IR to the fore by compelling us to think where we access knowledge and what it all adds up to, empirically and ideologically.

· ·

The second part of the article shows how Cuban agency was ignored/silenced in US-dominated accounts of the crisis. These emerged very soon after the resolution and were led by accounts by President John F. Kennedy and his advisers in ExComm, the hub of US decision-making at the time. These testimonials position the USA at the apex of the international hierarchy, as the defender of the free world. The Soviet Union was 'othered' as a barbaric, totalitarian state bent on imposing Communism on this free world. Cuba was but a puppet in the Soviet grand design (pp. 561–2). Its geographical position close to the USA coupled with the Castro revolution of 1959 had made Cuba seem like a grave threat to the USA. In US discourse this made Cuba another Soviet 'satellite' game for US counter-measures, including the failed Bay of Pigs invasion of 1961 and air surveillance by the USA to determine the state and extent of Cuban defence forces and armaments (pp. 562–3). Cuba was another territory in which the US–Soviet Cold War would play out, and its leadership was not party to the resolution of the missile crisis: 'Cubans were defined out of the crisis' (p. 563).

Scholarly histories and contemporaneous media accounts maintained the US-first ontology of the crisis, including what has since become *the* must-read work on foreign policy decision-making, Graham Allison's *Essence of Decision* (1971). However, the three meetings in 1989, 1991 and 1992 challenged this historiographical trend (historiography means the writing of history). How? In very simple terms, 'the subaltern spoke', especially in the Havana meeting of 1992 when Castro himself gave his account (pp. 564–5). The Cuban interpretation was that the crisis was caused by American aggression against the country: the missiles going into Cuba were a Soviet response, not the cause of the crisis (p. 565). Recapping the clash of historical narratives between the US and Cuban accounts, Laffey and Weldes argue that:

This is a very different view of the missile crisis; the spatial and temporal framing is shifted from the 13 days of heroic myth to a century of US-Cuban interaction, punctuated by repeated US interventions in Cuba and elsewhere. This history is not heroic, stressing instead imperial power and its meaning for the subaltern. (2008: 565)

Cubans pushed the sovereignty and non-interference angle. They defended the rights of small states in the international system (recall the Melian Dialogue from the Peloponnesian War, covered in the Realism chapter earlier in this book) and promoted the use of international law as a restraint on great power subversion of the sovereignty principle (a Liberal approach to international relations) (p. 566).

These accounts were tabled, Laffey and Weldes suggest, but the Cubans had much more difficulty in actually getting them *heard by* their US or indeed their Soviet interlocutors during the meetings. Indeed, in many ways the Cuban accounts were dismissed, ignored or subverted back into the previous hegemonic narrative. For example, US policy-makers overlooked the history of US policy towards (or meddling in) Cuba (pp. 566–9) in favour of an account that saw the crisis as a 'first bit of meddling'. Reading this article's account of great power reactions to the Cuban counter-narrative, it seems that extreme forms of cognitive dissonance were in play: there was a US story and its proponents stuck to it regardless of new evidence.

The final substantive section of the article weighs up the impact of the oral history project on later scholarship about the Cuban Missile Crisis. An unwillingness to come to terms with the reality of US imperialism, the authors suggest, has been one of the main reasons why the subaltern – Cuba – still struggles to get its side of the story across in scholarly accounts of the crisis. The power to gatekeep knowledge is thus real and lasting, and the opportunity to develop a Postcolonial framing of the events of October 1962 was lost (p. 572). To draw this case study to a close, Laffey and Weldes' article is a superb case study in both methods by which the subaltern can speak to promote Postcolonialism in IR, and the problems inherent in this exercise. The subtle and not so subtle exercise of power affects scholarship about IR, just as it informs practices of international relations on a daily basis.

QUESTIONS TO PONDER

'Discuss the affinities between Postcolonial, Constructivist and poststructuralist approaches to IR'

In planning an answer to this question you must first arrive at a suitable definition of each theory. Using your knowledge of each tradition, you might want to stress the diversity but also the common themes and issues writers discuss, using illustrative quotations and reference to the IRT scholarship to back your case. You will not have much space for this, given the demands of the question, so be sure to focus on the central themes and ignore the detail of each theory or the temptation to write everything you know about them. Obviously with this kind of question a working knowledge of all three theories needs to be demonstrated to get the very best marks.

Next, you have to weigh up the similarities between the three approaches to IR. One way might be to remove them from the realm of discrete 'theories' and use the language of loosely rated 'sensibilities'. In this chapter we referred to Said's take on language, representation, the role of ideas and education in constructing the Orient in the West. His point is that the Orient has been 'made' by human endeavour, it is not necessarily an accurate portrait of the 'reality' of the world 'out there'. Hence, you could link his work to 'thick' Constructivism and poststructuralist work on representation, discourse and signifier/signifieds. A standard answer would stop there. The highest achieving answers, however, will go on to note that, if anything, Postcolonialism shares just as much with other theories of IR such as feminism and Marxism. It all depends on the space and time available to you as to how far you can investigate these other overlaps. But if you can convey your sense of the nature of the interplay between Postcolonialism and these other theories, then you will get credit for exhibiting a thorough knowledge of the fabric of those other theories of IR.

All in all, this is a very difficult question because of the breadth of knowledge that it demands. Managing everything to fit the word and/or time limit would be extremely challenging. What this type of question illustrates is the importance of thinking strategically about which question/s you choose to answer for coursework assignments and exams. The better read you are during your course, the more options you have in terms of question choice.

'. . . an exercise in cultural strength'. What are the implications of Edward Said's description of *Orientalism* for the study of IR?

The nub of this question is to explain what Said means when he talks of the 'exercise of cultural strength', and to link that to a discussion of the dynamics of the Orientalist tradition more generally. For Said, Orientalism highlights the repressive dimensions of power (Power Political). However, we saw in his other three dimensions of power that he was at least as interested in the productive dimensions of the power, whereby individuals in the West defined, delimited and 'named' the Orient. In the process, they helped legitimize various techniques of colonial repression and exploitation based on everything from race and ethnicity, to the embellishment of cultural hierarchies, all linked to particular modes of knowledge production. Said's 'cultural strength' is therefore about the exercise of various forms of power, hard and soft. The best essays will do more than concentrate on the naked military or political forms of power, but will look at the reinterpretation of power by the likes of Said, possibly linked to Foucault and knowledge/power (see the previous chapter in this book).

Tracing the implications for the study of IR will involve assessing the impact of Said's work on the evolution of Postcolonialism as an intellectual movement. It is interesting that Said's early work did not mention Postcolonialism, but it galvanized an identifiable body of work to develop around this label, rather like Marx and Marx-inspired writers. You will not need to know in detail the sociology or politics of Postcolonialism as an intellectual movement, but you can tell how important Said and other writers are in this canon by the number of references to their ideas in textbook chapters and the like. Having established Said as a central figure you should be in a position to draw out three or four implications of this quote for the study of IR. Set out those you feel are most crucial and alert the reader to other points as you see fit. The kinds of implications you can consider would include: issues of race, ethnicity, identity, language, power, discourse, exploitation, systemic structures, oppression and the politics of disciplined knowledge.

REFERENCES TO MORE INFORMATION

van der Ree, G. (2014) 'International Relations 11: Postcolonialism', www.youtube.com/watch?v=gIwJFfNPj1M (accessed 25 August 2016).

Palestine Diary (2012) 'Edward Said on *Orientalism*', www.youtube.com/watch?v=fVC8EYd_Z_g (accessed 25 August 2016).
Said discusses the context within which the book was written, some of the main influences on his thought, and its relevance to the world today.

Fanon, F. (1968) *The Wretched of the Earth*, trans. C. Farrington. New York: Grove Press.
Opened up windows on the repressive practices of colonialism not just physically but also in terms of the knowledge that Europe's imperial masters produced about the world.

Bhaba, H.K. (1994) *The Location of Culture*. London: Routledge.

Chakrabarty, D. (2000) *Provincializing Europe: Postcolonial Thought and Historical Difference*. Princeton, NJ: Princeton University Press.

Chowdry, G. and Nair, S. (eds) (2002) *Power, Postcolonialism and International Relations: Reading Race, Gender and Class*. London: Routledge.

Spivak, G.C. (1987) *In Other Worlds: Essays in Cultural Politics*. London: Routledge.

Bush, B. (2006) *Imperialism and Postcolonialism*. Harlow: Pearson Education.
Explores the history, concept and dynamics of imperialism together with, in Chapter 6, the Postcolonial move in studies of Empire.

Doty, R. (1996) *Imperial Encounters: The Politics of Representation in North–South Relations*. Minneapolis, MN: University of Minnesota Press.

Darby, P. (2000) *At the Edge of International Relations: Postcolonialism, Gender and Dependence*. London: Continuum International Publishing Group.
Good on the wide-ranging challenge Postcolonialism poses for 'conventional' IR theory.

Darby, P. and Paolini, A.J. (1994) 'Bridging International Relations and Postcolonialism', *Alternatives*, 19(3): 371–97.

Ferguson, Y.N. and Mansbach, R.W. (1991) 'Between Celebration and Despair: Constructive Suggestions for Future International Theory', *International Studies Quarterly*, 35(4): 363–86.

Mohanty, C.T. (1988) 'Under Western Eyes: Feminist Scholarship and Critical Discourse', *Feminist Review*, 30(3): 61–88.

Muppidi, H. (2004) *The Politics of the Global*. Minneapolis, MN: University of Minnesota Press.

Hoogvelt, A. (2001) *Globalization and the Postcolonial World: The New Political Economy of Development*, 2nd edn. Baltimore, MD: Johns Hopkins University Press.

Parts 1 and 2 refresh you on the Marxist take on the global political economy, while Part 3 works the Postcolonial dimension region by region.

Walker, R.B.J. (ed.) (1984) *Culture, Ideology, and World Order*. Boulder, CO: Westview Press. Especially the chapters on civilizations, hegemonies and world order and the hegemony of Western reason.

Mignolo, W. (2003) *The Darker Side of the Renaissance: Literacy, Territoriality, and Colonization*, 2nd edn. Ann Arbor, MI: University of Michigan Press.

Krishna, S. (1993) 'The Importance of Being Ironic: A Postcolonial View on Critical International Relations Theory', *Alternatives*, 18(3): 385–417.
A review essay themed around works by critical and postmodernist scholars such as David Campbell and James Der Derian.

Ling, L.H.M. (2001) *Postcolonial International Relations: Conquest and Desire between Asia and the West*. Basingstoke: Palgrave Macmillan.
Challenges the 'clash of civilizations' thesis as a process of 'othering' that downplays the complex global interactions that shape cultural and individual identities.

George, J. and Campbell, D. (1990) 'Patterns of Dissent and the Celebration of Difference: Critical Social Theory and International Relations', *International Studies Quarterly*, 34(3): 269–93.

Krishnaswamy, R. and Hawley, J.C. (eds) (2008) *The Postcolonial and the Global*. Minneapolis, MN: University of Minnesota Press.
Wide-ranging collection covering everything from the politics of disciplined Western knowledge to World System Theory and resistance to Empire in a globalized world.

Loombe, A. (1998) *Colonialism/Postcolonialism*. London: Routledge.

Sajed, A. (2012) 'The Post Always Rings Twice? The Algerian War, Poststructuralism and the Postcolonial in IR Theory', *Review of International Studies*, 38(1): 141–63.

Sankaran, K. (2008) *Globalization and Postcolonialism*. London: Rowman and Littlefield.

14

GREEN INTERNATIONAL THEORY

Key terms

- Corporate Social Responsibility
- Ecoanarchy
- Ecocentrism
- Ecological citizenship
- Ecological security
- Regime
- State

> Environmental questions cannot be neatly boxed off from other political questions.
> (Paterson 1995: 214)

In Chapter 11 on feminism we saw how the concerns raised by this multifaceted social and political movement fed into IRT throughout the later 1980s and 1990s in the form of gender perspectives on world politics. We found it far too simple to portray feminist writings as being somehow tacked on to the existing core of the discipline of IR, and they certainly did not emerge from within IR itself. The critically inclined feminist literature challenges the fundamentals of what it means to say we study IR (the ontology of the discipline) and argues that the dominant methods and epistemologies of the discipline are inherently positioned in ways that marginalize women and women's experiences. 'Gender,' they say, is not a variable that can be added or removed from IR when we like, but it is always there and demands attention whenever we think about matters international. The same went for the other post-positivist theories of IR we covered in Chapters 8–13 of this book.

As you can appreciate from Matthew Paterson's quote above, international theorists foregrounding 'green' issues have much the same approach to IR. They do not see questions relating to the environment, ecological sustainability and development as ones that can be adequately addressed by a state-centric approach, either in the theory or practice of IR. Instead, they call for a thoroughgoing reassessment of the ways in which we think and act towards the environment, in the process calling into question the role of the state and statist approach to human security. While Green theorists may take a variety of positions and engage in heated debates amongst themselves 'they seem to share at least one core premise – that *our received wisdom about the relationship between nature (the natural environment) and culture (the human environment) must be questioned*' (Weber 2010: 192, original emphasis). In this chapter we explore this normative challenge to IRT in three parts: Green approaches to IRT; ecocentrism as ontology; and the idea of ecological citizenship.

'GREENING' IRT

Issues and debates surrounding the contemporary environment and the challenges humans face in providing development at a pace that is sustainable at a global level are constantly in the media and political spotlight. For example, the environment forms part of the remit of the UN, under its Office for Sustainable Development, established in 2011, which aims to help member states 'in planning and implementing sustainable development strategies through knowledge sharing, research, training, and partnerships' (UN undated). Meanwhile, massive global issues such as climate change remain ongoing bones of contention politically and scientifically. 'Water wars' and energy security, deforestation and desertification, fisheries and the reef systems are now all hot items on the international environmental agenda (Smith et al. 2011: 149–64). International and regional action on this matter, as with environmental issues more generally, cut across the (notional) borders between the domestic and the international. Citizens, civil society, small and large corporations, national governments and international institutions are all seen as part of the problem for the environment, but crucially also as parts of the solution. A strong legal framework and clear rules are deemed central to success in tackling this and other environmental challenges (see Paris UN Climate Change Conference 2015; for analysis and discussion of this conference see *The Guardian* 2016).

In tandem with growing action at UN level, the environment has featured on the agenda of regional organizations such as the EU for a number of years. This marks a break with past practices. It was not always acknowledged, for example, that trading relations between states impacted on the environment. Or, if it was acknowledged, the environmental damage caused by the production, delivery, consumption and disposal of manufactured items did not appear to warrant serious attention by states:

> The founding treaties of what is now the EU did not explicitly identify a power for the EU to act to protect the environment. Even at the time of the UK's accession to what was then the European Economic Community in 1973, the need to protect the environment was not a widely recognised issue, and indeed climate change was not considered until much later. *The initial drive for development of EU competence in this area was to improve the functioning of the Single Market.* (UK Government 2014, emphasis added)

In recent years, the 'market first, environment later' approach has been deemed unacceptable. Human survival itself has been brought into question if current manufacturing practices, levels of pollution and volume of consumption are maintained. By 2006, EU member states affirmed their commitment to a sustainable development agenda in words echoed precisely by the UN in 2008 (Council of the European Union 2006: 2). At the national level, various types of 'green' party have flourished in many countries. In the UK, for example, the Green Party is now a multi-issue party centring on creating a healthy environment for the present and in the years ahead, but with more than an eye on the international dimensions of its normative platforms (Green Party 2016).

It should be obvious from the manifold number of environmental issues now on the contemporary global agenda that theorizing them is no easy business. When we choose to buy re-usable carrier bags for our supermarket shopping, or when we donate money to charities providing clean water in desertified regions of Africa, we are responding to issues raised directly by the Green movement, which has grown rapidly since the 1960s (Eckersley 2016). In deciding to go for reusable carrier bags and giving money to the African water charity, we are also responding to the popular environmentalist call to 'think globally, act locally', a slogan that highlights the ways in which Green theorists cause us to rethink the state's role in dealing with environmental issues. The cross-cutting nature of environmental challenges poses acute problems for policy practitioners and IR theorists alike.

A useful way to get to grips with the goals of Green international theory is to summarize its take on the pitfalls of mainstream IR; we will do this using the work of Paterson (1995: 213–18; see also Hovden 1999):

- **A narrow agenda.** To use the terminology developed earlier in this book (see Chapter 3), Green international theorists see flaws in the ontological starting point for mainstream IR: state behaviour at the international level. Paterson identifies a problem with any approach that begins by asking what we can do internationally to, say, combat waste pollution of our rivers: it overlooks the domestic sources of those problems and the potential solutions to them. We can only 'think globally, act locally' if we either forget or reform the central place states occupy in dealing with environmental matters.

> For the purposes of Green international theory as Paterson developed it in the 1990s, 'mainstream' IR meant Neorealism and Neoliberalism. Do you think these theories still constitute the core of the discipline today?

- **Flaws in Neoliberal assumptions.** The knock-on point concerns the agreements that states make about the environment, such as the landmark Kyoto Protocol of 1997 (for the text of the treaty, see UN 1998) or the Copenhagen Climate Change Conference of 2009. In making these agreements, Paterson argues, the first assumption is that the signatory countries will want, and be able, to implement those agreements through appropriate regulation at the domestic level. What this overlooks, he remarks, is the influence of powerful corporate lobbies at the domestic level which can affect national climate policies against the spirit of international agreements (for example, the oil and coal lobbies). It is, he concludes, 'politically naïve' to ignore the impact of these organized interests and therefore theoretically flawed to talk about IR as the exclusive preserve of state actions and decisions. Non-governmental actors are hugely impactful where the environment is concerned, with the rise of Corporate Social Responsibility (see below in this chapter) a signal acknowledgement of the role that Multinational Corporations as well as small national businesses play in impacting on the environment (Smith et al. 2011: 154).

The second assumption is that scientists can provide 'objective' advice on the environment. The criteria they develop and the measurements they use to develop these criteria will always be politically skewed in some way. In the true spirit of post-positivist IRT, says Paterson, beware anyone who claims to be value-free or objective about any issue, however supposedly technical the subject matter.

Towards ecocentrism

The objections Green international theorists have to 'core' or state-centric IR theorizing have encouraged them to develop 'an alternative analysis of global ecological problems'. Green international theory exposes the problematic nature of Neoliberal assumptions and ethical values. Moreover, it encourages us to think about the environment in new ways which expand our IR horizons beyond states and interests to include ethics and values, and non-state actors such as transnational advocacy networks (Eckersley 2016: 269). In raising these questions about mainstream approaches, Green theorists 'see' a different world compared to the **anthropocentrism** of the Neoliberals (Dalby 2009), which 'only values the human species and is therefore only concerned with the survival of the human species' (Weber 2010: 193). Against this human-centred approach, an 'ecocentric' philosophy sees the world as made up of 'the larger web of life, made up of nested ecological communities at multiple levels of aggregation (e.g. gene pools, populations, species, ecosystems, and Earth system processes such as the hydrological, nitrogen, phosphorous, and carbon cycles)' (Eckersley 2016: 263). They see a world in which humans are not the only sentient beings for whom policies on the environment should be made. Rather, humans are 'part of nature, not above nature', the fate of the one hinging directly on the fate of the other (Weber 2010: 193).

Where feminists argue that IRT has been 'gender blind' and Marxists that IRT has been 'class blind', Green theorists argue that IRT has been 'Green blind', with a significant emphasis on a feminist 'ethics of care' informing their appreciation of the dynamics of world politics.

In the spirit of shifting our focus to the world and its long-term health and survival, Green theorists of many varieties think through the best way to respond to ecological challenges in ways that transcend the state-centricity of traditional IR approaches. The 'IPE wing' of Green international theory (Eckersley 2016: 267–8; Smith et al. 2011: 149–64) has already been discussed. It takes its cue from the flaws in Neoliberalism and proposes an alternative account of the causes and solutions to global ecological problems.

The 'green cosmopolitan' wing of Green theory brings together an array of individuals and groups committed to articulating new ways of thinking about ecology and proposing solutions 'at all levels of governance' above and below the state' (Eckersley 2016: 267). Their view is that we need to create new norms of 'environmental justice', which means:

- Ecological risks affect more than human beings alone and more than citizens of states but all peoples around the globe.
- Participation in decision-making on the environment should be massively expanded and democratized to include representatives of all those affected by such decisions.
- A minimization of risks vis-à-vis the wider community.
- All risks must be acceptable and they should be gauged democratically and with the input of all affected parties (a form of Critical Theory's theory of communicative action; see Chapter 8 above).
- Those suffering from the consequences of ecological problems should have adequate recourse to redress and compensation.

From within the 'green cosmopolitan' wing of Green theory there has emerged in recent years the notion of ecological citizenship and we can consider that the most fundamental challenge yet to state-based understandings of IRT – this is the theme of the next section.

Ecological citizenship and Corporate Social Responsibility (CSR)

Earlier forms of Green international theory were associated with rationalist microeconomic assumptions about the behaviour of states towards the environment in international organizations. In taking this approach to the subject matter the ontological positioning of this work was in line with what could be considered the 'core' of the discipline of IR to the early 1990s. More recently, Green international theory has reflected various 'post-' forms of social thought (in this case post-state) by departing from a focus on the costs and benefits of cooperation in the international arena to consider environmental attitudes and practices at the level of individual humans and non-state actors. Inspired by the work of Alan Dobson (2003) this sub-field of Green international theory is an attempt to rethink and in many cases go beyond cosmopolitan ideas and ideals (ibid. 2006a). Particular attention has been paid to new understandings of citizenship and the ways in which actors across the levels from humans to states, to non-state and supra-state actors 'manage' their behaviour by recasting the balance between rights/duties and responsibilities/obligations. Human responsibilities in Green cosmopolitan thought are universal – they do not stop at (always artificial) state borders (ibid. 2007).

For example, Neil Carter and Meg Huby do a good job of showing that actors such as ethical investors (individuals, businesses and fund managers) have sprung up around the globe in recent years. They act as ecological citizens, motivated by such concerns as nuclear power, ozone layer degradation, the Third World, armament proliferation and animal testing (Carter and Huby 2005: 262). They further show that while it is harder for companies to be 'black boxed' as ethical citizens in their own right, 'their activities are crucial to the achievement of ecological citizenship goals'. By engaging in practices such as Corporate Social

Responsibility (CSR), companies can provide the organizational rules and institutional norms for the promotion of ecological citizenship (ibid.: 262). For an excellent account of the historical rise of CSR from the 1950s onward, see Moura-Leite and Padgett (2011).

In turn, CSR has been encouraged by government laws and regulations put in place at the national, regional and international levels. For instance, the UK Department of Trade and Industry defines a 'responsible' organization as doing three things. First, recognizing that its activities have a wider impact on the society in which it operates. Second, a responsible organization takes account of the economic, social, environmental and human rights impacts of its activities across the world. Finally, it seeks to achieve benefits by working in partnership with other groups and organizations (DTI, cited in Carter and Huby 2005: 269). Organizations such as the EU (see the Taking it Further box below) and OECD are all involved in agreeing, promoting and enforcing CSR practices. For example, the updated OECD guidelines on responsible business practices for multinationals were agreed in May 2011 (OECD 2011). Accountability via visibility is provided by the publication of CSR statements on a regular basis, with global accountancy firms conducting insightful surveys of progress of global trends in CSR covering: first, the numbers of firms engaged in CSR reporting; second, the best and worst performing sectors of the economy; and third, the best and worst performing countries on CSR reporting (KPMG 2013).

· ·

 TAKING IT FURTHER

The EU and Corporate Social Responsibility

The European Commission is responsible for promoting responsible practices in the EU. It defines CSR as 'companies [not just multinationals] taking responsibility for their impact on society'. Companies are deemed to be responsible if they follow the law and if they integrate social, environmental, ethical, consumer and human rights concerns into both their business strategy and their operations (European Commission 2016). The agreement and enforcement of CSR at the European level is thus a classic case of states and firms working together to build trust, confidence, working relationships and sets of agreements that all will abide by – a classic IR problem. How does the EU do this for CSR?

- Enhancing the visibility of CSR and disseminating good practices.
- Improving and tracking levels of trust in business.
- Improving self- and co-regulation processes.
- Enhancing market rewards for CSR.
- Improving company disclosure of social and environmental information.
- Further integrating CSR into education, training and research.
- Emphasizing the importance of national and subnational CSR policies (European Commission 2016).

The Commission strategy is informed by a large and influential network of international agreements made in the following bodies: the UN, OECD (discussed above), the International Organization for Standardization (ISO) and the ILO. This shows how states, firms and international organizations have been working together to spread the 'norm' of CSR around the international system in recent years. CSR can be examined trough a number of theoretical lenses too. A Realist IR theorist might ask, what is the interest at stake in these 'moves' on CSR by states? A Neoliberal

IR theorist might ask, what functions have international organizations been performing in building thee agreements? A Constructivist might ask, has this now become an entrenched international norm, and how can we measure its take-up by states and companies?

. . . .

This and related work on ethical investment and CSR being undertaken way outside IR's disciplinary boundaries (see Palacios 2004; Hellsten and Mallin 2006) makes a compelling empirical case for theorizing ecological citizenship in tandem with the study of capitalism in the global political economy.

Many major companies publish their Corporate Social Responsibility objectives and have details on their websites about what they are doing to promote CSR in their local communities and more widely. A very engaging classroom exercise is for students to go away and research a CSR case study, answering such questions as:

1. How does the corporation studied define and implement CSR?
2. What are the current and future CSR challenges it identifies?
3. How committed does the corporation seem to promoting CSR – and why?

You can link your research and discussions to the KPMG (2013) and other surveys of global trends in CSR reporting.

Defining ecological citizenship: justice and order beyond state and time

One way of understanding ecological citizenship is to contrast it with traditional conceptions of democratic citizenship in political theory, whereby 'citizens should be under no duties and obligations towards the environment other than those laid down in political decisions resulting from just and legitimate processes'. Beyond this narrow, politically driven motivation for action, ecological citizenship promotes morally driven actions. It rests on the claim that 'the ecological crisis demands a new type of citizenship built on "non-reciprocal" morally derived responsibilities applicable to all human action' arising from the production of billions of ecological footprints the world over every day' (Martinsson and Lundqvist 2010: 531).

'A country's ecological footprint is the sum of all the cropland, grazing land, forest and fishing grounds required to produce the food, fibre and timber it consumes, to absorb the wastes emitted when it uses energy and to provide space for infrastructure' (WWF undated). See later in the chapter for more on ecological footprints.

According to this thicker conception of citizenship, human beings can aspire to live 'the good life', but they have morally binding obligations 'to take personal responsibility for restoring global justice'. An ecological citizen is one 'who embraces green values and attitudes and carries these out in practice' (Martinsson and Lundqvist 2010: 519–20). Reducing individual, community and national ecological footprints is a big part of the story in promoting good ecological citizenship.

Thus, ecological citizenship 'focuses on understanding the motivations and reasons for responsible actions' as far as the environment goes (Smith 2005: 16). It brings a feminist ethics of care into dialogue with work on solidarism, globalization and inequality associated with the English School and Marxists theorists. Perhaps more than any other IRT we study in this book, ecological citizenship is forward looking, rather than an attempt (as in Neorealism, for example) to freeze time and explain power configurations between major and minor powers at a given historical juncture. Ecological citizenship certainly deals with the present, but it stretches our horizons well beyond it. For example, the effects of deforestation highlight the need for justice on the planet now and in the future; water quality issues 'prompt awareness of our immediate successors' living on the planet; while the disposal or storage of nuclear waste 'raises obligations to distant future generations' (ibid.: 19).

We can summarize the core tenets of ecological citizenship with the help of Carter and Huby (2005: 256–57):

- First, it is *non-territorial*. Environmental problems such as acid rain do not stop at state borders, so ecological citizens have to operate within and beyond the state to achieve their collective goals. This is underlined by the work on bioregions, which suggests new ways of thinking about Green issues beyond the state by redrawing our conception of 'boundaries' in international relations (McGinnis 1999). The term bioregionalism was coined by Allen van Newkirk, who founded the Institute for Bioregional Research in the USA in the mid-1970s (for an excellent account of the emergence and take-up of this concept, see Aberley 1999).
- Second, it *takes place within the public and private realms*. Where conventional IRT focuses on state interactions 'out there' in the realm of 'the international', ecological citizens are aware that their low-level day-to-day actions have public ramifications, for example if they use plastic bags instead of recyclable multi-use canvas shopping bags.
- Third, ecological citizenship is associated with '*virtues that enable citizens to meet their obligations*', notably the social justice needed to ensure a fair distribution of ecological space for all humanity, and compassion defined as empathy with the plight of others on the planet now, along with those yet to be born.
- Fourth, it entails *non-contractual responsibilities*, for instance to ensure that ecological footprints are sustainable, without expectation that there will be reciprocity. In other words, do not expect you will get anything much in return for acting as an ecological citizen. By definition, future generations cannot pay you or thank you in advance!

Empirical and normative assumptions

The idea of ecological citizenship has been developed to provide an answer to the 'practical question' that animates Green theorists across the board: 'of how a sustainable society might be brought about' (Dobson 2006b: 450) when environmental concerns more often than not clash with perceptions of economic, political or material self-interest (ibid. 2007). The action that is clearly 'the right thing to do' can conflict with perceptions of our immediate wants, needs and interests. At the heart of this approach are empirical concerns with the nature and scale of the ecological footprint we leave behind: as humans going about our daily lives; as companies in the process of manufacturing and distributing goods and services; and as states *in toto* in terms of regulating environmental concerns at the international level. Its normative concern comes through in the cosmopolitan account of the political and moral obligations coming from individuals being united across national borders in a common humanity. One timely study of the links between identity with the 'world community' and global cooperation has described cosmopolitanism as a phenomenon that transcends the borders and boundaries of the state because of the cross-cutting nature of economic and environmental issues:

> Because of phenomena associated with global warming, destruction of rain forests, and instability in international markets, decisions made by actors in one locality have consequences for the physical environment and for the economic opportunities of people at remote distances. Addressing such problems requires cooperation that transcends national boundaries. (Buchan et al. 2011: 821)

Dobson describes the three commitments of cosmopolitanism as follows (all in Dobson 2006a: 167–8, unless otherwise stated):

1. **Scope: Who is obliged and to whom?** In principle the scope is universal across all human beings. As Dobson points out this universalist conception is well covered in Andrew Linklater's *The Transformation of Political Community* (1998). The problem cosmopolitans encounter is practical: we might be cosmopolitans in theory but find it difficult or impossible to put the theory into practice (Dobson 2006a: 169).
2. **Nature: What are we obliged to do?** Harder to capture, but writers coalesce around the following themes prevalent in Linklater's work: avoid deception and harm; cultivate and exercise certain virtues, for example compassion; and work towards the creation of open communities of discourse. Thomas Pogge adds that we should refrain from involving ourselves in unjust institutions and Charles Jones suggests that we should do justice wherever possible.
3. **Source of obligation.** Links to the motivation of human action. Legal sources are rule-bound obligations (fear of sanctions or reprisals for example). Dobson calls these 'perfect' obligations. 'Imperfect' obligations are ethical obligations and these are not sanctionable.

Ecological footprints

Ecological citizenship thus provides a related but deeper account of the ties that bind present and future generations, and the codes of justice that apply to our interaction with the environment, than does orthodox cosmopolitanism. Dobson looks to go beyond a 'thin' approach to cosmopolitan citizenship by introducing the idea that people are better motivated to act on an appreciation of their cosmopolitan responsibilities when they can be persuaded or made to feel causally responsible for the suffering of 'real' or 'imagined' others. This sentiment entrenches the appreciation of 'connected selves' because it encourages humans to feel morally responsible for injustice or harm (Dobson 2006a: 172). Recognition of environmental degradation and resource depletion caused by global warming could be one example of our globalized world producing 'literally *global* relations of causal responsibility' (ibid.: 175).

Our chances of generating 'thick' cosmopolitanism of the sort that transcends a 'thin' appreciation of our membership of a global human community thus turn on the extent to which we believe our individual/corporate/state ecological footprints bring with them a sense of needing to do justice – not just to other humans living on the planet now, but those billions who will live with the effects of our actions for centuries into the future:

> The idea of the ecological footprint enables us to think of the material impact we have on the biotic (including human) and abiotic [non-living] elements of the environment that lie within – or beneath – it. No one can avoid having an ecological footprint, and so everyone impacts on someone or something, all the time. (ibid.: 176–7)

Ecological citizenship encourages us to think beyond IR's conventional notions of space and time and to collapse the public–private distinction as a way of making better sense of the practical policy questions surrounding our 'being' in a globalized world of scarce resources, and how we make sense of these theoretically.

QUESTIONS TO PONDER

'Is Green international theory outside the remit of IRT?'

In organizing your response to this question you will have to take a direct position and back it up using evidence from two sets of literature. One is on the 'appropriate subject matter' or central agenda of IRT, and this is a matter of interpretation. The other literature you will need to know is Green international theory – its ontological positioning (what it studies) and how it can contribute to IR debates you deem to be significant. Your answer will turn on your definition of both the key concepts in the question: what are 'ecocentric issues' and what is 'the remit of IR'? What type of Green international theory do you take to be representative of the tradition: the 'reform the state' approach of writers such as Eckersley, the market-oriented solutions on offer in the practice and regulation of proponents of Corporate Social Responsibility, or the ecological citizenship ideas of Dobson? Where might the bioregionalists who ignore national borders in the construction of regional environmental challenges fit into this story? There is also a strong 'do away with the state' approach of ecoanarchists such as Murray Bookchin, which we have not even had space to cover in this chapter (see 'References to more information' below). You will have to allude to the commonalities across their thought as much as the divergences, so some general knowledge of the textbook chapters on Green international theory will help you see into the different agendas at work.

As for the remit of IR, you could reasonably take the conventional 'Neoliberal' position as representing an orthodox interpretation of IR's agenda. What Green international theorists ask, in common with Marxists, feminists and poststructuralists, is the extent to which this conventional agenda addresses issues in global politics today. If you agree that normative theory speaks more to our contemporary concerns than the positivist, state-centric approaches of Realism and Liberalism, then you will not think Green international theory is outside the remit of IR but fundamental to it. The very best answers will allude to the idea that Green international theory, like gender theory, cannot be treated as a 'variable' in IR to be addressed or forgotten about on a whim, but that it is always there organizing and regulating our knowledge about IR whether we choose to recognize it or not.

'Critically evaluate Dobson's idea of ecological citizenship as an approach to IRT'

Dobson's work on ecological citizenship has spawned a dedicated body of work in its own right. Hence, you can legitimately focus on Dobson whilst perhaps in the early stages of the answer showing how he links to Green international theory more widely. For example, he goes beyond anthropocentrism; he contributes to work on cosmo-politanism; and he theorizes along the lines of a feminist ethics of care. Many of the marks in this answer will be gained by defining and showing a good depth of knowl-edge about the concept of 'ecological citizenship'. Before you launch into criticisms of any theory you need to patiently establish your position by setting out exactly what you understand the theory (theorist in this case) to be saying. A robust understanding of ecological citizenship requires: one or more definitions from the relevant litera-ture; an explication of its core concepts such as the ecological footprint; and a general statement of its normative positioning within key IR debates about, for instance, the role of the state and the dynamics of contemporary international society in the era of advanced globalization. You might want to refer to 'real world' organizations such as the World Wildlife Fund that promote thinking on the ecological footprint (and/or use them for definitions), but do not get too distracted by the practical policy work at this stage – treat it as an illustrative add-on to the theoretical work.

The amount of marks you can pick up for the 'critically evaluate' segment will then rest on the extent to which you can present Dobson's case in the context of IRT more widely. Who agrees with him? Who disagrees with him, and why? Do you think that Green international theory 'fits' within what we might reasonably consider is encompassed by the 'field' of IRT (see the previous question to ponder)? Does it deal effectively with IR topics such as the role of the state, order and justice? You can bring to bear as many other theories as you like in making your argument. As long as you do so from a position of strength you can get mileage from any of the theories you cover on your IRT course.

REFERENCES TO MORE INFORMATION

Vogler, J. (2008) 'Environmental Issues', in J. Baylis, S. Smith and P. Owens (eds) *The Globalization of World Politics: An Introduction to International Relations*, 4th edn. Oxford: Oxford University Press, pp. 350–68.
More conventional treatment of Green theory than you will find in Paterson and Eckersley's critically inclined approaches.

Doran, P. (1995) 'Earth, Power, Knowledge: Towards a Critical Global Environmental Politics', in J. Macmillan and A. Linklater (eds) *Boundaries in Question: New Directions in International Relations*. London: Pinter, pp. 193–211.
Uses Foucault's idea of discursive regimes to expose the limits of environmental practices and policies put in place by states and international organizations.

Lövbrand, E. and Stripple, J. (2006) 'The Climate as Political Space: On the Territorialisation of the Global Carbon Cycle', *Review of International Studies*, 32(2): 217–35.

Smith, M.J. (1998) *Ecologism: Towards Ecological Citizenship*. Buckingham: Open University Press.
Opening chapter useful on the anthropocentric/ecocentric distinction.

Dobson, A. (2007) *Green Political Thought*, 4th edn. London: Routledge.
Wall, D. (2005) *Babylon and Beyond: The Economics of Anti-Capitalist, Anti-Globalist and Radical Green Movements*. London: Pluto.
Ecoanarchist take on Green theory, also useful for your understanding of Marxism and Anarchism.

Bookchin, M. (2005) *The Ecology of Freedom: The Emergence and Dissolution of Hierarchy*, 4th edn. Oakland, CA: AK Press.
Leading ecoanarchist writer. Or try:
Bookchin, M. (2007) *Social Ecology and Communalism*. Oakland, CA: AK Press.

Eckersley, R. (2004) *The Green State: Rethinking Democracy and Sovereignty*. Cambridge, MA: MIT Press.
The state-led approach to promoting environmental justice. Conflicts with the ecoanarchists' view of how to achieve the same ends.

Deudney, D. (1996) 'Ground Identity: Nature, Place, and Space in Nationalism', in Y. Lapid, and F. Kratochwil, (eds) *The Return of Culture and Identity in IR Theory*. London: Lynne Rienner Publishers, pp. 129–45.

Paterson, M. (1996) *Global Warming and Global Politics*. London: Routledge.
On the nature and limits of inter-state approaches to the environment.

Haas, P.M., Keohane, R.O. and Levy, M.A. (1993) *Institutions for the Earth: Sources of Effective Environmental Protection*. Cambridge, MA: MIT Press.
Conventional IR approach using regime theory to explain environmental outcomes.

Young, O.R. (1989) *International Cooperation: Building Regimes for Natural Resources and the Environment*. Ithaca, NY: Cornell University Press.
As with the Haas, Keohane and Levy book, critiqued by writers such as Paterson who advocate a wholesale rethink of the ways in which we think about the contemporary environment and act to sustain it into the future. For a regime-centric approach, see also:

Mitchell, R.B. (2006) 'International Environment', in W. Carlsnaes, T. Risse and B.A. Simmons (eds) *Handbook of International Relations*. London: Sage, pp. 500–16.

On ecological citizenship and cosmopolitanism:

Brown, G.W. and Held, D. (2010) *The Cosmopolitanism Reader*. Cambridge: Polity Press.

Dobson, A. and Bell, D. (eds) (2006) *Environmental Citizenship*. Cambridge, MA: MIT Press.

Gabrielson, T. (2008) 'Green Citizenship: A Review and Critique', *Citizenship Studies*, 12(4): 429–46.

Hailwood, S. (2005) 'Environmental Citizenship as Responsible Citizenship', *Environmental Politics*, 14(2): 195–210.

Hutchings, K. and Dannreuther, R. (eds) (1999) *Cosmopolitan Citizenship*. Edinburgh: Edinburgh University Press.

Smith, M. (1998) *Ecologism: Towards Ecological Citizenship*. Buckingham: Open University Press.

Walzer, M. (1994) *Thick and Thin: Moral Argument at Home and Abroad*. Notre Dame, IN: University of Notre Dame Press.

PART III

LECTURES, TUTORIALS, COURSEWORK AND EXAMS

The highest-achieving students on any module are usually those who manage their learning by taking responsibility for it. In an era when more and more students are asked to pay substantial fees for the privilege of going to university (in England and the USA, for example), the potential is there for some students to believe that because they fork out money they have a right to obtain a degree of their choosing. Nothing could be further from the truth. Whether we agree that universities should charge fees or not, your fees are paid for the right to study for the degree, not to be awarded the degree of your choice automatically. Think of it like joining a gym. You can pay all the membership fees you want, but if you never attend the gym, or use the equipment provided, you will not get fit. The same goes for university level study. The hardest-working students tend to get the best rewards. As many scholars will testify, universities are not staffed and peopled by natural geniuses, but people who work very hard and who are passionate about their subject.

Just like owning a car, therefore, you are buying the right to take *ownership of your learning* on your degree programme. Some car owners are careful with their vehicle, taking every care to keep it cleaned, polished and roadworthy. Others have a slapdash approach to car maintenance, meaning that over time their car becomes something of a dangerous, un-roadworthy rust bucket. It is up to you to decide what kind of owner of *your* learning you want to be. Your university tutors, friends, parents and relatives can help to a certain extent. However, your final degree classification will tell potential employers exactly what kind of owner of your learning you have been. The earlier you take responsibility, and the greater the level of responsibility you take, the better you will fare on your journey through university.

The following chapters give you tips and advice on how to take control of your learning. Chapter 15 takes you through how to make the most of theory in lectures and tutorials, including making use of different forms of feedback on your performance. Chapter 16 helps you make the most of theory in coursework essays and exam answers, including a section on how to avoid sloppy academic practice and plagiarism. Chapter 17 discusses examples of good practice in IRT essay-writing using extracts from real-life student essays. Chapter 18 considers revision and making the most of theory in exams, including tips on surviving an IRT exam.

CORE AREAS

15

MAKING THE MOST OF THEORY IN LECTURES AND TUTORIALS

In this chapter we examine two of the most widely used methods of delivering information at university: the lecture and tutorial. You can get the best out of theory in lectures and tutorials by taking a three-phase approach to them. Phase 1: Preparation. Phase 2: Learning during the lecture and tutorial. Phase 3: Consolidating your learning afterwards. Thinking seriously about managing your learning in all three phases will certainly help you get the most out of lectures and tutorials, which otherwise can become an impersonal and overwhelming experience. This chapter will begin with how to make the most of lectures, then move on to tutorials, and ends with some more general remarks on using feedback.

> Lectures and tutorials at university are an important part of the overall learning process, judged in terms of face-to-face contact time with your tutors. Taking ownership of your learning means knowing the advantages as well as the limitations of learning in the classroom.

MAKING THE MOST OF THE THEORY IN LECTURES

Attendance

The most obvious way to get the most out of lectures is to attend them! Sounds obvious right? But attendance at lectures tends to be relatively low, unbelievably so on some courses. 'They're boring.' 'It clashed with work.' 'It's too early.' 'I was tired after lunch.' 'I had soccer practice.' We can all find excuses not to do things, but excuses do not help you pass exams or get good academic references from your tutors when you graduate. Manage your life away from university studies in such a way that you prioritize your studies, not the other stuff you have going on. Clearly there will be sudden and unexpected events in your life, or genuine health issues, that can hinder your studies and attendance levels – in which case inform your home department. Universities have sophisticated welfare and pastoral care mechanisms in place to help you through troubled times. This chapter puts aside the unpredictable and unexpected trauma, working on the assumption that you are able fully to participate in your course of study.

Given the virtual and other learning technologies available today, the classic stereo-type of an academic lecturer standing at the front of a vast, dark, soulless lecture theatre droning on to a slumbering mass of students could not be further from the truth (for the vast majority of the time anyway – no one is perfect!). All lecturers differ in their approach, style, use of visual aids such as PowerPoint, video-clips, hand-outs and addi-tional resources. In this regard I was interested to read the reflections on IR theorist Karl Deutsch as teacher and lecturer by former student and now IR theorist, Richard Lebow: 'Karl,' he wrote, 'was not a gifted lecturer but always had the rapt attention of his audience' (2014: 188). There are two lessons in here. First, do not confuse style with substance. Just because a lecture is not all-singing, all-dancing with magic, fireworks and joke upon joke, it does not mean it will not be interesting if you listen attentively. Second, all lecturers have one thing in common regardless of individual style: they are passionate about their subject and they will want you to be passionate about it, too.

COMMON PITFALL

It is a mistake to believe lectures are only useful for subject-specific material that you can get from any old textbook. Attending lectures is the best way to 'get inside the head' of your lecturer and get a feel for how he or she approaches the subject.

The best way to feel a sense of enrichment through learning is, therefore, to attend all classes including lectures – even the dull ones. If you begin a course not attending lectures it becomes psychologically harder and harder to attend as the course goes on. Either you will feel embarrassed about your non-attendance or you will simply get into the habit of missing them and doing other things instead. Not doing something can become a habit in the same way that doing something regularly can – good or bad. So, make sure you attend the very first lecture of the course and maintain your participation through the module. Hearing the lecturer talk first hand you will gain a major advantage over students who do not attend regularly or at all.

Over the years I have kept records of the association between lecture attendance and marks gained by my students on IRT courses. There are exceptions, obviously, but the general finding has been that, year after year, those students who fre-quently attend lectures almost always scored better coursework and exam marks than regular non-attendees. Most importantly, they achieve the best marks that they themselves feel capable of achieving and that is important for their confidence going forward.

Reading

Your lecturer will either give you, or publish electronically, a list of suggested readings for each IRT lecture and tutorial on your course. Sometimes this will be in the form of a long, disaggregated list of sources. More often than not it will be divided into essential reading for each topic, backed up by desirable and/or further reading.

> Most tutors will recommend one or two essential textbooks as 'course reading' and you should start with these. See the Introduction in this book for a selection of IR and IRT books that are suitable places to begin your reading each week.

Before your lecture you should aim to read at least the essential reading and as much of the desirable reading as you can. There is no set amount that each tutor expects but, as a rough guide, if you are reading at least five book chapters and/or journal articles before each lecture you will stand a very good chance of grasping the fundamental points your lecturer will want you to take away from it. You will have time after the lecture to put the icing on the cake with further reading.

One way to approach your reading might be:

- Begin with general textbooks to get a feel for the main themes and debates, then move onto the tougher journal articles and monographs where the original academic research gets published.
- Set yourself realistic reading targets: trying to cover everything in one hour prior to class probably will not cut it. The mind needs time to digest complex new ideas.
- Learn how long it takes you to read one average textbook chapter and one average journal article and plan your reading on that basis.
- Learn *where* you read best: in your room, a study area or in the library?
- Find somewhere without too many distractions where you can concentrate and take focused, organized notes.
- Make a note of concepts/issues you do not understand and root around for further information on them. If necessary, contact your tutor, who will be happy to discuss them with you and advise where you can find information to enhance your understanding.

> Most tutors make their lecture notes and/or PowerPoint presentations available online in virtual learning rooms that support each module. Print them out and read them either before or after the lecture so you can pay particular attention to the areas you understand less well.

DURING THE LECTURE

The two most important things you can do to get the best out of lectures are, first, to go prepared and, second, to see them as an opportunity to engage creatively with the subject matter.

> The whole set-up of a lecture unfortunately tends to encourage the idea that the style of learning on offer is passive (lecturer talks; you listen). You need to think of ways to remain actively engaged over the course of the lecture. Being hydrated helps the brain stay focused, so taking a bottle of water in can help you maintain concentration over the duration.

Notes

If notes are available to you prior to the lecture, make sure you have read through them and identified any difficult concepts or ideas you do not understand. You can make additional notes either on these printouts or make your own notes from scratch. Either way, be sure to label your notes with the date and subject matter of the lecture so you can organize them properly. A simple A4 file with your notes divided by topic will help you organize them properly and find what you need to when writing essays and revising for exams.

Lecture notes should represent a *legible* account of the main ideas presented in the lecture. They can include some odd points to follow up and perhaps the references to academic and other writings the lecturer mentions which are not on the reading list, or which are particularly recommended. Lecturers will tend to present the 'big' picture in lectures and focus only on key concepts and ideas. It is up to you to put the flesh on the bones of the topics covered through preparation and post-lecture consolidation (see below).

> If a lecturer mentions an author or text that is not on the reading list, do not be afraid to ask him/her to spell out the author's name (by email after the lecture if you prefer) so you can trace the source easily in the library. In all likelihood the writer will have produced other works that can help you.

Lecturers will usually explain the meaning of new or difficult terms that crop up. If they are foundational to the module ('anarchy' might be one on an IRT course; 'power' might be another) they will return to them in various lectures so you will get other opportunities to hear about them. If at the end of the lecture you are still unfamiliar with a term – especially one that is germane to a particular IRT – you have two options to clarify things. First, try and find the term defined in the reading (glossaries at the ends of books are useful here). Second, contact your lecturer, who will be happy to explain its meaning or at least give you some help locating a relevant definition. If many writers define the same term differently, keep a record of all their definitions for use in essays and exam answers.

Note-taking

There is no guaranteed recipe for success as far as taking notes in lectures goes. If you try and take too many notes you will miss some or lots of what is said. If you take too few you will not generate a detailed enough picture of what was said for later reference. Do not worry if you do not get down everything that was said; the main thing is that you were present, that you listened attentively, did not sit looking at Facebook under the desk (lecturers have eyes – we can see this!), and that you leave with an idea of the big picture.

Use your first-year lectures in particular to work out a note-taking strategy that works for you, and which gives you the optimum balance between listening carefully and recording what was said on paper. Some students are very comfortable not making any notes at all because they want fully to digest what is being said. This is fine as part of an overall learning strategy backed by thorough reading. You have to do what works best for you – this is why taking ownership of your learning is the key message of this chapter.

COMMON PITFALL

If your lecturer talks too fast, he/she should not mind if you ask to record the lecture to play back at your leisure. Some institutions engage in lecture capture, where the lecture is recorded and uploaded to the virtual learning room. But remember: you do not need to tape every lecture and religiously copy out what was said. Repeating verbatim a lecturer's talk is not going to get you many marks.

AFTER THE LECTURE

Possibly the least recognized element of lecture-based learning is the post-lecture phase in which you consolidate and develop your knowledge.

Consolidation

This is all about establishing the foundations of the topic by confirming that you understand core concepts, the meaning of key terms and the texture of disciplinary debates in IRT:

- Take time to read through your notes after the lecture.
- Rewrite any lecture notes that are illegible.
- You could even rewrite the entire set of notes in a format that is clear and simple to understand, perhaps as a series of headline messages. This option is useful if you want to make it easy to retrieve information from an ordered, clearly structured stock of information at a later stage.
- Make a summary of the lecture in a series of bullet points at the top of your notes. This will help you establish your understanding and make it easy to find the relevant material for revision and so on.
- Make a note of any points made in the lecture that you are still unclear about.
- Make a list of any further reading mentioned by the lecturer and underline the main authors and texts that appeared in the talk.

Form a small study group (three to five people) to review your notes, pool ideas on difficult concepts and consolidate your understanding of the main issues covered in each lecture. This could become a routine gathering after each lecture where you can kick back, discuss the main themes and take stock of what was said. Peer-to-peer conversations of this nature can be absolute gold dust as part of a managed learning strategy.

Development

Having consolidated your knowledge of the lecture you are now in a position to develop that knowledge. You can do this in several ways:

- Do any essential or further reading you did not do prior to the lecture.
- Trace and read sources mentioned in the lecture, but which were not on the reading list (contact the lecturer or ask fellow students if they caught them, if necessary).
- Research around difficult concepts or ideas raised in the reading and lecture. A small student study group helps with this.
- Marry your lecture notes with notes from your reading. For example, if your lecturer talked about different theoretical traditions approaching an issue in IR from different perspectives, could you name writers who represent each of those traditions? If not, would you know where to look to find out?
- Practice questions: take a look at past exam papers for your course – these are akin to the 'Questions to ponder' included at the end of each chapter in Part II of this book. Could you now attempt an exam question on the lecture you have just listened to? If the answer is '*no*', you need to do more reading and research around the subject.

> Spend half an hour or so each week, or every other week, planning and drafting a 1,000-word answer to a past exam or essay question. This will be invaluable practice for the real thing. Very few students will do the same so your tutor would happily give you feedback on your answers.

MAKING THE MOST OF THEORY IN TUTORIALS

Tutorials offer you the opportunity to explore various perspectives on a given topic in depth. They expose you to different styles of learning and encourage you to think creatively around problems individually and in groups. Despite these benefits, tutorials are not always well attended by students, which seems strange when in the same breath students will say that contact time at universities can be insufficient for their perceived learning needs. This is a great shame because the tutorial environment encourages you to develop subject specific matter expertise as well as transferable skills for use outside the learning environment. If you aim to get the best out of IRT in tutorials you are giving yourself the very best chance of succeeding when it comes to the crunch in essays and exams. You will also be developing a series of inter-personal, teamwork and communication skills that will stand you in good stead in your future career: tutorials are very good for developing employability skills.

> I have used the term 'tutorial' to describe small-group learning at university. Some institutions call them seminars. I am getting at the idea that you will be in a room with somewhere between 5 and 20 other students, all discussing a pre-set module topic, usually linked to an accompanying lecture.

In this part of the chapter we will consider the nature of tutorial learning and how you can get the very best out of your tutorial time, with particular reference to tutorial learning, effort and presentations.

TUTORIAL LEARNING

Tutorials should play a dynamic part in helping you taking ownership of your learning at university. They help you generate a depth to your understanding of a given subject that lectures rarely can, however whizz-bang the lecturer. In IRT terms, the lectures will more than likely present a broad-brush overview of the main assumptions and explanations put forward by each school of theory, along with a flavour of the debates theorists engage in within and between traditions. In tutorials you will have time to consolidate your understanding of the basics, as well as debating the relative strengths and weaknesses of different theorists' interpretations of IR. Tutorials in IRT are where you can get prepared to do the basics as well as developing your critical faculties to get you towards the higher end of the marks spectrum in course essays and exams.

Initially, tutorial learning can seem a daunting prospect for three reasons. First, you may well be working with students you have not met properly before. Especially in larger departments that cater for several or many different degrees, tutorial groups are often mixed. See this as a plus: meeting and working with new people will be a part of your later career. Second, you may be asked to tackle questions you had not thought about prior to the tutorial, so you will have to learn the skill of thinking on your feet. This is also a great skill to develop. Third, teaching and learning in tutorials assume many forms. You will probably not know how you are going to be learning before you actually get to the tutorial room on the day. However the learning in tutorials is put together by the tutor, advance preparation is your best route to success.

COMMON PITFALL

Do not let the relative uncertainty about how you will learn in tutorials put you off attending. See it as a challenge and a way of proving that you are flexible and adaptable. Your tutor will look positively on those students who throw themselves wholeheartedly into group discussions and debates.

Here is a small sample of the kinds of tutorial learning you might experience at university:

- **Individual summaries/critiques.** You might be given a short extract from an IRT text and asked to spend 10 minutes reading it and summarizing/critiquing the main points it raises. Some tutors might ask you to pre-prepare summaries in advance of the class to give you more time to digest the material.
- **Pair work.** Discuss an IRT question/problem/perspective/issue with the person sitting next to you.

- **Group work.** Discuss an IRT question/problem/perspective/issue with a small number of other students in the tutorial, possibly leading to a 'group' answer which you present to the rest of the class.
- **Pyramid work.** All students start with the same issue to consider for five minutes. Then you work in pairs for five minutes. Finally, you discuss your ideas in groups for five minutes. It is called pyramid work because the number of 'units' involved decreases as the tutorial progresses, building up from a base of lots of students thinking about a problem to few pairs and finally even fewer groups.
- **Class debate.** As in parliaments you may be split into groups and asked to propose or oppose a motion. As an example, in recent years I have split my tutorial groups into two teams to debate the motion: 'This House believes the study of gender is vital to the study of IRT,' with one team proposing the motion and the other opposing it. Debates are good for helping you consider all sides of a problem, because not only do you have to work out your own position, you have to think about how to counter what the opposing team might argue. This form of intellectual flexibility and stretching yourself out of your comfort zone is a touchstone academic skill.
- **Whole group discussion.** Most common at the end of tutorials. A chance to wrap up big issues, ask questions, iron out any lingering misunderstandings and consolidate your knowledge from the lecture and tutorial reading.
- **Class 'votes'.** This is a good exercise for waking students up and getting everyone moving around. Students are asked to 'vote' on a motion (e.g. 'IRT is a waste of time – we should just *do* IR to learn about it'). Those who agree stand on one side of the room, those who disagree stand on the other. The tutor can then ask students why they are stood where they are – in other words, to justify their position. No abstentions are possible (the 'it all depends' syndrome). This can be a great way of getting a debate going and can also be an ice-breaker at the start of a session or midway through to perk up any flaggers.

All tutors organize tutorials differently and some can be set in their ways! If there are styles of tutorial learning you find particularly helpful, your tutor will consider using them if you alert him/her to your preference – politely.

YOU GET BACK WHAT YOU PUT IN

As with lectures, you tend to get as much out of tutorials as you put into them. If you find yourself sitting in tutorials unable to understand or discuss the basics of a given issue you have probably not done sufficient preparatory work. Here are some very basic tips on the kinds of things you can do to work confidently and rewardingly in tutorials:

- Do a realistic amount of preparatory reading. If your tutor has identified essential reading you should complete at least that.
- Take all your notes with you to each tutorial, plus pen and paper to jot down further notes during the tutorial. It amazes tutors how some students turn up without note-taking equipment. They rarely forget their phones though.

- If you are not sure you understand something: *ask*. Tutors are there to help you.
- Make sure you try and say something relatively early on in a tutorial, even if only to ask a basic factual question. Studies show that the longer you go without speaking, the harder it becomes to intervene as the tutorial progresses.
- At the end of the tutorial check through your notes to make sure that they are legible and identify any issues you may want to follow up on (see the sections on Consolidation and Development, above).

Sometimes, the problem is not that you have come to a tutorial unprepared, but that you are frightened of interjecting into a debate. In this case, remember the following:

- Very few people feel totally at ease at speaking in public, especially on subjects that are unfamiliar or new to them. Most university teachers I know still get nervous before giving lectures, even if they have been doing it for 20 years. Students are no different, and even if they *appear* confident you can be sure they are nervous inside.
- There really are no stupid questions. If you are unclear about something you are not the only one so do not fear speaking up.
- Your tutor is not there to tell you what to think. At university level, tutors are less like school teachers than facilitators for your learning.
- Disagreements among students in the tutorial group will be many and varied. This is entirely to be expected. As long as disagreements are aired politely and with due respect for each other's points of view then debate is actively to be encouraged.
- There are no right or wrong answers to questions about IRT. We may prefer one theory over another but no-one can shoot a theoretically informed opinion down by saying that it is definitively 'wrong'.
- Learning how to disagree and how to conduct rational arguments in a tutorial environment will help sharpen your critical thinking and communication skills.

> In pretty much any career you pursue after graduating you will have to speak in public in some environment, whether one-on-one with a boss or colleague or to larger groups at workshops and conferences. Use the university environment to generate confidence at public speaking.

PRESENTATIONS

Standing up and talking about academic matters can be a stressful business – ask any lecturer. In tutorials for IRT you may be asked to give a presentation on a set topic on your own. You might even have to work in pairs or groups to put something together and present your results. Either way, here are some tips on how to plan and deliver an effective presentation.

Planning your presentation

- Spend time preparing thoroughly and get started as early as you can, especially if working as part of a group. Get the deadline clear and work back from there with a series of targets that need to be met at each stage on the way.
- If working in pairs or a group, apportion work evenly and set realistic targets for each group member. Do not let one poor victim do all the work, however keen they might be. Set deadlines for each other and stick to them.
- Decide if you want to use visual aids such as hand-outs or PowerPoint and prepare these in advance. Make sure the text on the slides is visible and the images are relevant and engaging. Here is a tip: check the colours. Having a common form of colour-blindness I cannot see red font on green backgrounds, for example. Stick to neutral, pale backgrounds and darker writing to help out us colour-blind people!
- Clearly structure your presentation and centre it on one core argument or theme. Think of it like presenting an academic essay, with an introduction, middle and conclusion (see the next chapter in this book).
- Read as widely as you can and show you have a good knowledge of the field.
- Build practice time into your schedule, especially if you are using visual technologies such as PowerPoint. Whether presenting on your own or in a group run through the entire presentation at least once to check that it flows well and you cover the ground you need to in the allotted time.

Delivering your presentation

- If doing a group presentation, every member should try to say something.
- Stick to the allotted time. It is better to be slightly under the time than over it.
- Make eye contact with everyone in the audience at least once during the talk.
- Use a script if necessary but try to avoid reading out a one-to-one monologue or you will lose the audience's attention.
- Try and look and sound enthusiastic and confident (even if you are not!).
- If using PowerPoint do not turn around to talk to the screen – remember it is an aid, not the object or audience for your talk. I once had a student talk to the big screen for the duration of a 10-minute talk, facing away from the class. Not only was it hard to hear the student, but it was also very odd being addressed by the back of someone's head. The content of the talk was actually quite good, but because of the lack of eye contact the group got bored and lost interest very early on.
- Make sure your talk follows the structure of your hand-out or order of the PowerPoint slides (practicing in advance is critical here).
- Summarize the main argument of your talk at the end in a concluding section.

In tutorials you have a huge opportunity to establish confidence in your knowledge of IRT. The skills you develop in tutorials will be of great value in other tutorials and when you enter the world of work. Take them seriously and you will benefit enormously from them.

FEEDBACK: WHAT IS IT AND WHERE CAN I GET IT?

The best way to improve as a student of IRT – any subject – is to know what your strengths are and how to consolidate them, as well as what your weaknesses are and how to address them. If you cannot or do not understand your knowledge base and how to enhance it to meet the course learning objectives, then you need to take steps to do so. To repeat the message of this chapter: *take constructive and considered ownership of your learning.* This section will explain different forms of feedback at university and give you some tips on how you can get the best out of it.

Feedback comes in a variety of forms: numerical or summative (the score for an essay or presentation); narrative or formative (the written comments on performance, including 'feed forward' and/or areas for improvement); and oral or informal feedback, usually gleaned from chats with your tutor in out-of-classroom contact time, or in annual performance reviews with your personal tutor. Feedback also comes from a variety of sources. University tutors are where you look principally for feedback on your performance. Nevertheless, fellow students can also give feedback on your thinking in, for example, a tutorial exercise where you get to debate a given topic or theoretical approach. Being open to feedback is the way to improve your critical edge and get a head start in essays and exams.

Academic work only improves by listening carefully to constructive criticism. It is not an attack on you as a person, and while your ego may be slightly dented, it is not the end of the world but in fact a commonplace to accept and respond positively to feedback. As works of organizational behaviour and psychology show, a willingness to learn from less than perfect results is what makes the most successful people and organizations grow: 'It is no good spending an entire career cowering in fear of negative feedback, avoiding situations in which you might be judged, and thus scuppering any chance of improvement. You haven't given up; but you haven't progressed either' (Syed 2015: 282).

Summative feedback (yes, top level marks are available to *you* if you try hard)

This is the 'grading' element of feedback. The summative mark you are awarded for a piece of work tells you in a very quick and easy way where you are on the scale of achievement on a module. The lower down you are on the scale the more time you will have to spend working out what you need to do to improve. For example, if you receive a very low mark, in or around the 'fail' zone, you probably have to address your skills across the board: structuring your thoughts, developing an argument, sufficient reading and communication skills. If you score a fair-to-middling pass mark you know what to do but have not executed the piece of work very effectively, or the analysis is over-simplistic. If you are operating in the near the upper end of the scale, generally, you will have a decent grasp of the skills across the board and should be concentrating on the detail as a way of moving forward by fine tuning your wider reading, generating more critical depth in your work, and presenting it correctly from a technical point of view. If you achieve a very top mark you should be able to repeat that standard of work in the future and should be confident of doing well again, all things being equal. Things are never guaranteed though, so do not rest on your laurels. You are only as good as your last piece of work. Now the task will be to fine-tune your skills to reach for the even higher marks, which are – despite rumours – within reach for all the best students.

COMMON PITFALL

When you receive hard or online copies of assessed work back do not simply look at the mark and throw the essay away. Check through all the comments and feedback so that you know what you did well and where you need to enhance your skills or knowledge base. Discuss your performance with your tutor.

In sum, as your marks move higher up the scale, the better your tutor judges you to be meeting the essential and desirable learning outcomes for the module. But how do you know where precisely to improve? This is where formative feedback comes in.

Formative feedback

Summative feedback tells you where you are; formative feedback tells you how to get where you want to be. In other words, summative feedback is your score for the piece of work; formative feedback justifies why you were awarded that mark narratively. It should, delivered effectively, flag up the positive things the tutor liked about your work and spell out where you were weaker. Some formative feedback sheets invite the tutor to theme his or her comments around set headings such as 'structure of essay', 'logic of argument', 'analytical content', 'sources and presentation' (including academically important things like quality of referencing) and 'area(s) for improvement'. Assessment sheets that give the tutor scope to range freely over the essay can be harder to 'read' off, as it were, but do not let this put you off. All tutors look for the same kinds of qualities in university-level work (see the next chapter) and, even if idiosyncratically, they will try to help you understand where you went right and wrong in a piece of work. If you are unclear about what a tutor means in formative feedback: ask.

Perhaps the most important element of a feedback sheet is the 'area(s) for improvement' box. This is where your tutor will explain the skills you need to work on to improve in the future, taking your essay as a representative case of your hardest effort to achieve your potential. If your tutor writes that improvement has to come from reading some IRT, structuring an answer and presenting your work according to department guidelines, you probably will not have got a great mark because these are foundational skills. If, however, you are invited to read a few more authors to give you some depth and are asked to tidy up the presentation of your bibliography, it is probable that you have demonstrated a robust grasp of the essay basics and will have obtained a decent mark. This is more about fine-tuning than anything else. Whatever feedback you receive, take it seriously and ignore it at your peril. It is there for a reason!

If hard copies of essays are returned to you, with formative coversheets attached, some tutors will also have commented on your writing as they marked it. This can also be written into online submissions. In those comments you will get a little bit of extra useful detail about what they liked and what they disliked in the essay, helping you appreciate a bit better how you can improve for that tutor next time around. Tutors are happy to discuss the 'meaning' of written feedback should you be confused, but I would be wary about asking them to change your mark upwards!

Oral feedback

Very simply, this is the 'hot' or immediate feedback you will get from tutors in conversation in and around lectures and tutorials. It will also come to you in the tutorial room during presentations and group debates and discussion. It is a form of formative feedback not always valued that highly by students. However, if you listen carefully to what tutors to say to members of a tutorial group – not just to you personally – you will find a feast of hints and tips on which to draw to inform your understanding of the subject matter and how to impress that tutor in assessments (another reason to attend tutorials regularly). You may well receive formal summative and formative on oral presentations (see above), but oral feedback often comes a bit more conversationally. It is particularly useful when you do non-assessed work, when you can test whether you are on the right path by taking the work seriously and seeing if your work passes muster with your tutor.

There is another vital opportunity for you to receive feedback which in my experience all but a very few students take: one-to-one chats about your academic progress with the module tutor. This could be about a draft essay plan, to elicit formative feedback on assessed work, or even exam performance, which tends to be known to you in mark form only. Making an appointment to discuss your performance for quarter of an hour with your module tutor might make the difference down the line. It all adds up, and sometimes the little chats out of class can make a statistically significant difference to a final mark because something said in a different way from previously just 'clicks' with you.

Summary

If you think strategically about your learning at university you will take every scrap of feedback you can garner and put it to its very best use. In this section we have discussed how you make the most of theory in lectures and tutorials, and how to use feedback. The absolute crux of what was said in this chapter was to take ownership of your learning. Everything else flows from that. Attending lectures thoroughly prepared, along with taking effective notes, is the best start. Attending tutorials and interjecting regularly from an informed position is the best follow-up. Seeking out and taking on board constructive feedback is the icing on the cake, so to speak. Assessed work is where you receive the bulk of the feedback but there are many options in a non-assessed context to garner feedback from your tutors. If you apply what you learn from feedback on the non-assessed elements seriously you will be better prepared to succeed when it comes to the real thing. Feedback should be an integral part of your learning about IRT. Overall, *you* are responsible for your learning at university and it is only you who can improve when it matters at assessment time. Tutors are there to help you, but they cannot do the work for you and many of the best tutors will not spoon-feed you – they want you to stand on your own two feet by being independent learners. Understanding this, and taking the appropriate level of responsibility for your learning choices, is the surest route to success.

REFERENCES TO MORE INFORMATION

Here are some books dedicated to improving your tutorial communication and presentation skills:

Barrass, R. (2006) *Speaking for Yourself: A Guide for Students to Effective Communication.* London: Routledge.

Bonnett, A. (2011) *How to Argue: A Student's Guide*, 3rd edn. Harlow: Pearson Education.

Bradbury, A. (2006) *Successful Presentation Skills*, 3rd edn. London: Kogan-Page.

Gallo, C. (2009) *The Presentation Secrets of Steve Jobs: How to Be Insanely Great in Front of Any Audience.* New York: McGraw-Hill.

Girard, D. (2012) *Public Speaking Without Panic.* Methuen, MA: DanGir Enterprises.

Kroehnert, G. (1999) *Basic Presentation Skills.* Roseville: McGraw-Hill.

Stott, R. (2001) *Speaking Your Mind: Oral Presentation and Tutorial Skills.* Harlow: Longman.

van Emden, J. and Becker, L. (2016) *Presentation Skills for Students*, 3rd edn. Basingstoke: Palgrave Macmillan.

16

MAKING THE MOST OF THEORY IN ESSAYS

[T]here are several practices widely recognized as essential to good research. Among these are clarity of purpose, logical coherence, engagement with alternative arguments and the provision of good reasons (empirical evidence, corroborating arguments, textual interpretations, etc.). (Reus-Smit 2012: 532)

Essays (and other forms of extended academic writing) will probably be a significant part of the assessed work you do on your degree programme. Exams and/or tutorial presentations may feature too, but at some point on your course you will have to tackle a formal, fully referenced essay of 1,500 words upward. Learning what makes for a successful essay, and a critical approach to academic writing, is therefore vital at university level. The sooner you can develop the techniques for producing coherent, flowing, concise written responses to questions, the better you will fare on all your modules. Christian Reus-Smit's description above of the tenets of good academic research are exactly what tutors look to see you developing in your written submissions.

> The main components of a good coursework essay also make for good exam answers, so think of them as requiring the same skills. The only thing missing from exam answers are formal references and a bibliography.

This chapter covers essay skills in three parts. The first part studies sound essay basics, suggesting that the process of putting together a successful essay takes three things: sound preparation and planning, a structured approach to writing and presentation, and a solid amount of evidence to back your claims. The overall message of this and the remaining chapters in this book is that hard work consistently through your course will pay greater dividends than leaving it all to the night before an essay is due, or the night before you sit an exam. Engaging with the basics and more advanced IRT from the beginning of your course will give you the study momentum and confidence to tackle assessments effectively.

PLANNING AND PREPARATION

The keys to all successful essays are planning, time management, organization and hard work on the subject matter. You have got to know the assessment requirements, plan a coherent argument, write using a clear structure, use evidence appropriately and reference correctly. Do all those things and you will get a very high mark. Do some of them and you will pass. Do none of them and you will struggle. We will take each of them in turn in this section.

Know your enemy

Your initial undertaking from a planning perspective is to know the precise requirements to be met in your coursework. These will be available from your tutor either at or near the start of the module and are usually included in the module guide. The key things to note are:

- **Essay deadline.** Universities tend to punish late submissions quite heavily, unless there is very good reason for work being handed in after the deadline. Set yourself a realistic completion target and aim to finish at least one day before the due date to give yourself time to proofread the essay for errors, omissions or ambiguities in your argument, and to polish up your written English.

> Getting a friend or relative to read through your essay before you submit will help iron out any obvious problems with it. Their outsider perspective helps them spot things you may have missed because you are so 'close' to the essay. This requires finishing more than a day before the deadline, ideally, to give them time to peruse your work. Give proofreaders a very clear brief on what you want them to look out for.

- **Length of essay.** It is important to stick to the word limit. Check with your tutor if you are allowed to go slightly above or below the word limit and how far these bands extend. Ten per cent above or below is sometimes permitted but it will all depend on your tutor's and/or department guidelines. If you aim to come in up to 50 words under the limit you generally won't go far wrong. Going too far under a word limit makes the essay look 'thin' and under-researched.
- **Presentation and submission requirements.** Check your departmental guidelines and/or course handbook for all the details on how to set out your essays, how to provide references and where to submit your work. Tutors get bombarded with emails in the week leading up to the submission deadline and it does not look too good if you ask simple questions that are all answered in the handbook!
- **Lecture insights.** In lectures, tutors will often hint at ways of approaching essays that they feel pay dividends. This is another reason to attend lectures regularly.

> Attending lectures helps you learn more about subject matter and also gives you a feel for what your tutor expects to see in essays and exam answers. See the previous chapter for hints and tips on how to make the most of theory in lectures.

- **Deadline extensions.** If you have a valid claim for an extension contact your module tutor well in advance of the deadline. Check your department's guidelines on what you need to support your claim and keep all the relevant supporting evidence, for example, a doctor's note if you have been ill.

Plan your argument

Having oriented yourself to the requirements of the essay, and got clear in your mind the timeline to completion, you need to set about planning the essay. To get to this stage you will need to have carried out at least the essential reading on the topic. Ideally you will have ploughed through the desirable and some wider reading too. You can always carry on reading while you write, as long as you have most of it completed before you begin planning the essay.

> When tutors mark a big batch of essays, they get used to seeing the same authors and ideas rehashed over and over again. Doing wider reading will help your essay stand out from the crowd.

When you feel comfortable that you know the basics about the subject and are ready to put finger to keyboard, here are some tips on how to keep the essay focused, manageable and persuasive:

- **The main argument or central claim that makes the essay 'hang together'.** Your essay should unfold around a central argument, point of view, interpretation or opinion that you advance consistently through the narrative. You are effectively defending a position over an extended piece of writing. Your argument should be in the form of a direct response to the question set and this should appear as the focal point of your introductory section. The argument you make will be phrased according to the nature of the essay question, but the key thing is that you have a central argument and can explain it clearly and concisely. Without the focus an argument or central claim provides, you will not be able to give direction to the essay. If you are not clear about what you intend to argue, the reader will not be sure of where you are going in the essay either. Wandering around a range of topics hoping something might emerge is not the way to approach writing. You get the best marks for setting out a clear point of view and defending it with logic and academic evidence.

> It sounds formulaic, but you could even begin the essay with 'This essay will argue that …'. Few students have the confidence to lead off with their argument in this way, but it really helps a tutor to see exactly where you intend to go in the essay from the outset. They are then marking your ability to defend that claim. If you hide your claim away, or do not present one, do not expect them to be able to 'divine' it for you. You have to earn the marks in an essay, they are not awarded to you on a hunch about what you might have argued had you been bothered.

- **How many points to make?** Undergraduate essays vary in length, usually from 1,500 words upwards, so there are no hard and fast rules that will work in every situation. It is up to you, ultimately, to think this through in the context of your argument and structure (see below). To give an indication of the thought processes involved, take the following example. Assuming the introduction and conclusion together are approximately 10 per cent each of the entire word count (300 words between them), in a 1,500-word essay this would leave 1,200 words as the 'body' of the essay. This is not a lot of words. You will be able to cover effectively around four to five main points, so you will have to be selective about what to include and what to ignore. The less successful essays tend to be those that try to cover every single point made about a particular topic in the reading, that requrgitate points at will from the relevant lecture. Being selective is thus critical at the planning stage. Learning when to leave material out (or delete chunks of what you have just written) is a big part of developing effective writing techniques. It takes confidence and firmness of intent to stick only to the essentials that help you advance one core proposition.

- **Getting your own opinion across.** Some students worry if they do not include any of their own opinions in coursework essays. Do not worry about this. You are not expected to develop new theories of IR or never-thought-of-before critiques of the theories you examine in an essay. Your approach to the subject matter will come through in your main argument and the structure you give your answer. The 'originality' of the essay is, therefore, inherent in an essay that you have planned and written in your own words, and backed up by quotes and evidence from established sources.

> Remember that the same essay question can be answered in an infinite number of ways. In devising your response, using your own words, and structuring your answer, your work counts as original because it is your opinion you are conveying, even if you are using other people's writings to inform your perspective.

ESSAY STRUCTURE

If you ask any university student about essay structure they all tell you that they know what it means: beginning, middle and end. In my time teaching, I have increasingly come to the conclusion that this only tells a very small part of the story about essay structure. In fact, it might actually obscure as much as it reveals. Students grasp this basic 'macro' structure, but what about the middle or body of the essay? The essence of a robust structure is not just that the essay is in three parts, but that the various segments or paragraphs that make up those parts are also structured to fit together in a cohesive whole. It is at the 'micro' level of structure (the elements that go into each of the three 'macro' parts) that the vast majority of students trip up. The classic giveaway is an essay that starts with a coherent introduction and ends with a workable conclusion. But in the middle the essay jumps around at random with ideas, authors and concepts cropping up all over the place. The student has structured the essay at the macro level but forgotten about the micro level. This section will unpack essay structure basics at the macro and then the micro level.

If you think essay structure is all about introduction, body, conclusion, think again! There is much more to it than that. Structure applies on two levels: macro and micro, and successful essays pay attention to both levels.

Everyone knows about macro structure!

I will not dwell too much on the macro structure needed to write a successful essay. Suffice to say that you should be familiar with the basic idea and your tutor will usually be happy to look over a plan that comes in this format as a way of assuring you that your answer looks like a reasoned response to the essay question set. Figure 14 presents the essence of a 'macro' essay structure. An introduction setting out your main argument, a body of the essay presenting the evidence that supports your argument, and a conclusion reminding the reader where you went in the essay: these are the basics of any robust macro structure.

INTRODUCTION

- Aims of essay
- Core theme/argument
- Essay plan

BODY OF ESSAY

- The key points that help you advance your central case
- *Micro structure*

CONCLUSION

- Reminder of central argument
- Wider issues raised by essay

Figure 14   Macro essay structure

What is micro structure?

Less familiar might be the idea of micro structure. This is the structure of the individual sections themselves, particularly the body of the essay, which is the longest and most difficult to manage writing-wise. Why is micro structure important if you already have the macro structure in place? The whole idea of an essay is that you are showing your tutor that you are organized, well read-up on the subject matter of IRT, and able to construct a logical argument that flows nicely through the piece. If you do not structure at the micro level as well as the macro level, you risk losing your reader because they will probably not be able to follow where you go in the body of the essay. Do not expect tutors to be able to guess your thought processes, you need to tell them.

One way to structure the body of an essay is by using headings and subheadings. This helps the reader see how you have organized your answer.

Concentrating on micro structure is essential at both the planning and writing stages. You need to structure each section of your essay from introduction through body and conclusion. This means making sure the various paragraphs in each section follow logically from the one to the next, and 'fit' together to help you advance your central argument. Because it is the most difficult aspect of writing a good essay, let us concentrate on how a well-structured body of the essay looks from a micro perspective. We will assume an essay in four main parts, top and tailed by an introduction and conclusion. Depending on the word limit of the essay, each point in the body of the essay would be developed in roughly two to three paragraphs. Figure 15 sets out the micro structure of an essay.

Figure 15 reads quite formulaically, but do not be put off by this. Your tutor will be reading dozens, sometimes hundreds of essays. He or she will want to be told precisely what your argument is, why you put that case in your essay, and to know that *you* know

---

INTRODUCTION

- Aims of essay
- Core theme or argument you will make
- Essay plan: what you will cover in points 1 to 4

BODY OF ESSAY

- POINT 1
  - Summarize essence of point 1 (S)*
  - Make point 1
  - Explain how point 1 helps you advance your core argument and where you are going next in the essay (B)**

- POINT 2
  - Summarize essence of point 2 (S)
  - Make point 2
  - Summarize upshot of points 1 and 2 (S) and say where you are going next in the essay (B)

- POINT 3
  - Summarize essence of point 3 (S)
  - Make point 3
  - Summarize key findings from points 1, 2 and 3 (S) and say where you are going next in the essay (B)

- POINT 4
  - Summarize essence of point 4 (S)
  - Make point 4
  - Summarize key findings from point 4 and recap how they relate to points 1, 2 and 3 (S)

CONCLUSION

- Reminder of central argument
- Where you went in points 1 to 4
- Wider issues raised by essay

Figure 15 Micro structure of an essay

Notes:
* (S) denotes a signpost section (see below)
** (B) denotes a bridge section (see below)

why you travelled where you did in the answer. If you make this structure explicit you will stand out from the vast majority of students who will keep the marker guessing about their intellectual journey.

COMMON PITFALL

The basic requirement of a successful essay is that you take your reader on a journey that you have planned in advance. If you cannot (or do not) clearly explain your journey from start to finish, then do not expect your tutor to be able to follow you through it – at least not without getting frustrated or annoyed.

Techniques to help you develop your essay's micro structure

You only develop essay planning and writing skills by practicing writing. There is a huge amount of trial and error in getting to the point where you are happy with the finished product, and this can be time consuming. Do not expect a quality essay to be written at draft one stage. Here are a few things you can do to structure your essays clearly and explicitly.

Try implementing some or all of these techniques in your next essay. Also, try and identify good structuring techniques from the reading you do. Borrowing tips from the experts is a great way to learn essay skills.

- **Signposts.** Quite literally, you point the reader through the essay. Think of it like following road signs on a car journey. When they are in plentiful supply and easy to understand, it is dead simple to find your way to your destination. However, when there are no signs, or if they point the wrong way, or if they are unclear, then it becomes difficult for you to follow them. By inserting signpost sentences regularly, you give the reader the pointers they need to navigate their way through your thinking in the essay. After all, it is the quality and cogency of your thinking that you are being marked on.
- **Bridges.** Similar to signposts in that they give the essay direction, but they are used specifically to help the reader cross between two distinct parts of an essay. In the example above, bridging sections would be used to take the reader from the introduction to the body of the essay, from point 1 to point 2, from point 2 to point 3, from point 3 to point 4 and from point 4 to the conclusion. Hence, while signposts are used at the start of new sections or paragraphs to point the way ahead or recap a central theme in the essay, bridges are less frequent but play a crucial role in getting your reader into and out of sections.

Writing using signposts and bridges

There are three main varieties of signpost in an academic essay (Redman 2006: 64): (1) at the beginning of a new section to summarize what you will argue in it; (2) at the end of a section to recap the central theme of the section; and (3) where necessary to remind the reader of the subject of your essay and in particular your central argument – especially useful when you get to the later stages of an essay.

We will see practical examples of signposting in IR theory essays in the next chapter.

Signposts and bridges are similar in some respects because the idea of both is to help the reader through an essay. You can happily combine the two together if you wish. To illustrate, say you are tackling the essay question: 'Realism is the "common sense" theory of IR. Discuss.' This essay naturally falls into two parts: those who agree with that statement and those who disagree with it. At the end of all the 'for' points you could write: '*Having discussed three reasons why Realism is said to be the common sense approach to IR*, **the essay will now consider the arguments against this point of view by looking at the work of Liberal and feminist IRT**.' This sentence contains both a bridge (the bridge is in italics – it wraps up one section and transitions to the next section) and a signpost (the signpost is indicated by bold font – it points the reader to what will be covered next). Feel free to experiment with signposts and bridges and find what works best for you. However you use them, you will get credit for trying because you will be showing your tutor that you are organized and have thought seriously about how to write 'academically'. A crucial component of the mark will also come from how you handle evidence, and what evidence you bring to the table, so we will cover that next (this last sentence is a signpost sentence).

EVIDENCE

Successful essays and exam answers are built on a sound foundation of evidence. Academics use evidence to provide them with information about a subject and as a point of reference within a given debate. In IR, theorists get their evidence from many places: history, international events, political debates and policies, along with the work of other theorists, for example. Your tutor will recommend a series of readings for your course, and that is the first place you should look, but you are strongly encouraged to go beyond the recommended readings. Being creative with your research on a topic is a sign of initiative and your tutor will notice your work more if you have put in the effort to look beyond the basic texts.

A successful essay requires both technical proficiency and an in-depth knowledge of the subject matter. The volume and nature of the evidence you bring to bear in an essay will help guide the tutor to an assessment of how hard you worked on it.

By providing evidence you are showing your essay is built on more than a passing acquaintance with the subject, or what you heard your friends talking about in the Students Union bar the night before you submitted it. Cutting and pasting bits from open-edited sources such as Wikipedia is also a sure sign that something is wrong with an essay (see the plagiarism section below). No self-respecting IR theorist publishes work through Wikipedia and you should not be looking to non-peer-reviewed sites like that for evidence to include in an essay. Through the evidence you provide you are demonstrating a thorough engagement with the key literature as published in academic books and journals, and summarized in academic textbooks. A rich evidence base also establishes your familiarity with the technical concepts and an active involvement in the debates that take place between writers in the field. In sum, you are showing that you have made every effort to get inside the heads of the writers you have been asked to study on your course. You can only do this by reading widely and providing full references to the sources of information you used to construct the essay. We will deal with good referencing below.

COMMON PITFALL

Students routinely fail to provide evidence to back their assertions. You do not need a reference for every fact presented in an essay if it is common knowledge. For example, saying that the Second World War ended in 1945 would not need a reference. However, you do need to show the provenance or origin of every major argument, interpretation or point of view you discuss in an essay. For instance, if you set out the key assumptions of poststructuralism or alluded to the varieties of Critical Theory, you would need a clear reference to your source because these are NOT common knowledge, but your interpretations drawn from other people's texts.

Using evidence

You can use evidence from your reading in a variety of ways:

- **Quotations.** Use these if a writer makes a particularly succinct, cutting comment on a given issue, provides a suitable definition for a difficult concept, or has come up with an interpretation, theory or model that critically shaped a debate within a field. Try and limit the amount of quotations you use in an essay so that enough of your own words still come through. Quotations should support your ideas, not the other way around. Try to avoid using quotations of more than a few lines long. Common pitfalls with using quotations are that they are too long, do not stay focused on the relevant topic, and/or become just a series of unrelated sentences from writers with no explanation for why they appear where they do. The trick is to knit quotations together in a cohesive whole that shows you know what the writers are saying and how they help you make a particular point in an essay.

If you are quoting a writer who uses italics or bold font in their original work, make sure that you tell your reader that the emphasis in your essay has not been inserted by you but appears in the original. This level of technical detail is critical if you want to get the best marks. Faithful reproduction of original texts and sources is paramount.

- **Paraphrase/summary.** You may not always want to quote directly from authors but instead paraphrase them, usually in the form of a summary of their arguments. This is an equally valid way of introducing evidence from established sources into your essay. Remember that even if you do not quote directly you will still need to include a reference to the original source.

- **What to cite?** When providing references, you need only cite the source where you located the information. If you got all your information about poststructuralist writer X from textbook chapter writer B, then your reference will be to textbook chapter writer B. If you cite the original work by writer X your tutor will mistakenly assume you read that original piece. Do not pretend you have read an original work of IRT if you did not. If you got all your information about a theory from a textbook, be honest about it. It is sloppy practice to claim to have read things you have not, and is usually pretty obvious to the tutor.

Referencing

Before you start writing an essay acquaint yourself fully with your department's style guidelines on how to set out references and bibliographies. As a general rule you are likely to be asked for the following:

- If a reference appears in the essay (usually in brackets containing author surname, date of publication and page number if available) it will need to appear in the list of references at the end in a format that makes it easily identifiable to the reader.
- A bibliography includes all the sources you used to research an essay; a list of references only includes those sources you refer to in an essay.

> Do not be tempted to 'pad' a list of references and bibliography with many sources you did not read!

- Make sure you achieve consistency with dates, spelling of surnames and so on in your essay references and bibliography.
- Put your bibliography or list of references alphabetically by surname, and always start on a new page at the end of the essay. Do not include separate lists for, say, books and websites. The reason? To find your reference, a reader does not want to have to trawl through several different alphabetized lists to find the correct one. One holistic list makes tracking references easy.
- When referencing online sources do not include the full web address in the text of the essay, save it for the bibliography. In the essay you need a shortened reference fully traceable in the bibliography. For example, if you wanted to refer to UN Secretary-General Ban Ki-moon's August statement to regional groups of the UN in January 2008, this is available online. In your essay you would summarize or quote from it and your reference would read (Ki-moon 2008). See the References at the end of this book for the full reference to this document.
- Take another example. Say you want to refer to Barack Obama's January 2010 speech on the banking crisis which you located on *The Independent* website. You could decide whether to cite the actual online source of the speech (*The Independent* 2010) or because the speech is reproduced in full, and Obama was the author, you could legitimately use (Obama 2010) as your reference – the website address would indicate that it was reproduced on *The Independent* website. Either would do, but because the speech

appears verbatim (it has not been fragmented, commented upon, or 'interpreted' for you by the newspaper) as the author of the speech I would tend to go for (Obama 2010). A reminder: save the full web address for the bibliography, including the date you accessed the website, but do not include that detail in the in-text reference. What you must not do with the Obama speech is cite (*The Independent* 2010) but use (Obama 2010) in the bibliography because the reader would not have a clue where to look for it and would have to wade through the entire bibliography to track it down, if they could locate it at all. The name of author in the essay reference must match exactly that of the corresponding bibliographic reference. Go to my References now to see how I have set this one out.

> Some websites and written sources contain no author and/or date. In that case you simply say 'anonymous', 'no date' or 'undated' as applicable to the missing element. Give your marker as much information as possible so that they are able to trace your sources.

BAD ACADEMIC PRACTICE AND PLAGIARISM

Bad academic practice and plagiarism have been growing sources of concern at universities for a number of years now. The advent of new technologies and the availability of an ever wider range of electronic sources on all subjects has increased the opportunity and, unfortunately, the temptation for some students to be sloppy with their use of sources and/or try to pass off other people's work as their own. It is becoming increasingly common to put student essays through electronic plagiarism detection software such as Turnitin, which provides detailed reports on the provenance of written submissions as far as electronic material is concerned. Being poor at providing referencing or not knowing how to set references out is one thing; trying to claim you wrote something when you did not is an academic crime of an altogether different nature and you are liable to be accused of being a plagiarist if you take this route. Beyond all this there is a basic ethic at work: it is cheating, and it is a pretty hollow success. Many tutors I know refuse to write job references for students who have charges of plagiarism on their academic records. Let us take a look at what we mean by bad academic practice and plagiarism, by way of illustrating the key pitfalls to be avoided.

Bad academic practice

Spending time reading about violence, insecurity, and humans' failings towards each other make scholars of IRT perhaps as well aware as anyone that no one is perfect. It would be a strange world if we were. The whole point of university level teaching and learning has been built around subject matter expertise and skills development, so that students avoid falling into bad habits. Tutors understand that it can take time to grasp the detailed niceties of how to present academic work to the highest degree. Students whom they see trying to do the right thing will be cut a lot of slack. Sloppy academic practice (formally known as bad academic practice) is usually quite easy to spot. It shows a student not necessarily intending to deceive, but one who has not yet learnt how to cite correctly the sources of his or her knowledge using appropriate references.

Take the example of an essay which discusses anarchy in the international system. Student A has taken notes from Kenneth Waltz's *Theory of International Politics*, where he dissects the difference between anarchy and hierarchy. The student notes are later used when writing the essay. The relevant section of the student essay reads as follows:

> Anarchy is difficult to define. Those who view the world as a modified anarchy do so, it seems, for two reasons. First, anarchy is taken to mean not just the absence of government but also the presence of order and chaos … Second, the two simple categories of anarchy and hierarchy do not seem to accommodate the infinite social variety our senses record. Why insist on reducing the types of structure to two instead of allowing for a greater variety? That said, many scholars do seem to work with these two poles as their guiding influence (Waltz 1979: 114).

Reads quite well you might think, and you would be correct. This is because most of those words are from Waltz himself. This is how that section should have looked:

> Anarchy is difficult to define. 'Those who view the world as a modified anarchy do so, it seems, for two reasons. First, anarchy is taken to mean not just the absence of government but also the presence of order and chaos … Second, the two simple categories of anarchy and hierarchy do not seem to accommodate the infinite social variety our senses record. Why insist on reducing the types of structure to two instead of allowing for a greater variety?' (Waltz 1979: 114). That said, many scholars do seem to work with these two poles as their guiding influence.

In the first extract Waltz's words are masquerading as the student's own; in fact, the vast majority of that extract is from Waltz's book. The two are inseparable, and even though a source has been provided, the absence of speech marks is hiding the fact that Waltz wrote those words, not the student. You might agree with a writer and believe that they can express an argument far better than you can. However, if you quote directly from them you *must* give them the credit for expressing themselves in the manner they did.

Notice in the second extract I have moved the actual reference to just after the quotation itself rather than the interpretation that might be seen to flow from it, which Waltz might or might not have gone on to draw in his text. This clearly shows the delineation to the original text and my reading of it as a student of IR.

The reason I think most tutors would consider this bad practice is that the source of the quotation has not been hidden from view. More instances like this in the essay and it might be classed minor as opposed to major plagiarism in some universities, instead of plagiarism (at least on a first offence, and depending on the year of study). The student is telling the reader that he/she has read Waltz but, we trust, simply failed to convey that this was a direct quotation from the original. Perhaps the notes taken were ambiguous about what was a quotation from Waltz and what was not – it is your responsibility as a student to generate accurate notes. Barring evidence to the contrary, we would hope this was a problem with note-taking rather than intent to deceive. When you take notes from any source be sure to make clear what is a direct quote and what is a summary or your own opinion, so that when you reference you do not end up falling into the trap Student A did here. It might lead to a telling off, it could be worse depending on the institution it was submitted to. Plagiarism is a much more serious offence wherever you study, and that is the topic of the next section.

Plagiarism

The last two occasions on which I had to interview students charged with plagiarism, they blamed time pressures for their crime. They were poorly organized, had not done enough reading and just threw the essay together at the last minute before hand-in. They had gone to an e-book and Wikipedia and cut and pasted whole chunks from a biography of Hans Morgenthau and an article by Stephen Walt, which ended up being detected by the Turnitin plagiarism detection software. They were both found guilty of plagiarism.

> While they all agree on the principle, each university has a slightly different plagiarism policy and means of dealing with academic misconduct. Make sure you are clear on what constitutes plagiarism at your university before you submit assessed work. If in doubt, ask someone!

Let us take a fresh scenario to illustrate the issues at hand regarding plagiarism. Student B has been caught short of time on an IRT essay. She has left her essay until the last minute and is panicking that she does not know anything much about anarchy in the international system and its impact on international relations in the Cold War. However, she recalls that Kenneth Waltz does know something about IRT and the following segment of text appears in her essay:

> Those who view the world as a modified anarchy do so, it seems, for two reasons. First, anarchy is taken to mean not just the absence of government but also the presence of order and chaos ... Second, the two simple categories of anarchy and hierarchy do not seem to accommodate the infinite social variety our senses record. Why insist on reducing the types of structure to two instead of allowing for a greater variety? Anarchy often leads to a balance of power. As a theory, balance of power predicts that rapid changes in international power and status – especially attempts by one state to conquer a region – will provoke counterbalancing actions. For this reason, the balancing process helps to maintain the stability of relations between states. A balance of power system functions most effectively when alliances are fluid, when they are easily formed or broken on the basis of expediency, regardless of values, religion, history, or form of government.

Quite appropriately, given the theme of the essay, the student is exploring anarchy and the balance of power proposition that Waltz advances in his *Theory of International Politics*. Unfortunately, there are no speech marks or references to indicate that almost all of the words have been lifted from Waltz. The student has effectively claimed a deep knowledge of anarchy and the balance of power when in truth the appreciation is entirely someone else's.

The paragraph should have read:

'Those who view the world as a modified anarchy do so, it seems, for two reasons. First, anarchy is taken to mean not just the absence of government but also the presence of order and chaos … Second, the two simple categories of anarchy and hierarchy do not seem to accommodate the infinite social variety our senses record. Why insist on reducing the types of structure to two instead of allowing for a greater variety' (Waltz 1979: 114). Anarchy often leads to a balance of power. 'As a theory, balance of power predicts that rapid changes in international power and status – especially attempts by one state to conquer a region – will provoke counterbalancing actions. For this reason, the balancing process helps to maintain the stability of relations between states. A balance of power system functions most effectively when alliances are fluid, when they are easily formed or broken on the basis of expediency, regardless of values, religion, history, or form of government' (The IR Theory Knowledge Base 2015).

The student has contributed precisely eight words to the paragraph, linking the two quotations with '*Anarchy often leads to a balance of power*.' There is no acknowledgement that the first quotation is in fact a quotation, or that Waltz was the author. The second quotation is from a website of basic IRT definitions, but again there is no indication either that these are someone else's exact words or that the student has used the website as a source of information. Clearly the essay would need to be looked at in the round, and if Waltz and the IR Knowledge Base did not at least appear in the bibliography the student would be on very sticky ground. Even if the references did feature somewhere, and especially if the essay was replete with the same practice as here, this student is guilty of a form of plagiarism – trying to present other people's ideas as her own.

TIPS FOR AVOIDING PLAGIARISM

Avoiding plagiarism and/or bad academic practice is as easy as shelling peas. Simply know how your department wants you to present your assessed work, stick to those accepted guidelines and you will not go far wrong. *Any* plagiarism is too much plagiarism, even sticking in the odd sentence from someone else's text here and there without due acknowledgement of the source is cheating. Here is a list of just some of the most obvious ways you can avoid falling into this awful trap:

- **Leave yourself plenty of time** to write the essay and proofread it before submission. This has two advantages. First, it avoids putting you under the kinds of pressure where you might be tempted to cut and paste texts as your own to save time. Second, it gives you time to proofread your finished product to check you have referenced everything you need to, and that you have set out those references correctly.
- **Keep your notes organized** and written up in such a way that it is very clear when your notes are direct quotes, summaries of an author's interpretation of IRT or just your own musings on a book or article. Both of the first two would need referencing. Be certain to reference specific page numbers if quoting from a book or journal article. In the above example (Waltz 1979) is too vague for a reference. A specific

quote or summary of a particular passage demands (ibid.: 14). Increasingly tutors are finding that students are not bothering to give page numbers from books and journal articles, but you must include these. The rule of thumb is: we should be able to find the point of view or quotation you included in your essay in the original source as easily as possible. If it was from a book or article you should give us the page number(s) – otherwise, are you are expecting the reader to wade through long texts to find one specific quotation? *Transparency is what is needed.*

- **Do not include too many or too long quotations.** An essay should be an expression of *your* intervention in a given set of debates. By all means use authors in walk-on roles to scaffold your argument and to show where you looked for evidence and definitions, but the majority of an academic essay has to be in your own words. At the very least, 80/20 in favour of your own words is probably where you need to be. Large parts of the '80' will of course be you summarizing others' ideas – in which case you will still need to reference them, even lacking direct quotations.

- **You can under-reference an essay but, in truth, I have never worried if students over-reference.** If you are unsure about whether to include a reference to a 'fact', for example, then include it and let your tutor tell you it is unnecessary – they will not mark you down for it. If you under-reference an essay you run the risk of being accused (rightly or wrongly) of plagiarism or at the very minimum bad academic practice.

- **Quite simply, don't be tempted by the dark side: take pride in your work.** Plagiarism is unethical, intellectual theft and unbecoming of upstanding citizens such as students are supposed to be – the next generation of global leaders no less. Or, put yourself in the place of an academic who has spent decades developing and refining an approach to IRT. They struggle to gain a book contract and when they do, all their hard work and the hours they spent drafting and re-drafting their work fifteen times gets passed off as someone else's in the blink of an eye. They do not even get paid much for it. Hobbes' dictum that life is nasty, brutish and short may be true, but it is surely not too short to develop a working knowledge of a topic and to convey it in your own words.

REFERENCES TO MORE INFORMATION

There are many general texts on good practice in essay writing. Try any of the following:

Redman, P. (2013) *Good Essay Writing: A Social Sciences Guide*, 4th edn. London: Sage. Written specifically for social sciences students and contains lots of examples of good practice in essay writing. Good also on signposts and bridges.

Fowler, A. (2006) *How to Write*. Oxford: Oxford University Press.

Mcmillan, K. and Weyers, J. (2011) *How to Write Essays and Assignments*, 2nd edn. Harlow: Pearson Education.

Hennessy, B. (2002) *Writing an Essay: Simple Techniques to Transform your Coursework and Examinations*, 4th edn. Oxford: How To Books. Good on both the macro and micro sides of essay writing.

Kirton, B. (2007) *Just Write: An Easy-to-Use Guide to Writing at University*. Abingdon: Routledge.

Price, G. and Maier, P. (2007) *Effective Study Skills: Unlock Your Potential*. Harlow: Pearson Longman.
Includes writing skills in a discussion of good academic practice more generally.

Bailey, S. (2014) *Academic Writing: A Handbook for International Students*, 4th edn. London: Routledge.

Creme, P. and Lea, M.R. (2008) *Writing at University: A Guide for Students*, 3rd edn. Buckingham: Open University Press.

Levin, P. (2004) *Write Good Essays! A Guide to Reading and Essay Writing for Under-graduates and Taught Postgraduates*. Maidenhead: Open University Press.

Rose, J. (2007) *The Mature Student's Guide to Writing*. New York: Palgrave Macmillan.

There are also texts on writing specifically for political science students:

Scott, G.M. and Garrison, S.M. (2007) *The Political Science Student Writer's Manual*, 6th edn. Upper Saddle River, NJ: Prentice Hall.
Part One on writing and competent referencing is excellent.

Harrison, L. (2001) *Political Research: An Introduction*. London: Routledge.
Chapter 9 is on writing a politics dissertation but the same principles apply there as in an essay, so well worth a look.

17

EXAMPLES OF GOOD PRACTICE IN IR THEORY ESSAYS

This chapter uses extracts from genuine student essays on IRT to illustrate how three students more or less successfully deployed some of the essay techniques discussed in the previous chapter. All the essays responded to one question: 'How "scientific" is IR theory?' I am grateful to the students concerned for letting me use their essays. I have transcribed the extracts exactly as they appeared in the originals, including typographical errors, spelling/grammar errors and references. The essays were marked anonymously and it so happens that the three I selected for inclusion were all by male students. Hence, for simplicity below, I use 'he' to refer to the student authors when usually I would use the gender neutral 'he/she'.

MACRO STRUCTURE: INTRODUCTIONS

We saw in the previous chapter that macro structure (the need for a beginning, middle and end to an academic essay) is generally well understood by students. How do you convey that you have a macro structure in practical terms? Compare the opening paragraphs of the three student essays.

STUDENT 1

Purely by definition one could certainly suggest that students of International Relations theory undertake a very scientific approach to their studies. Indeed, the theory of any study could be deemed scientific, although outside the boundaries of how society would usually call a fact based science, those being, in general terms, biology, chemistry, physics and, to a certain extent, maths ... [*student then introduces definitions of 'science' from Reader's Digest Universal Dictionary*] ... However, it would be very easy

(Continued)

(Continued)

to argue over definitions without coming to any conclusions as to whether a study of theory has the right to be called a science or is simply an argument made without any evidence to support it. Some would say that without this actual, factual grasp on a subject a theory cannot be a science. Others would argue that the very approach to the production of a theoretical analysis earns it the right to be called a science. In today's world this is what we would call a social science, that is 'The study of society and of ... relationships in and [relating] to society' (Reader's Digest Universal Dictionary 1987, pg.1443).

STUDENT 2

This essay critically investigates the debate on 'How "scientific" is IR theory?'. I will start by outlining what the term 'scientific' means and then use this definition to question whether IR theory is a science, and if so, to what extent? As well as who supports or opposes this relatively new look on the subject to come to a qualified conclusion.

STUDENT 3

'Until the late 1980's, most social scientists in international relations (IR) tended to be positivist' (Baylis *et al.* 2001: 274). However, from then on numerous post-positivist theories have emerged, attacking positivist methodology, epistemology and ontology, questioning the validity of the underlying assumptions of positivism. Arguably, the discipline of IR is 'scientific' in nature and this essay aims to investigate and evaluate the nature of IR by exploring the construct and meaning of 'scientific', with respect to social and natural phenomena, and the underlying assumptions of positivist explanatory and post-positivist constitutive perspectives.

You can see three very different approaches here. Which do you think works best as an introduction? If you were the marker, which introduction would persuade you that the student was on top of the material being presented? Here are some things you would have to bear in mind.

- **Central argument.** Student 3 is the only student to set out a central argument that helps the answer 'hang together': 'Arguably,' he writes, 'the discipline of IR is "scientific" in nature.' Student 2 states that he intends to answer the question but forgets to tell us what his answer will be. Student 1 barely provides an introduction in the sense that he dashes into the different definitions of science and related debates without giving us any pointers as to where he will go in the essay.
- **Essay structure.** Student 3 clearly identifies how his central arguments will be advanced. In the final three lines of the paragraph he says that his argument that IR is 'scientific' will be made first by considering the definition of 'scientific' and then by considering the positivist versus post-positivist debates. This is an excellent use of signposting. Student 2 gets as far as saying that he will define 'scientific' but there the clues run out. Student 1 does not provide any direction but rushes off into the definitions themselves. Here we see the best essay *signposting* in Student 3's piece. Student 1 gives no signposts at all, and Student 2 manages just a smattering.

- **Subject matter expertise.** The introductions give a fair indication of the level at which the students are operating. Student 1 relies on two quotes from the Reader's Digest, while Student 3 uses an authoritative source writing in a major textbook, *The Globalization of World Politics*. Even after reading the introductions the marker would be persuaded that Student 3 was more on top of the reading than Student 1, even if the final judgement would wait until the end of the essay. However, first impressions are important and it helps if you can establish an authoritative position early in an essay.

TAKING IT FURTHER
Wikipedia and its reliability

Individual departments and tutors have differing opinions on the utility and validity of students using online dictionaries and resources such as Wikipedia. Even Wikipedia has a page pointing out the dangers of using Wikipedia in academic research, reminding us that user-edited encyclopedias such as this are useful starting points for (some) research but should never be the endpoint of your research (Wikipedia 2016). Check your course handbook and with your individual tutor to see if he/she has preferences. If in doubt, avoid such sites and stick to academic material only: credibility and reliability of sources is what is needed to make your claims in an essay stack up. It is not completely without its uses, but you have to be very careful what *type* of information you take from it and remember to check that off against other sources. The references and further readings can be helpful, for example, because they point you to readings you might not otherwise have found (for a good overview of the 'To Wikipedia or Not To Wikipedia' debate, see Coomer 2013).

There is a reason academic work is peer reviewed heavily in a way that much user-generated online material is not: to check for errors, the correct application of accepted methods, to iron out gross distortions not rooted in evidence, and to weed out other flaws that cast doubt on the reliability of the knowledge being presented. Of all sources you use at university, you should ask the following question: 'do I trust this source?' Wikipedia would score very low in the hierarchy of scores for different sources (Cornell University 2009). There is a very basic logic at work here as well: you are training to be scholars, so use scholarly materials.

- **Technical aspects.** Students 2 and 3 write in plain, unambiguous English. References are set out correctly and it is easy to follow their thoughts in the introduction. The quality of Student 1's written English is lower for the following reasons:

  o First, why does the definition of IR suggest that students of the subject take a 'very scientific' approach to the subject? The meaning of 'very scientific' is unclear so the logic of the statement is contentious. Can a method of researching an academic subject be 'quite scientific', and how would we measure which bits were scientific and which were not?

  o Second, Student 1's use of 'Some would say ...' and 'Others would argue ...' smacks of imprecision. Vagueness about who it is that takes positions in an academic debate (the 'some say .... others say ...' syndrome) is insufficient at this level. Precision is everything. Was it a woman in the pub who said it?

Or a bloke in a shop? At the very least a source would have been needed to clear up the confusion. Overall it adds to the impression that the student is not yet on top of the reading material on this topic.

  ○   Third, Student 1's references are incorrectly presented according to what were then my departmental guidelines on the Harvard system of referencing. Presentation of your notes and bibliography, as we have seen, is a key thing to get correct in essays. If you can spend time getting it right, you will show your tutor that you can present work 'academically' and you will be given your credit accordingly.

● Having read these introductions, the marker will be thinking that Student 3 is the most organized, well-prepared and logical student who can, moreover, express his ideas clearly and unambiguously. Student 2 is some way to understanding the basic requirements of an essay, while Student 1 is getting there but seems to be the least technically proficient student. Let us now drill down into the body essay and see how students deal with micro structure in their writing.

MICRO STRUCTURE

It is important to structure essays at the micro as well as the macro level so that the reader can follow the logic of your claims as you work through the piece. Here are some examples of signposting and bridging from the three essays which helped the students organize the body of their essays.

Signposting using questions

STUDENT 1 [OPENING PARAGRAPH OF BODY OF ESSAY]

But how do we undertake such an approach to studying issues as complex as classifying a state's identity in the contemporary world to understanding the balance of power and war and the significance of 9/11?

While there is a lot going on in the sentence, we can see that Student 1 is setting up the next paragraph or two by posing a question which, on being answered, should help him answer the essay question. The question acts as a different form of signpost compared to the declarative form of signpost discussed in the previous chapter.

STUDENT 2 [AFTER DEFINING 'SCIENCE']

In the purest meaning of the word is IR theory 'science'? Can IR be seen objectively and with only fact and figures?

The student goes on to analyse writers in the 'yes' camp, such as E.H. Carr. My critique of this part of the essay was that the student did not spend enough time looking at the 'no' camp. However, dropping in the odd question adds a useful structuring dimension to your writing so is definitely worth trying out.

Numbered points

STUDENT 3 [IN SECTION ON EMPIRICISM]

The positivist or naturalist 'scientific' perspective on IR has four main underlying assumptions, which are largely drawn from the main assumptions of logical positivism (Smith et al. 2006: 19). Firstly, they believe in the unity of science ... Secondly, facts and values are distinguishable ... Thirdly, positivists hold the social world to contain regularities ... Lastly, they hold the neutral nature of facts ... (Baylis et al. 2001).

Many texts list the characteristics of positivism in this way. You can see how replicating the numbered approach helps Student 3 take the reader smoothly through them. He also backs his case with reference to two authoritative sources. Providing micro structure to paragraphs achieves three things in academic writing. First, it helps you organize your thoughts when you put finger to keyboard. Second, it helps you write in coherent, well-balanced paragraphs. Third, it makes it easy for a marker to follow your thinking as it develops through a paragraph.

I micro structured that paragraph above using numbered points. The narrative form tends to read better than including them as bulleted lists, especially in essays. If you are producing other forms of academic writing, such as policy briefs, bulleted lists can work well. By all means think in bullet points, but write using narrative in an academic essay. If in doubt, check what your tutor prefers.

Micro structure: more on signposts and bridges

STUDENT 1 [ON THE DIFFERENT STRANDS OF REALIST THOUGHT]

First, the concept of 'procedural realism' stated that the rose-tinted view of the world that liberals so readily adopted 'must be succeeded by a stage of hard and ruthless analysis'. 'Scientific realism' continued claiming that 'no political utopia will achieve even the most limited success unless it grows out of political reality' and finally 'ideological realism' argued that 'realism is the necessary corrective to the exuberance of utopianism'.

Despite the fact that these are two of the most dominant theories in the world of IR, we can see that they are also just a fraction of the number of theories that do surround this study.

Unfortunately, we initially have to note the total absence of sources in the above. You can see that it is a distilled version of Crane's analysis of Realism (explored in Chapter 5 of this book), which in turn quotes Carr. As such the student needed at least one reference here to show the origin of his ideas.

Overlooking the bad practice vis-à-vis references, focus on the transition between paragraphs. After the summary of different types of Realism, the text does not just jump to a new point without warning. The student carefully explains where he goes next by alluding to the fact that there are many other theoretical perspectives on IR. This provides a bridge for the reader to cross from one paragraph to the next. In a perfect essay every break between paragraphs would be accompanied by a line either at the end of one paragraph or at the start of the next explaining the journey being taken. This is what Student 3's essay did very effectively.

STUDENT 3

In the same manner as evolutionary biologists, explanatory [positivist] theorists claim that by using theories as a starting point events can be reconstructed and explained ... [*summarizes explanatory theory*].

Conversely post-positivist theories are constitutive in nature. In this perspective theory is viewed to be a construct of the world [*summarizes constitutive theory*] ... Claiming that facts are neutral is 'simply a reflection of an adherence to a particular view of epistemology' (Baylis et al. 2001: 274).

Note here the improved use of quotes and reference to a key source compared to Student 1. Each paragraph is themed very neatly. The first covers explanatory theory, the second covers constitutive theory. These themes are clearly set out for the reader at the beginning of each paragraph, while at the end of the second paragraph there is a useful recap quote summarizing the nub of the matter.

The use of 'Conversely' at the start of the second paragraph is a pithy way of showing that the interpretation explored in paragraph 2 contradicts that set out in paragraph 1. The student is demonstrating that he has located divisions within the literature and is able to situate them for the reader. Equivalent techniques you can use to show differences of opinion between writers include:

- 'By contrast, ...'
- 'On one hand, ... On the other hand, ...'
- 'Nevertheless, X argues ...'
- 'Some writers argue ... Others suggest ...'. Make sure if you use this approach you provide references. Being vague about who the people are does nothing for your credibility as an academic author. Do not leave the reader guessing who you mean, otherwise it comes across as lacking evidence and rather as a 'straw man' approach to essay writing. Put simply, without a reference, a reader will be asking: 'Where is your proof?'

Taking time to wrap up at the end of a section is a great way of helping guide the reader through your essay. You can either use a quote or spend a line explaining the essence of your thinking in that section and relating it to the overall argument you are making.

MACRO STRUCTURE: ESSAY CONCLUSIONS

Now take a look at the conclusions by Students 2 and 3.

STUDENT 2

In Conclusion then a broad consensus is upon us as regards to International relations being a science in the broadest definition of the meaning but one must be cautious. International relations is a science with it's limitations. It would be wrong to approach politics purely from this angle without also understanding the human emotion behind the politics also. And I believe scientific realism does account for this ambiguity in that it accepts that one application of methods in one science is not necessarily the optimal method for other sciences.

STUDENT 3

In conclusion, the discipline of IR can claim to be 'scientific'. The social world and natural world differ with respect to the nature of the units and system of inquiry, implying that the epistemology and methodology of natural sciences are not necessarily applicable to study social phenomena. In the same manner, what constitutes a 'scientific' inquiry into natural phenomena does not necessarily constitute a 'scientific' inquiry into social phenomena. The term 'scientific' essentially represents valid and justified knowledge rather than certain epistemologies or methodologies and critical to this notion is the nature of the knowledge generated; it must contain objective elements. Essentially, the 'scientific' nature of IR is rooted in the communication of such knowledge. Even as theories operate with different epistemological, ontological and methodological perspectives the knowledge they generate can be viewed as constructive and applicable to the discipline of IR as a whole.

As with the introductions earlier, which conclusion do you think is better? If you were the marker, which conclusion would persuade you that the student knew most about how to answer the thorny question of whether or not IR was truly a 'science'?

- **Recap.** Student 3 summarizes the gist of his answer better than Student 2. It is firmly in line with the argument put forward in his introduction (see p. 272 above) and it explains the rationale as to why that was the answer given. Student 2 talks about scientific realism. However, the student does not reinforce an argument from the introduction where scientific realism is never mentioned and where we were in fact left guessing about the answer to be given in the essay. Bringing in new concepts late in the day is a dangerous tactic and indicates a lack of organization and pre-planning. Student 3 knows where he is going from the outset, whereas Student 2 seems to have built an answer as the essay progresses rather than before he started writing. Student 3 thus provides the most convincing and fully fledged macro structure.

- **Subject matter expertise.** Note the comparison in the language used in the two conclusions. Student 3's conclusion reads much more like an 'academic' piece of work because he uses terminology and expressions of which he has demonstrated ample knowledge of in the preceding essay. Student 2 raises new issues such as the 'human emotion' behind politics which were absent from the body of the essay. You should play it safe in conclusions by only bringing in concepts/themes/ideas you have thoroughly explored in the essay. Student 3 thus provides the more authoritative conclusion.

COMMON PITFALL

Only use long or technical words if you are absolutely sure that you know what they mean and have defined them for your reader. Trying to blind a marker with multisyllabic words (like 'multisyllabic' in fact) will never convince a marker if you do not demonstrate an in-depth understanding of these long words and the meanings and conceptual disagreements lying behind them. IRT is replete with essentially contested terms, so although you cannot spend a whole essay defining every word, think strategically about which you should be defining.

- **Written English.** The clarity of Student 3's conclusion is better than Student 2's. First, there are no typographical mistakes, as in 'International relations' or 'it's limitations'. Second, the quality of expression is greater, helped by sharper sentence construction (note the need for punctuation in the opening sentence of Student 2's conclusion). Finally, Student 3's conclusion is nearer the length expected for an essay of 1,500 words. Student 3's conclusion thus shows greater technical proficiency than Student 2's.

REFERENCING AND BIBLIOGRAPHY

Providing enough references and setting them out correctly are basic features of an essay (see Chapter 16). Your tutor will expect to see you getting this crucial feature of an essay right and you will be penalized if you cannot reference correctly. If your referencing is consistently bad you also risk being had up for bad academic practice or, worse, plagiarism. Of the three essays only Student 3 managed to present his references correctly. Student 1 routinely quoted without providing references or set the references out incorrectly. Student 2 provided more regular references but set them out incorrectly. On the quality of references, we have already noted the comparison between Students 1 (dictionary) and 3 (key text on IR from reading list). Student 2 also used a dictionary definition of 'science'.

There is no simple or straightforward correlation between the number of sources in a bibliography and the quality of an essay. However, certain inferences are possible from the three essays considered here. The most successful essay (Student 3's) had 10 sources listed in the bibliography. All of these were referred to at least once in the essay, and two of the articles cited were not on the module reading list, showing that the student had read around the subject. The submissions by Students 1 and 2 relied on about half that number of sources and this was reflected in the relative lack of critical depth they were able to achieve in their answers.

The previous chapter discussed the theory behind referencing and bibliographies, so all that is needed here is a reminder of the basics:

- Check how to set your references in your departmental handbook and/or module guide. If in doubt, check with your tutor – but only do so if your query is not answered somewhere else in your university/department/module materials.
- Reference only the place where you first found a piece of information.
- Every source you cite in an essay must appear in a list of references.
- A bibliography is wider than a list of references in that it can contain all sources you read when preparing an essay, even if you do not refer to them directly in the submission. It is generally best not to pad the bibliography too much or to have too much discrepancy between the bibliography and the sources you cite in the essay.
- A general rule is that better essays tend to be based on more sources, and more *credible* sources at that. Through wide reading, the author is able to generate balance and critical depth to an answer.

FINAL REMARKS

All these essays had different strengths and weaknesses. Student 3 scored a very high mark; Student 2 scored a middling mark; and Student 1 scored an above-pass mark. To attain the top grade, Student 3 did the basics very well and was able to demonstrate, even in this relatively constricted word limit, that he was organized, logical and had good knowledge of the subject. He also communicated his ideas effectively in plain English. Both the other essays showed promise, but displayed a weaker grasp of the subject matter and slipped up on basic presentational points such as referencing. As with academic subjects across the board, a successful essay in IRT requires technical proficiency and a comprehensive knowledge of the subject matter.

18

MAKING THE MOST OF THEORY IN EXAMS

Your IRT assessment programme will likely feature a coursework element (such as an essay, policy report, and/or presentation) and an exam element. Exam periods at university are stressful times and your performance can be badly hampered if you suffer from serious exam nerves. A bit of adrenalin and anticipation will help your performance under pressure. Full-blown panic will do you no good whatsoever. The way to avoid hitting the panic button is to approach your work on the module as a whole in as organized, logical and structured fashion as you can. Take ownership of your learning early on (see Chapter 15) and you will not go far wrong. That way, you are not starting to build up your subject knowledge and essay skills from scratch at the last minute, but simply applying them in new ways. In preparing for exams you should continue to practice the good working habits you have developed over the course as a whole.

START FROM DAY ONE

Revising for exams is not something that starts after a module ends, as if exams are somehow separate from the rest of the work you do on the course. As the final assessed element of the module, the capstone exercise if you like, exams should feature in your thinking throughout the module. Everything you do during the course should help gear you up to sit the exam paper in IRT. As Nicholas Walliman (2006: 169) puts it, 'You should be like the squirrel that stores up nuts for the winter. Do not waste any lecture, tutorial, tutorial, group discussion, etc. by letting the material evaporate into thin air.' When you are reading over your notes at the end of each lecture and tutorial make a list specifically for revision. On the list you could include:

- A list of key writers in a theoretical tradition.
- A list of the critics of each theory or theorist.
- A brief summary of the big debates that surround each theory covered.
- Definitions of all of the most contested terms in IR that crop up.

Early preparation will save you masses of time later on, allowing you to concentrate on the really important things like practicing exam answers and following up gaps in your knowledge in the library.

ORGANIZE YOUR NOTES

Put every note you take from reading, lectures and tutorials in a folder or ring binder, clearly separated by course topic or week. This will help you capture the sense of everything you learned and enable you to locate notes quickly and easily. If you are feeling really organized you could put together, electronically or by hand, a glossary of IRT key terms which you update each week with new entries.

PAST EXAM PAPERS

These will normally be made available in the module guide or in the online resources for your course. They will give you an idea of the kinds of themes that come up most often, and the ways in which questions tend to be framed. Keep copies of these in with your notes and pay particular care to the recent papers and those set by the tutor that convenes your course. The 'Questions to ponder' included near the end of each theory chapter in Part II of this book could be used as practice questions too.

COMMON PITFALL

Do not rote learn model answers to questions from past papers and repeat these in the exam. Every year the 'twist' to a question on a given theory varies slightly and you will not receive good marks for answering the question from last year's paper.

IDENTIFY GAPS IN YOUR KNOWLEDGE ... AND PLUG THEM

If you prepare thoroughly for each lecture and tutorial you should have an extensive and critically informed knowledge base from which to work at the start of the revision period. When rereading your notes identify areas where you consider your knowledge to be a bit sketchy. You might have gaps in your knowledge base if:

- You do not know the main claims of a given theory of IR.
- You cannot define a key term.
- You have not read an essential text.
- You do not understand a concept that featured in the reading or lecture.

Build time to research these areas into your revision timetable. It is tempting to ignore them and concentrate on revising the topics with which you are most comfortable.

However, you will reap the rewards if you work on your weaknesses and aim to turn them into strengths, because this will give you more flexibility when it comes to choosing which questions to tackle in the exam.

GROUP STUDY

Pooling ideas can be a great way of helping you consolidate and advance your knowledge. Get together with a small group of friends to go over key theories and discuss questions circulated in advance. For example, you could all practice writing an answer to the same exam question and then meet over a coffee to explore the relative merits of your individual approaches. The aim of group revision is not to generate 'model' answers or the same approach to a theory, but to help you think through the basics of each issue and how best to communicate responses to exam questions on a given topic or theory.

PRACTICE EXAM QUESTIONS

Group study can be an effective aid to individual study but remember that, in the final analysis, it is you who has to sit the exam and write the answer on your own. One of the best ways to prepare for the discomfort of sitting alone with an exam paper in front of you and a blank sheet of paper to fill in is to get used to being in that situation beforehand. You could therefore try the following:

- Empty your room of friends and turn off your mobile, television, radio, Instagram, Facebook and Twitter accounts, plus electronic gaming devices.
- Root out a past exam paper or practice essay question from an IR textbook.
- Give yourself 15 minutes to plan an answer. Identify and write out your central argument that you will defend in the essay and build a bullet point structure which works at the micro level.
- Write a 200-word introduction to the answer.
- Write a two-line summary of each of the main points you would cover in the essay.
- It is impossible to replicate exam conditions out of an exam room. Nevertheless, by answering practice questions on your own in a quiet room you will get a feel for the pressure of sitting the exam. The top sports people get there by consistent and hard practice and the same rule applies in academia.

VARY YOUR REVISION SCHEDULE

Although you need to be organized and methodical in your approach, revision can become a tedious business if you do the same things every day. Routine is one thing, going stale quite another. So, strike a good balance by varying your revision strategies (for example, alternating between group revision and self-directed study) and consider the following tips:

- You do not need to revise 24 hours a day 7 days a week. Try and keep to your usual waking, eating and sleeping patterns.
- Take regular exercise between revision sessions.
- Do not become a hermit! Make time for periods of relaxation and going out with friends and family.
- Learn which times of day you feel most active and work most effectively and tailor your revision programme to those peaks.
- Find out when the exam is and, if possible, write your practice exam answers in that same time slot to get yourself in the habit of thinking and writing during that part of the day.
- Remember that it is not only the naturally intelligent or gifted people who succeed at exams. It is also an easy get-out to do little or no revision and fall back on the line, 'I could have succeeded if I'd wanted to.' Put simply, that is a cop-out and a poor excuse for under-performance. Grafting hard through a module and paying close attention to what the examiner looks for in a good exam answer is the key, whatever you think your 'natural' level of ability is. Delivering logical, well-evidenced, well-communicated and critically incisive answers to the question set is the crux.

EXAM TIPS

I am not an expert on the psychological effects of stress, but from my experience of sitting exams and now working in a demanding job, I have learnt that the best way to deal with stress is to think about two things: (1) its causes, and (2) ways to combat it. From the students I have spoken to, exam nerves are generally brought on by a combination of lack of preparation and lack of confidence in their ability to write under pressure. Everything I have said so far in this book has been geared to making the exam period as stress-free as possible by seeing exams as another opportunity to put into practice the good working and writing habits you have developed through a module. Integrating the exam into your overall approach to learning on the module will help you leap the psychological barrier exams can sometimes become. In this final section we will consider a few of the tips you might deploy to get the very best exam mark you can.

The basics

Find out as early as you can where you will be sitting the exam, at what time, and what materials you can take into it with you (if any). Invest in a good alarm clock or ask friends to come and knock on your door if you are frightened of sleeping in for an early morning exam. Amazingly, some students fail to show up for exams, or arrive half an hour in. It goes without saying that this is a recipe for disaster. Make sure you have a good supply of pens that work and all the other stationary you will need. Arrive at the exam in plenty of time so that you can calm yourself down before entering the hall; the last thing you need is to be rushing in late all hot and bothered.

Planning your time

Find out before the exam how many questions you will have to answer. Typical exams are something in the region of two questions in two hours or three questions in three hours. In both scenarios you have one hour per answer. A good essay plan can take anything up to 10 minutes to put together. Do not mistakenly believe you are getting behind your peers if you do not start writing straight away.

> Have confidence in your ability to structure the exam to suit you and the IRT knowledge you possess. Play to your strengths. Know how much time you want to allocate to each part of the paper and stick to it.

If your exam is not all about writing essays, make sure you have worked out in advance how long you want to allocate for each part of the paper. For instance, there might be a multi-choice element, or a short summary element where you define key terms. However the paper is structured, make sure you leave enough time for each segment and that you have time at the end of each paper to read and correct each answer. When the exam begins try and get into your own little bubble ('in the zone' as the pro sports saying goes) to block out what is going on around you. Concentrate on the tasks ahead of you and manage your time accordingly.

Writing your answers

Spend a few minutes at the start of the exam deciding which questions you want to tackle. Pay attention at this point to the phrasing of the questions. There might be topics you are familiar with but for which the question is phrased in a complex or difficult way. Think carefully about what kinds of structure you could use for each question on offer and which of those structures helps you communicate your argument clearly and concisely given the stock of knowledge you possess about the relevant theory(ies).

Think strategically. Know before you go in whether you want to plan all the answers at the start of the exam and then write them, or whether you want to plan and write the answers one at a time. A practical advantage of the latter approach is that you give your writing hand a break while you plan the next answer. Moreover, switching from writing to planning and back to writing mid-exam will stimulate different parts of the brain and might keep you fresher and more focused. Whichever method you deploy keep an eye on the clock so that you do not spend too much time on one answer at the expense of the others.

> It is always tempting in an exam to spend disproportionate amounts of time on the question(s) you feel you know really well. However, a very long, overly detailed answer to one question will never compensate for short, thin answers elsewhere. Balance is vital. You do not want to be in the unhappy position of writing 'ran out of time' at the end of five lines of writing on the last question.

The essence of a good exam answer is that it is well structured, flows nicely from start to finish and is supported by a good range of credible, authoritative evidence. Your tutor will want to see that you have thought critically about the themes and issues raised by the question and that you can devise logical, well-reasoned responses to the questions you tackle. As in a coursework essay you are encouraged to use quotes from the books you have read and refer to key authors on whose work you have drawn to frame your arguments. If you can go beyond the basic course texts and into advanced and wider reading you will stand out from the vast majority of students who will churn out standard names, sources and interpretations.

COMMON PITFALL

The classic mistake in IRT exams is to write everything you know (or can remember) about a given theory. The 'scatter-gun' answer, as it is known, is a giveaway that a student has not prepared well for the exam. Sound revision and a robust essay structure will help limit the time you spend wandering off the subject.

Try not to repeat too much information from one answer in another because this indicates a thin knowledge base. To take a two-questions-in-two-hours exam: if you can show the examiner that you know, in detail, three or four theories of IR across your two questions, this looks better than if you can only demonstrate knowledge of two theories which you rehash in both answers.

In sum, the best exam marks go to students who do the following:

- Show sound knowledge of the subject matter.
- Answer the questions set rather than the question they want to see.
- Structure their answers around a few key points.
- Signpost their writing (see Chapters 16 and 17).
- Use appropriate, credible evidence to back their arguments. This can be presented in the form of short quotes or summaries of writers' arguments.
- It is an IRT exam, so make sure that you can reference theories of International Relations! Waffling on about the Iraq War, 9/11, the Eurozone crisis, intervention in Syria will only be relevant in the context of a theoretically informed approach. Reference to the 'real world' of IR is not ruled out, but it must be used appropriately to illustrate and critique theory, not as a substitute for it.

REFERENCES TO MORE INFORMATION

Cottrell, S. (2012) *The Exam Skills Handbook*, 2nd edn. Basingstoke: Palgrave Macmillan.

Mcmillan, K. and Weyers, J. (2011) *How to Succeed in Exams and Assessments*, 2nd edn. Harlow: Pearson Education.

Levin, P. (2005) *Sail Through Exams!: Preparing for Traditional Exams for Undergraduates and Taught Postgraduates*. Maidenhead: Open University Press.

Tracy, E. (2006) *The Student's Guide to Exam Success*, 2nd edn. Buckingham: Open University Press.
The focus here is on the emotional and psychological aspects of preparing for and sitting exams.

Holmes, A. (2005) *Pass Your Exams: Study Skills for Success*. Oxford: The Infinite Ideas Company.
A 'tips' book with useful advice on building up your confidence and playing the exam game and passing.

Burns, T. and Sinfield, S. (2012) *Essential Study Skills: The Complete Guide to Success at University*. London: Sage.
Excellent on academic reading, note-taking and essay-writing.

GLOSSARY

Actor   In this context it does not mean Will Smith, Daniel Craig or Angelina Jolie. In IR it means the unit of analysis (for example, the state or a supranational organization) whose behaviour theorists try to explain. Different theories tend to emphasize the significance of different actors in international affairs.

Aesthetics   The branch of philosophy dealing with the nature/appreciation of beauty and the beautiful. If you like the look of a piece of art, you could say it is aesthetically pleasing. There is a view that individuals are drawn to certain interpretations and theories about IR on aesthetic grounds as much as anything else.

Agency   There is a big debate within Politics and IR about the extent to which we explain people's/state's behaviour with reference to their own actions and ideas. Those people taking the latter view would believe in the priority of agency over structures or with reference to the impact of the structures that shape the lives and worlds of those people and states (agents).

Anarchy   When applied to IR, it means the lack of an orderer in the international system. This 'orderer' could be something like a world government but does not have to be as formal or powerful as that name implies.

Anthropocentrism   The idea that humans are the only creators of meaning in the universe and the only life form worth considering when we take decisions and make policies.

Balance of power   Centrepiece of Neorealist theory developed by Kenneth Waltz to explain how the structure of the international system explains the interactions of the units within it.

Bretton Woods System   Named after the place in the USA where the leading industrial powers met in 1944 to hammer out the rules for the management of their commercial and financial relations. Collapsed in 1971.

Colonialism   Has both formal and informal aspects. Formally it means the practice of one country controlling another by military, economic and/or political means, usually with the use of, or threat of, violence and local territorial infrastructures. Informally it can mean the exploitation or oppression of less developed and weaker countries by more developed and stronger ones through global structures such as international institutions. A key component of Marxist and Postcolonial theories of IR.

Cosmopolitanism   A political theory that denies the relevance of the state in determining individual morality and justice. Usually contrasted with communitarianism, which charges states with a central place in shaping individual attitudes on these issues.

Deconstruction   Associated with the thought of Jacques Derrida. Deconstruction is a vital tool for postmodernist IR scholars who use it to probe, unsettle, unhinge and pull apart supposedly settled core IR concepts such as the 'state' and 'sovereignty'. One of the most popular ways they achieve this is through the double reading of texts.

Defensive Realism   A Realist approach focusing on states seeking security in a balance of power. Kenneth Waltz's Neorealism is a good example. Critiqued by the offensive Realists (see below).

Determinism   The philosophical proposition that human beliefs, actions and decision are causally determined by prior events and circumstances. In IRT the debate plays out between those who believe that the structure of the international system decisively shapes state behaviour (the determinist position) and those who believe states themselves have the capacity to 'author' the international system (Constructivists and poststructuralists).

Diplomacy   The official conduct of relations between two or more states, or two or more groups of states. Usually carried out by government ministers and civil servants, or diplomats, it entails negotiation, communication and the drawing up of treaties, agreements and the like. Can also include unofficial dimensions such as cultural exchanges. Political disagreements between countries can mean diplomatic ties being cut as a sign of disapproval by one state at the actions of another.

Discourse   Means much more than a conversation between two people. Associated with the work of Michel Foucault, it refers to the way in which language is used to structure our accounts of, and give meaning to, the social world. The study of discourse is usually undertaken for critical purposes, to reveal something about power relations in a society or set of human relationships.

Empiricism   A theory of knowledge that suggests knowledge should be generated through direct observation and other sensory experience.

Epistemology   Theory about how we know things and what is regarded as hard and fast knowledge in a given discipline; or the origins and legitimacy of knowledge.

Essentially contested   If we say that an object, event or process is essentially contested it implies that while it has been observed to exist there is no agreement on its meaning, implications or potential uses. For example, we might all assert that the 'Arab Spring' has changed the conduct of national politics in countries such as Egypt, but the wider meaning of Arab Spring is itself much harder to pin down – its origins, impact and likely future outcomes. The 'Arab Spring' is an essentially contested concept.

Etymology   The study of the origin, development and derivation of words.

Falsification   The process of proving a theory to be flawed, for example, because a prediction generated through its application turns out to be wrong.

Functionalist integration theory   Developed by David Mitrany. Explains how economic and social integration increases levels of interdependence between states and can therefore lead to peace and security for the states involved.

Genealogy   Associated with Michel Foucault, an investigation into the historical practices which create subjects through discursive closures, exclusions and marginalizations. Not a history in the conventional sense of understanding how things come to be. In IR we undertake genealogies to probe how the discipline makes sense of the world: what has IR had to forget or overlook to make knowledge about international affairs seem like the 'truth'?

Gender   The social meanings given to the concepts 'male' and 'female' and the supposed characteristics that flow from them in terms of those that are held to be 'masculine' and those we associate with 'femininity'.

General Agreement on Tariffs and Trade (GATT)   Set up at the Bretton Woods Conference in 1944 to promote the reduction of barriers to international trade such as tariffs and quotas.

Generic skills   See *transferable skills*.

Globalization   Extremely difficult to define in a few words! Widely taken to imply the widening, deepening and/or intensification of economic, political, technological, cultural, social and environmental interactions across state borders. Products of globalization include rolling 24/7 news media and social media such as Twitter, which have sped the pace of cross-border communication.

Hegemony   Concept used in IR to chart the relative position of states in the international system, measured by their power (loosely defined). For example, the USA is said to have been a hegemonic power since the end of the Cold War especially but not exclusively in military terms. In Critical Theory the definition broadens so that it is less about dominance by force than subtle forms of consent and consensus-building. In this interpretation, hegemony becomes the dynamics of order that comes from states getting into positions whereby their ideas/practices are accepted by other states without the threat or use of force. Includes the use of international organizations to spread norms and thereby shape the system in almost unnoticed ways, for instance the International Monetary Fund (IMF).

Hypothesis   A prediction about the state of the world and/or relationships between variables within that world. For example, we might want to test the hypothesis that students who attend more lectures and seminars/tutorials achieve higher marks in essays and exams than those who attend fewer lectures and seminars/tutorials. We would test this hypothesis by studying attendance registers and correlating them with the marks achieved for each student. If marks generally rise as attendance rises we have proved the hypothesis.

Ideational   That feature of the study of IR dealing with ideas that transcend state borders and which can come to be shared either as tight value sets or influences on state behaviour. Used in later Liberal, Neoliberal English School and Constructivist thought on international institutions and the spread of norms in international systems/societies.

Interdependence   The idea that the political, economic and social connections among states or groups of states have reached a point where the actions of one or other of those states directly affects the other states, intentionally or not. Linked to the concept of globalization and usually contrasted with independence.

International organization   A body created by states to which they delegate authority to carry out action at the international level. The United Nations is the most comprehensive global international organization operating today.

International regime   A term associated with Neoliberal IRT. Highlights the idea that international cooperation is about more than the formalized, rule-bound cooperation we see in the establishment of international organizations. Institutions and international organizations also promote informal modes of inter-state cooperation via regimes.

International system   All the states that exist in the world today constitute the international system. IR scholars disagree about the nature of this system. Some (e.g. Realists) see the system as inherently conflict ridden, others (e.g. Liberals and English School theorists) argue that even without a world government, state behaviour tends to be structured and regulated, thus avoiding the worst excesses of perpetual war and violence.

Metatheory   Theory about theory; theory about the rules and standards by which theories count as theories how they make sense of their subject matter, and how we measure theoretical contributions to a given field. Metatheory focuses on the philosophical assumptions underlying theories, so is explicitly concerned with questions of ontology, epistemology and methodology.

Methodology   In the social sciences, the procedures by which we generate knowledge. For example, research using quantitative methods might interpret statistical data whereas qualitative research interprets meanings, beliefs and attitudes of subjects. In the natural sciences, rules and guidelines on how to set up experiments and interpret the data.

Multinational corporation   A company or business that has headquarters, offices and/or means of production such as factories located in different countries around the world, such as Barclays Bank, McDonald's and Coca-Cola. Used interchangeably with 'transnational corporation' and sometimes shortened to 'multinational' or MNC.

Nation-state   Used interchangeably with 'state' in much IR literature. Has a specific meaning whereby members of a territorially bounded population share more in common than merely their land borders, including ethical codes of conduct and values which come from them sharing a common language, tradition and sense of history: who they are and where they are going, collectively speaking.

Naturalism   The view that the social world and the natural worlds can be studied using the same methods. It was arguably the dominant theoretical approach within IR until the 1980s (especially as practiced in the USA) when normative theory became more prominent within the discipline.

Norm(s)   Norms are socially shared sets of understandings and expectations about how it is appropriate to behave for agents with given identities. Norms are not always written down but they can be formalized in laws, for example, governing the relations between states on the global stage. They feature prominently in theories of IR such as Liberalism, Neoliberalism and Constructivism.

Offensive Realism   The 'human nature' image of international relations in which the innate lust for power combines with the security dilemma in anarchy to give rise to constant instability in the system. This is the insurmountable 'tragedy' of international politics for writers such as Mearsheimer.

Ontology   Theory connected with the things, properties and events that exist in the world; what exists to be investigated.

Paradigm   Popularized by Thomas Kuhn's 1962 book *The Structure of Scientific Revolutions*. Scientists who work in a particular research paradigm 'are committed to the same rules and standards for scientific practice' and work to continue that particular research tradition (Kuhn 1996: 11). IR theories can be likened Kuhnian paradigms in that they set down precise research agendas and validate work against certain benchmarks and practices.

Patriarchy   A system of rule or governance by men. Such systems can be openly patri-archal, where men have greater legal, political, religious and social freedoms than women. Or they can be covert, in that women are discriminated against institutionally, in the workplace (in terms of pay and conditions) and so on. Feminist scholars have deepened our understanding of the overt and covert sources of patriarchy in IR both within states and in the international system at large.

Pax Americana   Describes the period of relative international peace (or absence of world war) since 1945. Replaced the Pax Britannica evident in the mid-nineteenth century centred on the 'order' provided by the British Empire.

Pluralism   A position within English School theory concerning the appropriateness of contravening state sovereignty to achieve ethical ends, for example a humanitarian inter-vention such as Libya. The debate revolves around normative positions taken on such values as order and justice in IR and pluralists believe order trumps justice except in acute emergencies. See *solidarism* for the countervailing view.

Positivism   Both a philosophy about scientific research and an epistemological approach to the study of IR. Positivists try and apply the methods and practices of the natural sciences to the social sciences. They assume that we can produce objective knowledge about the world through the careful application of the scientific method of observation, reporting and testing the properties of a world external to us.

Post-positivism   Refers to the approach taken by a range of writers who critique but do not necessarily seek to overthrow positivist ways of generating knowledge. Some of them we explore in this book, such as Critical Theorists, feminists and poststructuralists. In US literature tends to be called 'reflectivism'.

Rationalism   The idea that actors are utility-maximizers, which has come to IR from economic theory. In IR, states are rational actors if they identify their main interests – economic, security, diplomatic – and select the most efficient means of securing those interests. Calculation not emotion is what drives state behaviour. This might mean collective action in international organizations/institutions, or it might mean 'going it alone' as Britain has chosen to do in the June 2016 Brexit referendum.

Reductionism   Using the behaviour of a component part to explain the behaviour of the environment or system within which it operates. For example, Realist IR theorists explain the behaviour of states by treating them like humans in a state of nature, implying that in a given situation states act as humans would do. This is a contested approach to explaining IR because it privileges interests, takes them as given, and ignores the identity-driven sources of foreign policy action.

Reflectivism   Another name given to different forms of normative theory. Reflectivism is often used interchangeably with labels such as 'new', 'post-positivist', 'post-structuralist' 'alternative', or even 'radical' approaches to IRT, to differentiate it from older, conventional, or rationalist accounts of IR (see Aalberts and van Munster 2008).

Reification   The process of attributing to some phenomenon (for example, 'anarchy') human, living or 'real-life' properties which it cannot or does not possess. In IR, Social Constructivists say that Realist scholars 'reify' anarchy; in other words Realists take this abstract, literally non-existent thing to be something real and tangible when it does not exist out there at all, only 'in our heads'.

Security dilemma   Classic concept dating back to the work of John Herz in the 1950s, whereby a state seeking to maximize its security makes other states in the international system feel less secure. Constant fear of the 'other' is what produces and reproduces patterns of insecurity and the potential for conflict between states existing in an anarchic international system.

Solidarism   A position within English School theory concerning the appropriateness of contravening state sovereignty to achieve ethical ends, for example a humanitarian intervention such as Libya. The debate revolves around normative positions taken on such values as order and justice in IR. Solidarists believe that the needs of basic justice for humanity override the necessity to maintain a sovereign state order. See *pluralism* for the countervailing view.

Sovereignty   A state is said to possess internal sovereignty when it exercises ultimate legal and political authority over a named territory. It possesses external sovereignty when other states respect its jurisdiction in these matters. Proponents of humanitarian intervention suggest that state sovereignty can and should be violated in cases of urgent need, such as crimes against humanity or genocide.

State   Used to refer to two things: a bounded, populated territory and/or the body that governs that particular territory. Said to have emerged with the Treaty of Westphalia in 1648, the modern state is said to be sovereign in that it and it alone has the right to pass laws to regulate its own affairs and population. The state was held to be the main actor in international relations by many early theorists such as those writing in the Realist and Liberal traditions. Newer approaches in IRT think about the implications of global politics conducted 'beyond' the state.

Structure   IRT, like the study of politics and society more widely, is interested in the interactions between units – often but not always states – and different structures in which they operate at the international level. These structures can be material 'real world' entities such as international organizations, or 'ideational', meaning the sets of norms, values and associated beliefs that shape state actions.

Subaltern   Means lower in rank or subordinate: originally used in the British military to denote a rank lower than captain. Now, the word has been claimed by Postcolonial scholars to refer to work by and about individuals, states and regions long silenced or marginalized by IR and other scholars propagating a Western- or Euro-centric view of the world. Subaltern Studies is one way of promoting attention to these gaps and closures in our knowledge too long left at IR's disciplinary borders.

Subnational actor   One that operates at a level below that of the state of which it is a part. Local councils in England are subnational actors, politically and administratively. Others might include: media, churches and religious groups, pressure groups, interest groups, think-tanks and economic organizations.

Supranational actor   A body set up by states to advance their common political, security and economic interests by making and executing legislation that affects the state signatories. The European Union is an example of a supranational organization.

Theory   Systematically describes aspects of the world, categorizes these aspects and considers their interrelationships with the intention of making sense of complexity and developing law-like generalizations.

Transferable skills   Also go by the name of generic skills or employability skills. Generally encompasses the following: reading, writing and arithmetic; listening, speaking, thinking; time and project management; information skills; design and presentation; problem identification, definition and solving; and personal knowledge. It is useful to keep a log of these skills you acquire during your degree programme to enhance your CV and employability prospects.

REFERENCES

Aalberts, T.E. (2010) 'Playing the Game of Sovereign States: Charles Manning's Constructivism *Avant-la-lettre*', *European Journal of International Relations*, 16(2): 247–68.

Aalberts, T.E. and Munster, R. (2008) 'From Wendt to Kuhn: Reviving the "Third Debate" in International Relations', *International Politics*, 45(6): 720–746.

Abbot, K.W. and Snidal, D. (1998) 'Why States Act through Formal International Organizations', *Journal of Conflict Resolution*, 42(1): 3–32.

Aberley, D. (1999) 'Interpreting Bioregioalism: A Story from Many Voices', in M. McGinnis (ed.) *Bioregionalism*. London: Routledge, pp. 13–42.

Abrahamsen, R. (2007) 'Postcolonialism', in M. Griffiths (ed.) *International Relations Theory for the Twenty-First Century*. London: Routledge, pp. 111–22.

Acharya, A. (2014) *Constructing a Security Community in Southeast Asia: ASEAN and the Problem of Regional Order*, 3rd edn. Abingdon: Routledge.

Adler, E. (1997a) 'Imagined (Security) Communities: Cognitive Regions in International Relations', *Millennium: Journal of International Studies*, 26(2): 249–77.

Adler, E. (1997b) 'Seizing the Middle Ground: Constructivism in World Politics', *European Journal of International Relations*, 3(3): 319–63.

Adler, E. and Barnett, M. (eds) (2008) *Security Communities*. Cambridge: Cambridge University Press.

Alker, H. and Biersteker, T. (1995) 'The Dialectics of World Order: Notes for a Future Archeologist of International *Savoir Faire*', in J. Der Derian (ed.) *International Theory: Critical Investigations*. Basingstoke: Macmillan, pp. 242–76.

Allison, G. (1971) *Essence of Decision: Explaining the Cuban Missile Crisis*. New York: Longman.

Anderson, B. (2006) *Imagined Communities*, 2nd edn. London: Verso.

Anievas, A. (2010) 'On Habermas, Marx and the Critical Theory Tradition: Theoretical Mastery or Drift?', in C. Moore and C. Farrands (eds) *International Relations and Philosophy: Interpretive Dialogues*. London: Routledge, pp. 144–56.

Aradau, C. (2010) 'Derrida: Aporias of Otherness', in C. Moore and C. Farrands (eds) *International Relations and Philosophy: Interpretive Dialogues*. London: Routledge, 107–18.

Arrival (2016) dir. Denis Villeneuve.

Ashcroft, B., Griffiths, G. and Tiffin, H. (1994) *The Empire Writes Back: Theory and Practice in Post-Colonial Literatures*. London: Routledge.

Ashley, R.K. (1986) 'The Poverty of Neorealism', in R.O. Keohane (ed.) *Neorealism and its Critics*. New York: Columbia University Press, pp. 1–26.

Ashley, R. (1995) 'The Powers of Anarchy: Theory, Sovereignty, and the Domestication of Global Life', in J. Der Derian (ed.) *International Theory: Critical Investigations*. Basingstoke: Macmillan, pp. 94–128.

Axford, B., Browning, G.K., Huggins, R. and Rosamond, B. (2006) *Politics: An Introduction*, 2nd edn. London: Routledge.

Babst, D.V. (1964) 'Elective Governments – A Force for Peace', *Wisconsin Sociologist*, 3: 9–14.

Badon, M. (2010) 'Red Light, Green Light: The Invention of the Traffic Signal', The Design Observer Group, 14 June, http://designobserver.com/feature/red-light-green-light--the-invention-of--the-traffic-signal/8627/ (accessed 5 August 2016).

Bailey, J.L. (2008) 'Arrested Development: The Fight to End Commercial Whaling as a Case of Failed Norm Change', *European Journal of International Relations*, 14(2): 289–318.

Bain, W. (2000) 'Deconfusing Morgenthau: Moral Inquiry and Classical Realism Reconsidered', *Review of International Studies*, 26(3): 445–64.

Baudrillard, J. (1995) *The Gulf War Did Not Take Place*, trans. P. Patton. Bloomington, IN: Indiana University Press.

Baylis, J., Smith, S. and Owens P. (eds) (2008) *The Globalization of World Politics: An Introduction to International Relations*, 4th edn. Oxford: Oxford University Press .

Baylis, J., Smith, S. and Owens, P. (2014a) 'Introduction', in J. Baylis, S. Smith and P. Owens (eds) *The Globalization of World Politics: An Introduction to International Relations*, 6th edn. Oxford: Oxford University Press, pp. 1–14.

Baylis, J., Smith, S. and Owens, P. (eds) (2014b) *The Globalization of World Politics: An Introduction to International Relations*, 6th edn. Oxford: Oxford University Press.

BBC (undated) 'IMF voting powers' (image), http://newsimg.bbc.co.uk/media/images/46443000/gif/_46443360_pledge3a_466.gif/ (accessed 15 August 2016).

Bellamy, A.J. (ed.) (2005) *International Society and its Critics*. Oxford: Oxford University Press.

The Big Short (2015) Dir. Adam McKay, Paramount Pictures.

Blits, J.H (1989) 'Hobbesian Fear', *Political Theory*, 17(3): 417–31.

Bishop, T., Reinke, J. and Adams, T. (2011) 'Globalization: Trends and Perspectives', *Journal of International Business Research*, 10(1): 117–30.

Biswas, S. (2016) 'Postcolonialism', in T. Dunne, M. Kurki and S. Smith (eds) *International Relations Theory: Discipline and Diversity*, 4th edn. Oxford: Oxford University Press, pp. 219-35.

Blair, T. (1999) 'Doctrine of the International Community', speech, Chicago, 24 April, www.britishpoliticalspeech.org/speech-archive.htm?speech=279 (accessed 4 August 2016).

Blair, T. (2001) Leader's speech, Brighton, 2 October, www.britishpoliticalspeech.org/speech-archive.htm?speech=186 (accessed 4 August 2016).

Blair, T. (2006) 'Tony Blair's Speech to the Foreign Policy Centre', *The Guardian*, 21 March, www.guardian.co.uk/politics/2006/mar/21/iraq.iraq1 (accessed 9 August 2016).

Boddy, C. (2011) 'The Corporate Psychopaths Theory of the Global Financial Crisis', *Journal of Business Ethics*, 102(2): 255–9.

Booth, K. and Wheeler, N.J. (2008) *The Security Dilemma: Fear, Cooperation and Trust in World Politics*. Basingstoke: Palgrave Macmillan.

Bowen, J.D. (2011) 'Theory in Action: Liberalism', www.youtube.com/watch?v=tZbD-MUaqwE8, 11 May (accessed 1 September 2016).

Brown, C. (2001) *Understanding International Relations*, 2nd edn. Basingstoke: Palgrave.

Buchan, N.R., Brewer, M.B., Grimalda, G., Wilson, R.K., Fatas, E. and Foddy, M. (2011) 'Global Social Identity and Global Cooperation', *Psychological Science*, 22(6): 821–8.

Bull, H. (1977) *The Anarchical Society: A Study of Order in World Politics*. London: Macmillan.

Burchill, S. and Linklater, A. (2013) 'Introduction', in S. Burchill and A. Linklater (eds) *Theories of International Relations*, 5th edn. Basingstoke: Palgrave Macmillan, pp. 1–31.

Buzan, B. (1993) 'From International System to International Society: Structural Realism and Regime Theory Meet the English School', *International Organization*, 47(3): 327–52.

Buzan, B. (2004) *From International to World Society? English School Theory and the Social Structure of Globalisation*. Cambridge: Cambridge University Press.

Buzan, B. (2014) *An Introduction to the English School of International Relations*. Cambridge: Polity Press.

Cabrera, M.A. (2005) *Postsocial History: An Introduction*, trans. M. McMahon. Lanham, MD: Lexington Books.

Cafruny, A.A. (2006) 'Historical Materialism: Imperialist Rivalry and the Global Capitalist Order', in J. Sterling-Folker (ed.) *Making Sense of International Relations Theory*. Boulder, CO: Lynne Rienner Publishers, pp. 209–24.

Cameron, D. (2006) 'A New Approach to Foreign Affairs – Liberal Conservatism', speech to the British American Project, 11 September, www.conservatives.com/News/Speeches/2006/09/Cameron_A_new_approach_to_foreign_affairs__liberal_conservatism.aspx (accessed 28 July 2016).

Cameron, F. (2010) 'The European Union as a Model for Regional Integration', Council on Foreign Relations, September, www.cfr.org/world/european-union-model-regional-integration/p22935 (accessed 25 July 2016).

Campbell, D. (1996) 'Violent Performances: Identity, Sovereignty, Responsibility', in Y. Lapid, and F. Kratochwil (eds) *The Return of Culture and Identity in IR Theory*. London: Lynne Rienner Publishers, pp. 163–80.

Campbell, D. (1998) *Writing Security: United States Foreign Policy and the Politics of Identity*. Manchester: Manchester University Press.

Campbell, D. (2007) 'Poststructuralism', in T. Dunne, M. Kurki and S. Smith (eds) *International Relations Theory: Discipline and Diversity*. Oxford: Oxford University Press, pp. 203–28.

Campbell, D. (2016) 'Poststructuralism', in T. Dunne, M. Kurki and S. Smith (eds) *International Relations Theory: Discipline and Diversity*, 4th edn. Oxford: Oxford University Press, pp. 196–235.

Carlsnaes, W., Risse, T. and Simmons, B.A. (eds) (2006) *Handbook of International Relations*. London: Sage.

Carr, E.H. (2001a) *What is History?* Basingstoke: Palgrave.

Carr, E.H. (2001b) *The Twenty Years' Crisis 1919–1939*. Basingstoke: Palgrave.

Carter, N. and Huby, M. (2005) 'Ecological Citizenship and Ethical Investment', *Environmental Politics*, 14(2), 255–72.

Central Intelligence Agency (CIA) (undated) 'International Organizations and Groups', www.cia.gov/library/publications/the-world-factbook/appendix/appendix-b.html (accessed 26 July 2016).

Chemaly, S. (2014) '20 Facts Everyone Should Know about Gender Bias in Movies', 24 November, www.huffingtonpost.com/soraya-chemaly/20-mustknow-facts-about-g_b_5869564.html (accessed 22 August 2016).

Cheng, A. and Lu, T.K. (2012) 'Synthetic Biology: An Emerging Engineering Discipline', *Annual Review of Biomedical Engineering*, 14: 155–78.

Chomsky, N. (1991) 'Force and Opinion', *Z Magazine*, July–August, https://chomsky.info/199107__/ (accessed 9 August 2016).

Cocoyoc Declaration (1974) 23 October, http://helsinki.at/projekte/cocoyoc/COCOYOC_DECLARATION_1974.pdf (accessed 18 August 2016).

Commons Select Committee (2016) 'Mike Ashley Must be Accountable for Sports Direct Working Practices', 22 July, www.parliament.uk/business/committees/committees-a-z/commons-select/business-innovation-and-skills/news-parliament-2015/working-practices-at-sports-direct-report-published-16-17/ (accessed 19 August 2016).

Coomer, A. (2013) 'Should University Students Use Wikipedia?', *The Guardian*, 13 May, www.theguardian.com/education/2013/may/13/should-university-students-use-wikipedia (accessed 2 September 2016).

Cornell University (2009) 'Using Wikipedia', www.digitalliteracy.cornell.edu/tutorial/dpl3222.html (accessed 2 September 2016).

Council of the European Union (2006) 'Review of the EU Sustainable Development Strategy: Renewed Strategy', 9 June, http://register.consilium.europa.eu/doc/srv?l=EN&f=ST%2010117%202006%20INIT (accessed 30 August 2016).

Cox, R.W. (1996a) 'Social Forces, States and World Orders: Beyond International Relations Theory', in R. Cox and T.J. Sinclair (eds) *Approaches to World Order*. Cambridge: Cambridge University Press, pp. 85–123.

Cox, R.W. (1996b) 'Gramsci, Hegemony and International Relations: An Essay in Method', in R. Cox and T.J. Sinclair (eds) *Approaches to World Order*. Cambridge: Cambridge University Press, pp. 124–43.

Crane, G. (1998) *Thucydides and the Ancient Simplicity: The Limits of Political Realism*. Berkeley, CA: University of California Press. http://publishing.cdlib.org/ucpressebooks/view?docId=ft767nb497&brand=ucpress (accessed 28 July 2016).

Crawford, N.C. (2009) 'Jürgen Habermas', in J. Edkins and N. Vaughan-Williams (eds) *Critical Theorists and International Relations*. London: Routledge, pp. 197–8.

Curtis, M. (2003) *Web of Deceit: Britain's Real Role in the World*. London: Vintage.

Daddow, O. (2006) 'Postmodernism and the Politics of Historiography', in A.L. Macfie (ed.) *The Philosophy of History: Talks Given at the Institute of Historical Research, London, 2000–2006*. Basingstoke: Palgrave Macmillan, pp. 155–72.

Daddow, O. (2009) '"Tony's War?" Blair, Kosovo and the Interventionist Impulse in British Foreign Policy', *International Affairs*, 85(3): 547–60.

Daddow, O. (2011) *New Labour and the European Union: Blair and Brown's Logic of History*. Manchester: Manchester University Press.

Daddow, O. (2012) 'The UK Media and "Europe": From Permissive Consensus to Destructive Dissent', *International Affairs*, 88(6): 1219–36.

Daddow, O. (2015) 'Constructing a "Great" Role for Britain in an Age of Austerity: Interpreting Coalition Government Foreign Policy, 2010–2015', *International Relations*, 29(3): 303–18.

Dalby, S. (2009) 'What Happens if We Don't Think in Human Terms?', in J. Edkins and M. Zehfuss (eds) *Global Politics: A New Introduction*. London and New York: Routledge, pp. 45–69.

Davis, D.E. (2009) 'Non-State Armed Actors, New Imagined Communities, and Shifting Patterns of Sovereignty and Insecurity in the Modern World', *Contemporary Security Policy*, 30(2): 221–45.

Der Derian, J. (1995) 'A Reinterpretation of Realism: Genealogy, Semiology, Dromology', in J. Der Derian (ed.) *International Theory: Critical Investigations*. Basingstoke: Macmillan, pp. 363–96.

Der Derian, J. (2009) 'Critical Encounters in International Relations', *International Social Science Journal*, 59(191): 69–73.

Deutsch, K.W. (1957) *Political Community and the North Atlantic Area: International Organization in the Light of Historical Experience*. Princeton, NJ: Princeton University Press.

Devetak, R. (1995a) 'Incomplete States: Theories and Practices of Statecraft', in J. Macmillan and A. Linklater (eds) *Boundaries in Question: New Directions in International Relations*. London: Pinter, pp. 19–39.

Devetak, R. (2001) 'Critical Theory', in S. Burchill et al. *Theories of International Relations*, 2nd edn. Basingstoke: Palgrave, pp. 144–78.

Devetak, R. (2013a) 'Critical Theory', in S. Burchill and A. Linklater (eds) *Theories of International Relations*, 5th edn. Basingstoke: Palgrave Macmillan, pp. 162–186.

Devetak, R. (2013b) 'Post-structuralism', in S. Burchill and A. Linklater (eds) *Theories of International Relations*, 5th edn. Basingstoke: Palgrave Macmillan, pp. 187–216.

Dictionary.com (2016) http://dictionary.reference.com/search?q=an- (accessed 18 July 2016).

Dictionary.com (2016b) http://dictionary.reference.com/browse/archon (accessed 18 July 2016).

Dobson, A. (2003) *Citizenship and the Environment*. Oxford: Oxford University Press.

Dobson, A. (2006a) 'Thick Cosmopolitanism', *Political Studies*, 54(1): 165–84.

Dobson, A. (2006b) 'Ecological Citizenship: A Defence', *Environmental Politics*, 15(3): 445–51.

Dobson, A. (2007) 'Environmental Citizenship: Towards Sustainable Development', *Sustainable Development*, 15(5): 276–85.

Donnelly, J. (1996) 'Twentieth-Century Realism', in T. Nardin and D.R. Mapel (eds) *Traditions of International Ethics*. Cambridge: Cambridge University Press, pp. 85–111.

Doyle, M. (1983) 'Kant, Liberal Legacies, and Foreign Affairs', *Philosophy and Public Affairs*, 12(3) and 12(4): 205–35 and 323–53, respectively.

Doyle, M. (1986) 'Liberalism and World Politics', *American Political Science Review*, 80(4): 1151–69.

Drezner, D. (2011) *Theories of International Politics and Zombies*. Princeton, NJ: Princeton University Press.

Duffield, J. (2007) 'What are International Institutions?', *International Studies Review*, 9(1): 1–22.

Dunne, T. (2005) 'The New Agenda', in A.J. Bellamy (ed.) *International Society and its Critics*. Oxford: Oxford University Press, pp. 65–79.

Dunne, T. (2014) 'Liberalism', in J. Baylis, S. Smith and P. Owens (eds) *The Globalization of World Politics: An Introduction to International Relations*, 6th edn. Oxford: Oxford University Press, pp. 113–25.

Dunne, T. (2016) 'The English School', in T. Dunne, M. Kurki and S. Smith (eds) *International Relations Theory: Discipline and Diversity*, 4th edn. Oxford: Oxford University Press, pp. 107–26.

Dunne, T. and Schmidt, B.C. (2008) 'Realism', in J. Baylis, S. Smith and P. Owns (eds) *The Globalization of World Politics: An Introduction to International Relations*, 4th edn. Oxford: Oxford University Press, pp. 90–106.

Dunne, T., Kurki, M. and Smith, S. (eds) (2016) *International Relations Theory: Discipline and Diversity*, 4th edn. Oxford: Oxford University Press.

Dunoff, J.L. (2003) 'Is the International Trade Regime Fair to Developing States?', *Proceedings of the Annual Meeting (Annual Society of International Law)*, 97(2–5 April): 153–7.

Dyson, S.B. (2015) *Otherworldly Politics: The International Relations of* Star Trek, Game of Thrones, *and* Battlestar Galactica. Baltimore, MD: Johns Hopkins University Press.

Eagleton, T. (1998) 'Postcolonialism and "Postcolonialism"', *Interventions: International Journal of Postcolonial Studies*, 1(1): 24–6.

Eckersley, R. (2016) 'Green Theory', in T. Dunne, M. Kurki and S. Smith (eds) *International Relations Theory: Discipline and Diversity*, 4th edn. Oxford: Oxford University Press, pp. 259-80.

The Economist (2010) 'Facebook Population: Status Update', 22 July, www.economist.com/node/16660401 (accessed 2 September 2016).

Edkins, J. (2003) *Trauma and the Memory of World Politics*. Cambridge: Cambridge University Press.

Edkins, J. and Zehfuss, M. (2005) 'Generalising the International', *Review of International Studies*, 31(3): 451–72.

Elshtain, J.B. (1995) 'Feminist Themes and International Relations', in J. Der Derian (ed.) *International Theory: Critical Investigations*. Basingstoke: Macmillan, pp. 340–60.

Encyclopedia of World Biography (2005–6) 'On Hans J. Morgenthau', www.bookrags.com/biography/hans-j-morgenthau/ (accessed 28 July 2016).

Enloe, C. (2001) *Bananas, Beaches and Bases: Making Feminist Sense of International Politics*. Berkeley, CA: University of California Press.

Epstein, C. (2008) *The Power of Words in International Relations: Birth of an Anti-Whaling Discourse*. Cambridge, MA and London: MIT Press.

Europa (2016a) 'The History of the European Union', http://europa.eu/about-eu/eu-history/index_en.htm, 26 May (accessed 25 July 2016).

Europa (2016b) 'Foreign and Security Policy', http://europa.eu/pol/cfsp/index_en.htm, 15 January (accessed 25 July 2016).

European Commission (2016) 'Corporate Social Responsibility (CSR)', http://ec.europa.eu/growth/industry/corporate-social-responsibility_en, 25 August (accessed 30 August 2016).

Evans, G. (2004) 'The Responsibility to Protect: Rethinking Humanitarian Intervention', 1 April, www.gevans.org/speeches/speech103.html (accessed 4 August 2016).

Ferguson, Y.H. and Mansbach, R.W. (1996) 'The Past as Prelude to the Future? Identities and Loyalties in Global Politics', in Y. Lapid and F. Kratochwil (eds) *The Return of Culture and Identity in IR Theory*. London: Lynne Rienner Publishers, pp. 21–44.

Finnemore, M. and Sikkink, K. (1998) 'International Norm Dynamics and Political Change', *International Organization*, 52(4), 887–917.

Finnemore, M. and Sikkink, K. (2001) 'The Constructivist Research Program in International Relations and Comparative Politics', *Annual Review of Political Science*, 4(1): 391–416.

Forde, S. (1996) 'Classical Realism', in T. Nardin and D.R. Mapel (eds) *Traditions of International Ethics*. Cambridge: Cambridge University Press, pp. 62–84.

Foucault, M. (1991) 'Truth and Power', in P. Rabinow (ed.) *The Foucault Reader: An Introduction to Foucault's Thought*. London: Penguin, pp. 51–75.

Foucault, M. (1995) *Discipline and Punish: The Birth of the Prison*, trans. A. Sheridan. London: Penguin.

Foucault, M. (1998a) *The Care of the Self: The History of Sexuality: 3*, trans. R. Hurley. London: Penguin.

Foucault, M. (1998b) *The Will to Know: The History of Sexuality: 1*, trans. R. Hurley London: Penguin.

Foucault, M. (1998c) *The Will to Know: The Use of Pleasure: 2*, trans. R. Hurley. London: Penguin.

Foucault, M. (2001) *Madness and Civilization*, trans. R. Howard. London: Routledge Classics.

Foucault, M. (2002) *The Archaeology of Knowledge*, trans. A.M. Sheridan Smith. London: Routledge Classics.

Fowler, R. (1992) *Language in the News: Discourse and Ideology in the Press*. London: Routledge.

Freyberg-Inan, A. (2006) 'World System Theory: A Bird's Eye View of the World's Capitalist Order', in J. Sterling-Folker (ed.) *Making Sense of International Relations Theory*. Boulder, CO: Lynne Rienner Publishers, pp. 225–41.

Friedman, G. (2008) 'Identifying the Place of Democratic Norms in Democratic Peace', *International Studies Review*, 10(3): 548–70.

Fukuyama, F. (1992) *The End of History and the Last Man*. New York: Free Press.

Fuller, T. (2006) '"Sweatshop Snoops" Take on China Factories', *International Herald Tribune*, 16 September, www.nytimes.com/2006/09/15/world/asia/15iht-inspect.282 7852.html?_r=0 (accessed 8 August 2016).

Gallagher, A. (2016) 'Conceptualizing Humanity in the English School', *International Theory*, 8(2): 341–64.

Gaskarth, J. (2011) 'Entangling Alliances? The UK's Complicity in Torture in the Global War on Terrorism', *International Affairs*, 87(4): 945–64.

Geis, A. (2011) 'Of Bright Sides and Dark Sides: Democratic Peace Beyond Triumphalism', *International Relations*, 25(2): 164–70.

Giddens, A. (1974) 'Introduction', in A. Giddens (ed.) *Positivism and Sociology*. London: Heinemann, pp. 1–22.

Gill, S. (ed.) (1993) *Gramsci, Historical Materialism and International Relations*. Cambridge: Cambridge University Press.

Gill, S. (2008) *Power and Resistance in the New Global Order*, 2nd edn. Basingstoke: Palgrave Macmillan.

Gilmore, J. (2014) 'The Uncertain Merger of Values and Interests in UK Foreign Policy', in T. Edmunds, J. Gaskarth and R. Porter (eds) *British Foreign Policy and the National Interest: Identity, Strategy and Security*. Basingstoke: Palgrave Macmillan, pp. 23–42.

Gilpin, R.G. (1984) 'The Richness of the Tradition of Political Realism', *International Organization*, 38(2): 287–304.

Glaser, C.L. (1994–5) 'Realists as Optimists: Cooperation as Self-Help', *International Security*, 19(3): 50–90.

Global Firepower (2016) www.globalfirepower.com/ (accessed 8 September 2016).

The Godfather Part III (1990) Dir. Francis Ford Coppola, Paramount Pictures.

Gov.UK (2014) 'Global Summit to End Sexual Violence in Conflict', www.gov.uk/government/news/uk-and-canada-respond-to-sexual-violence-by-isil-in-iraq (accessed 31 May 2016).

Gowa, J. (2011) 'The Democratic Peace after the End of the Cold War', *Economics and Politics*, 23(2): 153–71.

Green Party (2016) 'What We Stand For', www.greenparty.org.uk/we-stand-for/ (accessed 30 August 2016).

Griffiths, M. (2011) *Rethinking International Relations Theory*. Basingstoke: Palgrave Macmillan.

Groom, A.J.R. and Taylor, P. (1975) *Functionalism: Theory and Practice in International Relations*. London: University of London Press.

The Guardian (2016) 'COP21: UN Climate Change Conference', *The Guardian*, October, www.theguardian.com/environment/cop-21-un-climate-change-conference-paris (accessed 30 August 2016).

Guilhot, N. (2011) 'One Discipline, Many Histories', in N. Guilhot (ed.) *The Invention of International Relations Theory: Realism, the Rockefeller Foundation, and the 1954 Conference on Theory*. New York: Columbia University Press, pp. 1–32.

Guzzini, S. and Leander, A. (2006) 'Wendt's Constructivism: A Relentless Quest for Synthesis', in S. Guzzini and A. Leander (eds) *Constructivism and International Relations: Alexander Wendt and his Critics*. London: Routledge, pp. 73–92.

Haas, E.B. (1958) *The Uniting of Europe: Political, Social and Economic Forces, 1950–1957*. Stanford, CA: Stanford University Press.

Haas, E.B. (1964) *Beyond the Nation–State: Functionalism and International Organization*. Stanford, CA: Stanford University Press.

Haggard, S. (2013) 'Liberal Pessimism: International Relations Theory and the Emerging Powers', *Asia and the Pacific Policy Studies*, 1(1): 1–17.

Hague, W. (2009) 'The Future of British Foreign Policy', speech to the International Institute for Strategic Studies, 21 July, http://conservative-speeches.sayit.mysociety.org/speech/601323 (accessed 28 July 2016).

Haynes, J., Hough, P., Malik, S. and Pettiford, L. (2011) *World Politics*. Harlow: Pearson Education.

Hellsten, S. and Mallin, C. (2006) 'Are "Ethical" or "Socially Responsible" Investments Socially Responsible?', *Journal of Business Ethics*, 66(4): 393–406.

Henrikson, A.K. (2002) 'Distance and Foreign Policy: A Political Geography Approach', *International Political Science Review*, 23(4): 437–66.

Herz, J. (1950) 'Idealist Internationalism and the Security Dilemma', *World Politics*, 2(2): 157–80.

Hobbes, T. (2007) *Leviathan*. University of Adelaide ebook, https://ebooks.adelaide.edu.au/h/hobbes/thomas/h68l/ (accessed 1 September 2016).

Hobolth, M. (2011) 'European Visa Cooperation: Interest Politics and Regional Imagined Communities', IDEAS Working Paper Series from RePEc. St Louis, MO: Federal Reserve Bank of St Louis.

Hobson, C. (2011a) 'Towards a Critical Theory of Democratic Peace', *Review of International Studies*, 37(4): 1903–22.

Hobson, C. (2011b) 'The Sorcerer's Apprentice', *International Relations*, 25(2): 171–7.

Hoffman, S. (1985) 'Raymond Aron and the Theory of International Relations', *International Studies Quaterly*, 29(1): 13–27.

Hoffman, S. (1995) 'An American Social Science: International Relations', in J. Der Derian (ed.) *International Theory: Critical Investigations*. Basingstoke: Macmillan, pp. 212–41.

Holden, G. (2002) 'Who Contextualizes the Contextualizers? Disciplinary History and the Discourse about IR Discourse', *Review of International Studies*, 28(2): 253–70.

Hollis, M. and Smith, S. (1991) *Explaining and Understanding International Relations*. Oxford: Clarendon Press.

Hollis, M. and Smith, S. (2000) 'The International System', in A. Linklater (ed.) *International Relations: Critical Concepts in Political Science*. London: Routledge, pp.849–68.

Holsti, K.J. (1985) *The Dividing Discipline: Hegemony and Diversity in International Theory*. London: Unwin Hyman.

Hooghe, L. and Marks, G. (2008) 'A Postfunctionalist Theory of European Integration: From Permissive Consent to Distraining Dissensus', *British Journal of Political Science*, 39(1): 1–23.

Hooper, C. (2006) 'Masculinities, IR and the "Gender Variable"', in R. Little and M. Smith (eds) *Perspectives on World Politics*. Abingdon: Routledge, pp. 376–85.

Hovden, E. (1999) 'As if Nature Doesn't Matter: Ecology, Regime Theory and International Relations', *Environmental Politics*, 8(2): 50–74.

The Huffington Post (2015) 'Facebook is now Bigger than the Largest Country on Earth', 28 January, www.huffingtonpost.com/2015/01/28/facebook-biggest-country_n_6565428.html (accessed 9 August 2016).

Huggan, G. and Tiffin, H. (2008) 'Green Postcolonialism', *Interventions: International Journal of Postcolonial Studies*, 9(1): 1–11.

Human Rights Watch (2012) 'Women's Rights', http://hrw.org/women/ (accessed 18 August 2016).

Human Rights Watch (2016) *World Report 2016, Cuba: Events of 2015*, www.hrw.org/world-report/2016/country-chapters/cuba (accessed 19 December 2016).

Hutchings, K. (1999) *International Political Theory*. London: Sage.

International Labour Organization (ILO) (2012) '21 Million People are Now Victims of Forced Labour, ILO Says', 1 June, www.ilo.org/global/about-the-ilo/newsroom/news/WCMS_181961/lang--en/index.htm (accessed 8 August 2016).

International Telecommunication Union (ITU) (2016) 'Overview of ITU's History', www.itu.int/en/history/Pages/ITUsHistory.aspx (accessed 26 July 2016).

The IR Knowledge Base (2015) *Balance of Power*. Available at: www.irtheory.com/know.htm (accessed 26 January 2017).

Ish-Shalom, P. (2011) 'Don't Look Back in Anger', *International Relations*, 25(2): 178–84.

Jackson, R. and Sørensen, G. (2015) *Introduction to International Relations: Theories and Approaches*, 6th edition. Oxford: Oxford University Press.

James, A. (1993) 'System or Society?', *Review of International Studies*, 19(3): 269–88.

James, M. (2015) *A Brief History of Seven Killings*. London: OneWorld Publications.

Jarvis, D.S.L. (2001) 'Identity Politics, Postmodern Feminisms, and International Theory: Questioning the "New" Diversity in International Relations', in R.M.A. Crawford and D.S.L. Jarvis, *International Relations: Still an American Social Science?: Towards Diversity in International Thought*. Albany, NY: State University of New York Press, pp. 101–29.

Jeffery, R. (2006) *Hugo Grotius in International Thought*. Basingstoke: Palgrave Macmillan.

Jervis, R. (1978) 'Cooperation under the Security Dilemma', *World Politics*, 30(2): 167–214.

Jervis, R. (1994) 'Hans Morgenthau, Realism, and the Study of International Politics – Sixtieth Anniversary, 1934–1994: The Legacy of Our Past', *Social Research*, 61(4): 853–76.

Jervis, R. (2001) 'Was the Cold War a Security Dilemma?', *Journal of Cold War Studies*, 3(1): 36–60.

Jervis, R. (2008) 'Bridges, Barriers, and Gaps: Research and Policy', *Political Psychology*, 29(4): 571–92.

Jervis, R. (2010) 'Thinking Systematically about Geopolitics', *Geopolitics*, 15(1): 165–71.

Jervis, R. (2013) 'Do Leaders Matter and How Would we Know?', *Security Studies*, 22(2): 153–79.

Joker Scene from *The Dark Knight* (2008) www.youtube.com/watch?v=GGwHUr0b4yE (accessed 18 July 2016).

Jørgensen, K.E. (2010) *International Relations Theory: A New Introduction*. Basingstoke: Palgrave Macmillan.

Joynt, C.B. and Corbett, P.E. (1978) *Theory and Reality in World Politics*. Basingstoke: Macmillan.

Kadir, D. (1995) 'Postmodernism/Postcolonialism: What Are we After?', *World Literature Today*, 69(1): 17–21.

Kantengwa, J. (2013) 'Why Rwanda has the Most Female Politicians in the World', 17 September, http://leftfootforward.org/2013/09/rwanda-has-the-most-female-politicians/ (accessed 19 August 2016).

Keohane, R.O. (1982) 'The Demand for International Regimes', *International Organization*, 36(2): 325–55.

Keohane, R.O. (1986a) 'Realism, Neorealism and the Study of World Politics', in R.O. Keohane (ed.) *Neorealism and its Critics*. New York: Columbia University Press, pp. 1–26.

Keohane, R.O. (ed.) (1986b) *Neorealism and its Critics*. New York: Columbia University Press.

Keohane, R. (1995) 'International Institutions: Two Approaches', in J. Der Derian (ed.) *International Theory: Critical Investigations*. Basingstoke: Macmillan, pp. 279–307.

Keohane, R.O. (1998) 'International Institutions: Can Interdependence Work?', *Foreign Policy*, 110, Special Edition: Frontiers of Knowledge: 82–96.

Keohane, R.O. and Nye, J.S. (1977) *Power and Interdependence: World Politics in Transition*. Boston: Little Brown and Co.

Ki-moon, B. (2008) 'Statement to Regional Groups of Member States', 10 January, www.un.org/apps/news/infocus/sgspeeches/search_full.asp?statID=170 (accessed 1 September 2016).

Koschut, S. (2014) 'Regional Order and Peaceful Change: Security Communities as a Via Media in International Relations Theory', *International Relations*, 49(4): 519–35.

KPMG (2013) *The KPMG Survey of Corporate Social Responsibility Reporting 2013*, www.kpmg.com/Global/en/IssuesAndInsights/ArticlesPublications/corporate-responsibility/Documents/corporate-responsibility-reporting-survey-2013-exec-summary.pdf (accessed 30 August 2016).

Krasner, S.D. (ed.) (1983) *International Regimes*. Ithaca, NY: Cornell University Press.

Kratochwil, F. (1982) 'On the Notion of "Interest" in International Relations', *International Organization*, 36(1): 1–30.

Kratochwil, F. (1989) *Rules, Norms and Decisions*. Cambridge: Cambridge University Press.

Kratochwil, F. (2000) 'Wendt's "Social Theory of International Politics" and the Constructivist Challenge', *Millennium: Journal of International Studies*, 29(1): 73–101.

Kratochwil, F. and Ruggie, J.G. (1986) 'International Organization: A State of the Art on an Art of the State', *International Organization*, 40(4): 753–75.

Kreisler, H. (2003) 'Theory and International Politics: Conversation with Kenneth N. Waltz', Institute of International Studies, University of Berkeley, http://globetrotter.berkeley.edu/people3/Waltz/waltzcon0.html (accessed 25 August 2016).

Kuhn, T.S. (1996) *The Structure of Scientific Revolutions*, 3rd edn. Chicago, IL, and London: University of Chicago Press.

Kumar, M.P. (2011) 'Postcolonialism: Interdisciplinary or Interdiscursive?', *Third World Quarterly*, 32(4): 653–72.

Laffey, M. and Weldes, J. (2008) 'Decolonizing the Cuban Missile Crisis', *International Studies Quarterly*, 52(3): 555–77.

Lamy, S.L. (2014) 'Contemporary Mainstream Approaches: Neo-Realism and Neo-Liberalism', in J. Baylis, S. Smith and P. Owens (eds) *The Globalization of World Politics: An Introduction to International Relations*, 6th edn. Oxford: Oxford University Press, pp. 126-40.

Langlois, A.J. (2007) 'Worldviews and International Political Theory', in M. Griffiths (ed.) *International Relations Theory for the Twenty-First Century*. London: Routledge, pp. 146–56.

Lapid, Y. (1996) 'Culture's Ship: Returns and Departures in International Relations Theory', in Y. Lapid, Y. and F. Kratochwil (eds) *The Return of Culture and Identity in IR Theory*. London: Lynne Rienner Publishers, pp. 3–20.

Lapid, Y. and Kratochwil, F. (eds) (1996) *The Return of Culture and Identity in IR Theory*. London: Lynne Rienner Publishers.

Lebow, R.N. (2003) *The Tragic Vision of Politics: Ethics, Interests and Orders*. Cambridge: Cambridge University Press.

Lebow, R.N. (2014) 'Karl Deutsch and International Relations', *International Relations*, 28(3): 288–95.

Lebow, R.N. (2016) 'Classical Realism', in T. Dunne, M. Kurki and S. Smith (eds) *International Relations Theory: Discipline and Diversity*, 4th edn. Oxford: Oxford University Press, pp. 34–50.

Lehane, D. (2003) *Shutter Island*. London: Bantam Press.

Lenin, V.I. (2010) *Imperialism: The Highest Stage of Capitalism*. London: Penguin.

Linklater, A. (1990) *Beyond Realism and Marxism*. London: Macmillan.

Linklater, A. (1995) 'Neo-Realism: Theory and Practice', in K. Booth and S. Smith (eds) *International Relations Theory Today*. Cambridge: Polity Press, pp. 241–61.

Linklater, A. (1998) *The Transformation of Political Community*. Cambridge: Polity Press.

Linklater, A. (2010) 'Global Civilizing Processes and the Ambiguities of Human Connectedness', *European Journal of International Relations*, 16(2): 155–78.

Linklater, A. (2013) 'Marxism', in S. Burchill and A. Linklater (eds) *Theories of International Relations*, 3rd edn. Basingstoke: Palgrave Macmillan, pp. 113–37.

Linklater, A. (2016) *Violence and Civilization in the Western States-Systems*. Cambridge: Cambridge University Press.

Little, R. (1995) 'International Relations and the Triumph of Capitalism', in K. Booth and S. Smith (eds) *International Relations Theory Today*. Cambridge: Polity Press, pp. 62–87.

Little, R. (2005) 'The English School and World History', in A.J. Bellamy (ed.) *International Society and its Critics*. Oxford: Oxford University Press, pp. 45–63.

Lopez-Lucia, E. (2015) 'Regional Powers and Regional Security Governance: An Interpretive Perspective on the Policies of Nigeria and Brazil', *International Relations*, 29(3): 348–62.

Lupovici, A. (2009) 'Constructivist Methods: A Plea and Manifesto for Pluralism', *Review of International Studies*, 35(2): 195–218.

Lygdamus.com (undated) 'The Melian Dialogue', trans. Rex Warner, http://lygdamus.com/resources/New%20PDFS/Melian.pdf (accessed 28 July 2016).

Lynch, M. (2006) 'Critical Theory: Dialogue, Legitimacy, and Justifications for War', in J. Sterling-Folker (ed.) *Making Sense of International Relations Theory*. Boulder, CO: Lynne Rienner Publishers, pp. 182–97.

Macmillan, J. (2003) 'Beyond the Separate Democratic Peace', *Journal of Peace Research*, 40(2): 233–43.

Mann, M. (1993) 'Nation-States in Europe and other Continents: Diversifying, Developing, Not Dying', *Daedalus*, 122(3): 115–40.

Mansbach, R.W. and Rafferty, K.L. (2008) *Introduction to Global Politics*. Abingdon: Routledge.

Martinsson, J. and Lundqvist, L.J. (2010) 'Ecological Citizenship: Coming "Clean" without Turning "Green"?', *Environmental Politics*, 19(4): 518–37.

Marx, K. (2008) *Capital: A New Abridgement*. Oxford: Oxford University Press.

Marx, K. and Engels, F. (1998) *The Communist Manifesto*. Oxford: Oxford University Press.

McCarthy, T. (2015) *Satin Island*. London: Jonathan Cape.

McGinnis, M. (ed.) (1999) *Bioregionalism*. London: Routledge.

McLuhan, M. and Powers, B.R. (1989) *The Global Village: Transformations in World Life and Media in the 21st Century*. New York: Oxford University Press.

Mearsheimer, J.J. (2001) *The Tragedy of Great Power Politics*. London: W.W. Norton and Co.

Milner, H.V. (1998) 'International Political Economy: Beyond Hegemonic Stability', *Foreign Policy*, 110, Special Edition: Beyond Frontiers of Knowledge: 112–23.

Mingst, K.A. and Snyder, J.L. (2011) *Essential Readings in World Politics: An Introduction*, 4th edn. London: W.W. Norton and Co.

Mishra, V. and Hodge, B. (2005) 'What was Postcolonialism?', *New Literary History*, 36(3): 375–402.

Mitchell, D. (2015) *The Bone Clocks*. London: Sceptre.

Mitrany, D. (1933) *The Progress of International Government*. New Haven, CT: Yale University Press.

Molloy, S. (2008) 'Hans J. Morgenthau Versus E.H. Carr: Conflicting Conceptions of Ethics in Realism', in D. Bell (ed.) *Political Thought and International Relations: Variations on a Realist Theme*. Oxford: Oxford University Press, pp.83–104.

Moravcsik, A. (1998) *The Choice for Europe: Social Purpose and State Power from Messina to Maastricht*. Ithaca, NY: Cornell University Press.

Morgenthau, H.J. (1985) *Politics Among Nations: The Struggle for Power and Peace*, 6th edn. New York: Knopf.

Morris, J. (2005) 'Normative Innovation and the Great Powers', in A.J. Bellamy (ed.) *International Society and its Critics*. Oxford: Oxford University Press, pp. 265–81.

Morris, J. (2011) 'How Great is Britain? Power, Responsibility and Britain's Future Global Role', *British Journal of Politics and International Relations*, 13(3): 326–47.

Moura-Leite, R.C. and Padgett, R.C. (2011) 'Historical Background of Corporate Social Responsibility', *Social Responsibility Journal*, 7(4): 528–39.

Myrdal, G. (1974) 'What is Development?', *Journal of Economic Issues*, 8(4): 729–36.

Namaste, K. (1994) 'The Politics of Inside/Outside: Queer Theory, Poststructuralism, and a Sociological Approach to Sexuality', *Sociological Theory*, 12(2): 220–31.

Navon, E. (2001) 'The "Third Debate" Revisited', *Review of International Studies*, 27(4): 611–25.

Naylor, B. (2016) 'Obama: Globalization is "Here" and "Done"', *NPR*, National Public Radio, Washington, DC, 29 June, www.npr.org/2016/06/29/484087513/obama-globalization-is-here-and-done (accessed 9 August 2016).

Neal, A.W. (2009) 'Michel Foucault', in J. Edkins and N. Vaughan-Williams (eds) *Critical Theorists and International Relations*. London: Routledge, pp. 161–70.

Neethling, T. (2004) 'The Development of Normative Theory in International Relations: Some Practical Implications for Norm-Based and Value-Based Scholarly Enquiry', *Koers*, 69(1): 1–25.

Nexon, D.H. and Neumann, I.B. (eds) (2013) *Harry Potter and International Relations*. Lanham, MD: Rowman and Littlefield.

Nye, J.S. and Welch, D.A. (2011) *Understanding Global Conflict and Cooperation: An Introduction to Theory and History*. London: Pearson.

Obama, B. (2010) 'Barack Obama's Speech on Banking Reform: In Full', *Independent*, 21 January, www.telegraph.co.uk/finance/newsbysector/banksandfinance/7046668/Barack-Obamas-speech-on-banking-reform-in-full.html (accessed 1 September 2016).

Onuf, N.G. (1989) *A World of Our Making: Rules and Rule in Social Theory and International Relations*. Columbia, SC: University of South Carolina Press.

Onuf, N. (1998) 'Constructivism: A User's Manual', in V. Kubálková, N. Onuf and P. Kowert (eds) *International Relations in a Constructed World*. Armonk, NY: M.E. Sharpe, pp. 58–78.

Onuf, N. (2002) 'Institutions, Intentions and International Relations', *Review of International Studies*, 28(2): 211–28.

Onuf, N. (2009) 'Structure? What Structure?', *International Relations*, 23(2): 183–99.

Organisation for Economic Co-operation and Development (OECD) (2011) 'OECD Guidelines for Multinational Enterprises 2011 Edition', www.oecd.org/daf/inv/mne/48004323.pdf (accessed 30 August 2016).

Organization for Security and Cooperation in Europe (OSCE) (undated) 'Participating States', www.osce.org/states (accessed 8 August 2016).

Owen, J.M. (2011) 'Liberal Tradition not Social Science', *International Relations*, 25(2): 158–63.

Palacios, J.J. (2004) 'Corporate Citizenship and Social Responsibility in a Globalized World', *Citizenship Studies*, 8(4): 383–402.

Paris UN Climate Change Conference (2015) 30 November to 12 December, www.cop21.gouv.fr/en/ (accessed 30 August 2016).

Pasic, S.C. (1996) 'Culturing International Relations Theory: A Call for Extension', in Y. Lapid, and F. Kratochwil (eds) *The Return of Culture and Identity in IR Theory*. London: Lynne Rienner Publishers, pp. 85–104.

Paterson, M. (1995) 'Radicalizing Regimes?: Ecology and the Critique of IR Theory', in J. Macmillan and A. Linklater (eds) *Boundaries in Question: New Directions in International Relations*. London: Pinter, pp. 212–27.

Pedersen, S. (2007) 'Back to the League of Nations', *American Historical Review*, 112(4): 1091–1117.

Peoples, C. (2009) 'Theodore Adorno', in J. Edkins and N. Vaughan-Williams (eds) *Critical Theorists and International Relations*. London: Routledge, pp. 7–18.

Permanent Mission of Ukraine (2016) Statement on 'Russia's Ongoing Aggression against Ukraine and Violations of OSCE Principles and Commitments', 3 March, www.osce.org/pc/226596?download=true (accessed 8 August 2016).

Peterson, V.S. (1992) 'Introduction', in V.S. Peterson (ed.) *Gendered States: Feminist (Re)Visions of International Relations Theory*. Boulder, CO: Lynne Rienner Publishers, pp. 1–29.

Phillips, T., Harvey, F. and Yuhas, A. (2016) 'Breakthrough as US and China Agree to Ratify Paris Climate Deal', *The Guardian*, 3 September, http://mahb.stanford.edu/library-item/breakthrough-us-china-agree-ratify-paris-climate-deal/ (accessed 5 September 2016).

Prebisch, R. (1981) 'Third World Lecture 1981: Capitalism: The Second Crisis', *Third World Quarterly*, 3(3): 433–40.

Puntigliano, A.R. and Appleqvist, Ö. (2011) 'Prebisch and Myrdal: Development Economics in the Core and on the Periphery', *Journal of Global History*, 6(1): 29–52.

Puzo, M. (1991) *The Godfather*. London: Arrow Books.

Ralph, J. (2011) 'A Difficult Relationship: Britain's "Doctrine of International Community" and America's "War on Terror"', in O. Daddow and J. Gaskarth (eds) *British Foreign Policy: The New Labour Years*. Basingstoke: Palgrave Macmillan, 123–38.

Ramakrishnan, A.K. (1999) 'The Gaze of Orientalism: Reflections on Linking Postcolonialism and International Relations', *International Studies*, 36(2): 129–63.

Redman, P. (2006) *Good Essay Writing*, 3rd edn. London: Sage.

Reiter, D. (2015) 'Should we Leave Behind the Subfield of International Relations?', *Annual Review of Political Science*, 18: 481–99.

The Report of the Iraq Inquiry (2016) Her Majesty's Stationary Office, 6 July, www.iraqinquiry.org.uk/the-report/ (accessed 4 November 2016).

Reus-Smit, C. (2002) 'Imagining Society: Constructivism and the English School', *British Journal of Politics and International Relations*, 4(3): 487–509.

Reus-Smit, C. (2005) 'The Constructivist Challenge after September 11', in A.J. Bellamy, A.J. (ed.) *International Society and its Critics*. Oxford: Oxford University Press, pp. 81–94.

Reus-Smit, C. (2012) 'International Relations, Irrelevant? Don't Blame Theory', *Millennium: Journal of International Studies*, 40(3): 525–40.

Reus-Smit, C. (2013) 'Constructivism', in S. Burchill and A. Linklater (eds) *Theories of International Relations*, 5th edn. Basingstoke: Palgrave Macmillan, pp. 217–40.

Ricks, T.E. (2006) *Fiasco: The American Military Adventure in Iraq*. London: Allen Lane.

Roe, P. (1999) 'The Intrastate Security Dilemma: Ethnic Conflict as "Tragedy"?', *Journal of Peace Research*, 36(2): 183–202.

Rosato, S. (2003) 'The Flawed Logic of Democratic Peace Theory', *American Political Science Review*, 97(4): 585–602.

Rosenau, J.N. (1976) 'International Studies in a Transnational World', *Millennium*, 5(1): 1–20.

Rosenau, J.N. (2002) 'Unfulfilled Potential: Sociology and International Relations', *International Review of Sociology*, 12(3): 545–9.

Rosenau, J.N. (2003) 'The Theoretical Imperative: Unavoidable Explication', *Asian Journal of Political Science*, 11(2): 7–20.

Rosenau, J.N. (2004) 'Many Globalizations, One International Relations', *Globalizations*, 1(1): 7–14.

Rosenau, J.N. and Durfee, M. (1995) *Thinking Theory Thoroughly: Coherent Approaches to an Incoherent World*. Oxford: Westview Press.

Rosenberg, J. (2000) *The Follies of Globalisation Theory: Polemical Essays*. London: Verso.

Rosenberg, J. (2001) *The Empire of Civil Society: A Critique of the Realist Theory of International Relations*. London: Verso.

Rosenberg, J. (2005) 'Globalisation Theory: A Post-Mortem', *International Politics*, 42(1): 2–74.

Rosenberg, J. (2010) 'Basic Problems in the Theory of Uneven and Combined Development. Part II: Unnevenness and Political Multiplicity', *Cambridge Review of International Affairs*, 23(1): 165–89.

Rosenberg, J. (2013) 'Kenneth Waltz and Leon Trotsky: Anarchy in the Mirror of Uneven and Combined Development', *International Politics*, 50(2): 183–230.

Rosenberg, J. (2016) 'International Relations in the Prison of Political Science', *International Relations*, 30(2): 127–53.

Ruane, K. (2000) *The Rise and Fall of the European Defence Community: Anglo-American Relations and the Crisis of European Defence, 1950–55*. Basingstoke: Macmillan.

Ruggie, J.G. (1993) 'Territoriality and Beyond: Problematizing Modernity in International Relations', *International Organization*, 47(1): 139–74.

Ruggie, J.G. (1998a) *Constructing the World Polity: Essays on International Institutionalization*. London: Routledge.

Ruggie, J.G. (1998b) 'What Makes the World Hang Together? Neo-Utilitarianism and the Social Constructivist Challenge', *International Organization*, 52(4): 855–85.

Rupert, M. (2009) 'Antonio Gramsci', in J. Edkins and N. Vaughan-Williams (eds) *Critical Theorists and International Relations*. London: Routledge, pp. 176–86.

Rupert, M. (2016) 'Marxism', in T. Dunne, M. Kurki and S. Smith (eds) *International Relations Theory: Discipline and Diversity*, 4th edn. Oxford: Oxford University Press, pp. 127–44.

Russett, B. (1995) 'Correspondence on The Democratic Peace: "And Yet It Moves"', *International Security*, 19(4): 164–75.

Ruzicka, J. (2014) 'A Transformative Social Scientist: Karl Deutsch and the Discipline of International Relations', *International Relations*, 28(3): 277–87.

Sachs, J. (1998) 'International Economics: Unlocking the Mysteries of Globalization', *Foreign Policy*, 110, Special Edition: Frontiers of Knowledge: 97–111.

Said, E. (1994) *Culture and Imperialism*. London: Vintage Books.

Said, E. (2003) *Orientalism*. London: Penguin.

Salter, M.B. (2010) 'Edward Said and Post-Colonial International Relations', in C. Moore and C. Farrands (eds) *International Relations and Philosophy: Interpretive Dialogues*. London: Routledge, pp. 129–43.

Scarface (1983) Dir. Oliver Stone, Universal Pictures.

Schenk, R. (1997–2006) 'A Case of Unemployment', http://ingrimayne.com/econ/EconomicCatastrophe/GreatDepression.html (accessed 28 July 2016).

Schmidt, B.C. (2006) 'On the History and Historiography of International Relations', in W. Carlsnaes, T. Risse and B.A. Simmons (eds) *Handbook of International Relations*. London: Sage, pp. 3–22.

Scholte, J.A. (1997) 'Global Capitalism and the State', *International Affairs*, 73(3): 427–52.

Scholte, J.A. (2005) 'Premature Obituaries: A Response to Justin Rosenberg', *International Politics*, 42(3): 390–9.

Scholte, J.A. (2008) 'Defining Globalisation', *The World Economy*, 31(11): 1471–502.

Schweller, R. (2011) 'Theory in Action: Realism', 4 May, www.youtube.com/watch?v=UnKEFSVAiNQ&feature=relmfu (accessed 1 September 2016).

Scriven, M. (1994) 'A Possible Distinction between Traditional Scientific Disciplines and the Study of Human Behaviour', in M. Martin and L.C. McIntyre (eds) *Readings in the Philosophy of Social Science*. Cambridge, MA: MIT Press, pp. 71–7.

Searle, J. (2005) 'What is an Institution?', *Journal of Institutional Economics*, 1(1): 1–22.

Shinko, R.E. (2006) 'Postmodernism: A Genealogy of Humanitarian Intervention', in J. Sterling-Folker (ed.) *Making Sense of International Relations Theory*. Boulder, CO: Lynne Rienner Publishers, pp. 168–81.

Sinclair, T.J. (1996) 'Beyond International Relations Theory: Robert W. Cox and Approaches to World Order', in R.W. Cox and T.J. Sinclair (eds) *Approaches to World Order*. Cambridge: Cambridge University Press, pp. 3–18.

Smallman, S. and Brown, K. (2011) *Introduction to International and Global Studies*. Chapel Hill, NC: University of North Carolina Press.

Smith, M.J. (2005) 'Obligation and Ecological Citizenship', *Environments*, 33(3): 9–23.

Smith, M.R. (2016) *Normative Issues in International Relations: Bridging the Communitarian/Cosmopolitan Divide*. CreateSpace Independent Publishing Platform.

Smith, R., El-Anis, I. and Farrands, C. (2011) *International Political Economy in the 21st Century*. Harlow: Pearson Education Limited.

Smith, S. (1995) 'The Self-Images of a Discipline: A Genealogy of International Relations Theory', in K. Booth and S. Smith (eds) *International Relations Theory Today*. Cambridge: Polity Press, pp. 1–37.

Smith, S. (1997) 'Power and Truth: A Reply to William Wallace', *Review of International Studies*, 23(4): 507–16.

Smith, S. (2004) 'Singing our World into Existence: International Relations Theory and September 11', *International Studies Quarterly*, 48(3): 499–515.

Smith, S., Booth, K. and Zalewski, M. (eds) (1996) *International Theory: Positivism and Beyond*. Cambridge: Cambridge University Press.

Smith, T. (2011) 'Democratic Peace Theory: From Promising Theory to Dangerous Practice', *International Relations*, 25(2): 151–7.

Spiro, D. (1995) 'Correspondence on The Democratic Peace: The Liberal Peace – "And Yet it Squirms"', *International Security*, 19(4): 177–80.

Statista (2016) 'Number of Monthly Active Twitter Users Worldwide from 1st Quarter 2010 to 2nd Quarter 2016', www.statista.com/statistics/282087/number-of-monthly-active-twitter-users/ (accessed 9 August 2016).

Sterling-Folker, J. (2006a) 'Liberal Approaches', in J. Sterling-Folker (ed.) *Making Sense of International Relations Theory*. Boulder, CO: Lynne Rienner, pp. 55–62.

Sterling-Folker, J. (ed.) (2006b) *Making Sense of International Relations Theory*. Boulder, CO: Lynne Rienner.

Sterling-Folker, J. (2006c) 'Historical Materialism and World System Theory Approaches', in J. Sterling-Folker (ed.) *Making Sense of International Relations Theory*. Boulder, CO: Lynne Rienner, pp. 199–208.

Sterling-Folker, J. (2006d) 'Postmodern and Critical Theory Approaches', in J. Sterling-Folker (ed.) *Making Sense of International Relations Theory*. Boulder, CO: Lynne Rienner, pp. 157–67.

Sterling-Folker, J. (2006e) 'Realism', in J. Sterling-Folker (ed.) *Making Sense of International Relations Theory*. Boulder, CO: Lynne Rienner, pp. 13–17.

Stiglitz, J. (1998) 'International Development: Is it Possible?', *Foreign Policy*, 110, Special Edition: Frontiers of Knowledge: 138–51.

Suganami, H. (2005) 'The English School and International Theory', in A.J. Bellamy (ed.) *International Society and its Critics*. Oxford: Oxford University Press, pp. 29–44.

Sutch, P. and Elias, J. (2007) *International Relations: The Basics*. London: Routledge.

Syed, M. (2015) *Black Box Thinking: The Surprising Truth about Success (And Why Some People Never Learn from their Mistakes*. London: John Murray.

Sylvester, C. (2014) 'Post-Colonialism', in J. Baylis, S. Smith and P. Owens (eds) *The Globalization of World Politics: An Introduction to International Relations*, 6th edn. Oxford: Oxford University Press, pp. 184-97.

Tang, S. (2009) 'The Security Dilemma: A Conceptual Analysis', *Security Studies*, 18(3): 587–623.

The Telegraph (2010) 'Barack Obama's Speech on Banking Reform: In Full', 21 January, www.telegraph.co.uk/finance/newsbysector/banksandfinance/7046668/Barack-Obamas-speech-on-banking-reform-in-full.html (accessed 1 September 2016).

Teschke, B. and Cemgil, C. (2014) 'The Dialectic of the Concrete: Reconsidering Dialectic for IR and Foreign Policy Analysis', *Globalizations*, 11(5): 605–25.

Thucydides (2004) *History of the Peloponnesian War*, trans. R. Crawley. Mineola, NY: Dover.

Tickner, J.A. (1988) 'Hans Morgenthau's Principles of Political Realism: A Feminist Reformulation', *Millennium: Journal of International Studies*, 17(3): 429–40.

Tickner, J.A. (1996) 'Identity in IR Theory: Feminist Perspectives', in Y. Lapid and F. Kratochwil (eds) *The Return of Culture and Identity in IR Theory*. London: Lynne Rienner Publishers, pp. 147–62.

Tickner, J.A. and Sjoberg, L. (2016) 'Feminism', in T. Dunne, M. Kurki and S. Smith (eds) *International Relations Theory: Discipline and Diversity*, 4th edn. Oxford: Oxford University Press, pp. 179–95.

UK Government (2014) *Review of the Balance of Competences Between the United Kingdom and the European Union: Environment and Climate Change*, February, www.gov.uk/government/uploads/system/uploads/attachment_data/file/284500/environment-climate-change-documents-final-report.pdf (accessed 30 August 2016).

UK in a Changing Europe (2016) 'A Three-Minute Guide on Democracy and Sovereignty', http://ukandeu.ac.uk/explainers/a-three-minute-guide-to-democracy-and-sovereignty/ (accessed 18 July 2016).

Ullmann-Margalit, E. (1977) *The Emergence of Norms*. Oxford: Clarendon Press.

United Nations (UN) (1974) 'Declaration on the Establishment of a New International Economic Order', General Assembly, Sixth Special Session, 1 May, www.un-docu ments.net/s6r3201.htm (accessed 20 July 2016).

UN (1997) 'A Summary of United Nations Agreements on Human Rights', www.hrweb. org/legal/undocs.html#Geneva (accessed 1 September 2016).

UN (1997–2010) 'Women Watch', www.un.org/womenwatch/directory/statistics_and_ indicators_60.htm (accessed 18 August 2016).

UN (1998) 'Kyoto Protocol to the United Nations Framework Convention on Climate Change', http://unfccc.int/resource/docs/convkp/kpeng.pdf (accessed 30 August 2016).

UN (2013) 'A Declaration of Commitment to End Sexual Violence in Conflict', 24 September, www.gov.uk/government/uploads/system/uploads/attachment_data/file/274724/A_DECLARATION_OF_COMMITMENT_TO_END_SEXUAL_VIOLENCE_IN_CONFLICT.pdf (accessed 31May 2016).

UN (2015) Organization Chart, www.un.org/aboutun/chart.html (accessed 24 July 2016).

UN (2016a) 'History of the United Nations', www.un.org/en/sections/history/history-united-nations/index.html (accessed 24 July 2016).

UN (2016b) 'Growth in United Nations Membership, 1945–Present', www.un.org/en/sections/member-states/growth-united-nations-membership-1945-present/index.html (accessed 24 July 2016).

UN (2016c) 'Preamble', www.un.org/en/sections/un-charter/preamble/index.html (accessed 24 July 2016).

UN (undated) 'United Nations Office for Sustainable Development', www.unosd.org/index.php?menu=17 (accessed 30 August 2016).

UN Women (2016) 'Facts and Figures: Leadership and Political Participation', January, www.unwomen.org/en/what-we-do/leadership-and-political-participation/facts-and-figures (accessed 19 August 2016).

van der Ree, G. (2014) 'International Relations 10: Post-Structuralism', www.youtube. com/watch?v=0IVSA2mETqM (accessed 23 August 2016).

van Hoorn, A. (2015) 'The Global Financial Crisis and the Values of Professionals in Finance: An Empirical Analysis', *Journal of Business Ethics*, 130(2): 253–69.

Varadarajan, L. (2009) 'Edward Said', in J. Edkins and N. Vaughan-Williams (eds) *Critical Theorists and International Relations*. London: Routledge, pp. 292–304.

Vasquez, M. (2002) 'Cultural Integrity in Non-Traditional Societies: Cuba Encounters the Global Market System', *Cultural Dynamics*, 14(2): 185–204.

Viotti, P.R. and Kauppi, M.V. (2014) *International Relations Theory*, 5th edn. Harlow: Pearson Education Limited.

Wæver, O. (2016) 'Still a Discipline after All these Debates?', in T. Dunne, M. Kurki and S. Smith (eds) *International Relations Theory: Discipline and Diversity*, 4th edn. Oxford: Oxford University Press, pp. 300–21.

Wainwright, M. and Carvel, J. (2006) 'Blair Heralds End of "Nanny State" Health Advice', *The Guardian*, 26 July, http://politics.guardian.co.uk/publicservices/story/0,,1830167,00.html (accessed 1 September 2016).

Walker, R.B.J. (1993) *Inside/Outside: International Relations as Political Theory*. Cambridge: Cambridge University Press.

Walker, R.B.J. (1995) 'History and Structure in the Theory of International Relations', in J. Der Derian (ed.) *International Theory: Critical Investigations*. Basingstoke: Macmillan, pp. 308–39.

Wallace, W. (1996) 'Truth and Power, Monks and Technocrats: Theory and Practice in International Relations', *Review of International Studies*, 22(3): 301–21.

Wallerstein, I. (1974) *The Modern World System, Vol. 1: Capitalist Agriculture and the Origins of the European World-Economy in the Sixteenth Century*. New York and London: Academic Press.

Wallerstein, I. (1980) *The Modern World-System, Vol. II: Mercantilism and the Consolidation of the European World-Economy, 1600–1750*. New York and London: Academic Press.

Wallerstein, I. (1989) *The Modern World System, Vol. III: The Second Era of Great Expansion of the Capitalist World Economy, 1730s–1840s*. New York and London: Academic Press.

Walliman, N. (2006) *Social Research Methods*. London: Sage.

Walt, S.M. (1998) 'International Relations: One World, Many Theories', *Foreign Policy*, 110, Special Edition: Frontiers of Knowledge: 29–46.

Waltz, K.N. (1959) *Man, the State and War*. New York: Cambridge University Press.

Waltz, K.N. (1979) *Theory of International Politics*, 1st edn. Boston, MA: McGraw-Hill.

Walt, K.N. (1997) 'Evaluating Theories', *American Political Science Review*, 91(4): 913–917.

Waltz, K.N. (2010) *Theory of International Politics*. Long Grove, IL: Waveland Press.

Watson, A. (1990) 'Systems of States', *Review of International Studies*, 16(2): 99–109.

Watson, A. (2001) *The Evolution of International Society*. London: Routledge.

Watson, A.M.S. (2006) 'Children and International Relations: A New Site of Knowledge?', *Review of International Studies*, 32(2): 237–50.

Weber, C. (2010) *International Relations Theory: A Critical Introduction*, 3rd edn. London: Routledge.

Weber, C. (2013) *International Relations Theory: A Critical Introduction*, 4th edn. London: Routledge.

Weigley, S. (2013) '10 companies profiting most from the war', *USA Today*, 10 March. Available at: www.usatoday.com/story/money/business/2013/03/10/10-companies-profiting-most-from-war/1970997/(accessed 26 January 2017).

Welch, D.A. (2003) 'Why IR Theorists Should Stop Reading Thucydides', *Review of International Studies*, 29(3): 301–19.

Wendt, A. (1992) 'Anarchy is What States Make of It: The Social Construction of Power Politics', *International Organization*, 46(2): 391–425.

Wendt, A. (1996) 'Identity and Structural Change in International Politics', in Y. Lapid and F. Kratochwil (eds) *The Return of Culture and Identity in IR Theory*. London: Lynne Rienner Publishers, pp. 47–64.

Wendt, A. (1999) *Social Theory of International Politics*. Cambridge: Cambridge University Press.

Wendt, A. (2000) 'On the Via Media: A Response to the Critics', *Review of International Studies*, 26(1): 165–80.

Wexler, L. (2003) 'The International Deployment of Shame, Second-Best Responses, and Norm Entrepreneurship: The Campaign to Ban Landmines and the Landmine Ban Treaty', *Arizona Journal of International and Comparative Law*, 20(3): 562–606.

Wheeler, N.J. (2008) '"To Put Oneself into the Other Fellow's Place": John Herz, the Security Dilemma and the Nuclear Age', *International Relations*, 22(4): 493–509.

Wheeler, N.J. and Dunne, T. (1996) 'Hedley Bull's Pluralism of the Intellect and Solidarism of the Will', *International Affairs*, 72(1): 91–107.

Wight, M. (1987) 'An Anatomy of International Thought', *Review of International Studies*, 13(3): 221–7.

Wight, M. (1995) 'Why is there No International Theory?', in J. Der Derian (ed.) *International Theory: Critical Investigations*. Basingstoke: Macmillan, pp. 15–35.

Wikipedia (2016) 'Wikipedia: Academic Use', 25 March, https://en.wikipedia.org/wiki/Wikipedia:Academic_use (accessed 2 September 2016).

Williams, J. (2005) 'Pluralism, Solidarism and the Emergence of World Society in English School Theory', *International Relations*, 19(1): 19–38.

Wilson, W. (1918) 'President Woodrow Wilson's Fourteen Points', 8 January, http://avalon.law.yale.edu/20th_century/wilson14.asp (accessed 24 July 2016).

Windschuttle, K. (1996) *The Killing of History: How Literary Critics and Social Theorists are Murdering our Past*. San Francisco, CA: Encounter Books.

Women in National Parliaments (2016) World Classification, 1 June, www.ipu.org/wmn-e/classif.htm (accessed 19 August 2016).

Woods, N. (1999) 'Order, Globalization, and Inequality in World Politics', in A. Hurrell and N. Woods (eds) *Order, Globalization, and Inequality in World Politics*. Oxford: Oxford University Press, pp. 8–35.

WWF (undated) 'What is an Ecological Footprint?', www.wwf.org.au/our_work/people_and_the_environment/human_footprint/ecological_footprint/ (accessed 30 August 2016).

Yale Law School (2007) 'The Covenant of the League of Nations', http://avalon.law.yale.edu/20th_century/leagcov.asp (accessed 24 July 2016).

Young, G. (2016) *Women, Naturally Better Leaders for the 21st Century*, Transpersonal Leadership Series: Whitepaper 2. London: Routledge.

Zalewski, M. and Enloe, C. (1995) 'Questions about Identity in International Relations', in K. Booth and S. Smith (eds) *International Relations Theory Today*. Cambridge: Polity Press, pp. 279–305.

Zehfuss, M. (2003) 'Forget September 11', *Third World Quarterly*, 24(3): 513–28.

Zehfuss, M. (2006) 'Constructivism and Identity: A Dangerous Liaison', in S. Guzzini and A. Leander (eds) *Constructivism and International Relations: Alexander Wendt and his Critics*. London: Routledge, pp. 93–117.

Zehfuss, M. (2009) 'Jacques Derrida', in J. Edkins and N. Vaughan-Williams (eds) *Critical Theorists and International Relations*. London: Routledge, pp. 137–49.

Zheng, J. (2016) Constructing "A New Type of Great Power Relations": The State of Debate in China', *British Journal of Politics and International Relations*, 18(2): 422–42.

INDEX

English School *cont.*
  order 121–2
  and Realism 118, 121, 126–7
  security communities 144
  solidarism and pluralism 123–5
  state 119
  systems 119–20
  Uneven and Combined Development (U&CD) 166
'environmental justice' 229
Erasmus 63
essay writing 255–69, 271–9
  argument 257–8, 272
    number of points 258
  bad practice 265–7
  bibliography 279
  evidence 262–4
    citations 264
    quotations 263, 273, 274
  feedback 251–3
  plagiarism 267–9
  proofreading 256
  referencing 264–5, 278–9
  requirements
    deadline 256
    deadline extensions 257
    lecture insights 256
    length 256
    presentation and submission 256
  structure 258–62
    headings and subheadings 259
    macro structure 259
      conclusions 277–8
      introductions 271–4
    micro structure 259–61, 274–6
    signposts and bridges 261–2, 272, 274
  use of Wikipedia 273
  written English 256, 273, 278
European Bank of Reconstruction and
  Development 64
European Central Bank 179
European Coal and Steel Community (ECSC) 71
European Court of Justice 110
European Defence Community (EDC) 71, 72
European Economic Community (EEC) 71
European security 71
European Union (EU) 56, 70–1, 80
  Brexit 46, 70, 75, 141, 143
  corporate social responsibility (CSR) 230–1
  development 70–1
  Euroscepticism 143
  Eurozone crisis (2008) 70, 109–10, 141
  and human rights 75
  Maastricht Treaty 70–1
  and New Labour 143
  protecting the environment 226–7
  as security provider 72
  social processes in cooperation 141
  'zone of peace' 75
evidence 56

exams 281–6
  gaps in knowledge 292–3
  group study 283
  notes 282
  past papers 282
  planning time 285
  practical preparation 284
  practice questions 283
  revision 281, 283–4
  stress 284
  writing 285–6

Facebook 156
feedback 251–4
  constructive criticism 251
  formative 252
  oral 253
  summative 251–2
feminism 50, 137, 185–94
  Constructivist feminism 190
  Critical feminism 189–90
  female representation in politics 190–1
  feminist perspectives 188
  gender 186–7, 189–90
  liberal feminism 188–9
  postcolonial 185, 192–3
  poststructural 191–2
films and IRT 37, 38
financial crisis 2008 43, 157
Finnemore, Martha and Sikkink, Kathryn 134, 140–1,
  143, 145, 147, 148
Foucault, Michel 197, 199, 200–1, 202, 203, 204, 214
France 71, 155, 179
Frankfurt School 174–5
free trade 67, 92, 154, 160
functionalist integration theory 72, 141, 293

'game-playing' 74
Geena Davis Institute 189
gender 186–7
  and deconstruction 200
  definitions 186, 293
  female representation in politics 190–1
  in film 189–90
  maleness and femaleness 187
  masculine and feminine characteristics 187, 191, 192
  and power 191–2
  reasons for gendering IR 187
  as unseen structure 189
genealogies 204–5, 293
  and Critical Theory 204
General Agreement on Tariffs and Trade (GATT)
  65–6, 107, 179, 293
Geneva Convention 122
George, Jim 52
Germany 65, 68, 71, 109, 155, 168, 179
  aftermath of 9/11 205
  Critical Theory 174
  reunification 45